Cambridge Studies in medieval life and thought

CLEMENT VI

Cambridge studies in medieval life and thought
Fourth series

General Editor:
J. C. HOLT
Professor of Medieval History and
Master of Fitzwilliam College, University of Cambridge

Advisory Editors:
C. N. L. BROOKE
Dixie Professor of Ecclesiastical History and
Fellow of Gonville and Caius College,
University of Cambridge

D. E. LUSCOMBE
Professor of Medieval History, University of Sheffield

The series Cambridge Studies in Medieval Life and Thought was inaugurated by G. G. Coulton in 1920. Professor J. C. Holt now acts as General Editor of a Fourth Series, with Professor C. N. L. Brooke and Professor D. E. Luscombe as Advisory Editors. The series aims to bring together outstanding work by medieval scholars over a wide range of human endeavour extending from political economy to the history of ideas.

Frontispiece Pope Clement VI, from the dedication page of Bartholomew of Urbino, *Milleloquium Sancti Augustini*, MS Paris, Bibliothèque Nationale, latin 2120, fol. 1r

CLEMENT VI

The Pontificate and Ideas
of an Avignon Pope

DIANA WOOD

Lecturer in History, University of East Anglia

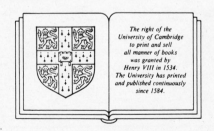

The right of the
University of Cambridge
to print and sell
all manner of books
was granted by
Henry VIII in 1534.
The University has printed
and published continuously
since 1584.

CAMBRIDGE UNIVERSITY PRESS

CAMBRIDGE

NEW YORK   PORT CHESTER   MELBOURNE   SYDNEY

Published by the Press Syndicate of the University of Cambridge
The Pitt Building, Trumpington Street, Cambridge CB2 1RP
40 West 20th Street, New York, NY 10011, USA
10 Stamford Road, Oakleigh, Melbourne 3166, Australia

First published 1989

Printed in Great Britain at the University Press, Cambridge

British Library cataloguing in publication data
Wood, Diana
Clement VI.
1. Christian church. Clement VI, Pope, 1291–
1352
1. Title
262'.13'0924

Library of Congress cataloguing in publication data
Wood, Diana, 1940—
Clement VI: the pontificate and ideas of an Avignon pope
Diana Wood.
p.   cm. – (Cambridge studies in medieval life and thought;
4th ser., 14)
Bibliography.
ISBN 0-521-35460-9
1. Clement VI, Pope, ca. 1291–1352.   2. Popes – Primacy – History of
doctrines – Middle Ages, 600–1500.   1. Title.   11. Series.
BX1297.W66 1989
282'.092'4 – dc 19   88–30459   CIP

ISBN 0 521 35460 9

In Memoriam
G.M.S.
et
Gratias ago tibi
V.H.P.

CONTENTS

ILLUSTRATIONS

PREFACE

'Suit the action to the word': this book is an attempt to explore the extent to which Pope Clement VI (Pierre Roger) managed to do this in terms of the preordained 'word' of the papal office. Was he ruled totally by the dictates of the papal-hierocratic theory, entirely identified with the office of the successor of St Peter and vicar of Christ on earth, or did he occasionally manage to act as an individual guided by his own political ideas or personal preferences? And if he did so, did this result in any adjustments to earlier papal theory?

Clement VI was a fascinating and controversial figure. He has often been regarded as the most typical of the Avignon popes, and has therefore tended to be the most vilified of them. He has been seen as the symbol of the period of 'Babylonish captivity', a period said to be decadent and devoid of ideas, and sullied with nepotism and vice, a period when the popes were entirely in thrall to the French monarchy. This apart, his pontificate, 1342–52, was an exceptionally eventful one. It was a time of political and social turmoil – of imperial pretenders and rebellious kings, of incessant European warfare, of unchecked Islamic expansion and aggression, and of suffering brought about by plague and economic uncertainty. The pontificate also boasted a successful imperial election, an official jubilee year, and more than its share of revolutions. Yet, despite the opportunities such events might seem to afford, the political theory of Clement VI has been relatively little studied.

It may be that potential Clementists have been deterred by the seeming scarcity of material. After all, Clement wrote no *magnum opus* as such, and not all of his letters are extant. But at least these limitations are compensated for by the preservation of his sermon literature, which provides an exceptionally rich source for papal theory. The secondary purpose of this book, now that there is a growing and welcome interest in medieval sermons, is to use those of Clement VI as a case study to demonstrate the value of sermons as historical evidence, and, in particular, as a source for political theory.

xi

Preface

For this reason I have concentrated largely on the thirty or so political *collationes* – the sermons which Clement preached in consistory on occasions of political importance – rather than his more pastoral and theological compositions, many of which were delivered in his pre-papal years. Some of his most important sermons are now available in modern editions, but others, notably those concerned with the cardinals, have still to be edited. Where an unreliable printed edition exists, or where an alternative reading seems preferable, I have ventured to use my own transcription. In most cases footnote references to the sermons have been made according to the numbered list which appears as appendix 3. Biblical references are to the Latin Vulgate. Since the wording of this sometimes differs from English versions, translations of biblical quotations are partly according to the Authorised Version and are partly my own.

The authority of the medieval papacy was considered to be universal in scope, and to do Clement VI justice this book should have been the same. But time, space, and economics have dictated the adoption of a thematic approach and the examination of specific problems to orchestrate it. The chapters which follow are not intended to be an exhaustive study of the Pope, for no such work could afford to ignore his efforts to combat heresy or his dealings with the religious Orders, or to dismiss so briefly his Eastern policy and his relationship with the Italian city-states. Much could be added, too, on his relationship with the Christian rulers who do not feature in the book. And the career of Pierre Roger, his involvement in current theological controversies, both at Paris and at Avignon, and his political and diplomatic services to both the papacy and the French monarchy, would merit a volume of its own.

I am glad of the opportunity to acknowledge generous financial assistance from the University of London, the Institute of Historical Research, and the University of East Anglia, which made possible the basic research for this book. Acknowledgement is also due to the Librarians of the Bibliothèque Nationale and the Bibliothèque Sainte-Geneviève, Paris, of the Universitätsbibliothek, Graz, the Stiftsbibliothek, Klosterneuburg, the Stadtbibliothek, Frankfurt, the Bibliothèque Royale Albert Ier, Brussels, and to the Prefect of the Biblioteca Apostolica Vaticana, Vatican City, for kindly supplying me with microfilms, and to members of the staff of numerous libraries in which I have worked, especially to those of the Bodleian Library. An earlier version of chapters 3 and 4 was awarded the

Norman Hepburn Baynes Memorial Prize for 1973, for which I should like to thank the adjudicators. My thanks are also due to Christopher Ligota of the Warburg Institute, University of London, for kindly giving permission for me to cite material from his unpublished Cambridge doctoral dissertation, *Petrus, Petra, Ecclesia Lateranensis: A Study in the Symbolic Aspects of Papal Authority in Their Bearing on the Investiture Contest*, and to the editors of *Studies in Church History* for permission to reproduce material originally published in volumes XI (1975), XX (1983), XXI (1984), and subsidia 4 (1985).

Medieval hagiographers often proclaimed their insufficiency to perform the work they had undertaken. Clement VI is no subject for the hagiographers, but this does nothing to decrease my sympathy with their sentiments. I alone am responsible for the errors and omissions in the book: they are in no way a reflection on those who have been generous enough to help me in my task.

It is always a pleasant duty to record personal debts of gratitude, and I have been especially fortunate in the help and encouragement I have received from the late Beryl Smalley, from Sir Richard and Lady Southern, from Katherine Walsh, from my colleagues Jane and Andrew Martindale, and from Michael Brandon Jones. The late Professor Walter Ullmann read an earlier version of the work, and I owe much to his constructive criticism and stimulating advice. But undoubtedly my warmest thanks must be to Michael Wilks, who first suggested Clement VI to me as a subject for research, and from whose teaching, advice, and friendship I have profited so greatly over a number of years. My grateful thanks are also due to David Luscombe for giving up so much of his time to advise me during the final stages of the work, and for saving me from many errors, and, at the Press, to Andrea Smith for her tireless and meticulous subediting. My final debt of gratitude is a private one to the dedicatees of this book: they alone know how much I owe to them.

ABBREVIATIONS

Note: References to the sermons of Clement VI (Pierre Roger) in the footnotes follow the numbering of appendix 3. Biblical references are to the Latin Vulgate.

AFP	*Archivum Fratrum Praedicatorum*, Rome, 1931ff.
AHP	*Archivum Historiae Pontificiae*, Rome, 1963ff.
Baluze-Mollat	S. Baluzius, *Vitae Paparum Avenionensium*, ed. G. Mollat, 4 vols., Paris, 1914–27.
BEC	*Bibliothèque de l'école des chartes*, Paris, 1838ff.
BEFAR	*Bibliothèque des écoles françaises d'Athènes et de Rome*, Paris, 1876ff.
BJRL	*Bulletin of the John Rylands Library*, Manchester, 1903ff.
BL	British Library, London
BN	Bibliothèque Nationale, Paris
Briefwechsel	*Briefwechsel des Cola di Rienzo*, eds. K. Burdach and P. Piur, 5 parts, Berlin, 1912–29
Brussels 359	MS Brussels, Bibliothèque Royale Albert Ier, 359 (11437–40)
CC	*Corpus Christianorum*, Turnhout, 1952ff.
Cerasoli	F. Cerasoli, ed., 'Clemente VI e Giovanna I di Napoli. Documenti inediti dell' Archivio Vaticano', *Archivio storico per le provincie Napoletane*, XXI (1896), pp. 3–41, 227–64, 427–75, 667–707; *ibid.*, XXII (1897), pp. 3–46
CHR	*Catholic Historical Review*, Washington, D.C., 1915ff.

Clem.	*Constitutiones Clementis Papae V*, ed. Ae. Friedberg, *Corpus Iuris Canonici*, ii, Leipzig, 1879, cols. 1132ff.
Coulon	*Lettres secrètes et curiales du Pape Jean XXII relatives à la France*, eds. A. Coulon and S. Clémencet, Paris, 1900–62
CSEL	*Corpus Scriptorum Ecclesiasticorum Latinorum*, Vienna, 1866ff.
Daumet	*Benoît XII, lettres closes, patentes et curiales se rapportant à la France*, ed. G. Daumet, Paris, 1899–1920
Decretales	*Decretales Gregorii IX*, ed. Ae. Friedberg, *Corpus Iuris Canonici*, ii, Leipzig, 1879, cols. 6ff.
Déprez	*Clément VI. Lettres closes, patentes et curiales se rapportant à la France*, eds. E. Déprez, J. Glénisson, and G. Mollat, Paris, 1910–61
Déprez-Mollat	*Clément VI. Lettres closes, patentes et curiales intéressant les pays autres que la France*, eds. E. Déprez and G. Mollat, Paris, 1960–61
Deutsches Archiv	*Deutsches Archiv für [Geschichte*, Weimar, 1937–43] *Erforschung des Mittelalters*, Cologne and Graz, 1950ff.
DHGE	*Dictionnaire d'histoire et de géographie ecclésiastiques*, eds. A. Baudrillart, *et al.*, Paris 1912ff.
DS	*Dictionnaire de spiritualité, ascétique et mystique*, ed. M. Viller, Paris, 1932ff.
Dykmans	*Le Cérémonial papal de la fin du Moyen Age à la Renaissance*, ii, *De Rome en Avignon ou Le Cérémonial de Jacques Stefaneschi*, ed. M. Dykmans, Brussels and Rome, 1981
EHR	*English Historical Review*, London, 1886ff.
Extrav. Comm.	*Extravagantes Communes*, ed. Ae. Friedberg, *Corpus Iuris Canonici*, ii, Leipzig, 1879, cols. 1237ff.
Extrav. J. XXII	*Extravagantes Ioannis Papae XXII*, ed. Ae. Friedberg, *Corpus Iuris Canonici*, ii, Leipzig, 1879, cols. 1205ff.
FRB	*Fontes Rerum Bohemicarum*, ed. J. Emler, iii–v, Prague, 1882–93

FRG	*Fontes Rerum Germanicarum*, ed. J. Fr. Böhmer, 4 vols., Stuttgart, 1843–68
Gasnault-Laurent	*Innocent VI, lettres secrètes et curiales*, eds. P. Gasnault and M.-H. Laurent, Paris, 1959–68
Genèse et débuts	*Genèse et débuts du Grande Schisme d'Occident*, Avignon, 25–28 septembre 1978, Paris, 1980 = *Colloques internationaux du C.N.R.S.*, 586
Gratian	*Decretum Gratiani*, ed. Ae. Friedberg, *Corpus Iuris Canonici*, i, Leipzig, 1879
HLF	*Histoire littéraire de la France*, Paris, 1733ff.
JEH	*Journal of Ecclesiastical History*, Cambridge, 1950ff.
JHI	*Journal of the History of Ideas*, London, 1940ff.
JTS	*Journal of Theological Studies*, London, 1899ff.
JWCI	*Journal of the Warburg and Courtauld Institutes*, London, 1937ff.
Klicman	*Acta Clementis VI*, ed. L. Klicman, *Monumenta Vaticana Res Gestas Bohemiae Illustrantia*, i, Prague, 1903
Léonard	E. G. Léonard, *La Jeunesse de Jeanne Iere, reine de Naples, comtesse de Provence*, 2 vols., Monaco and Paris, 1932
Mélanges	*Mélanges d'archéologie et d'histoire de l'école française de Rome*, Paris, 1881–1970
MGH Const.	*Monumenta Germaniae Historica, Constitutiones*
MGH, SRG	*Monumenta Germaniae Historica, Scriptores Rerum Germanicarum*
MGH, SRGUS	*Monumenta Germaniae Historica, Scriptores Rerum Germanicarum in Usum Scholarum*
MGH, SsM	*Monumenta Germaniae Historica, Staatsschriften des späteren Mittelalters*
PBA	*Proceedings of the British Academy*, London, 1903ff.
PG	*Patrologia Graeca*, ed. J. P. Migne, 161 vols., Paris, 1857–66

PL	*Patrologia Latina*, ed. J. P. Migne, Paris, 1841–64
Potthast	*Regesta Pontificum Romanorum*, ed. A. Potthast, ii, Berlin, 1875
QF	*Quellen und Forschungen aus italienischen Archiven und Bibliotheken*, Rome and Tübingen, 1897ff.
RA	*Registra Avenionensia*
Raynaldus	O. Raynaldus, *Annales Ecclesiastici*, iv–vii, Lucca, 1749–52
RB	*Revue bénédictine*, Maredsous, 1884ff.
RHE	*Revue d'histoire ecclésiastique*, Louvain, 1900ff.
RIS	*Rerum Italicarum Scriptores*, ed. L. A. Muratori, Città di Castello, 1723–51, series 2, 1900ff.
RNI	*Regestum Innocentii III Papae super Negotio Romani Imperii*, ed. F. Kempf, *Miscellanea Historiae Pontificiae*, xii, Rome, 1947
RS	*Rerum Brittanicarum Medii Aevi Scriptores*, 99 vols., London, 1858–1911 = *Rolls Series*
RTAM	*Recherches de théologie ancienne et médiévale*, Louvain, 1929ff.
RV	*Registra Vaticana*
SCH	*Studies in Church History*, London and Oxford, 1964ff.
Schmidinger	H. Schmidinger, 'Die Antwort Clemens' VI. an die Gesandtschaft der Stadt Rom vom Jahre 1343', *Miscellanea in onore di monsignor Martini Giusti = Collectanea Archivi Vaticano*, vi, Vatican City, 1978, pp. 323–65
Sext.	*Liber Sextus Decretalium Bonifacii Papae VIII*, ed. Ae. Friedberg, *Corpus Iuris Canonici*, ii, Leipzig, 1879, cols. 937ff.
Ste-G. 240	MS Paris, Bibliothèque Sainte-Geneviève, 240
Tautu	*Acta Clementis Papae VI (1342–52)*, ed. A. L. Tautu, *Pontificia Commissio ad Redigendum Codicem Iuris Canonici Orientalis, Fontes*, series 3, ix, Vatican City, 1960

Theiner, *Cod. Dip.*	*Codex Diplomaticus Dominii Temporalis Sanctae Sedis*, ed. A. Theiner, ii, Rome, 1862
Theiner, *Mon. Hung.*	*Vetera Monumenta Historica Hungariam Sacram Illustrantia*, ed. A. Theiner, i, Rome, 1859
Theiner, *Mon. Pol.*	*Vetera Monumenta Poloniae et Lithuaniae Historiam Illustrantia*, ed. A. Theiner, i, Rome, 1860
TRHS	*Transactions of the Royal Historical Society*, London, 1871ff.
TU	*Texte und Untersuchungen zur Geschichte der altchristlichen Literatur*, Leipzig and Berlin, 1882ff.
Valbonnais	*Mémoires pour servir à l'histoire de Dauphiné*, ed. J. P. Moret de Bourchenu de Valbonnais, Paris, 1711
Vidal	*Benoît XII, lettres closes et patentes intéressantes les pays autres que la France*, ed. J.-M. Vidal, Paris, 1913
Werunsky	*Excerpta ex Registris Clementis VI et Innocentis VI*, ed. E. Werunsky, Innsbruck, 1885
ZSSR, Kan. Abt.	*Zeitschrift der Savigny-Stiftung für Rechtsgeschichte, Kanonistische Abteilung*, Weimar, 1911ff.
ZSSR, Rom. Abt.	*Zeitschrift der Savigny-Stiftung für Rechtsgeschichte, Romanistische Abteilung*, Weimar, 1880ff.

Chapter 1

INTRODUCTION

When fourteenth-century writers described the appointment of a pope they sometimes observed that a change of name meant a change of man: he who before had been pure man had now become the vicar of God on earth. Much of the interest which Clement VI, formerly Pierre Roger, has occasioned concerns the official and unofficial sides of him – the man and the office – and leads to a questioning of the extent to which he managed to separate the two in the challenging circumstances of the fourteenth century. Did he ever allow his private affections and interests to predominate over the rigid dictates of the office he filled?

This question arises partly because historians have hailed Clement as the forerunner of the Renaissance popes and have emphasised his 'humanism'. Indeed, as early as the fifteenth century he won the approval of the humanist papal biographer Bartolomeo Platina (d. 1481), who described him as 'liberal in all things, kind, and very humane – *perhumanus*'.[1] In our own century, Fournier, for example, has written:

Lui-même humaniste, entouré de savants, de lettrés et d'artistes, Clément VI ressemble par de nombreux traits au papes du XVe siècle et en est comme le précurseur.[2]

Anneliese Maier endorsed this nearly thirty years later by referring to Clement as 'der Humanistenpapst des 14 Jahrhunderts',[3] while for Lenzenweger in 1983 he was 'der prächtige Papst' (the magnificent pope).[4] Wrigley's verdict was that the life of Pierre Roger exemplified the spirit of humanism, and that Clement was 'the first modern pope' and 'a pope too modern for his time'.[5] Burnham wrote that 'although Clement pursued his career entirely within the Church, he thought and acted in terms that were thoroughly humanistic'.[6] The

---

[1] Bartolomeo Platina, *Liber*, pp. 272–3.
[2] Fournier, 1983b, p. 220.
[3] Maier, 1964, p. 99.
[4] Lenzenweger, 1983, col. 2144.
[5] Wrigley, 1965a, p. liii.
[6] Burnham, 1978, p. 373.

only biography of Clement to be published this century is by Antoine Pélissier (Brive, 1951). He too recognised Clement's Renaissance characteristics and enshrined them in the title he chose: *Clément VI, le magnifique.*

The question of Clement's 'Renaissance humanism' is closely related to the theme of man and office, for one of the hallmarks of the Renaissance popes was that they did not succeed in making the necessary separation between the two. For them, a change of name did not always mean a change of man. Writing about the late-fifteenth-century papacy, Walter Ullmann observed that 'It was no longer the impersonal office with its powers that was determinative, but the personal character of the pope – his "humanity"'.[7]

One of the problems in deciding whether or not Clement VI was a humanist pope is the uncertainty about both the definition and provenance of Renaissance humanism.[8] In general, humanism focused attention on the hu*man*ity of man, his human nature. It gave a positive value to all his purely natural, human abilities and potentialities, including his powers of natural reasoning, and encouraged him to use them to the full. This being so, the manifestations of humanism were many and various. In political terms it was to lead eventually to the liberation of the layman from his hitherto passive role in a universal Christian society dominated by the priesthood, and to his recognition as a citizen, one who had a claim, indeed, a natural right, to participate actively in government. But such developments could take place only if the whole nature of the community were altered: if society were to be viewed as a natural creation, the product of men's desire to associate with one another, and if it catered for natural human needs. They could not occur within the confines of a universal Christian society orientated towards a divine purpose. Unlike the Christian society, the basic principles of which could lead logically only to a monarchic structure of government, the community which emphasised the natural human rights and abilities of man and aimed at fulfilling merely terrestrial needs tended to stress man himself as the source of political power. Such ideas owed much to the natural law concepts which the renewed interest in Roman law, followed by the reintroduction of

[7] Ullmann, 1972b, p. 318.
[8] For example, Burckhardt, tr. Middlemore, 1878; Ullman, 1941; Campana, 1946; Ferguson, 1948; Weinstein, 1972; Skinner, 1978, pp. 3–65; and Ullmann, 1977, pp. 1–13 where further bibliography is given.

Aristotelian learning into Western Europe in the twelfth and thirteenth centuries, had nourished.[9]

By the late-medieval period an entirely new wind was blowing, destroying the old emphases on divinity and authoritarianism and scattering seeds of independence and individualism, of secularism and humanism, on every aspect of life. Society was indeed changing: what had been in theory a universal and corporate Christian society, united under the sovereign sway of the pope, was gradually becoming a collection of separate, national churches, whose loyalty and obedience to the papacy was often imperfect. The imperial authority, traditionally seen, like the papacy itself, as an expression of the unity and universality of that society was being eroded and was fragmenting into a group of independent sovereign states, whose lay rulers would acknowledge no temporal superior. New and dangerous, and, above all, anti-papal political ideas were emerging, such as those propounded by Marsilius of Padua and William of Ockham. Demands were being made for participation, for representation, even for consent to decisions at different levels of society, both in the secular and the ecclesiastical spheres, from members of the Sacred College at the top to humble lay people at the bottom. All this profound political turmoil and theoretical change formed the background to Clement's pontificate. But this is not to suggest that the time was right for the appearance of a 'humanist' pope. The fifteenth-century popes, by allowing their own personalities to predominate over the dictates of their divinely ordained office, by their lifestyle, and by embroiling themselves in local Italian politics, in effect, dragged themselves down to the level of merely secular rulers and so contributed to the destruction of the universal character of the papal office. But by then the gradual changes in the nature and purpose of society were more advanced. By then too the papacy had suffered the loss of prestige caused by the Great Schism of 1378–1417 and the conciliar movement. Clement VI, however, ascended the papal throne only forty years after Boniface VIII's reaffirmation of the universality of papal authority in *Unam Sanctam* (1302), which declared it absolutely necessary for salvation to be achieved that every human creature should be subject to the Roman pontiff.[10]

Political humanism was just one aspect, for humanism could reveal itself in anything which emphasised or glorified human nature

---

[9] Ullmann, 1977, pp. 118–48 and 1967, pp. 99–151.
[10] *Extrav. Comm.*, I, xiii, 1.

or catered for natural needs. On a trivial level it was demonstrated in the self-indulgent lifestyle of Renaissance princes. It was manifested more seriously in literature, especially in the rediscovery of classical writing; in fine arts, where the emphasis was on the realistic representation of nature and on portraiture and sculpture from life; and in music, where religious polyphonic techniques were applied to secular works. It emerged too in the empirical study of natural science and in medical research. This stimulating cultural atmosphere also formed part of the background to Clement's pontificate. Renaissance popes such as Nicholas V and Sixtus IV were to be great patrons of humanist culture and scholarship, and in this sense it is possible that Clement, by anticipating them, could be termed a 'Renaissance pope'.

Clement himself was an enigma – a puzzling combination of the secular and the ecclesiastical. Antoine Pélissier, despite the Renaissance title of his biography, recognised the dichotomy in Clement's attitude and was able to emphasise a different side of him: Clement VI followed in the footsteps of Innocent III (1198–1216) in trying to preserve papal power, and in the defence of the prestige of the Church.[11] More recently, in 1978, Kurt Huber confessed himself puzzled by Clement's apparent lack of consistency. For him, the Pope's worldliness and Renaissance traits did not square with his theological commitments and his insight into mystical literature. He went on to question how sincere Clement was in the performance of his official duties, and how far motivated by true Christian charity when he acted generously.[12] In addition to the questions posed by Huber, there is that raised by the disagreement between Lenzenweger and Guillemain about Clement's thought. Lenzenweger writes that Clement 'combined knowledge with eloquence and original thought',[13] while Guillemain considers that he was not an original thinker.[14]

Even in his own century opinions about Clement were polarised, usually following nationalistic lines, with the French eulogising and the others condemning him. In France, clearly, the warmth of his personality, coupled with his undoubted abilities, had 'brought golden opinions from all sorts of people'. These were conveniently summarised by one of his biographers, probably Jean la Porte

[11] Pélissier, 1951, p. 137.
[12] Huber, 1978, p. 108.
[13] Lenzenweger, 1983, col. 2144.
[14] Guillemain, 1982, p. 216.

d'Annonay (Ardèche), writing *c.* 1367.[15] Not only was he the mirror of clemency, the dispenser of charity, the father of mercy, the disciple of piety, and the minister of liberality, but he was also a fighter for justice, an athlete of equity, an author of concord, and a lover of peace.[16] Many writers echo the play on Clement's name:[17] indeed, he himself suggested that he had been twinned with mercy from his mother's womb and wedded to clemency.[18] His love of peace was equally well known,[19] while his generosity was legendary. Apparently the 'general grace' which he issued at the beginning of his pontificate[20] occasioned such a shower of petitions from poor clerics that the following year he complained about the danger of stones wrapped in petitions being thrown at him in consistory, or worse, when he was out riding.[21] The Pope was a frequent and lavish almsgiver,[22] and subscribed to the imperial motto that no one should leave the presence of the prince dissatisfied.[23] Jean went on to hail him as the norm of modesty, the pattern of religion, the basis of faith, and the flower of eloquence.[24] His outstanding ability as an orator and his academic brilliance did in fact win him universal acclaim. The French preacher of his funeral oration marvelled at the breadth of his knowledge, his fluent eloquence, the depth of his wisdom, and the charm of his conversation, renowned throughout the world.[25] The Englishman Walter Burley praised his teaching skill, his oratory, and his memory – an opinion shared by Thomas Walsingham.[26] An Italian chronicler described the magnetism of his preaching, and how in his pre-papal days at Paris the whole city would rush to hear him whenever he prepared to preach.[27] A

[15] Baluze-Mollat, *Tertia Vita*. On Jean's probable authorship see Mollat, 1917, pp. 36–40.

[16] Baluze-Mollat, *Tertia Vita*, p. 288, lines 33–5.

[17] Baluze-Mollat, *Prima Vita*, p. 260, lines 5–6; *Secunda Vita*, p. 272, line 18; *Tertia Vita*, p. 275, lines 18–20 and p. 276, line 28.

[18] Clement VI, sermon 34, Ste-G. 240, fol. 360v: 'Et ideo licet ab infantia creverit mecum miseratio et de utero matris meae egressa sit mecum, et licet clementiam desponsaverim . . .' Cf. Job, xxxi. 18.

[19] Baluze-Mollat, *Prima Vita*, p. 259, lines 17–21; Henry of Diessenhoven, *Chronica*, p. 86. See also n. 16 above.

[20] Déprez, no. 162.

[21] Déprez-Mollat, no. 329.

[22] Baluze-Mollat, *Prima Vita*, pp. 260–1.

[23] Baluze-Mollat, *Tertia Vita*, p. 275, lines 22–4.

[24] Ibid., p. 288, lines 35–7.

[25] Jean de Cardaillac, MS BN, lat. 3294, fol. 267r. On him see Mollat, 1974.

[26] Walter Burley, *Epistola dedicatoria*, pp. 95–6; Thomas Walsingham, *Historia Anglicana*, p. 254.   [27] *Historiae Romanae Fragmenta*, ch. 12, p. 344.

German also remarks on his great knowledge and outstanding eloquence.[28]

Clement's detractors tended to be his political opponents, and were therefore most likely to be German, Italian, or English. The issues which aroused the most passion were his promotion of Charles of Moravia as king of the Romans, his alleged partiality for France during the Hundred Years War, and his reluctance to take the papacy back to Rome from Avignon. In general, he was censured for extravagance, extortion, and misappropriation of the Church's wealth, for nepotism in the promotion of his ill-qualified friends and relations to high office, and for fornication. Matthew of Nuremberg, for example, depicts him as greedy for women, for honour, and for power, and reports how he gave both himself and the curia a bad reputation for simony.[29] Henry of Diessenhoven reports on Clement's 'generosity' to friends and relations, and how he promoted several of them to the cardinalate despite their insufficient age and knowledge.[30] Even one of his French biographers echoes this criticism.[31] Henry Taube of Selbach comments on the 'new and unheard of' reservations of benefices which Clement made, and the hurried and uncanonical way in which he conferred holy orders.[32] From Italy, Petrarch and Matteo Villani, both of whom felt passionately about the Roman question, delighted in perpetrating scandals about the Pope's private life,[33] while Cola di Rienzo compared him with Mahomet, who had seven wives.[34] William of Ockham accused him of procreating illegitimate children whom he subsequently promoted to ecclesiastical dignities. This was not, as Ockham censoriously observed, according to the doctrine of the Apostles.[35] The smear campaign reached a crescendo by the end of

---

[28] Henry of Diessenhoven, *Chronica*, p. 86.

[29] Matthew of Nuremberg, *Chronica*, ch. 69, p. 188.

[30] Henry of Diessenhoven, *Chronica*, p. 86.

[31] Baluze-Mollat, *Prima Vita*, p. 261, lines 5ff.

[32] Henry Taube of Selbach, *Chronica*, p. 70.

[33] Matteo Villani, *Istorie Fiorentine*, bk iii, ch. 42, cols. 186–7, where the Pope's name was linked with that of Cécile, countess of Turenne. Petrarch attacked Clement's way of life in *Eclogues* VI and VII (see Francis Petrarch, ed. Piur, 1925, pp. 56–7; Wilkins, 1955, p. 48). For vindication of Clement's reputation see Mollat, 1961 and 1964, pp. 96–7; and Wrigley, 1965b).

[34] 'Il commento di Cola di Rienzo alla *Monarchia* di Dante', p. 698.

[35] William of Ockham, *De Electione Karoli IV*, ch. 4, p. 352. Commentators have doubted Ockham's authorship of this work since it is extant only in Conrad of Megenberg's *Tractatus contra Wilhelmmum Occam*, and Conrad himself (p. 11) allows only that it was attributed to Ockham. For discussion see Miethke, 1969, pp. 133–6. Baudry, 1949, p. 237, endorses Ockham's authorship and this view has been followed here.

the century, when Thomas Burton, the chronicler of Meaux, sympathised with Clement's confessor, to whose pleas for sexual abstinence Clement would retort that what he did was *ex consilio medicorum* – on the advice of his doctors. He then went on to advance the bizarre notion that Clement used to keep a little black book in which he recorded the names of all promiscuous popes in order to show that they had been better governors of the Church than the celibate ones.[36] If this were true it would add a new and interesting dimension to the political theory of the medieval papacy, but in fact twentieth-century scholarship has vindicated Clement's moral reputation.[37]

Different facets of Clement's life and personality – the ecclesiastical or the secular, the official or the unofficial – were emphasised according to the political sympathies or the nationality of the appraiser. It does seem, however, that in his earlier career Pierre Roger had benefited equally from ecclesiastical and secular influences, and had been as much at home in royal Paris as in papal Avignon. He was born at Maumont, in Corrèze, in 1291 or 1292, the second son of a family of the lesser nobility. He was to have two brothers and two sisters. The family seems to have been a close-knit and expanding one – his elder brother had thirteen children – and its members were to reap many advantages from Pierre's success. At the age of ten he was sent to the Benedictine abbey of Chaise-Dieu, in the Auvergne, where he was to make his profession as a Benedictine monk.[38] At fifteen, due to his unusual promise, he was sent to the University of Paris. There he studied arts, philosophy, and finally theology,[39] and excelled both as a scholar and as a preacher. In his mid to late twenties he started to attract attention. On the basis of two fragments from an early work of his on papal power, Anneliese Maier has deduced his involvement in the controversy surrounding the views of the Paris theologian Jean de Pouilli,[40] who opposed the privileges of the Mendicant Orders, especially their right of hearing confession in competition with the secular clergy. The debates soon widened to embrace the whole question of papal authority, and one

[36] Thomas Burton, *Chronicon Monasterii de Melsa*, iii, pp. 89–90.
[37] See p. 6, n. 33 above.
[38] On his profession as a monk see Baluze-Mollat, ii, p. 342. On his early life see Wrigley, 1970. On his career and influence in general see Mollat, 1953, and 1964, pp. 89–103; Fournier, 1938b; Pélissier, 1951; Huber, 1978; Guillemain, 1982; Lenzenweger, 1983.
[39] Baluze-Mollat, *Secunda Vita*, p. 264; *Tertia Vita*, p. 274.
[40] MS Vat. Lat. 14606, fols. 131v, 194v: Maier, 1967, pp. 510–16. On the controversy see Sikes, 1949; Fournier, 1938a, pp. 46, 62–71.

of de Pouilli's main themes was that bishops and priests, as successors of the Apostles and disciples, held their authority directly from Christ, rather than through the medium of the papacy. Pope John XXII not surprisingly took exception to this, and after a trial which lasted on and off for four years, he condemned de Pouilli's views in *Vas electionis* (24 July 1321). Among those who supplied John with theological ammunition to use against de Pouilli at his trial was the Dominican Pierre de la Palu. Significantly Pierre Roger copied much of the Dominican's *De Potestate Papae*, written in this connection, into the commonplace book he kept at Paris.[41] His own involvement has attracted far less attention. The first manuscript fragment analysed by Maier implies that the Pope had asked him for his opinion on de Pouilli's first defence (July 1318), while the second, which was apparently to be read out in consistory, refuted de Pouilli's views on the origins of priestly power.

Concurrently with the de Pouilli affair, in 1320–1, Pierre was participating in a series of spectacular university disputations on the *Sentences* of Peter Lombard. His chief, but not sole, opponent was the Franciscan François de Meyronnes, and this part of the debate has been edited.[42] The arguments were on trinitarian theology, and the Benedictine adopted a 'Thomist' viewpoint in opposition to that of the more *avant garde* 'Scotists', who tried to apply the theory of formal distinction to the three persons of the Trinity. Pierre maintained the indivisibility of the Trinity.[43] Of the two standpoints, Pierre's was the more orthodox, and this orthodoxy was to be reflected later, during his pontificate, when he condemned the nominalist opinions (partly based on those of Ockham) of the Paris theologians Nicholas of Autrecourt (1346) and John of Mirecourt (1347).[44] Pierre's admiration for Aquinas was also to be demonstrated in three sermons he preached in his honour in 1324, 1326, and 1340, and in the catalogue of his works which he compiled.[45]

Pierre's prominent role at Paris was soon to be rewarded, for he benefited from both royal and papal favour. When, on 12 May 1323, John XXII commanded the Chancellor of the University to confer

[41] MS Vat. Borghese 247, fols. 13r–16v: Maier, 1967, pp. 308, 509–10.
[42] *François de Meyronnes-Pierre Roger: 'Disputatio'*, ed. J. Barbet (Paris, 1961). For discussion see introduction, pp. 22–35; Ruello, 1965.
[43] Barbet, 1961, p. 29.
[44] H. Denifle and A. Chatelain, *Chartularium Universitatis Parisiensis*, ii, nos. 1124, 1147, pp. 567–87, 610–13.
[45] Laurent, 1931.

the mastership in theology, a chair, and the *licencia docendi* (licence to teach) upon Pierre it was partly as a result of a supplication from Charles IV of France. These honours were to be bestowed despite the fact that he had not read the *Sentences* for the statutory six years, as the Pope pointed out. He was also younger than other masters, for the customary age for the mastership to be conferred was thirty-five, and Pierre was only thirty or thirty-one.[46]

As a master, the Benedictine lectured on canon law as well as theology.[47] Soon after his promotion, probably in 1325, he composed a postill (commentary) in support of John XXII's bull *Quia quorundam mentes*.[48] This had been issued against the 'Spiritual' wing of the Franciscan Order in 1324 on the vexed issue of the poverty of Christ and his Apostles, the issue which had earlier split the Order. John denied that Christ and the Apostles had practised poverty or that they had been devoid of legal rights. He also reaffirmed the pope's absolute right to define matters of doctrine. Pierre strongly supported John. Drawing on Gratian he explained that while Christ and the Apostles had not possessed estates, fields, and houses, they had possessed the price of them – in legal terms they had possessed movable rather than immovable goods. They had not wanted to be encumbered with immovables because they foresaw that the future of the Church lay elsewhere, with the Gentiles, but this did not mean that they had abdicated their right to use such goods.[49]

Pierre was to return to this theme at the Council of Vincennes in 1329. This council was summoned by Philip VI to try to settle disputes which had arisen in France about the respective spheres of jurisdiction of the ecclesiastical and the civil courts. Pierre acted as spokesman for the bishops, defending them against the opposing views of Pierre de Cugnières, and preached on the theme 'Fear God and honour the king' (I Peter, ii. 17).[50] Using arguments from divine, natural, civil, and canon law, and appealing also to custom

[46] Denifle and Chatelain, ii, no. 822, pp. 270–1. For the age at which the mastership was conferred see Powicke and Emden, 1936, i, p. 472.

[47] As witnessed by the canonist Johannes Gaufredi (see Fournier, 1938b, p. 526, n. 2) and the poet-chronicler Aegidius li Muisis, *De Domino Papa Clemente Sexto*, p. 308, lines 35–9.

[48] Brussels 359, fols. 25r–67v. For discussion of John's bull (*Extrav. J. XXII*, xiv, 5) see Leff, 1967, pp. 241–6: Tierney, 1972, pp. 171–204.

[49] Brussels 359, fol. 63r. Cf. Gratian, II, C.xii, q. 1, c. 15. On the poverty dispute in general, see Douie, 1932; Leff, 1967, pp. 51–255; Lambert, 1961, and 1977, pp. 183–206.

[50] Pierre Roger, sermon 15. For analysis of the proceedings see Martin, 1909. See also Posthumus Meyjes, 1978, where the influence of Pierre Roger's discourse upon Gerson is examined.

and privilege, he proved the total competence of the Gallican Church to hear not just cases involving the Church, but also personal suits between laymen. In so doing he rehearsed all the traditional papal arguments to demonstrate the superiority of the priesthood over the laity, and to show that the priests possessed both spiritual and temporal jurisdiction. Probably his promotion to the archbishopric of Rouen the following year was in recognition of the considerable abilities he had shown at Vincennes.

It is difficult to know how much of Pierre's success to attribute to papal favour and how much to royal: doubtless it was a combination of the two. The young monk's first promotion had been to the priory of St Pantaléon (1316), followed by that of Savigny, in the diocese of Lyons (1323), and finally that of St Baudil, in Nîmes (1324). These houses were all dependents of Chaise-Dieu. His next promotion came in 1326 to the abbacy of the major house of Fécamp. His most dramatic rise in the ecclesiastical hierarchy, however, was in the years immediately following the accession of Philip VI Valois in 1328. He became successively Bishop of Arras (3 December 1328), Archbishop of Sens (24 November 1329), and finally Archbishop of Rouen (14 December 1330).[51]

Ecclesiastical responsibilities also entailed involvement in secular politics. Immediately after Philip's coronation Pierre was sent to England to demand Edward III's homage for Aquitaine, and later that year supervised the confiscation of the revenues of the Duchy, which Philip had decided to seize.[52] About the same time he was appointed to the *Chambre des Enquêtes*. Since this dealt with judicial inquiries it was unusual to find someone with theological rather than legal qualifications being appointed to it, and it may well indicate that Pierre had some expertise in civil as well as canon law.[53] Two years later he became Président of the *Chambre des Comptes*.[54] It seems unlikely, however, that he became Chancellor of France, as is sometimes suggested. The most likely explanation of a puzzling passage in Jean la Porte's *Vita* is that the Archbishop of Rouen held the office of *garde des sceaux* (in effect that of Vice-Chancellor) for a few weeks early in 1334.[55] What is certain is that he was one of the King's most valued councillors: indeed, his biographers reported

---

[51] Baluze-Mollat, *Secunda Vita*, p. 263; *Tertia Vita*, p. 274.
[52] Wrigley, 1970, pp. 456–65; Déprez, 1902, pp. 39–43.
[53] Cazelles, 1958, p. 345.
[54] Ibid.
[55] Wrigley, 1970, p. 462; Pélissier, 1951, p. 26, on the basis of Baluze-Mollat, *Tertia Vita*, p. 274. For correction see Tessier, 1957, pp. 362–4.

that so great was Philip's affection for him, and so unwilling was the King to lose his counsel and his agreeable conversation, that he deliberately blocked Pierre's promotion to the Sacred College by John XXII.[56] During the 1330s the Archbishop continued to be employed on vital diplomatic missions in connection with Anglo-French affairs. He was also heavily involved in promoting the projected crusade to the Holy Land, and made three visits to Avignon in connection with it. On the third occasion, in July 1333, his eloquent preaching persuaded John XXII to confer the leadership of the expedition on Philip VI.[57] The Pope then authorised Pierre to preach the crusade officially.

Sometimes Pierre's loyalties must have been divided. This was true, for example, of the affair of the English Dominican Thomas Waleys, who preached against John XXII's provocative view on the Beatific Vision. In two sermons John had declared that the souls of the blessed do not enjoy the vision of God after death, but must await the Day of Judgement and the reunion of soul and body.[58] John expected the Archbishop of Rouen to explain the scriptural basis of his view to Philip and his Queen. Pierre failed to do this, for he too disagreed with the Pope's view, and at the examination which took place at Avignon in 1333 he did what he could to prevent, or at least delay, Waleys's condemnation. He subsequently attended a meeting of French theologians convoked by the King which condemned John's teaching.[59] Pierre Roger seems to have been in an even more difficult position during the early years of Benedict XII's pontificate. On the one hand he was expected to promote the cause of France in the war against England for Philip, while on the other he was expected to promote the cause of peace for Benedict. This was made no easier by Philip's wish to divert the tenths collected for the crusade, which had been cancelled, into his war coffers. He expected Pierre to plead his case at Avignon.[60] It says much for the Archbishop that he retained the esteem of both Pope and King. He was created Cardinal-priest of St Nereus and Achilleus in 1338,[61] and in this role continued to exercise a special responsibility for Anglo-

---

[56] Baluze-Mollat, *Secunda Vita*, p. 263; *Tertia Vita*, p. 274. On Pierre as a councillor see Cazelles, 1958, pp. 91, 137.
[57] Wrigley, 1970, p. 261. The text of the sermon is in Ste-G. 240, fols. 289v–305r; and 495v–505v.
[58] For a summary of John's views, Offler, 1956b, pp. 20–2.
[59] Käppeli, 1936, pp. 22–9. On Waleys see Smalley, 1954.
[60] Wrigley, 1970, pp. 462–4; Déprez, 1902, pp. 142–3.
[61] Daumet, no. 540 (19 December 1338).

French affairs. On Benedict's death in April 1342 Philip sent his son John, Duke of Normandy, to press for Pierre's election as pope – needlessly as it turned out, for by the time the Duke reached Avignon, Pierre Roger was already recognised as Pope Clement VI.[62]

No pope could have ascended the papal throne at a more exciting or difficult time. Quite apart from the long-term challenge to the traditional papal conception of the universal Christian society, Clement was beset by specific problems. To name but a few: he was confronted with an imperial 'usurper' in the shape of the heretical Louis of Bavaria, whom it was impossible to recognise or approve, and to whom there appeared to be no suitable alternative candidate; the growth of the lay spirit and nationalism in the regional kingdoms, accompanied by incessant warfare among them; a climax in the Anglo-French struggle; turmoil in Naples under his ward, the defiant but inexperienced Queen Joanna; popular revolution in the papal city of Rome, led by the flamboyant demagogue Cola di Rienzo, coupled with demands that the papacy should leave Avignon and return there, further complicated by Clement's declaration of 1350 as a jubilee year; the failure of the crusades to check Islamic expansion or heal the Greek Schism; the social tensions generated by plague and economic uncertainty; and, at the end of the reign, an unprecedented show of 'constitutionalism' among the Pope's closest advisers, the cardinals, who staged a palace revolution. All these troubles, and many more, had to be surmounted at a time of growing financial hardship for the curia.

Such eventful years give ample scope for assessing Clement's pontificate and ideas, and the extent to which the person predominated over the office. But of course the historian is always dependent upon evidence, and in this case there are many imperfections. The glaring problem is the lack of any *magnum opus* containing the Pope's views. In the absence of this there are only registers and sermons, neither of which is ideal. The papal registers appear particularly unpromising: heavy with traditional formulae, and often drastically abbreviated ones at that, they do not seem likely to convey Clement's personal views.[63] Indeed, there are at least two instances in the

---

[62] Déprez, 1902, pp. 389–91.

[63] For a table giving the distribution of the Vatican Registers for the pontificate see *Sussidi per la consultazione dell'Archivio Vaticano*, i, pp. 61–4. On alterations in the arrangement of the secret letters during the pontificate see Opitz, 1938–9; Bock, 1941, p. 43. From *c.* 1350 the *communes* and *de curia* letters gradually ceased to be copied from *RA* to *RV*: see Bock, esp. pp. 8–11; Boyle, 1972, pp. 114–23.

printed correspondence where Clement seems to have appropriated letters written by Benedict XII (1334–42), his predecessor, and reissued them under his own name, sending them to different recipients.[64] So impersonal are some of the letters that there has been confusion in their registration. One of Clement's registers, *RV* 216, has turned out to contain nine folios of letters belonging to Benedict XII.[65] Yet some minutes thought to be those of Innocent VI (1352–62) were shown by Renouard to belong to Clement VI.[66] Despite their impersonal character, there are occasional indications that Clement was at least partly responsible for the contents of his registers. Some of the letters are marked by references to secret *cedulae*. These were documents written in the Pope's own hand, and contained confidential material which he did not wish to be registered. They were then enclosed with the official letters, the contents of which Clement must obviously have known. Needless to say the information contained in the *cedulae* would have been invaluable to the historian.[67] Occasionally the letters contain personal details, which argue for Clement's authorship, as when he described the agonies of having a tooth out to Queen Joan of France,[68] or when he gave details of his parlous state of health to various royal correspondents.[69]

The Pope's participation in the composition of at least some of his letters makes the loss of all his Year I secret letters particularly frustrating. His first year, when he was relatively inexperienced, and still in reasonably good health, is the time when he might have been expected to take a personal interest in the workings of the curia. Later, curial business might have become routine, and his almost constant illnesses might well have disposed him to let the bureaucratic machine run itself.[70] Almost certainly these letters

[64] Cf. Déprez, no. 94 (31 May 1343) with Benedict XII's letter of 23 June 1337, Daumet, no. 305, and Theiner, *Mon. Pol.*, i, no. 713, which repeats Benedict's letter in Theiner, *Mon. Hung.*, i, no. 958: cited by Knoll, p. 152, n. 34.

[65] Kyer, 1978a.

[66] Renouard, 1935.

[67] Mollat, 1956–7. See also Clement's sermon 13, Ste-G. 240, fol. 545v, where he admits to having written letters in his own hand to the rebel Archbishop of Milan, Giovanni Visconti: '. . . nos per multiplicatas litteras et bullas apostolicas et postmodum per litteras *manu nostra scriptas* voluissemus eum a tam nefando opere retrahere'.

[68] Mollat, 1957.

[69] See, for example, Déprez, no. 500 to John of Normandy; Déprez–Mollat, no. 2565 to Peter of Aragon and his Queen. See also Léonard, 1932, ii, p. 328; Wrigley, 1964, pp. 621–4.

[70] On Clement's precarious health see Waquet, 1912; Déprez, 1900; Wrigley, 1964.

would have contained the initial negotiations in his plan to engineer the election of Charles of Moravia as king of the Romans, and also valuable material on his early efforts to mediate between England and France in the Hundred Years War. The loss is all the more tantalising because St Clair Baddeley gives a reference to 'Arch. Secr. Vatic. f. 147, Anno I', which implies that the secret letters for that year were available at the end of the nineteenth century when he was writing.[71] The chance discovery by Déprez of a register containing letters Clement wrote in connection with Anglo-French affairs between his election and his coronation, although full of interest, is scant compensation.[72]

The greatest compensation, however, is provided by Clement's sermons, which are an exceptionally rich source.[73] The fact that there are nearly 120 sermons extant (although admittedly not all of them complete), and that they are distributed in some ninety manuscripts throughout Europe bears witness to their popularity. Among them are university sermons, preached in the 1320s, sermons preached while he was in the service of the King of France, sometimes at Paris, sometimes at Avignon, and often in connection with either the Anglo-French war or the crusade, and both the political *collationes* he preached as pope in consistory and occasional pulpit sermons dating from the pontificate. Obviously the papal sermons are the most valuable to the historian, but sometimes Pierre Roger's early theological and political views can be gleaned from the Paris sermons, which enable comparisons to be made with the attitudes he expressed later as pope. The consistory sermons, however, expand on the formulae of the papal letters. Sometimes they will provide the odd personal 'aside', but their greatest value is that they enable the historian to assess Clement's political principles and motives and to follow the interplay between political theory and practice. Clement seems to have been especially keen to preach in consistory, and there are about thirty *collationes* preached on important political occasions. Some, but by no means all, have been edited.[74] There are several sermons connected with the deposition of Louis IV of Bavaria and the election of Charles IV. There are pieces

---

[71] St Clair Baddeley, 1897, p. 269.

[72] Déprez, 1903.

[73] On Clement's sermons see Mollat, 1928; Schmitz, 1929 and 1932; Schneyer, 1972, pp. 757–69; Fournier, 1938b; Wood, 1975. For discussion of MS Innsbruck Universitätsbibliothek 234, containing sermons of Pierre Roger and Richard FitzRalph, see Walsh, 1981b.

[74] See app. 3, pp. 211–15 below.

about the deposition and subsequent reinstatement of the tyrant Archbishop Giovanni Visconti of Milan, about the crusade, the Jubilee Year of 1350, the murder of Prince Andrew of Hungary, and many other topics. There are two about the creation of a king of the Fortune (or Canary) Islands. Finally, there are about a dozen *collationes* connected with the cardinals – their appointments to the Sacred College, their promotions, and their legations. Clement himself claimed that he established the custom of preaching in consistory whenever a cardinal legate or nuncio returned to Avignon after an assignment.[75]

In structure the political *collationes* are much like other sermons of the period in that they have a biblical theme, which is then divided into distinctions and subdistinctions to illustrate particular points. These are weighted with biblical, patristic, and other authorities.[76] Clement was an acknowledged master of the scholastic method, but this is not to suggest that all of his compositions follow a uniform plan, far less that they all adhere strictly to the guidelines recommended in contemporary *artes praedicandi*.[77] What makes these *collationes* a distinctive genre is that their biblical themes are adapted to expound a political rather than a purely theological or moral message.

Of course they are not a perfect source of evidence. Incidental references show that some of the consistory pieces are not extant.[78] Then there are problems of identification, and in one case of interpolation.[79] And while the list of his compositions is a growing

---

[75] Clement VI, sermon 18, Ste-G. 240, fols. 69v–70r: '. . . audivimus quod in regressu legati vel nuncii non sunt aliae tales collationes fieri consuetum, licet dominus Benedictus fecerit in regressu domini Cardinalium Hispani et de Monte Favencio et in regressu Cardinalium Penestrini et Tusculani'. See also Dykmans, ch. 118, 'De creatione cardinalium legatorum vel nuntiorum', § 17, p. 499: 'Dicta namque collatio que fit per papam in adventu nuntiorum vel legatorum, fuit introducta per dominum Benedictum papam XII, et observata per dominum Clementem VI. Tamen, temporibus domini Clementis V et domini Iohannis XXII non observatur'. Dykmans, p. 246, considers that this paragraph was added to the *Ceremonial* during Clement's pontificate.

[76] On Clement's use of the Bible see Wood, 1985.

[77] See, in general, Charland, 1936, esp. pp. 111–65, and Caplan, 1970.

[78] These include a sermon against Louis of Bavaria, referred to by Cola di Rienzo, 'Il commento', pp. 705–6 (see Wood, 1985, p. 237); a sermon preached in support of the Mendicant Orders in 1351, described by Jean de Venette, *Continuatio Chronici*, pp. 224–5; an election sermon parodied by Matthew of Nuremberg, *Chronica*, ch. 69, pp. 187–8; and a sermon preached before the French court on 31 July 1335, which described Philip VI's plans to send 6,000 men at arms to help the Scots against England, described in the *Chronique parisienne anonyme*, pp. 164–5.

[79] Offler, 1974.

one,[80] it is not usually the political discourses which come to light. Moreover, Clement was an accomplished plagiariser: his sermons are so redolent with other men's flowers that it is often a job to disentangle his own words from the thicket of others' verbiage. His favourite writers were Aristotle, Seneca, Augustine, Ambrose, and Bernard. While Archbishop of Sens (1329–30) he had made his own collection of excerpts from the works of Bernard,[81] and so great was his enthusiasm for the other four authors that he employed a group of scholars at the curia to compile dictionaries of quotations from their works, so that he might use them in his own.[82] It seems like poetic justice that some of Clement's sermons were to be plagiarised and preached at the Council of Constance (1415–17).[83] The fact that the sermons could be re-used, unacknowledged, after some seventy years is indicative of their often impersonal quality, and shows the limitations of their use as a source of evidence for the personal views of their author. There is also the problem faced by most scholars of the medieval sermon – that of authenticity. True, there are some good, near-contemporary manuscripts, in which the words of the sermons, where they appear in more than one manuscript, are very similar. But they are not always identical, and this, and the fact that Clement's sermons are rarely preserved in autograph manuscripts, suggests that their copyists may have been relying on the words of *rapporteurs*, a common practice at the time.[84] In the interpretation of medieval political theory the use or omission of a particular word can be crucial, and the history of the texts which have survived is a limitation which needs to be borne in mind.

The sermons are not an easy source to use. Even when their reader has sorted out which words were actually Clement's as opposed to those of earlier writers, and whether they are authentic, there is still the problem of Clement's rhetoric. A great deal of what he said was mere sound and fury, declaimed partly to conform to scholastic rules of sermon composition, but above all for poetic and rhetorical effect.

[80] The most recent list is that by Schneyer, 1972, iv, pp. 757–69, where 101 *incipits* are listed. Taking into account the fragmentary compositions found in Vat. Borghese 247, the total can be shown to be about 120.

[81] Paris, BN, nouvelle acquisition latine, 2627, fols. 59r–149r. Fol. 59r reads: 'Incipit liber primus exceptionum collectarum de diversis opusculis b. Bernhardi . . . editus ab episcopo Petro Senenensi'.

[82] See app. 1 below, nos. 1, 2, 6, and 7.

[83] Wood, 1975, pp. 168–72.

[84] Bataillon, 1980.

The emotional atmosphere he produced is caught by the fourteenth-century chronicler Aegidius li Muisis:

Praedicans verbum divinum
Nullum ponebat terminum
In ipsius sermonibus,
Sed saepe coram omnibus
Verbum Dei proponebat
Et populum incitabat
Deum summum adamare,
Atque semper honorare.[85]

Clement's rhythmic, assonant, and poetic style was renowned, and he excelled in the ability to rhyme the words of the subdivisions of his themes, all of which must have helped to captivate his audience.[86]

In addition to Clement's sermons and registers there are the narrative sources, the seven lives of him which form part of Baluze's *Lives of the Avignon Popes (Vitae Paparum Avenionensium)*, now edited by Mollat. Of these, the third, that of Jean la Porte (c. 1367) is the most valuable, and adds many details to the closely related second life, with which it shares a common source.[87] The first life is thought to date from c. 1404–6 and takes part of its material from a chronicle of Werner, canon of Bonn (d. 1384).[88] The fourth life reproduces a chronicle of the time of Urban V (1362–70), and appears to date from after 1413: it mentions a fire at the Papal Palace,[89] and we know that one took place then.[90] The fifth life, that of Peter of Herenthals, relies on the chronicle of Conrad of Halberstadt, which finished in 1353. It devotes a lot of space to preserving a forged jubilee bull attributed to Clement. Apart from that, its brevity is disappointing, particularly since the author says that he was himself in Avignon in 1342.[91] The sixth life is of little value since it merely provides excerpts from Werner of Bonn's work.[92] The final life is that of Werner himself, who was an eyewitness of the canonisation of St Yves at Avignon in 1347.[93]

---

85 Aegidius li Muisis, *De . . . Clemente Sexto*, p. 312, lines 147–54.
86 Charland, 1936, p. 154.
87 Mollat, 1917, pp. 34–43.
88 Ibid., pp. 58–80.
89 Ibid., pp. 18–21: Baluze–Mollat, i, p. 293, line 20 refers to the fire.
90 Laclotte and Thiébaut, 1983, p. 37.
91 Baluze–Mollat, i, p. 298, line 19. Mollat, 1917, pp. 106–8.
92 Mollat, 1917, p. 44.
93 Baluze–Mollat, i, p. 546, lines 30–1.

The problems of the sources, especially the sermons, reflect the problems of interpreting Clement's pontificate and ideas. How much is just a matter of form, and how much expresses the genuine ideas of the writer or preacher? How much can be attributed to Pierre Roger the man, and how much to Pope Clement VI in his official capacity? To suppress individual interests and preferences would be practically impossible for anyone to achieve: to what extent did Clement manage to do so? And in the challenging conditions of the fourteenth century, with an ever widening chasm opening between theory and practice, did he ever make deliberate adjustments to the strict letter of the papal theory of government to meet new situations? Such questions can be answered only by examining the man, his conception of the papal office, and the way in which he exercised papal authority in the solution of some of the major problems of the universal Christian society.

Chapter 2

CLEMENT VI'S CONCEPTION OF THE PAPAL OFFICE

Pierre Roger was far from unique in facing the problem of submerging his own personality to conform with the dictates of his new office. Any Christian office-holder, be he pope or bishop, emperor or king, was expected to be totally identified with his office, to enter into a spiritual union with it, and this 'matrimonial' relationship was signified by the ring bestowed at ordination or coronation ceremony. The assumption of office involved so great a change that it was as if its new holder had been totally reborn as a new and different being, his private *persona* having been cast aside, and the more exalted the office, the greater the metamorphosis. In the case of the pope, Christ's earthly vicar, the change was of such incalculable magnitude that he took an official name to show that he had become a new man: 'a change of name creates a change of man', as fourteenth-century canonists declared.[1] The German publicist, Conrad of Megenberg, one of Clement VI's most loyal defenders, provided by far the best contemporary explanation of why he, like his predecessors, had changed his name. Gregory X had been called Theobald; Clement VI had been called Pierre. 'Why change their own names?' Conrad asked. He replied, with a flash of humour, that it had not been in order to commit the sort of fraud forbidden by law: it had been to show that a miraculous transformation had taken place, whereby a human being had become a terrestrial god, above

---

[1] Johannes Andreae, *Glossa Ordinaria ad Proemium Sext.*, col. 2: 'ostendatur ad permutationem nominis, factam mutationem hominis, cum enim prius esset purus homo nunc vicem veri Dei gerit in terris'; Johannes Calderinus, *ad Proemium Decretalium*, ii, fol. 2r: 'unde dicunt alii quod hoc est inductum ad ostendendum ad [*sic*] mutationem nominis factam esse mutationem hominis, quia qui primo erat purus homo, factus est Dei vicarius in terris'; Johannes Gaufredi, *ad Proemium Decretalium*, fol. 1r: 'Sed quare mutatur nomen pape in sui creatione? Dicendum quod ad [*sic*] significationem quod quantum ad perfectionem debet fieri novus homo . . .' On the pope's change of name see Krämer, 1956; Poole, 1934.

all worldly princes – to show that he could achieve no higher position on earth.[2]

Logically, a terrestrial god – one above all worldly princes – would have to preside over a universal society. Clement VI had no doubt about the universal extent of the *Ecclesia*, the Church, or the fullness of power which he wielded over it. Christianity was spread everywhere, not limited to certain lands or provinces, but diffused throughout the whole world, he declared,[3] echoing an idea which originated in patristic thought; while in correspondence he referred to the Christian society as the universal Church, diffused throughout the whole world.[4] But it meant more than this, for the *Ecclesia* existed not merely on the visible, earthly level, but also on the celestial. On earth it was the Church Militant, and in heaven it was the Church Triumphant, the society of the blessed. In origin the idea is traceable to Plato's conception of the ideal and the actual levels of being, which was adapted and given Christian expression by Augustine and Pseudo-Denys. As in the Platonic system, the purpose of human society was the realisation of the ideal on earth. Christians believed that at the end of time the visible and invisible churches would merge, on the scriptural basis of Apocalypse, xxi. 2: 'And I saw the heavenly Jerusalem descending from the sky' – a text which Clement cited.[5] But until then Christians on earth were engaged in an arduous pilgrimage towards their heavenly destination. They were encouraged along the route by members of the Church Triumphant, to whom they were united by a chain of charity. Adapting the words of Augustine's *Enchiridion*, Clement

---

[2] Conrad of Megenberg, *Yconomica*, iii, 3. ch. 1, pp. 359–60. Cf. Johannes Andreae, *Glossa Ordinaria ad Proem. Sext.*, col. 3: 'lex autem de mutatione nominis fraudulenta intelligitur'. Among canonists' opinions about the pope as God see Johannes Andreae, *Glossa Ordinaria ad Proem. Clem.*, col. 800: '*Papa*. Id est admirabilis. Et dicitur a pape quod est interiectio admirantis, et vere admirabilis: quia vices Dei in terris gerit'; William of Monte Lauduno, *ad Clem*. V, x, 4, fol. 167v: 'Omnis enim summitas et celsitudo est in Papa qui non hominis sed veri Dei vices gerit in terris . . . et ideo dicitur a Papae interiectione admirantis quasi quid admirabile in terris . . .' See Gillmann, 1915, and Rivière, 1922 and 1924.

[3] Clement VI, sermon 45, Ste-G. 140, fol. 337v: 'Patet ergo quomodo Christianitas est ubique dilatanda, nec ad certas terras seu provincias coartanda, sed per totum orbem diffundenda'. Cf. Gratian, D. XI, c. 8, on which see Wilks, 1963a, p. 411, n. 1. For similar ideas in the work of Cyprian see Bévenot, 1971, pp. xxi–xxiii. On Pseudo-Denys's observation that God, as goodness, is a principle of diffusion, and for its later use, see Peghaire, 1982, and in general Rutledge, 1964. For further bibliography see Altaner and Struiber, 1966, pp. 501–5.

[4] Tautu, no. 26, par. 101. Cf. John XXII, Raynaldus, v, ch. 17, p. 553, ch. 19, p. 555, and ch. 21, p. 22.

[5] Clement VI, sermon 40, p. 157; sermon 19, Ste-G. 240, fol. 27r.

explained how the Church of the Blessed had to help the Church Militant, which was still journeying, because, as he said, 'the two will become one in the fellowship of the City, and now are one through a bond of charity'.[6]

For heaven to become a reality on earth the Church Militant had to be orientated towards God's purpose. To show this, Clement likened the *Ecclesia* to the cloud described in Numbers (ix. 17–18), at whose motion the Children of Israel moved, and at whose halting they paused and pitched their tents.[7] As far as possible the earthly Church had to mirror the heavenly. Clement proclaimed that the Church Militant 'literally took its example' from the Church Triumphant.[8] It had not merely to imitate the perfection of its heavenly counterpart, but its structure had also to be the same. Drawing on Pseudo-Denys and on Bernard, Clement maintained that the earthly hierarchy imitated the heavenly: there was one supreme being set over the celestial hierarchy, therefore the same was true of the terrestrial one. Just as the seraphim and cherubim and the others, even to the angels and archangels, were ordered under the headship of the one God, so on earth Christians were ordered under the supreme pontiff,[9] the implication being that the pope fulfilled the role of God on earth, and the priesthood that of the angelic hierarchy.

Members of the priesthood, and above all the supreme pontiff, were marked out from the laity by their ordination. They were the only ones qualified by their knowledge of divinity to guide society to its heavenly destiny. The most common way to express this was to liken priesthood and laity to soul and body respectively,[10] as Clement himself did, echoing Hugh of St Victor.[11] As head of the earthly

---

[6] Clement VI, sermon 19, Ste-G. 240, fol. 40v. Cf. Augustine, *Enchiridion*, ch. 56, *PL*, 40, 258–9. Clement substituted the word *civitatis* for the original *aeternitatis*, underlining his debt to the *De Civitate Dei*. Cf. Denifle and Chatelain, ii, no. 1125, p. 588, where Clement wrote, 'et civitatem Dei, universalem videlicet Ecclesiam...'

[7] Clement VI, sermon 40, p. 159.

[8] Clement VI, sermon 19, Ste-G. 240, fol. 27r.

[9] Clement VI, sermon 40, p. 157. Cf. Pseudo-Denys, *De Ecclesiastica Hierarchia*, *PG*, 3, 371ff; Bernard, *De Consideratione*, bk iii, ch. 18, p. 445. See also similar passages in Herman of Schildiz, *Contra Hereticos*, i, ch. 3, p. 12; John of Legnano, *De Principatu*, ch. 4, pp. 434–5, and further examples in Wilks, 1963a, p. 48, n. 2. The relationship between the hierarchies was much debated in the late thirteenth and early fourteenth centuries: see Congar, 1961, esp. pp. 114–45. For the use of Pseudo-Denys see pp. 114–38, and for the views of Aquinas, pp. 129–34. For the influence of Pseudo-Denys before the thirteenth century see Luscombe, 1980.

[10] See Ullmann, 1966b, pp. 92ff, and 1967, pp. 46–8.

[11] Clement VI, sermon 40, p. 154. Cf. Hugh of St Victor, *De Sacramentis*, II, ii, 4, *PL*,

hierarchy, it was the pope's responsibility to ensure the salvation both of the whole Christian society and of each individual soul within it.

In order to fulfil this function the pope needed to wield a plenitude of jurisdictional (as opposed to sacramental) power. It was this which made him Christ's earthly vicar. The concept of the papal plenitude of power had become so familiar by the fourteenth century that there was rarely any need to elaborate on it. It was only when dealing with people who were ignorant of papal theory, or intentionally blind to it, that it needed enlargement. In a catechism drawn up to test the faith of the schismatic Armenians, Clement asked whether they believed that:

the Roman pontiffs of the past, and we who are now the Roman pontiff, and those who will be successively in future . . . have accepted and will accept immediately from Christ Himself all the jurisdictional power over the whole and universal body of the Church Militant which Christ Himself as head possessed in His earthly life.[12]

This forceful and highly condensed passage serves as an epitome of Clement's ecclesiology and views on papal power. It raises a number of issues. Firstly, by combining past, present, and future popes as if they were indistinguishable he was emphasising the continuity of the papal office, just as John XXII had done.[13] There would be a pope so long as the Christian society endured. Then he expanded on the vicariate of Christ. Each pope had been directly empowered by Christ. In the same catechism Clement wrote that each one 'held the place of blessed Peter',[14] using an idea which originated with Leo I (440–61). Because an heir was considered to be legally identical with his principal, each pope was thought to have experienced the Petrine commission of Matthew, xvi. 18–19 directly, and to have succeeded to Peter himself rather than to another pope. Each held exactly the same plenitude of jurisdictional power – the power to bind and to

---

176, 418. Among other examples see Galvaneus Flamma, *Chronica Galvagnana*, ch. 109, p. 182; John of Legnano, *De Principatu*, p. 433; Alvarus Pelagius, *De Planctu Ecclesiae*, bk i, ch. 37, p. 48.

[12] Tautu, no. 192, par. 641. On the papal plenitude of power see Buisson, 1958, esp. pp. 74ff; Benson, 1967; Watt, 1965; Miethke, 1978.

[13] John XXII, Raynaldus, v, ch. 47, p. 104: 'manet igitur, etiam istis reclamantibus, et usque ad finem seculi permanebit apud Romanum praesulem sicut summa auctoritas, sic immensa potestas'. Cf. Richard FitzRalph, *Summa de Quaestionibus Armenorum*, bk vii, ch. 14, fol. 48v: 'Petrus sicut et ceteri successores in sua dignitate usque ad consummationem seculi fuerat permansurus'; ibid., ch. 13, fol. 48v. On *dignitas non moritur* see Kantorowicz, 1957, pp. 383ff.

[14] Tautu, no. 192, pars. 637, 638.

loose, the power of the keys of heaven – as Peter had done.[15] Since the individual office-holders became indistinguishable, since they all in effect merged into one, it made little difference whether Clement VI or St Peter occupied the papal throne. By the same token, the personality of an individual office-holder could not change the nature of the office.

The pope's jurisdictional power was exercised over a corporate society – the universal body of the Church Militant, as Clement called it. Elsewhere he used the powerful expression, the *corpus Christi mysticum*, the mystical body of Christ, which had first been sanctioned by Boniface VIII.[16] The provenance of this idea was the Roman law theory of corporations, which had passed into the mainstream of Christian thought through the work of Paul and Augustine.[17] The term which the lawyers preferred to use from the time of Cicero was *populus*, a people.[18] Occasionally Clement used the term too, referring to Christians as the people of Israel, or the peculiar people of God, which signified not merely the Pauline idea that they were the heirs of the Israelites, but also their legal, corporate status.[19] In one sermon he spoke of the *collegium*, the college, of the holy Church, using a purely juristic term which, through its etymological derivation from *colligere*, to bind together, denoted the indissoluble unity of its members.[20] The cohesion among the members of a people was so great that they became as one man; they became a fictitious legal person, the individual identity of

---

[15] Ibid., par. 640: 'credidisti, tenuisti vel credere paratus es . . . quod omnes Romani Pontifices, qui beato Petro succedentes canonice intraverunt et canonice intrabunt, ipsi beato Petro Romano Pontifici successerint et succedent in eadem plenitudine iurisdictione potestatis, quam ipse beatus Petrus accepit a Domino Jesu Christo super totum et universum corpus Ecclesiae militantis?' Cf. John XXII, Raynaldus, v, ch. 40, p. 566; Richard FitzRalph, *Summa*, bk vii, ch. 14, fol. 48v. On the Roman law theory that an heir became the principal see Schulz, 1951, pp. 211ff., and for its application to the papacy Ullmann, 1975b, no. 4, pp. 33–4.

[16] See *Unam Sanctam* [*Extrav. Comm.*, I, viii, 1]: 'unum corpus mysticum cuius caput Christus'. On the development of the distinction between the terms *corpus Christi mysticum* and *corpus Christi verum* (the sacramental body of Christ) see De Lubac, 1948, esp. pp. 116–35; Mersch, 1951; Kantorowicz, 1957, pp. 193–206; and Struve, 1978, p. 57, n. 56 (on the distinction made by Augustine).

[17] In general see Gillet, 1927; Gierke, 1927, pp. 22ff.; Ehrhardt, 1953, pp. 299–347; Wilks, 1960, 1963a, pp. 22–5, and 1966; Struve, esp. pp. 44–67, 87–98, and 329–38.

[18] Augustine, *De Civitate Dei*, xix, 21, pp. 687–8, quoting Cicero, defined a people as a multitude united in pursuit of a common sense of right and a community of interest.

[19] Clement VI, sermon 40, p. 159; Pierre Roger, sermon 15, p. 468. See Cerfaux, 1959, pp. 59–79.

[20] Clement VI, sermon 11, p. 362: 'expellitur a collegio sancte Ecclesie'.

each member being merged within the fictitious whole. The whole accordingly took precedence over the parts, for once a man had been integrated into a people he had no existence apart from it. This was a theory of extreme realism, for the existence of the universal transcended that of the parts, and the universal, in that it was an abstraction, a 'fictitious' person, existed in a more real sense than the individuals who comprised it. In political terms the whole concept was akin to modern theories of the totalitarian state.[21] But in the fourteenth century the civilian Baldus de Ubaldis penned one of the clearest definitions of a people, linking it directly with the concept of the mystical body:

Separate men do not make a *populus*; for a *populus* strictly speaking is not men, but a binding together of men in one body, mystical and existing independently, whose significance is invented by the intellect.[22]

Baldus's words about an abstract person, which was not men but *a* man, were very close to the language of ecclesiology. There was, however, an all-important difference: the legal person depicted by Baldus was indeed a fiction, one whose significance existed in the mind. But the person of Christ was in effect a true fiction, for the Christian did not regard his Saviour as something mythical: He was real both in the modern sense of the term, and in the Platonic sense that He existed as a reality on the level of ideals.

The practical problem posed by a mystical or fictitious person was that there had to be someone of flesh and blood to speak for it, to give it physical representation. The representative had to 'become' the person of the corporation and take on all its attributes, indeed, to be totally identified with it: hence the casting aside of his private *persona*, and the bestowal of a 'matrimonial' ring at coronation and consecration ceremonies. Since he came to epitomise the wills and rights of the individuals who were united or contracted into the mystical body, he was really the embodiment of sovereignty. Cicero's expression was that he 'bore' the person of the State.[23]

This too is what Clement VI said. Drawing on Bernard, and ultimately on Augustine, he declared that he, although unworthy, bore the person in the *Ecclesia*:

I, although unworthy, bear in the Church the person of whom Bernard said

---

[21] Wilks, 1966, p. 488.

[22] Baldus de Ubaldis, Additio ad c. 7, 53, 5: quoted by Wahl, 1970, p. 312, n. 24. See also Canning, 1987, throughout and esp. p. 187, and Canning, 1980.

[23] Cicero, *De Officiis*, bk i, ch. 34, p. 126: 'Est igitur proprium munus magistratus intellegere se gerere personam civitatis debereque . . .'

. . . 'Let us inquire very carefully who bears the person in the Church of God. Who are you? The high priest, the supreme pontiff . . .'[24]

In more familiar terms this meant that the pope was the vicar of Christ: he acted both for and as Christ; and as such he exercised 'all the jurisdictional power over the whole and universal body of the Church Militant which Christ Himself had possessed in His earthly life', as Clement had expressed it. The theory of the representation of the mystical body of Christ and that of the vicariate of Christ were really complementary ways of justifying papal sovereignty.

There was nothing new in Clement's ecclesiology or his idea of the papal office. If anything, he seemed concerned to stress his identity with his office and his monarchic powers even more than his predecessors. This emerged in a number of subtle ways, many of them linked directly or indirectly with the ceremonial sequence for the creation of a pope, the effecting of the 'miraculous transformation' whereby a human being became a terrestrial god.

It emerged firstly in the name he chose, because this could be linked with claims to divinity. 'Clement' did not mean simply 'mild tempered', as in the dictionary definitions: the quality of clemency could be exercised only by one who was sovereign, by one who was omnipotent, and therefore very often by one who was, or who claimed to be, divine. The use of clemency involved the imposition of deliberate self-restraint by one who was all-powerful, but who voluntarily limited himself in the exercise of supreme power. To Clement the best illustration had been provided by Christ the King, who had voluntarily humbled Himself by coming to earth to minister to others as a servant.[25] In origin the idea was pre-Christian, and clemency had come to be regarded as one of the virtues associated with the Roman emperors, who themselves had claimed to be divine.[26] Clement's numerous citations from Seneca's *De Clementia*, including one in the panegyric he preached on Clement I,[27]

---

[24] Clement VI, sermon 35, Ste-G. 240, fol. 243v. Cf. Bernard, *De Consideratione*, bk ii, ch. 8, p. 423.

[25] Clement VI, sermon 39, MS Klosterneuburg Stiftsbibliothek, 204, fol. 166v: 'Scribitur Proverb. xx [28] *quod misericordia et veritas custodiunt regem et stabilietur clementia thronus eius*. Et ideo clementissimus rex, Dei filius benedictus, dicebat Luc. xxii [27], *Ego in medio vestrum sum, sicut qui ministrat*, quia *filius hominis non venit ministrari, sed ministrare, et animam suam ponere pro multis*, Matt. xx [28]. Ecce secundum ista, dignitas et praeeminentia, ecce humilitas et clementia'.

[26] On the origin and meaning of clemency and its association with the Roman emperors see Weinstock, 1971, pp. 233–43; Charlesworth, 1937, pp. 112–13; Adcock, 1964, pp. 75, 103–4. On the divinity of the emperors see Cerfaux and Tondriau, 1957, esp. pp. 269ff.; Taylor, 1931; Weinstock, pp. 281ff.

were probably more than coincidence, for he obviously had a predilection for the work. Seneca's Emperor Nero, to whom his work was dedicated, bore the vicariate of the pagan gods on earth:[28] Clement VI bore the vicariate of the Christian God. In practice, clemency was most frequently exercised in a judicial context: indeed, as Clement explained to the heretical Louis of Bavaria, clemency could not be exercised without justice.[29] The text chosen by the Pope for his sermon on St Clement was therefore an apt one: 'In his tongue is the law of clemency (Proverbs, xxxi. 26)'.[30] More specifically, clemency could be exercised only by one with supreme judicial powers, and there was no doubt about Clement's possession of these. Traditionally the pope was considered to be a living law, *lex animata*, and, like the Roman emperors, he was thought to possess the laws within his breast.[31] Clement's intimation to the Armenians that he was a norm of right living, an example to his people, was simply a corollary of this.[32] As the *lex animata* the pope alone could authorise new legislation; he alone could judge all matters, and all people, both lay and ecclesiastical, as the supreme judge, the universal ordinary of mankind.[33] There was, moreover, no escape from his judgement,[34] and no appeal against it.[35] He had, as he emphasised, 'supreme and pre-eminent authority and juridical power', and quoting Gregory VII, reminded the Armenians that he himself could be judged by no man, but was subject solely to the judgement of God.[36] Nevertheless, despite this omnipotence, indeed, in a sense because of it, the pope voluntarily imposed restraint upon himself in passing sentence.

[27] Clement VI, sermon 32, MS Vat. Lat. 2541, fol. 233v: 'Clementia in quamcumque domum pervenerit, eam felicem tranquillamque praestabit'. Cf. Seneca, *De Clementia*, I, v, 4, p. 370.

[28] Seneca, *De Clementia*, I, i, 2, p. 356.

[29] Clement VI, sermon 34, Ste-G. 240, fol. 360v: 'licet clementiam desponsaverim, tamen clementia non est sine iustitia, et misericordia sine veritate'.

[30] MS Vat. Lat. 2541, fols. 233v–36r.

[31] Cf. Boniface VIII, *Sext.*, I, ii, 1, on which see Gillmann, 1912, and for further examples, Wilks, 1963a, pp. 162–3, 301–2. For the Roman law origins of the idea see Lear, 1965, pp. 68–9; Ullmann, 1975a, pp. 61, 92.

[32] Tautu, no. 4, par. 26: 'ut nedum populo sibi [scil. papae] commisso *recte vivendi normam* tribuant . . . sed sibi ipsis per vitae meritum et eorum subditis proficiant per exemplum'. See also no. 41, par. 132.

[33] Clement VI, sermon 24, Ste-G. 240, fol. 376r: 'Ymmo omne iudicium in terris pape datum est, et nec est qui possit effugere iudicium eius'. Cf. Herman of Schildiz, *Contra Hereticos*, i, ch. 4, p. 13: 'nullus in mundo potest esse de iure exemptus a iurisdictione Ecclesiae'.

[34] Tautu, no. 192, pars. 642, 646. [35] Ibid., par. 643.

[36] Ibid. Cf. Gregory VII, *Dictatus Papae*, c. 19, p. 206.

If the pope was a living law, he was also the living Faith. He alone could pronounce authentically on doubtful points of the Faith. He demanded total adherence to his judgements on what was true and catholic, and what was false and heretical, for such judgement was made by the authority of the keys.[37] This was the vital point. Deviation from such judgements, heresy, was not merely a case of doctrinal eccentricity; it was a case of disobedience to the authority which had authenticated that doctrine. Clement therefore regarded the heretic Louis of Bavaria as being 'in contempt of the keys'.[38] The matter was made more serious by the Pope's claim to be divine. Borrowing from Hellenistic and Byzantine theories of divine emperorship the popes considered that they possessed *maiestas* – majesty. This was simply a way of expressing the divine and absolute status of the universal sovereign of mankind. Impiety or heresy was therefore a deliberate affront to a divine ruler. To underline his divine status Clement termed Louis' creation of an anti-pope 'idolatry'.[39] His heresy constituted the most serious of all crimes, *lèse majesté*, or treason, a crime, as Clement explained, not against merely human majesty, but against divine majesty itself.[40]

The monarchic role of the pope was an awesome one, involving the exercise of divine, sovereign power. It was this which led him to draw the distinction between the man and the office. The obvious occasion upon which to point the contrast was in the official letters announcing his coronation. Clement strained every nerve to convey a sense of the vast abyss which separated the heavenly office from the earth-bound man. The majestic opening (common to all his 'coronation' letters) deliberately set out to give the impression of height: 'In the loftiest throne of the divine height is the summit of wisdom, the

---

[37] Ibid., par. 651: 'Si credidisti et adhuc credis, solum Romanum Pontificem, dubiis emergentibus circa fidem catholicam, posse per determinationem authenticam, cui sit inviolabiliter adhaerendum, finem imponere et esse verum et catholicum, quidquid ipse auctoritate clavium sibi traditarum a Christo determinat esse verum; et quod determinat esse falsum et haereticum, sit censendum?' Cf. Herman of Schildiz, *Contra Hereticos*, ii, ch. 9, p. 76: 'Primo probandum est, quod ad Romanum Pontificem prae omnibus aliis pontificibus pertinet determinare dubia circa articulos fidei et circa sacram Scripturam'.

[38] Clement VI, sermon 5, p. 134: 'claves ecclesie non solum contempnando, ymmo negando'; *MGH Const.*, no. 378, p. 425: 'non tamen in contemptum clavium'.

[39] Ibid., p. 136: 'antipapam creando, ydolum in ecclesia constituendo'.

[40] Clement VI, sermon 24, Ste-G. 240, fol. 375v: 'Videmus enim hominem vel demonem notatum gravissimo scelere quia de heresi, quod est gravissimum crimen, quia crimen lese maiestatis, non maiestatis humane, sed divine . . .' Cf. *Digest*, XLVIII, iv, 1: 'Proximum sacrilegio crimen est quod maiestatis dicitur' (Ulpian).

sublimity of power, and the fullness of discretion . . .'[41] He had, as he enlarged, been elected on the one hand to ascend to the zenith of the apostolic office, and on the other to sink under the awful burden of the government of the whole world.[42] He was numbed with fear at the thought of assuming the apex of such dignity: his shoulders were too weak to support such a load. Eventually, trusting in Him who renders his yoke sweet and His burden light to those who bear them patiently, Clement VI was persuaded to submit his neck to the yoke of apostolic servitude.[43] The more he could emphasise this gigantic burden bearing down upon his shoulders, the more he could abase himself as a mere man and stress his personal unworthiness (hence the frequent use of the phrase 'although unworthy' in his writing), the more lofty and illustrious did the office appear, and the more exalted was he as its occupant: he did indeed become a terrestrial god. Looked at from one viewpoint the separation between the person and the office was simply a device to enable the Pope to stress his sovereign status.

The yoke of apostolic servitude recalls another image Clement used to stress his identity with his office, the marriage metaphor. As the vicar of Christ, the Pope was able to apply to himself the text of Ephesians, v. 25–7, where Christ had appeared as the bridegroom of the Church, an idea which had figured in official sources since the fifth century.[44] Clement was especially fond of the image, and his work abounds in references to himself as the spouse of the Church. The most striking examples occurred in two *collationes* he delivered on the suspension from office and the subsequent deposition of the heretical Archbishop of Mainz, Henry of Virneberg. In the first, Clement explained how in marriage two became one, so that to despise the Church was also to despise her bridegroom, Christ Himself.[45] He returned to this in the second piece when he accused the miscreant of wishing to subject, to abuse, even to kill Christ 'in His members and His bride, Holy Mother Church'.[46] But it was in

---

[41] Déprez, no. 4, cols. 2–3.
[42] Ibid.: '[cardinales] . . . vota sua concorditer direxerunt, nos ad conscendendam speculam apostolici culminis et subeundam gravissimam totius orbis regiminis sarcinam eligentes'.   [43] Ibid.
[44] See, for example, Tautu, no. 26, par. 100: 'sacrosanctam Ecclesiam, non habentem maculam neque rugam, congregatam in unum ex gentibus et Judaeis'. On this concept see Chavasse, 1940; Cerfaux, 1959, pp. 242, 348–51.
[45] Clement VI, sermon 22, p. 339: 'Deinde cum contempnitur ista Ecclesia, non contempnitur ipsa sola, sed eciam Christus sponsus ejus, cum ipse dicit Luce. x [16]: *Qui vos audit, me audit, et qui vos spernit me spernit*'.
[46] Clement VI, sermon 11, p. 359.

the earlier sermon that he drew out the marriage metaphor to its logical conclusion by envisaging Christians as the progeny of the pope, Christ's earthly vicar, and the Church:

We and our predecessors and this Holy Mother Church procreated a son, Henry, Archbishop of Mainz, and not merely procreated, but rather nurtured him most indulgently, brought him up, and then exalted him by immediately promoting him to one of the most important churches.[47]

The judicial side of the pope's marriage to the universal Church was thought to be effected at his election, for it was this which conferred his judicial powers upon him. The important point was that in juristic terms *consensus facit matrimonium*, consent creates matrimony.[48] The pope's consent to his marriage came to be identified with his formal consent to election which was enshrined in the ceremonial orders in use for the creation of a pope.[49] The consent was also recalled in the 'coronation' letters sent to all the officials of Christendom, for to be completely valid a marriage also had to be publicly announced.[50] Once the consent had been given, the elect, duly robed by the Prior of the Deacons, was solemnly invested with the words: 'I invest you with the Roman papacy that you may preside over the City and the world.' The ring, symbol of his marriage to the Church, was then handed to him, and the mitre, symbol of priestly supremacy, was placed upon his head.[51] It was at this point, the legal change having been effected, that he was asked by what name he wished to be known.[52] He was then formally enthroned, to demonstrate publicly that he had taken physical possession of the *Ecclesia*. In Roman law the moment when the heir actually 'became' the deceased, for all practical and legal purposes,

---

[47] Clement VI, sermon 22, p. 334. On the origins of the concept of the *Ecclesia* as mother see Plumpe, 1943a; James, 1959, pp. 192–227.

[48] Gratian, C. XXVII, q. ii, c. 2: 'Consensus . . . qui solus matrimonium facit . . .' For discussion and further canon law examples see Esmein, 1929, i, pp. 101–3, 185–9; Joyce, 1949, pp. 58–74. For discussion of the Roman law precepts on marriage, ibid., pp. 40–3; Buckland, 1963, pp. 113–14.

[49] Dykmans, ch. 10, §2, p. 267: 'et eo electioni de se facte consensum prestante'. The ceremonial *ordines* in use at Avignon are thought to be those of Cardinal Jacques Stefaneschi, which were formerly known as OR XIV (in Mabillon's numbering). Schimmelpfennig, 1973, argues for composite authorship, but considers that it was in use at Avignon, see pp. 62–100, esp. 66–71, where the election and consecration of the pope are discussed. See also Nabuco, 1966, p. 14. On the evolution and significance of the papal coronation see Wasner, 1935; Klewitz, 1941; Eichmann, 1951; Ullmann, 1970, pp. 310–19; Benson, 1968, pp. 150–67.

[50] See ch. 8, pp. 156–7 below.

[51] Dykmans, ch. 10, § 3, p. 267.

[52] Ibid.

was when he took possession of the inheritance. Interestingly the original meaning of *possidere*, to possess, was 'to sit upon'.[53]

Once the pope was invested with his powers he was entitled to enter on the administration of the papal office, despite the fact that he was uncrowned. Clement VI accordingly immersed himself in peacemaking negotiations between England and France. The chance discovery of a register of the letters he wrote in this connection, however, shows that at this stage he used the demi-bull, as was customary, and that he also adopted the traditional style: 'Clement, elect, servant of the servants of God'.[54] Although he possessed jurisdictional power as pope, in his capacity as bishop of Rome he was still merely 'elect'.

In the fourteenth century there was confusion over whether elections or coronations really forged the identity between man and office, and this was as true of the imperial office as of the papal. Discussing the papacy, Baldus de Ubaldis sensibly suggested that the pontifical year should begin from the pope's election day.[55] Surprisingly enough Gregory XI was the only Avignon pope to follow this.[56] The registers of Clement VI and the others show that letters began to be registered in Year I from the pope's coronation day. In Clement's case there is the added testimony that the letters written between election and coronation were recorded in a separate register,[57] indicating that he regarded them as apart from those of the pontificate. When Clement started to register his letters in the normal way, however, he took the trouble to begin a new section with the heading *de coronatione*, unlike his predecessors, who had

[53] Ibid., ch. 10, § 4, p. 268. See Schulz, 1951, pp. 282ff.

[54] Déprez, 1903, pp. 58–76. The use of the demi-bull and the title *electus* was described as customary by Johannes Andreae in the conclusion to *Glossa Ordinaria ad Sext.*, *De regulis iuris*, LXXXVIII, col. 784. Compare Conrad of Megenberg, *Yconomica*, iii, 3, ch. 1, p. 360.

[55] Baldus de Ubaldis, *ad Decretales*, I, vi, 6, fol. 66r: 'Ergo statim, cum est electus in papam, incipit annus pontificatus, et potest scribere se in pontificem'. See Herman of Schildiz, *Contra Hereticos*, ii, ch. 8, p. 73: 'Romanus pontifex in electione succedit Petro in plenitudine potestatis et iurisdictionis'.

[56] Gregory XI was elected on 30 December 1370 and consecrated on 5 January 1371. The letter he wrote to Charles V of France announcing his election on that day [Mirot and Jassemin, no. 2] was dated 'Datum Avinione, iii. kalendas januarii, susceptus a nobis apostolatus officii anno primo': clearly this date was thought to fall within the first year of the pontificate. Letters started to be registered in Year II from 1 January 1372, and in Year IV on 4 January 1374: see nos. 571, 1479, respectively.

[57] Clement's coronation letter to Philip VI, dated 21 May 1342, opened *RV* 152 at fol. 1r and *RV* 214 at fol. 1r: see Déprez, no. 4. On the separate register containing letters written between his election and coronation see Déprez, 1903, p. 4.

registered their coronation letters *de curia*.[58] Clement obviously attached some importance to his coronation.

Traditionally the pope was thought to be *sanctus*, a saint, in his capacity as the successor of St Peter.[59] Preaching at Avignon as a cardinal, Pierre Roger emphasised that Christ had beatified Peter (Matthew, xvi. 17), because Peter alone had recognised Him as the Christ, son of the living God.[60] As pope, Clement regarded Peter's confession as an essential part of the Petrine commission. The implication was that Clement, in line with his predecessors, and with contemporary thinkers, saw himself as *sanctus*.[61] This did not mean that he succeeded to the personal merits of St Peter: he was always Peter's successor 'although unworthy'. It did mean, however, that as pope he acquired another self, one which existed on the ideal level. This was perfectly logical given the existence of the Church itself on two levels. It also explains Clement's assertion, in the words of Isaiah, that the sky was his see.[62]

It is difficult to decide at what moment the pope actually became *sanctus*, but for Clement it seems likely that it was at his coronation. It was a happy coincidence that the anniversary of the death of the Breton priest Ivo Hélory was also the anniversary of his coronation, 19 May. It was the obvious day upon which to canonise Ivo as St Yves, for it enabled him to stress that both of them had received 'heavenly crowns' on the same date.[63]

The pope's status as *sanctus* meant that when he used the power of the keys to bind and loose on earth, they also bound and loosed in heaven. This applied especially to eschatological matters. As Clement explained to Louis of Bavaria, when the Church excommuni-

---

[58] Bock, 1941, p. 8.

[59] Ullmann, 1975b, no. 11, pp. 248–51.

[60] Pierre Roger, sermon 37, Ste-G. 240, fol. 126r: 'ex hoc [confessione] Christus ipsum proferentem beatificavit . . . Unde ibidem subiungitur in textu [Matt., xvi. 17] *Beatus es* . . . Ecce quomodo eum beatificavit . . .'

[61] Cf. Johannes Andreae, *ad Proemium Sext.*, col. 4: 'Quis enim sanctum dubitet, quem apex tantae dignitatis attolit?'; Alvarus Pelagius, *De Planctu Ecclesiae*, bk i, ch. 54, p. 139: 'ideo universalis pastor Ecclesiae dicendus est sanctus. Nam etsi persona, quae praeest, possit esse non sancta . . . locus et status est sanctus in hac vita et summe perfectus'.

[62] Clement VI, sermon 28, Ste-G. 240, fol. 62r: 'sicut descendit ymber et nix de celo, id est isti nuncii ab ista sancta sede. *Celum enim michi sedes est.* Ysa. lxvi [1]' and sermon 47, Ste-G. 240, fol. 416v.

[63] Clement VI, sermon 23, Ste-G. 240, fol. 531r: 'iste dominus Yvo anno etatis sue quinquagesimo et xix^a die maii coronatur in celis. Ego autem anno etatis mee quinquagesimus ad statum istum, licet immeritus, assumptus xix^a die mensis maii coronatus fui'. For Clement's bull of canonisation see Perarnau, 1980, pp. 362–6.

cates someone on earth, he is excommunicate in heaven, and when reconciled on earth, he is reconciled in heaven.[64] This was borne out after Louis' death as an excommunicate by references to him as 'of damned memory',[65] in contrast to other deceased Christians who were 'of blessed memory'. A shorthand device for this idea, often used by Clement, was that *extra Ecclesiam non est salus*: outside the Church there is no salvation.

During Clement's reign two important events allowed him to stress especially his sovereign powers on both the terrestrial and the celestial levels. These were the declaration of indulgences in connection with the jubilee year of 1350, and the canonisation of St Yves. Some confusion surrounds Clement's doctrine of indulgences, largely because of the existence of several forged contemporary bulls. One in particular, *Cum natura humana*, preserved by Peter of Herenthals and the jurist Albericus de Rosate,[66] caused a storm, because it ordered the angels to convey the souls of any confessed and penitent pilgrims straight to heaven.[67] Wyclif accordingly condemned Clement for 'manifest blasphemy',[68] and his criticisms were echoed through to the end of the seventeenth century.[69] The first indulgence for the dead was actually issued by Sixtus IV in connection with the church at Xaintes in 1476,[70] and made no reference to Clement.

In his genuine bull, *Unigenitus Dei filius*, issued on 27 January 1343, Clement VI elaborated fully the Church's doctrine of indulgences in writing for the first time,[71] although he had already done so in consistory, in a *collatio* preached to an embassy from the Roman

---

[64] Clement VI, sermon 5, p. 135: 'Cum excommunicat Ecclesia, in celo ligatur excommunicatus; cum reconciliatur ab Ecclesia, in celo solvitur reconciliatus'. Cf. Augustine, *In Ioann. Evangel.*, tr. l, ch. 12, p. 438.

[65] *MGH Const.*, viii, no. 372, p. 417; no. 376, p. 320; no. 390, p. 434; no. 590, p. 596; no. 638, p. 615. Cf. Innocent III, Reg. vii, 1, *PL*, 215, 278: '. . . omnes qui extra Ecclesiam inventi fuerint, in judicio damnabuntur'.

[66] Baluze–Mollat, *Quinta Vita*, pp. 299–302; Albericus de Rosate, *Dictionarium Iuris*, fols. 163v–4r. Albericus, who had attended the celebrations in Rome in 1350, was doubtful about the bull's authenticity: see fol. 164r. For opinions about it see Baluze–Mollat, ii, pp. 431–2; Paulus, 1913, and 1923, ii, pp. 114–23; Lea, 1896, ii, p. 203, n. 1. In general, Foreville, 1974.

[67] Baluze–Mollat, *Quinta Vita*, p. 300.

[68] Wyclif, *Trialogus*, ch. 32, p. 357. See also *Tractatus de Blasphemia*, p. 16.

[69] See, for example, Philip de Mornay du Plessis, *The Mystery of Iniquity*, 1612, p. 475 and Anon, *Sodom Fair*, 1688, p. 32.

[70] Ed. Lea, 1896, ii, p. 585. See pp. 345–51 for discussion.

[71] *Extrav. Comm.*, V, ix, 2. For discussion see Lea, ii, pp. 14–65; Stickler, 1977.

people.[72] It was the only decretal which he was to issue,[73] in contrast to Boniface VIII, who had issued twelve, John XXII with nearly fifty, and even the cautious Benedict XII with a couple.[74]

Surprisingly Boniface VIII, who had decreed the first jubilee year of 1300,[75] had not elaborated the theory fully. It was therefore Clement who was the target for Luther's attack in his *Ninety-five Theses* on the subject. Although not mentioned specifically in the *Theses*, *Unigenitus* was taken as a basis upon which to examine Luther at his Augsburg trial in 1518 by Cardinal Cajetan.[76] The foundation of the theory was the notion that the Church was a vast treasury, as Clement explained. Within it was reserved all the spiritual grace accumulated by the merits of Christ and the saints.[77] One of the fullest explanations was given by William of Monte Lauduno, a canonist from Toulouse (d. 1343), who pointed out that the merit accumulated by Christ and the saints far outweighed all the penalties due from living Christians.[78] It was thought that each Christian had an account of spiritual grace with God, which was in credit or debit according to the life lived by the individual. All sins were debited from the account, and the resulting debt had to be paid. The individual was usually unable to settle the account himself, and the treasury therefore had to be unlocked, and the sinner granted an indulgence of the spiritual grace he needed, usually in return for some pious act, such as the taking of a crusading vow or performance of a jubilee pilgrimage, or, increasingly during the late-medieval period, a money payment towards a good cause, or in

---

[72] Sermon 14. From a comparison of Schmidinger's edition, based largely on MS Vat. Borghese 41, with my edition, based largely on Ste-G. 240, it appears that in several cases the wording of Ste-G. 240 is preferable, and in many instances it has therefore been retained.

[73] The constitution he issued in 1351 mitigating the severity of the conditions in conclave might well have ranked as one. *Licet in constitutione*, Raynaldus, vi, ch. 25, p. 550. See also Baluze–Mollat, *Prima Vita*, p. 210.

[74] Friedberg, *Corpus Iuris Canonici*, ii, p. lxvi.

[75] *Extrav. Comm.*, V, ix, 1: *Antiquorum habet fida relatio.*

[76] See Fife, 1957, pp. 293–5. For bibliography see Benzing, 1965; Edwards, 1984.

[77] Clement VI, sermon 14, Ste-G. 240, fol. 150v: 'Ecclesia habet thesaurum ex merito passionis Christi et ex sanguine martirorum [*sic*] et ex orationibus sanctorum'.

[78] William of Monte Lauduno, *ad Clem.*, III, xvi, 1, fol. 161v: 'Sed quid est ille thesaurus Ecclesie? Dico quod est superabundantia meritorum quae multi sancti ultra mensuram debitorum suorum supererogaverunt etiam impenderunt tribulationes quas iniuste sustinuerunt, quorum meritorum . . . excedit omnem poenam debitam nunc viventibus, et praecipue passio Christi . . .' See also Conrad of Megenberg, *Yconomica*, iii, 3, ch. 2, pp. 362–4.

commutation of a vow.[79] An indulgence did not, as some thought, absolve from both punishment and from guilt – *a pena et a culpa*, but merely remitted some of the punishment. Guilt could be removed only through the sacrament of penance and absolution, and indulgences were therefore supposed to be granted only to the penitent who had been so absolved. The authorising of grants of indulgence was a purely jurisdictional act, performed by the pope out of his plenitude of power, using the Petrine keys.[80]

The whole idea of the treasury administered by the pope was a corollary of the corporate status of the *Ecclesia* and the pope's role as its representative. One of the hallmarks of a corporation was that as a *persona ficta* it could own property, and for practical purposes ownership became vested in its representative, in this case, the pope.[81] The fact that spiritual grace was itself an abstraction did nothing to invalidate the theory. The same held good for all the material wealth of the Church: it too was administered by the supreme pontiff. When the idea was elaborated to its fullest extent the *Ecclesia* was seen to be a double treasury, comprising both material wealth, on the earthly level, and spiritual grace, on the celestial level.[82] As Pierre Roger had observed, Christ had both a right and a left hand. On the basis of Proverbs, iii. 16: 'Length of days is in her right hand, and in her left hand riches and honour', the scriptural interpretation of 'right' was spiritual goods, and of 'left' temporal goods.[83]

Arguably the pope's ability to canonise saints was the most interesting of his sovereign rights. In Clement's case this was so because his canonisation of St Yves brought into focus the controversial issue of infallibility.[84] During the canonisation process the

[79] In general see Lea, 1896, ii, pp. 14–29; Adnès, 1971.

[80] See Clement's explanation in Tautu, no. 155, par. 517: 'quem quidem thesaurum . . . per beatum Petrum, caeli clavigerum eiusque successores, suos in terris Vicarios, commisit fidelibus salubriter dispensandum et pro piis ac rationabilibus causis nunc pro totali nunc pro partiali remissione poenae temporalis pro peccatis debitae, tam generaliter, quam specialiter . . . *vere poenitentibus et confessis* misericorditer applicandum'. See also no. 155, par. 517.

[81] Cf. William of Sarzano, *Tractatus de Potestate Summi Pontificis*, ch. 7, pp. 1044–5: 'licet rerum ecclesiasticarum proprietas, jus et dominium pertinere possit diversis personis singulariter vel communiter viventibus, diversis quoque ecclesiis, monasteriis, vel colegiis [*sic*], quasi secundariis administratoribus . . . primo tamen et principaliter omnium proprietas, jus et dominium ad personam summi pontificis pertinere videtur . . . videtur quod ipse omnium facultatum ecclesiasticarum sit dominus et dispensator principalis tanquam unius thesauri'.

[82] See Wilks, 1963a, pp. 180–1.   [83] Pierre Roger, sermon 7, p. 353.

[84] Controversy centres on Tierney, 1972, and started with the review by

pope examined the life, miracles, and virtues of the candidate on the basis of reliable testimony, and if he was satisfied, he would then apply the Petrine keys to unlock the gates of heaven and admit the candidate to the society of the blessed. He was henceforth entitled to be venerated as a saint by all Christians. The reason why canonisation had become a papal prerogative, as Clement, citing Aquinas, explained, was because the honour accorded to the saint and the belief in his glory was in a sense a profession of faith.[85] In the early Church canonisation had been left to 'particular' churches, which venerated their own saints, but 'particular' churches, unlike the universal Church, might err in such matters. It was impossible for the universal Church to err in a matter of faith.[86] Clement adduced several reasons why the *Ecclesia* could not err, some based on its corporate status, for there was the added underlying support of the legal commonplace that a corporation could not err. Clement himself based one argument on the spiritual marriage of Christ, and by implication his vicar, to the Church. Christ loved the *Ecclesia* and gave Himself for it, so that He might present it to Himself, a glorious Church, not having spot or wrinkle, but so that it could be holy and without blemish (Ephesians, v. 25–7). But how could this happen, he questioned, if she fornicated and erred in those things which pertained to salvation? How could she remain an immaculate virgin if she had the stain of error in her intellect and judgement?[87] Obviously this was impossible, and Clement concluded in the belief that God would not permit him to err in the matter of canonisation: 'trusting confidently that God will not allow *us* to err in this . . .',[88] showing that he saw himself as identified with the Church.

A. M. Stickler in *CHR*, LX (1974), pp. 427–41, continuing in LXI (1975), pp. 265–73. See now Turley, 1975 and 1982; Heft, 1982, and Tierney, 1982b.

[85] Clement VI, sermon 19, Ste-G. fol. 37v: 'Dicit etiam quod canonizatio sanctorum . . . quia etiam honor quem sanctis exhibemus est quaedam professio fidei qua sanctorum gloriam credimus pie credendum est, quod etiam in hiis iudicium Ecclesie errare non possit'.

[86] Ibid.: 'Et forte ista est causa quare papa sibi soli retinuit iudicium et auctoritatem canonizandi sanctos, quod non fiebat in primitiva ecclesia, ubi quelibet particularis ecclesia viros iustos et sanctitate vite et miraculis preeminentes pro sanctis venerabatur post mortem, quia iudicium universalis Ecclesie non potest errare in talibus, ut dictum est supra, quod forte posset particularis'. The rendering of Aquinas, *Quodlibet*, IX, qu. viii, art. 1 [16], p. 194 is a free one. For analysis of the passage see Schenk, 1965, pp. 74–8; 160–94; and esp. 171–7. For canonisation as a papal prerogative see Kemp, 1948, pp. 82–106; Kuttner, 1938; Vauchez, 1981, pp. 71–120.

[87] Clement VI, sermon 19, Ste-G. 240, fols. 39v–40r.

[88] Ibid., fol. 42r.

Other arguments were based on the strength of the Church's foundation. Christ had founded the Church upon Himself, and He had said, 'I am the truth, the way, and the life'. If truth could not err, then neither could the Church which was founded upon it. The Pope then turned to the sempiternity of the Church, borrowing from John Chrysostom and quoting Matthew xvi, that the gates of hell would not prevail against it. It would be easier for the sky to vanish or the earth to perish than for the Church to endure wrong.[89] Again there was a convenient underlying legal maxim that a corporation could not die, and elsewhere Clement had been quite specific about the Church's sempiternity.[90] Another reason why the pope could not err, according to Clement, was Christ's intercession for Peter's faith that it should not fail, to which was joined the intercession of the Church Triumphant and the 'just' members of the Church Militant. Such intercession preserved the Church from error. And of course what was said about Peter applied equally to his successors on the basis of the Petrine commission.[91]

Clement seemed to be telling his subjects that as pope he could not err, and indeed when dealing with Louis of Bavaria he went so far as to refer to himself as the 'vicar of Him who could not and did not wish to err'.[92] In his official capacity Clement seemed to differ from John XXII, who had not thought of himself as infallible.[93] John's view was the one held by most contemporary canonists, who maintained that the pope's sovereignty enabled him to alter or revoke the 'erroneous' decrees of a predecessor.[94] Clement's view

---

[89] Ibid., fol. 38v. See also sermon 5, p. 139, and Pierre Roger, sermon 37, Ste-G. 240, fol. 126v. See also Nicholas Rosselli's explanation of the gates of hell, *Tractatus de Jurisdictione Ecclesie super Regnum Apulie et Siciliae*, iv, p. 470: 'Portae enim inferi dicuntur omnes Tyranni, omnes Schismatici, et omnes rebelles Ecclesiae, quibus semper male cessit non obediendo, nec deferendo eidem'.

[90] Clement VI, sermon 40, p. 158: 'Unde est regnum Ecclesie, *quod in eternum non dissipabitur, quod comminuet et consumet universa regna, et ipsum stabit in eternum.* Daniel II [44]'. Cf. Hostiensis, *Commentaria, ad Decretales*, III, x. 8, fol. 147v: 'quia Ecclesia non moritur'. On the sempiternity of the *populus* according to Baldus see Canning, 1987, p. 189, n. 15.

[91] Clement VI, sermon 19, Ste-G. 240, fol. 40v: 'Quinta ratio sumitur ex parte intercessionis. Christus enim oravit pro Petro, Luc. xxii [32] ut non deficeret fides sua. Quod autem dictum est de Petro dicitur de se et successoribus suis, sicut apparet Mt. xvi° de collatione clavium. Ecclesia autem triumphans erat et valde sollicita est pro Ecclesia militante . . . Patet ergo ratione intercessionis tam Christi, qui propter sui reverentiam meruit exaudiri, quam etiam Ecclesie triumphantis quam etiam iustorum qui sunt in Ecclesia militante. Ipsa enim Ecclesia militans ab errore primo servatur'.

[92] Clement VI, sermon 34, Ste-G. 240, fol. 359r.

[93] Tierney, 1972, pp. 186–96. See also his summary of his views in Tierney, 1971.

[94] See, for example, Turley, 1982.

was more progressive, like that of the Carmelite Guido Terreni.[95]

The implication of the theory of papal infallibility was that no pope could be or ever had been wrong when pronouncing on a matter of faith. Infallibility was essentially an attribute of divinity, and the arguments which Clement advanced were based on his identification with one of the Three Persons of the Trinity. This meant that anything said about the pope must apply also to God Himself, which leads to difficulty in trying to reconcile the apparently incompatible qualities of sovereignty and infallibility.[96] The problem is that if the pope was, and had always been, inerrant, then it should follow that he could not reverse or contradict either his own previous legislation or that of a predecessor (given that all holders of the papal office merged into one). If he did, it would imply that the pope had erred on a previous occasion. This would be to imply that God, whose earthly representative the pope was, could Himself err. But of course this could not be so. If, on the other hand, the pope regarded himself as bound by his own legislation or that of his predecessors, then clearly he could not be truly sovereign. And once again he would appear to be imposing an impossible limitation on the Almighty, who would be limited by His own utterances and deprived of the freedom to change His mind: in which case He would no longer be almighty.

As pope, Clement did not discuss the issue of wrong legislation. It was no part of his role to suggest lines of attack to his opponents. In his youth, however, he had faced the issue in the postill he had written to justify John XXII's *Quia quorundam mentes*, which appeared to reverse Nicholas III's legislation on Apostolic poverty.[97] Here Pierre Roger had tried to support the conclusion that a pope could legislate against the determination of his predecessors. He achieved this by borrowing a verse from Esther (xvi. 9), which justified it on the grounds of changed circumstances and the common good:

The pope is able (to establish canons) against what has been determined by his predecessors, and even by himself, in accordance with Esther, xvi [9]: 'Neither must you think if we command different things, that they come from the levity of our mind, but that we give sentence according to the quality and necessity of the times, as the good of the commonwealth requires'.[98]

[95] On him see Tierney, 1972, pp. 259–69, and Turley, 1975.
[96] One of the merits of Tierney's thesis is to draw attention to this: see 1972, esp. pp. 1–13.
[97] *Extrav. J. XXII*, xiv. 5. See above, p. 9, nn. 48–9.
[98] Brussels 359, fol. 27r.

Wisely, he did not enlarge on this citation, for he was on dangerous ground. He had managed to preserve sovereignty intact, but he had weakened infallibility by robbing it of its permanence. The legislation was originally right, but if circumstances changed, which in the turmoil of the fourteenth century was more than likely, then it could be reversed. Circumstances could change the nature of right.

Strictly speaking infallibility applied only to matters of faith and, as pope, Clement discussed it only in connection with canonisation. In the medieval period, however, matters of jurisdiction were not easily separable from matters of faith.[99] Clement had an underlying reluctance to reverse any papal legislation or action. It was something which needed to be justified. He clearly felt strongly about Clement V's *Pastoralis cura*, which limited the territorial extent of the empire, but he made no attempt to reverse it or to discuss its unwisdom.[100] The only time he appeared to change his mind was over Giovanni Visconti, Archbishop of Milan. He had been a partisan of Louis of Bavaria, and had even accepted a red hat from his anti-pope, Nicholas V (Peter of Corbara, O.F.M.). After being restored to the unity of the Church, Clement had provided him to the archbishopric of Milan. Notwithstanding his archiepiscopal status, he had then occupied the papal territory of Bologna, for which Clement excommunicated him. Yet only two years later the Pope appeared to commit a complete *volte face* by coming to terms with him and appointing him his vicar in Bologna for twelve years.[101] This meant that he had to be received back into the grace of the Church, and Clement was faced with the difficult task of explaining why he had appeared to reverse his earlier action, despite Visconti's blatant lack of contrition. He chose to do this by turning once again to a verse from Esther, combining biblical precedent with the, originally Thomist, idea of reason of state, by which a sovereign ruler could act above the law in emergency circumstances if the common good demanded it. The text of Clement's sermon was Esther, xv. 11: 'And God changed the king's spirit into mildness',[102] from a chapter which amply demonstrated the *maiestas* of the king and his use of the imperial attribute of clemency. He thought that in this and similar affairs God had made a 'wonderful and glorious

---

[99] Tierney, 1982a, p. 788.
[100] For discussion see pp. 146–8 below.
[101] On the relationship between Clement and the Visconti during the early years of the pontificate see Biscaro, 1927.
[102] Clement VI, sermon 9, Ste-G. 240, fols. 458r–63r.

change'.[103] He argued that his own action was 'for the universal good and for that of the commonwealth', proving it by reference to both biblical precedent and the current political situation. When he absolved the impenitent, he did so in such a way as to remove all doubt about the correctness of his original decision. Sacraments had a dual significance: they marked the reception of spiritual grace, but they also had a legal or political purpose. Thus marriage was both a spiritual union effected through the reception of God's grace, and a civil contract. On this occasion Clement explained that there were two sorts of absolution. One related to jurisdiction over inward, spiritual matters, and required contrition. This type of absolution absolved from blame and it was clearly a sacramental act. The other was a matter of outward form and absolved merely from the sentence of excommunication. It was a purely jurisdictional act, and therefore could be performed by an official who had not even reached the rank of subdeacon (presumably with papal permission, though Clement did not state this).[104]

Seemingly, Clement had managed to preserve his sovereignty and his infallibility intact. The most telling way in which he did this was to identify himself with the Holy Ghost, the spirit of truth. The *Ecclesia* was unable to err because the Holy Ghost, the spirit of truth, governed it; and the Pope produced a whole cluster of quotations in support.[105] Since the Pope himself fulfilled the role of governor of the Church, this can be taken to mean that he identified himself with the spirit of truth. Guido Terreni had argued similarly.[106]

---

[103] Ibid., fol. 458v.
[104] Ibid., fols. 461v–62r: 'absolutio non potest impendi nisi contrito. Sed iste non videtur contritus . . . Sed ad hoc potest faciliter responderi . . . Est enim absolutio in foro prima interiori, et alia absolutio in foro exteriori, scilicet absolutio a sentencia excommunicationis. *Et ista non exigit de necessitate contritionem.* . . . prima non potest dari nisi per sacerdotem; secunda autem datur per non sacerdotem, sicut per officialem non dum eciam subdyaconum. Item prima est sacramentalis, secunda non. Item prima absolutio a culpa, secunda autem a pena . . . Et ille est maxime contumax et contempnens, qui absolvi non vult, et absolvi non potest, dicit sic respondendo: dicendum quod etiam remanente contumacia potest aliquis discrete excommunicationem etiam iuste latem remittere, si videat saluti illius expedire, in cuius medicina excommunicatio lata est'. On these two types of excommunication see Vernay, 1912, pp. lxiv–lvi. In general and for bibliography see Vodola, 1986, esp. pp. 35–43.
[105] Clement VI, sermon 19, Ste-G. 240, fol. 40r: 'Quarta ratio sumitur ex parte gubernationis. Ecclesia enim gubernatur per Spiritum Sanctum qui est spiritus veritatis, Jo. xv [1], et docet omnem veritatem, Jo. xiv [17]. Unde Crisostomus . . .'
[106] Guido Terreni, *Quaestio de Magisterio Infallibili Romani Pontificis*, p. 15: 'Ergo eadem actoritate [*sic*] summus pontifex et Ecclesia Romana per Spiritum Sanctum directa absque errore docet et determinat veritatem in hiis que ad fidem pertinent,

It is perhaps in the light of this special relationship that the symbolism attached to Clement's coronation can be fully appreciated. Why else should he have made the profoundly significant choice of Whit Sunday – the only pope from Innocent III to Gregory XI to make such a choice – the very day when the Apostles were infused with the grace of the Holy Ghost?[107] So important did the popes consider Whitsun that they used to keep a nocturnal vigil at the tomb of Peter in celebration.[108] The pentecostal symbolism was not lost upon Jean la Porte, who poetically likened the gleaming carbuncle on the tip of Clement's tiara to the tongues of flame which had descended on the heads of each of the Apostles. It looked as if the Holy Ghost had descended on Clement VI.[109] But it was left to Guido Terreni, in his tract on infallibility, to draw out the full significance of the descent. Once the Apostles had been confirmed in grace, after the reception of the Holy Spirit, they were unable to commit mortal sin, and since an error in faith is a mortal sin, so he enlarged, the implication was that they had acquired infallibility.[110] And so it can be argued that Clement VI at his coronation had become the spirit of truth, specially identified with the Holy Ghost: as such he had become infallible in matters of faith.

The Pope's identification of himself with the Holy Ghost, the

nec in hiis Spiritus Sanctus, qui docet omnem veritatem, permitteret summum pontificem aut ecclesiam errare'.
[107] Of the Avignon popes Clement V, John XXII, and Urban V were crowned on Sundays after Trinity, Benedict XII on the first Sunday after Epiphany, Innocent VI on the first Sunday after Christmas, and Gregory XI on the second Sunday after Christmas.
[108] Schimmelpfennig, *Die Zeremonienbücher*, app. 1, § 29: 'Dominica pentecostes statio ad Sanctum Petrum, ubi dominus pontifex ad vesperam vigilie cum omnibus ordinibus venit in nocte ad matutinum sicut in nocturnis stationibus, ad corpus sancti Petri vigilias facit'.
[109] Baluze–Mollat, *Tertia Vita*, p. 276: 'ita quod sicut in apostolos singulos illa die [Spiritus Sanctus] prout lingua ignis apparuit, sic in hunc summum pontificem per carbunculum lapidem pretiosum lucentem ignis, ad instar in thiare seu diadematis culmine positum, descendisse seu apparuisse monstratur'. Cf. *Secunda Vita*, p. 263. Herman of Schildiz, *Contra Hereticos*, ii, ch. 8, p. 73 also makes the connection between the papal coronation and the Whitsun sequence: 'Cum ergo ex electione ipsa . . . Romanus pontifex consequatur plenitudinem potestatis . . . rationabiliter dubitatur, quid eius consecratio superaddat. Ad quod probabiliter potest dici quod quandam confirmationem divinam per Spiritum Sanctum datum ad robur in illo gradu, quo Petrus fuit datus in die Pentecostes'.
[110] Guido Terreni, *Quaestio de Magisterio Infallibili*, p. 31: 'cum error in fide sit peccatum mortale, sed ut communiter dicitur, apostoli confirmati in gratia post receptionem Spiritus Sancti non potuerunt peccare mortaliter'. Cf. Herman of Schildiz, *Contra Hereticos*, ii, ch. 8, p. 74: 'videtur quod apostoli nunquam mortaliter peccaverunt postquam Spiritum Sanctum ad robor acceperunt'.

spirit of truth, was a way of identifying himself with the will of God. Ultimately what was true and therefore right was determined by the will of God. And if God were seen as omnipotent there was nothing to prevent Him from changing His mind about what was right. If He did so, however, the whole nature of right would alter – a problem which had not escaped Ockham and others.[111] As the vicar of God on earth the Pope was therefore pushed into the position of having to change the nature of right itself. And from this standpoint the problem of 'wrong' legislation, and the attendant issues, did not arise. If the nature of right and wrong changed, previous legislation could not be condemned as erroneous. The argument was a stronger one than 'changed circumstances' and necessity.

Clement VI saw himself as sovereign and infallible: the physical representative of God on earth. In the final analysis he would probably have agreed with his English contemporary John of Athona that he had no power to change things which related to truth alone, any more than he could create white from black.[112] But he could at least turn squares into circles.[113] The question remains, however, of why Clement was so anxious to stress his role as God on earth and to express the theory of papal sovereignty in such extreme terms. Almost certainly it was because he was on the defensive about it, for it was under fierce attack. Lay rulers had always resented the inferior role which the papal-hierocratic system allotted to them, making them subject to papal jurisdiction, even in secular matters. Over the centuries the protests became increasingly articulate and forceful, reaching a crescendo in the fourteenth century. While papal opponents did not go so far as to divide the Christian society into the two autonomous units of 'Church' and 'State', they nevertheless asserted a duality of powers within the one society. This relegated the pope's authority to 'spiritual' affairs and gave the lay ruler

---

[111] See Leff, 1957, pp. 188ff.

[112] John of Athona, *ad Const. Ottobuoni, Praef.*, p. 76: 'In his quae solum veritatem facti respiciunt, nullam potestatem obtinet [papa] immutanti; non enim facere posset album de nigro'. Cf. William of Monte Lauduno, *ad Clem.*, III, ii, 4. John of Athona was a pupil of Archbishop John Stratford (1332–48) and probably wrote his commentaries on the constitutions of the thirteenth-century legates Otto and Ottobuono between 1334 and 1344.

[113] John of Athona, *ad Praef. Ottobuoni*, p. 76: 'Papa vivens in terris . . . possit volvere quadrata rotundis'. This idea seems to have come from Hostiensis, *Commentaria, ad Decretal.* II, i, 12, fol. 5r: '[Cum venissent] . . . Sed et quamvis dicatur dominus: quia quamdiu vivit potest mutare quadrata rotundis; et omnia disponere tanquam dominus salva violatione fidei'. See also Johannes Andreae, *Commentaria, ad Decretal.* II, i, 12, fol. 8v.

supreme temporal authority. It was not easy to differentiate between these two realms, but the limitation of the pope's competence to spiritual affairs alone meant in effect the destruction of the papal plenitude of power.[114] Thus Louis of Bavaria, who had 'usurped' the imperial office according to the papal viewpoint, condemned John XXII for 'usurping' imperial power. On the basis of such biblical quotations as 'Render unto Caesar the things that are Caesar's' and 'My kingdom is not of this world', Louis argued that Christ had never intended 'spiritual' and 'temporal' power to be united in the same hands.[115]

During Clement's pontificate the attack was continued, especially by Louis' supporter Ockham, who regarded Clement as a heretic and usurper, and referred to him contemptuously as 'the lord Clement who names himself pope the sixth'.[116] In his *De Imperatorem et Pontificum Potestate*, written *c.* 1347, Ockham gives a valuable insight into Clement's attitude. He reports that the Pope had vetoed university discussion on the subject of papal power, even that which was 'rightly intentioned'. He adds that if the Pope is afraid of discussion about his power the suspicion must arise that he is a tyrant – that he is not content with the 'legitimate bounds' of that power, but rules over his subjects tyrannically.[117] It is true that tyranny is often born of fear, but while Clement may well have been afraid of the continuing attacks on his plenitude of power, there was nothing in his exercise of it in practice which could have substantiated the accusation of tyranny. His fear was more likely to have been a sign that he was on the defensive, and it is this which explains his concern to emphasise his role as a terrestrial god – to show that 'a change of name created a change of man'.

---

[114] On this see Wilks, 1963a, pp. 65–83.

[115] *MGH Const.*, IV, 1, no. 436, p. 347.

[116] William of Ockham, *De Electione Karoli IV*, ch. 4, p. 356.

[117] William of Ockham, *De Imperatorem et Pontificum Potestate*, ch. 15, p. 470. Cf. Kelley, 1987, p. 16. On the dating see McGrade, 1974, p. 21, n. 72. For the many works written on papal power and the structure of the Church in the first half of the fourteenth century see Miethke, 1980.

Chapter 3

THE RENAISSANCE POPE AND *NOVA ROMA*

We understand from some of our brethren that there have now been two hundred or two hundred and six supreme pontiffs, and all save a few have lived in their own see – their *propria sedes*. And because we are not there we reproach ourselves and say bitterly that now thirty-eight years have elapsed since Mass was celebrated at the altar of the Apostles, except by the Antipope or anti-Christ [Nicholas V], and that was not celebration but profanation. Therefore I long to see you: *desidero videre vos* [Rom., i. 11–12].[1]

This is how Clement VI summed up the problem of the papacy's self-imposed exile at Avignon when preaching to a delegation of Roman citizens in 1343. They had come, *inter alia*, to petition for the return of the papacy to Rome. But both the sincerity and the mathematics of the Pope's statement were somewhat limited. It was actually thirty-nine years since a pope had lived in Rome. Benedict XI (1303–4) had left the city in 1304, and the first so-called Avignon pope, Clement V (1305–14) had taken the papacy to Avignon on a temporary basis, intending to stay north of the Alps only until after the Council of Vienne (1311). When he died the curia was actually at Carpentras.[2] John XXII, his successor, had been bishop of Avignon from 1310 until he became a cardinal, and this doubtless prompted him to move the curia back to Avignon. Nevertheless, despite his fondness for Avignon, Henry of Diessenhoven records a story that John had taken an oath at his election at Lyons that he would never mount a horse or mule again except to go to Rome. Henry says that John went by boat from Lyons to Avignon and then approached the papal residence on foot. After that he did not venture out at all, except to the cathedral, which conveniently adjoined the palace.[3] Although the anecdote is demonstrably false, it is an interesting contemporary observation on John's attitude to the Avignon–Rome

---

[1] Clement VI, sermon 14, Ste-G. 240, fol. 149v. On the embassy see Schmidinger, 1978, pp. 323–43, and Schmidinger, 1979.
[2] Mollat, 1964, pp. 18–19; Guillemain, 1962, pp. 76–7.
[3] Henry of Diessenhoven, *Vita Joannis XXII*, p. 177.

problem.[4] At the time conditions in Rome were bloodthirsty and unstable, due to the internecine wars of its leading families, and the Papal State (that is, the lands in central Italy owned by the papacy) was in a state of anarchy. The situation was aggravated further in 1328 by the illegal coronation of Louis of Bavaria as 'emperor' by the Romans, and the appointment of his anti-pope, Nicholas V, he who 'profaned' the altar of the Apostles. John therefore turned his attention to Bologna, where extensive building preparations were made to receive pope and curia, but again political conditions prevented the move.[5] Like John, Benedict XII was initially keen to go to Rome. In July 1335 he took a decision to go, promising the Romans that he would set a date that October.[6] But by then the wishes of the cardinals were so 'dissonant and diverse', as he wrote to Philip VI, that he had to defer the decision.[7] In 1337 a combination of the Italian political situation and the outbreak of Anglo-French hostilities compelled him to refuse the Romans' petition to return.[8] Once he had decided to stay in Avignon he started to build the Papal Palace and had the archives brought from Assisi.[9]

The more settled the popes became in Avignon, the more difficult it was to make a move, and the more intense became the criticism and the loss of prestige which resulted from being away from Rome. Most contemporaries felt that the successor of St Peter ought to live in Rome. But Avignon had many advantages, among them its peace and security, its situation on the main trade routes, and the relative ease of communication with both north and south, which made it an ideal centre of government. It was ruled not by France, but by the Angevin rulers of Naples, who held it as a fief of the Empire as counts of Provence, but who were also, as rulers of Naples, vassals of the Holy See. In Clement VI's time the nominal ruler was the troublesome Queen Joanna, granddaughter of King Robert the Wise, who was still a minor and therefore under the Pope's wardship.

Unlike John and Benedict, Clement never had any intention of travelling to Italy. The Limousin Pierre Roger, surrounded by his largely French College of Cardinals, simply did not want to leave Provence. But officially, as Pope Clement VI, it was not politic to

[4] Mollat in Baluze–Mollat, ii, p. 295, points out that John rode after his coronation.
[5] Mollat, 1964, p. 20.
[6] Ibid., p. 21.
[7] Daumet, no. 112. See also Guillemain, 1962, p. 136.
[8] Vidal, no. 1434, letter to the Romans of 31 July 1337.
[9] Renouard, 1970, p. 41.

admit this to the Romans – hence the recurrence of the text like a rondo theme throughout his discourse that he 'longed to see them'. The only practical reason that he could muster officially for staying in Avignon was that the warring kings of England and France, of Aragon and Majorca, might accuse him of deserting them in their hour of need, and think that the Church did not care about them. If he were to move anywhere he felt that it should be to one of the territories of the belligerents. After all, as he reasoned, supreme pontiffs had left Rome before and had travelled to other parts of the world with far less justification.[10] Benedict XII had also used the suffering and disturbed state of western areas to explain his decision not to leave Provence when writing to the Romans in 1337.[11]

Clement VI professed himself anxious to avoid the vituperation and reproaches which were being levelled at him for not going to Rome,[12] which meant that he had to justify himself on theoretical as well as practical grounds. Given his views on papal sovereignty, he was not likely to accept any arguments which appeared to limit him in any way. To regard the pope as bound to Rome and therefore obliged to live there was to place a definite limitation on papal power – to restrict the pope's freedom of choice and movement. Moreover, the corollary of such a view could only be that papal power was something inherent in the see of Rome rather than in the papal office. This in turn could stir up a whole swarm of problems, not the least of which was that the pope could be regarded as the successor of St Peter, and therefore as having inherited St Peter's plenitude of power, only by being in physical possession of St Peter's see, as demonstrated by his residence at Rome. This could do irreparable damage to the pope's claims to wield universal powers, for how could a ruler be seen as a universal monarch if he could live only in one place? Even worse, it was but a short step from this for extremists to conclude that if the pope left Rome, then he left behind him his plenitude of power, and automatically ceased to be pope. This was a line of argument which had not escaped Louis of Bavaria and his partisans. In one of his 'imperial' constitutions, aimed at John XXII, Louis laid down that a pope who persisted in absenting himself from his see, despite requests by the Roman clergy and people to return, was *ipso iure* deprived of his office.[13]

[10] Clement VI, sermon 14, Ste-G. 240, fol. 150r: cf. Schmidinger, p. 352.
[11] Vidal, no. 1434.
[12] Clement VI, sermon 14, Ste-G. 240, fol. 148r: 'Movemur ex septem causis ut Romam deberemus accedere . . . septimo ex vituperii seu improperii vitatione'.
[13] *MGH Const.*, VI, 1, no. 438, p. 362.

Clement was able to counter such arguments quite easily. Christ Himself, so he explained, had been given all power, as Matthew, xxviii. 18 showed. St Peter was Christ's vicar, and he, Clement VI, was Peter's most unworthy successor. The question of Rome simply did not come into it. The pope's authority was universal because he was the vicar of Christ. The Roman pontiff, Clement declared, could not be said to rule the world just because he happened to rule the city of Rome: on the contrary, he ruled the city because he ruled the world.[14] His arguments were very much in line with those of contemporary publicists. Alvarus Pelagius, for example, maintained that it was heresy to say that the pope lost his jurisdiction when he was away from Rome. This was contrary to sacred Scripture, because wherever the pope was, there was the Roman Church and the apostolic see and the head of the Church. Because the Church was the mystical body of Christ, it could not be confined by walls, and wherever it was, there was its head, namely the pope.[15] Albericus de Rosate stated simply that Rome and the Roman curia was where the Roman pontiff was, and then gave a list of texts in support.[16] Conrad of Megenberg argued that the pope could move any distance from Rome and live in another city if he preferred, for where the pope is, there is Rome – *ubi papa, ibi Roma* – that is, the authority of the Roman Church.[17] Later in the century, about 1370, the biblical commentator John of Hesdin reasserted the view that the pope could reside wherever he chose for the advantage of the catholic faith – *pro utilitate fidei catholice*, and that wherever this happened to be, there was his see. He then quoted the *ubi papa* phrase with the assurance of one using a cliché.[18] The logical result of this was that Avignon came to be seen by some as Rome during the fourteenth century. Opicinus de Canistris, who was employed in the papal penitentiary during Clement's pontificate, referred to it as *Nova*

---

[14] Clement VI, sermon 14, Ste-G. 240, fol. 148r: 'Dicit Christus, Mt. xxviii° [18], cuius vicarius remansit Petrus, cuius licet immeriti, ymmo immeritissimi successor sumus, *Data est michi omnis potestas*. Nec Romanus pontifex preest orbi quia preest urbi, ymmo econverso, quia preest orbi, preest urbi'. For discussion on the subject see Wilks, 1963a, pp. 396–400.

[15] Alvarus Pelagius, *Collirium adversus Hereses*, p. 506.

[16] Albericus de Rosate, *Dictionarium*, p. 296.

[17] Conrad of Megenberg, *Yconomica*, iii, 3, ch. 13, p. 404.

[18] John of Hesdin, *Invectiva contra Fr. Petrarcham*, p. 126: 'Nonne etiam ille summi et altissimi Domini Vicarius . . . in aliqua parte terrae patitur exilium? Nonne solis Romanis debitor est? Absit. Ubicumque enim, pro utilitate fidei Catholicae, statuit residere, sedes sua est, nec sine causa dictum est: *ubi papa, ibi Roma*'. On John of Hesdin see Smalley, 1961 and 1963. For further examples of the maxim and discussion see Wilks, 1963a, pp. 396–407.

Roma in a note to one of his maps.[19] The 'prophet' John of Roquetaillade, writing in 1354, endorsed this.[20] Petrarch called it *Parva Roma*, though he preferred to call it Babylon.[21] He also informed his readers that part of the new Papal Palace was referred to as Rome.[22]

In theory Clement did not regard himself as wholly bound to Rome, but this did not necessarily mean that he was committed to Avignon. Being 'bound' to any see would threaten his universal sovereign powers. But this did not alter the fact that he was personally drawn to Avignon and determined to stay there. His attitude was demonstrated in two important ways. Firstly, he tried to give the papal residence there an air of permanence, as evidenced in his purchase of the city from Queen Joanna of Naples and his additions to the Papal Palace. Secondly, he tried to build up Avignon as the intellectual and artistic nucleus of Christendom by drawing people to it – many of them Italians – through patronage. His generosity was extended especially to humanist scholars, writers, architects, natural scientists, and musicians, and it is this aspect of the pontificate above all which has led historians to label Clement as a 'Renaissance' pope.

To some extent Clement had been anticipated in both these aspects by John XXII and Benedict XII. Like Clement, John too had wanted to surround himself with scholars, perhaps to compensate for the cultural lead which the papacy had lost by leaving Rome. Among those he patronised were Pierre Bersuire, Marsilius of Padua (briefly, at least), John Grauntson, and Nicholas Trevet. Part of his policy seems to have been to encourage Italians to settle at Avignon. Above all, it was John who summoned Petrarch, the real founder of the early humanist movement, from Bologna to Avignon in 1326.[23] It is probable that Italian painters started to come to Avignon during John's pontificate: indeed, Vasari preserves some evidence which suggests that Giotto may have worked in the city.[24] Like Clement, John was an enthusiast for classical learning. When Nicholas Trevet

---

[19] Salomon, 1953, p. 57. See also Wilks, 1963a, p. 404, n. 5.

[20] Bignami–Odier, 1952, p. 133. On Jean's life and works see Bignami–Odier, 1981.

[21] Petrarch, *Ep. Fam.*, xv, 7: 'Nam de ipsa quam inhabitas, parva ut aiunt Roma, ut ego vocitare soleo Babylone novissima', quoted by Piur, 1925, p. 80, n. 4.

[22] Petrarch, *Ep. Sen.*, vii, p. 913: 'Fama est esse palatii tui partem, quae Roma dicitur . . .' Cf. Piur, p. 81, n. 1.

[23] Simone, 1969, pp. 44–5.

[24] Giorgio Vasari, *Le Vite*, ii, p. 117. For a discussion of John's patronage see Laclotte and Thiébaut, 1983, pp. 9–10.

offered to comment on the Pentateuch for him, the Pope instead invited him to comment on Livy.[25] It was John, too, who started to collect manuscripts for the papal library, and although he amassed many orthodox theological works, he also went out of his way to indulge his own taste for classical learning and to acquire manuscripts of classical authors.[26] Benedict's real anticipation of Clement was to endow the papal residence on the Rhône with an air of permanence by building his palace, now known as the Old Palace, on the site of John's episcopal palace. His chief architect was a Frenchman, Pierre Poisson, and his chief artist was Jean Dalbon, but he seems to have employed Catalan, English, and Italian painters as well as French.[27] During Benedict's pontificate Simone Martini arrived at Avignon. Although there is no evidence that he was patronised by either Benedict or Clement, or that he worked on the palace, he appears to have been responsible for the frescoes in the porch of the cathedral of Notre-Dame-des-Doms, which may have been commissioned by Cardinal Jacques Stefaneschi. He also painted a portrait of Cardinal Napoleon Orsini, now lost. Simone's brother Donato and, later, his brother-in-law Lippo Memmi were also with him in Avignon.[28]

Clement's aim to give the papacy a settled existence at Avignon was demonstrated in his purchase of the city from Joanna of Naples in 1348. He seems to have been especially keen to acquire it. By diplomatic timing, at which he was adept, he manoeuvred the Queen into an impossible situation. She and Louis of Taranto, her second husband, had fled from Naples to Provence to escape an invasion by Louis of Hungary, which was ostensibly to avenge the murder of his brother, Andrew, who had been Joanna's first husband. Both Joanna and Louis were suspected of complicity in the crime. To make matters worse, they had been secretly married the previous August without papal dispensation, and Joanna was five months pregnant. The Queen, as a ward of the Holy See, was expressly forbidden to marry without papal approval, added to which the couple were within the prohibited degrees of consanguinity. While Clement may have been in favour of the union privately, it would have been very unwise to have enraged the

---

[25] Simone, pp. 285–6.
[26] Ibid., pp. 48–9.
[27] Laclotte and Thiébaut, p. 25.
[28] Ibid., pp. 15–22. For the suggestion about Stefaneschi see Martindale, 1988, pp. 46–7. In general see Enaud, 1963.

avenging Louis of Hungary even further by granting a dispensation, although when faced with a *fait accompli* Clement did so retrospectively. When the Queen took refuge in the plague-ridden city of Avignon – for the Black Death was at its height – she was faced with uncertainty about the legality of her marriage, with the prospect of standing trial before the Sacred College for the murder of Andrew, and with the problem of how to get back to Naples without money. By 'mortgaging' Avignon she could buy the Pope's goodwill and raise enough money to get home.[29]

Controversy surrounds the sale of Avignon. Joanna herself claimed on several subsequent occasions that Clement had made her a verbal promise in the presence of six cardinals that the transaction was to be treated as a mortgage: in other words, she could redeem the city as soon as she could afford it.[30] But the terms of the contract of sale leave no doubt that Clement intended the transfer to be permanent.[31] Then there is the question of the price. Opinion is divided over whether the 80,000 gold florins paid was a fair price.[32] Probably it was not. In the deed of sale Joanna was made to admit that Avignon was worth more than this amount, or at least that it might become so in future, but she was aware that it was 'more blessed to give than to receive'.[33] As an added safeguard to the transaction she was also made to promise that she would not cause or allow any litigation, debate, or controversy against the Holy See in future concerning the sale.[34] Clement had obviously driven a hard bargain, and his biographers liken him to the Argus, the beast with a

---

[29] For these events see Léonard, 1932, ii, pp. 125–32; St Clair Baddeley, 1897, pp. 281–448.

[30] Two of the three letters preserved by Nicola d'Alife, Joanna's chancellor, in connection with this are edited by Léonard, 1932, ii, pp. 489–90. One is a letter of Joanna to the Seneschal of Provence, which gives a list of the cardinals who apparently witnessed Clement's promise; the other is to a member of the Sacred College on the accession of Innocent VI, when Joanna tried to redeem Avignon.

[31] Pfeffel, 'pièce justificative', no. 11, p. 101: 'vendimus, cedimus et *ad perpetuam quitammus* pro nobis et haeredibus ac successoribus nostris . . . titulo procuratio perpetuae venditionis transferimus irrevocabiliter pleno iure, ad habendum, tenendum, et perpetuo ac pacifice possidendum per dictum dominum nostrum papam et ejus successores ad Romanam Ecclesiam'.

[32] Léonard, p. 131, thinks that the price was a fair one, against St Clair Baddeley, p. 444.

[33] Pfeffel, no. 11, p. 103: 'Et nunc quidquid dicta civitas Avenionensis cum ejus territorio, pertinentibus et districtu, juribus supradictis plus valet seu in futuram plus valebit pretio ante dicto; considerantes quod secundum apostolorum verba Domini Jesu memorantem beatius est dare quam accipere'.

[34] Ibid., p. 108.

hundred eyes, out to observe his opportunity and use it to advantage.[35]

The role of Charles IV, the emperor-elect, is also instructive. As the suzerain of Provence he surrendered all his feudal rights over the city of Avignon to Clement and his successors in gratitude for the 'immense benefits and honours' which Pope and *Ecclesia Romana* had bestowed upon him and the Empire. Given the long papal stay at Avignon, Charles recognised the advantages to the status of the Roman curia which would result if the papacy possessed the city. Finally he considered it 'indecent' that a place which the papacy had for so long graced with its presence should be temporally subject to anyone else.[36] One of Clement's biographers quotes from another document written by Charles in which again he outlined the advantages to the papacy, emphasising that Avignon was the safest place in the world for the popes to live.[37] All this lends support to the view that the sale was no temporary measure. Clement's establishment of the papal mint at Avignon confirms this.[38]

The policy of the popes towards the episcopal see of Avignon is also significant. John XXII had been succeeded as bishop by his nephew Jacques de Via. In 1317 it was a simple matter for John to create him a cardinal and to take the temporalities of the see into his own hands, although he made provision for its administration by the bishop of Marseilles.[39] This enabled him to return to his former home, the bishop's palace, to which he made several alterations. Benedict XII, once he had decided to stay at Avignon, provided John of Corjordan to the see, in April 1336,[40] giving him a different palace. In return, John was persuaded to make over the original palace to the Pope, which allowed him to demolish it to make way for the new building.[41] Clement VI kept John in office so long as Avignon remained in Neapolitan hands. Once the purchase was completed, however, Clement appointed two vicars-general, one 'in spirituals', the other 'in temporals', to administer the see on his

---

[35] Baluze–Mollat, *Secunda Vita*, pp. 266–7.

[36] *MGH Const.*, viii, no. 676, p. 680.

[37] Baluze–Mollat, *Prima Vita*, p. 259: 'cum hodie non habeat locum alium in toto orbe in quo liberius et securius commoretur'. The author did not acknowledge his quotation, but it was identified by Pfeffel, who edited it as 'pièce justificative', no. 12 (see p. 111). Both Mollat and the *MGH* editor, Zeumer, assumed that there was only the one document.

[38] Renouard, 1970, p. 47.

[39] Eubel, 1913, i, p. 126; Guillemain, 1962, p. 501.

[40] Albanès and Chevalier, vii, no. 1155. Renouard, p. 41.

[41] Renouard, p. 41; Guillemain, 1962, p. 501.

behalf. About three weeks later John was translated elsewhere.[42] The implication is that Clement saw himself as bishop of Avignon, although it would have been impolitic to have admitted this in view of the fact that he was also the bishop of Rome. Avignon continued to be administered by vicars during the pontificate of Innocent VI. But as soon as a pope who was seriously concerned to return to Rome ascended the throne, that is, Urban V in 1362, a bishop of Avignon was once more appointed.[43]

Clement's concern to bind himself to Avignon is reflected in the interest he took in the city and the welfare of its citizens. In December 1342, for example, he accorded indulgences to anyone who contributed to the repair of the bridge, which presumably had been damaged in the floods of 1342.[44] It is as if Avignon were a holy city. During the Black Death Clement supervised nursing care and burial arrangements at his own expense. He purchased a field just outside the city to be used as a cemetery, and he also consecrated the Rhône to be used for the same purpose.[45] Clement also showed the deepest concern for the poor. According to a contemporary eyewitness, Louis Sanctus of Beringen, chaplain to Cardinal Giovanni Colonna, the number of loaves distributed to them each day by the papal almonry, the *Pignotte*, was about 30,000. Under John XXII it had been only about 10,000.[46] When Clement died, the uncharacteristic simplicity of his funeral ceremonies at Avignon was the result of his wish that the money which might otherwise have been spent on them should be distributed to the city's poor.[47]

Clement's attitude to Avignon was soon publicly demonstrated in his alterations and extensions to Benedict's papal palace to make it vast and grandiose enough to house the prince of Christendom. In practical terms this also meant big enough to house not only the stream of distinguished lay visitors whom Clement entertained so royally, but also his family, including the women and children, who

---

[42] Albanès and Chevalier, no. 1312. Clement's letters were 1 November 1348 and 1 January 1349. The vicars were appointed on 8 January 1349. John was translated on 23 January 1349: ibid., no. 1313.

[43] On 12 December 1363: see Albanès and Chevalier, no. 1335.

[44] Ibid., no. 1289, 21 December 1343. On the effects of the flood see Baluze–Mollat, *Prima Vita*, p. 242.

[45] Baluze–Mollat, *Prima Vita*, p. 252; *Secunda Vita*, p. 268; *Tertia Vita*, pp. 284–5. See also Louis Sanctus of Beringen, *Tractatus de Pestilentia*, p. 467. In general and for bibliography see Bulst, 1979.

[46] Louis Sanctus of Beringen, p. 469. See Mollat, 1964, p. 515; Guillemain, 1962, pp. 411–13.

[47] Déprez, 1900, pp. 236–7.

seem to have moved in with him. The atmosphere must have been distinctly secular. To judge from his sermons the Pope acted as a father and took responsibility for bringing up at least one of his nephews.[48] One of his nieces was christened at the Papal Palace in December 1350.[49] The children, for their part, seem to have run riot in the gardens, and on one occasion at least managed to break a spout on the elaborate fountain which their uncle had had constructed.[50] As well as friends, relations, and ambassadors, there was also the Pope's menagerie to be housed. This included a lion and a bear.[51]

Clement's lifestyle seems to have been that of an extravagant Renaissance prince: he lived in 'pomp, and feast, and revelry'.[52] The anonymous account of the now famous banquet given for him by Cardinals Annibaldus de Ceccano and Pedro Gomez, with its nine 'services' of three courses and dessert, each separated by a lavish intermezzo with music, and its fountain flowing with five different wines, is an outstanding example. It was at this banquet that the celebrated practical joke was played. An unsafe, fake bridge was constructed across the river, in the hope that inquisitive onlookers, attracted by the noise of the feasting, would be lured into crossing it, and would be thrown into the water, which was precisely what happened.[53] Clement's coronation banquet, at which some 200 casks of wine were consumed, probably ran the Cardinals' banquet a close second for sheer ostentation and extravagance.[54]

Clement's building operations were undertaken not just to pro-vide him with a suitable setting for his ostentatious Renaissance lifestyle. The New Palace was a demonstration that Avignon was in every sense the capital of Christendom: on one level it was the centre of papal government, on another it was to be the intellectual and artistic centre of the Christian world. Clement started by building one or two extensions to the Old Palace, notably the kitchen and the

---

[48] Clement VI, sermon 33, Ste-G. 240, fol. 527r: 'quia vere est sibi pater, quia ipsum virtuose nutruit et prudenter et sollicite promovit, et ipse libenter recepit, et vere ipsum nutruit in virtute'. See also sermon 4, Ste-G. 240, fol. 526r: 'Et iste Nicolaus est filius meus ratione cognationis, ratione nutritionis, et ratione vocationis'.

[49] Gasnault, 1964, p. 122.

[50] Burnham, 1978, p. 378. The repair cost one florin.

[51] Pélissier, 1951, p. 37, n. 1, quotes an entry from the papal accounts concerning the custody and provisioning of the Pope's lion.

[52] Peter of Herenthals, *Vita Clementis VI*, p. 298: 'Ipse sumptuosissimum tenuit statum et multum pomposum ac secularem, prout audivi et *pro parte cognovi*'.

[53] De Loye, 1974; Zacour, 1975, pp. 440–1; Mollat, 1964, pp. 508–9.

[54] Werner of Bonn, *Vita Clementis VI*, p. 543: 'coronatus est cum pompa et gaudio'. For the expenses see Schäfer, 1914, pp. 184–91.

Tower of the Garde-Robe (Wardrobe). He also commissioned the painting of frescoes on many of the walls of Benedict's building. The area of the new palace roughly doubled that of the previous one (see figure 1). While Clement's buildings maintained the defensive character of Benedict's, their style was different. The Old Palace had

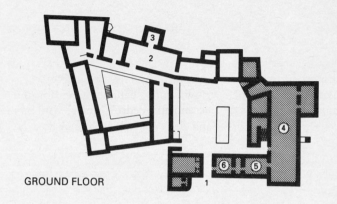

GROUND FLOOR

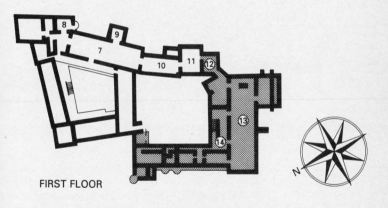

FIRST FLOOR

☐	Old Palace (Benedict XII)	▨	New Palace (Clement VI)

1 Porte des Champeaux   8 Kitchen
2 Consistory Hall   9 Chapel of St Martial
3 Chapel of St John   10 The State Chamber
4 Grand Audience   11 Bed Chamber (Angels' Tower)
5 Small Audience   12 Chambre du Cerf
6 Guards' Room   13 Great Chapel of St Peter
7 Banqueting Hall   14 Gate of Great Chapel

1 Plan of the Papal Palace, Avignon

2 The 'Porte des Champeaux', Papal Palace, Avignon, with the arms of
Clement VI above it

been built in a severe Roman style, whereas the facade of the New
Palace is Gothic in character. This is seen especially in the two
defensive turrets with their small crocketed spires above the Porte
des Champeaux, originally called the Gate of St Peter and St Paul[55]
(see figure 2). Clement placed his coat of arms – the Roger or 'Rosier'
roses – with the triple tiara and the keys of St Peter above this gate
(see figure 3). Something of the wonder the palace inspired in
contemporaries is conveyed by two of Clement's biographers, who
term it *valde misteriosum et pulchrum*, very mysterious and beautiful;[56]

[55] Gagnière, 1985, p. 76. On the palace in general see Gagnière and Labande, 1925.
[56] Baluze–Mollat, *Secunda Vita*, p. 271; *Tertia Vita*, p. 287. See also *Prima Vita*,
pp. 257–8 for description of the buildings.

3 Arms of Clement VI above the 'Porte des Champeaux'

while one of Benedict's later biographers, referring to his own time, probably the first decade of the fifteenth century, describes it as 'of solemn and wondrous beauty in its dwellings, and of immense fortitude in its walls and towers'.[57]

Clement's chief architect was Jean de Louvres from the Isle de France.[58] His most impressive work was in the design of the Grand Audience, started in 1345 (see figure 4) and the Great Chapel, dedicated to St Peter and completed in 1351, immediately above it (see figure 5). Clement was able to celebrate a Mass of thanksgiving

---

[57] Baluze–Mollat, *Prima Vita Benedicti XII*, p. 197, lines 22–4.
[58] Gasnault, 1964.

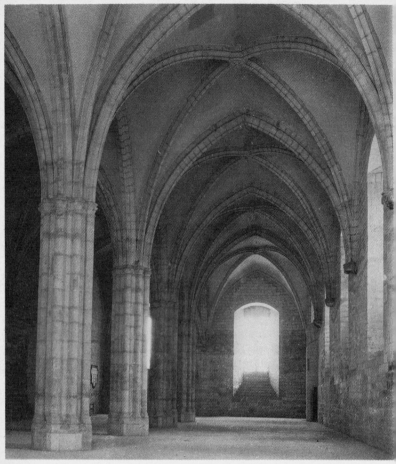

4 The Grand Audience, Papal Palace, Avignon

there for the completion of the palace and to preach an eloquent sermon on All Saints Day 1352, five weeks before he died.[59]

The decoration of the palace, especially the walls of the papal bed chamber in the Angels' Tower, has generated a good deal of interest. The room is richly adorned with a geometric pattern of foliated

[59] Baluze–Mollat, *Tertia Vita*, p. 288. Unfortunately the All Saints Day sermon (no. 36, app. 3) preserved in Ste-G. 240, fols. 49v–51v gives no hint that it was preached on this occasion. The fact that it is macaronic (Latin and French) possibly indicates that it was a pre-papal sermon.

5 The Great Chapel of St Peter, Papal Palace

scrolls on a blue background, and with vines and branches of oak, alive with birds and woodland animals. The most spectacular feature, however, is the three-dimensional bird cages which decorate the recesses of the windows, and which appear to be suspended from Gothic arches (see figure 6). It used to be thought that Clement

6 Bird cages on the wall of the papal bed chamber, Papal Palace (Angels' Tower)

commissioned the decoration of this room and that it was a replacement for the earlier and more austere decorations of Benedict XII.[60] Debate centred on whether the paintings were executed under the direction of Matteo Giovannetti of Viterbo, seemingly Clement's official artist, or were done by native workmen under Robin des Romans.[61] But scholars now consider that Jean Dalbon was responsible for the work during Benedict's pontificate on the basis of some entries in the papal accounts.[62] It is admitted, however, that such an imaginative and exuberant setting for the papal slumbers would fit the tastes of Pierre Roger better than those of the Cistercian Bene-

[60] Gagnière, p. 26; Laclotte, 1960, pp. 41–2.
[61] Roques, 1960.
[62] Castelnuovo, 1962, p. 30; Laclotte and Thiébaut, p. 25: see also pp. 145–7 for description of the room and summary of views.

7 Bird-catcher, Chambre du Cerf, Papal Palace (photo: Georges Gaud, 77950 Moisenay, France)

dict.[63] Even if the attribution to Jean Dalbon is accepted it does not settle the origin of the bird cages, which present such a stylistic contrast to the rest of the room, and which might well have been added later. It is still possible that Matteo Giovannetti could have influenced their creation.[64]

The room which undoubtedly reflects Pierre Roger's individual and profane tastes is the Chambre du Cerf (Room of the Stag), which was his study. The luxuriant, bird-filled forests painted on the walls provide a backcloth for scenes of secular seigneurial pleasure – falconry, fishing, stag-hunting (hence the name of the room), and bird-catching (see figure 7). On the south wall there is a scene of

[63] Laclotte, 1960, p. 41, and Laclotte in Laclotte and Thiébaut, p. 25.
[64] Castelnuovo, 1962, pp. 30–3; Laclotte, 1960, p. 42.

8 Hunting and fishing scenes, Chambre du Cerf (photo: Georges Gaud, 77950 Moisenay, France)

either women or children (perhaps the papal nephews?) bathing in a river.[65] The fishing scene on the north wall is especially interesting for the attempted use of perspective in the rectangular fishpool (see figure 8). Again, this may well have been influenced by Matteo Giovannetti. The room as a whole is thought to be the work of several hands and displays a mixture of French and Italian influences.[66] We know that the Italians in Matteo's *atelier* included Riccone and Giovanni of Arezzo, Giovanni of Lucca, Niccolò and Francesco of Florence, and Pietro of Viterbo.[67] The paintings in the Chambre du Cerf provide an unexpectedly secular setting for the composition of papal sermons.

The decorations of the Pope's private apartments display what are often considered to be 'Renaissance' features, such as the realistic representation of natural objects, the desire to capture the beauty of nature, and the use of perspective. The same features are discernible in Giovannetti's known surviving works in the palace, notably in the

---

[65] Laclotte and Thiébaut, p. 152.
[66] Ibid., p. 45, and see pp. 148–54 for description and reproductions.
[67] Ibid., p. 45.

9 Matteo Giovannetti, a miracle of St Martial, detail from a fresco in the Chapel of St Martial (photo: Georges Gaud, 77950 Moisenay, France)

Prophets on the fresco in the Grand Audience, the lively and realistic scenes depicted in the Chapel of St Martial, Clement's private chapel (see figure 9), and the episodes from the lives of the two Johns, St John the Baptist and St John the Evangelist, in the Chapel of St John. Tragically much of Matteo's work has been destroyed – his work in the Great Chapel, the Banqueting Hall, and the Consistory Hall in particular.

Matteo Giovannetti is described in the papal accounts as *pictor papae*[68] – the painter of the Pope. Clement was not only his patron, but also his subject, for it is possible that he painted him three times: once incorporating him into the Crucifixion scene in the Chapel of St Martial,[69] once in 1344 in a portrait now lost but seen in the seventeenth century,[70] and possibly also in a scene of a pope receiving a book from John the Good of France.[71] Vasari says that

[68] Schäfer, 1914, p. 313, for the account of 17 March 1346.
[69] App. 2, no. 5, p. 209 below. It seems that the identification by Labande, 1925, ii, pp. 50–64, of St John the Baptist next to the Pope (adopted by Heck, 1980) is no longer accepted: see Laclotte and Thiébaut, p. 165.
[70] App. 2, no. 4, p. 209 below.
[71] Ibid., no. 6.

Clement was also portrayed by Andrea di Cione Orgagna in a fresco in Santa Croce in Florence.[72] In addition to these there are some half dozen or so miniature representations in the initial letters of various documents (see frontispiece). How 'realistic' these portraits are is open to question, particularly in the case of the Florentine fresco. Probably the closest likeness of Clement was that on his tomb at the abbey of his profession, Chaise-Dieu, in the Auvergne.

From the start of his pontificate Clement showed special favour to Chaise-Dieu, the 'abbey he had always loved', and granted it many privileges.[73] In 1344 his attention turned to the buildings, and he decided that the Romanesque church of the founder, St Robert (d. 1067), by then 'consumed by age and nearly in ruins',[74] should be rebuilt. It was to be 'in much more solemn state' than the original one, a papal biographer says.[75] The resulting church, designed by Hugues Morel, from the south of France, is indeed magnificent (see figure 10). As in the case of the palace, the interior was as important as the exterior, and Matteo Giovannetti's paintings were obviously a central feature of the decorations. But the real centrepiece was Clement's tomb. This was of black marble, with the figure of the Pope, sculpted in white marble, lying on top, fully robed and wearing the triple tiara (see figure 11). Sadly this is all that remains of it, due to destruction by Huguenot vandals in 1562, but the other details have been reconstructed.[76] Round the recumbent figure of the Pope knelt not saints or angels, as might have been expected, but six of Clement's closest relatives, including his brother Cardinal Hugues Roger, and three of his cardinal-nephews. Around the base, set in Gothic niches, were statuettes of all the other friends, relations, and counsellors who had formed part of the funeral cortège on its long journey from Avignon. Many of them were laymen and women, and among them was his married sister Aliénor with her immediate family (see figure 12). The whole tomb comprised some forty-four or forty-five realistic statues, all of which had been fashioned at Avignon. The materials were bought in 1346, although the work did not actually start until 1349, being completed in 1351, when the tomb was installed. It was executed by Pierre Roye or Boye, from the north, helped by Jean de Sanholis and Jean David.[77]

[72] Ibid., no. 7.
[73] Gaussin, 1962, p. 422.
[74] Baluze–Mollat, *Prima Vita*, p. 258.
[75] Ibid. For an account of its construction see Faucon, 1904.
[76] Fayard, 1962; Gounot, 1962; Wetterlöf, 1975, pp. 206–21.
[77] Fayard, p. 42; Wetterlöf, p. 207.

10 The Abbey Church of Chaise-Dieu

The idea of adorning a tomb with 'weepers', as the statuettes were
called, was relatively new in 1349, and its origins were both French
and secular as opposed to Roman and ecclesiastical.[78] The monu-
ment provides an unspoken comment on the distinction between the
man and the office, between the formal figure of the pope, resplen-
dent with all the trappings of office, and the nepotistic Renaissance
prince, who could not bear to be separated from those he loved even
in death.

In his lavish patronage of builders, painters, and sculptors Clement anticipated the popes of the fifteenth century, and in paying his
artists to create realistic representations and to capture the beauties of

[78] On these see the catalogue to the exhibition held at the Musée des Beaux-Arts at
Dijon in 1971, *Les Pleurants dans l'art du moyen âge en Europe*. See also Martindale,
1967, pp. 115–18.

11 *Gisant* of Pope Clement VI on his tomb at the Abbey Church of Chaise-Dieu

nature he was indirectly contributing to the development of Renaissance values. What is more difficult to assess, however, is whether his patronage in other fields of humanist learning sprang from his personal interest in humanist topics, or whether they were simply part of his general intention to make his court the forum for the outstanding intellects of his time.

Due to Anneliese Maier's work on manuscripts in the Vatican Borghese collection, some of them in Pierre Roger's hand, we can form some impression of his early interests apart from theology. The contents of the autograph manuscript Vatican Borghese 247, into which Pierre copied anything which took his fancy, are so rich and varied that it has some claim to be regarded as the forerunner of

12 Bas-relief from the tomb of Clement VI, showing his sister Aliénor (left), her two daughters who were abbesses, two married daughters (behind), and her son (behind, right) (see Fayard, 1962, p. 41 on the identification)

the commonplace books of the Renaissance.[79] The manuscripts as a whole reveal an interest in astronomy, astrology, and medicine. Pierre had also copied part of the Hebrew alphabet into his commonplace book, which suggests that he had tried to learn Hebrew, something often associated with Renaissance scholars.[80] Reflecting these interests, in 1342 Clement VI commissioned the translation from Hebrew into Latin of part of an astronomical–philosophical

[79] For descriptions of Vat. Borghese 247 see Maier, 1952, pp. 295–30 and 1967, pp. 309–12. The other manuscripts written wholly or partly in Pierre's hand are Vat. Borghese 69, 83, 157, and 204.

[80] Maier, 1952, p. 298.

treatise written by the Rabbi Levi ben Gerson, and he may later have commissioned a second.[81] In 1344 he summoned the music theorist and astronomer Jean de Murs to Avignon. With Firman de Beauval he was to head a commission of theologians, mathematicians, and astrologers, which attempted a reform of the Julian calendar.[82] Jean de Murs also apparently gave Clement political advice based on astrology.[83] Both he and Levi ben Gerson tried to explain the Black Death of 1348 in astrological terms.[84]

Clement sought his own explanations, and it is in his unofficial attitude to the plague, and the contrast it presents to his official attitude, that the possible humanist bent of his mind is revealed. The Black Death, which swept Europe killing vast numbers of people, reached Avignon at Candlemas 1348. More than half the population died, and conditions in the city were appalling. The chroniclers tell how, as in the biblical plagues, the living were not sufficient to bury the dead, nor the cemeteries large enough to contain them.[85] Fathers abandoned their sons on their deathbeds and sons their fathers. Even the animals died – dogs and cats, cocks and hens, and others, so we are told.[86] Clement's official reaction to the situation was to grant indulgences to the dying,[87] to preach a sermon attributing the cause of the scourge to God's judgement on a sinful world,[88] and to write a mass of intercession.[89] With the accent on sin, Louis Sanctus explained that many thought that the epidemic was God's retribution for the murder of Prince Andrew of Hungary,[90] and the arrival of Joanna and her second husband in Avignon that spring may well have added fuel to this. The Pope also apparently encouraged processions of barefooted, chanting penitents, who flagellated themselves. Louis Sanctus says that Clement even went out and joined the processions himself when they came within the precincts of the palace,[91] but this does not seem very likely: the penitents sound little

---

[81] See app. 1, nos. 12 and 13 below.
[82] Déprez, 1899; Thorndike, 1934, pp. 268–80.
[83] Tomasello, 1983, p. 15.
[84] Ibid., pp. 15–16.
[85] Baluze–Mollat, *Tertia Vita*, p. 284: cf. Wisdom, xviii. 12.
[86] Baluze–Mollat, *Prima Vita*, p. 251.
[87] Baluze–Mollat, *Tertia Vita*, p. 285.
[88] Clement VI, sermon 31, Ste-G. 240, fol. 435r where he speaks of 'pestilentia vel epidemia, que a Domino, vel propter peccata mea et aliorum propositorum, vel propter peccata subditorum videtur esse inflicta'.
[89] Ed. Viard, 1900. See also Coville, 1938a.
[90] Louis Sanctus of Beringen, *Tractatus de Pestilentia*, p. 468.
[91] Ibid.

different from the heretical Flagellants, the sect which he was to condemn only the following year.[92]

Clement also took a scientific interest in the epidemic, justified neither by theology nor astrology. Louis Sanctus tells us that he ordered post-mortem examinations to be performed on plague victims at Avignon to discover the cause of the outbreak.[93] Such examinations were not unknown at this time: the 1340 statutes of the University of Montpellier, for example, enjoined the Chancellor to provide a corpse for the students to dissect at least once every two years.[94] They were, however, unusual outside the universities. And for a pope to have initiated them officially at that time would have been extraordinary. Ecclesiastical opposition to interference with the human cadaver was strong, based as it was on the belief, enshrined in the Creed, in the ultimate resurrection of the body. Such opposition had been strengthened by Boniface VIII's legislation of 1299 against the division of corpses and the burial of limbs in different places[95] (although Clement did grant dispensations for members of the French royal family to practise this[96]). It is significant that there is no trace of a papal decretal ordering, or even allowing, the post-mortems to take place. It seems that their performance sprang from the personal interest of Pierre Roger in medical science, and as such it presents an interesting contrast to the theological acceptance of bodily suffering as the will of God.

Many scholars hold that the rediscovery of classical antiquity is the real touchstone of Renaissance humanism.[97] Clement's interests certainly included classical learning as well as natural sciences. Manuscripts in the Vatican and other European libraries which can be shown to have belonged to him reveal him as an avid bibliophile and book collector.[98] His first purchase, in 1312, contained a com-

---

[92] Raynaldus, vi, ch. 21, p. 495.

[93] Louis Sanctus of Beringen, *Tractatus de Pestilentia*, p. 466: '. . . est enim facta anatomia per medicos in multis civitatibus Ytalie, et etiam in Avinione, *ex jussu et precepto pape*, ut sciretur origo morbi huius, et sunt aperta et inscisa multa corpora mortuorum'. For discussion see Campbell, 1931, p. 111; Welkhuysen, 1983, p. 482.

[94] Demaitre, 1975.

[95] Boniface VIII, *Detestandae feritatis abusum* [*Extrav. Comm.*, III, vi, 1].

[96] Brown, 1981.

[97] For example, Kristeller, 1961; Bolgar, 1954; Smalley, 1960. The term *studia humanitatis* from which the term humanism is derived originally meant the study of classical literature: see Campana, 1946.

[98] Ehrle, 1890, p. 585, says that Pierre would note in his books the name of the seller, the price he paid, and the date of the purchase. On the manuscripts concerned see Maier, 1952, pp. 75, 177–9; 354–7, 417–18 on MSS Vat. Borghese

mentary on Cicero.[99] A catalogue which he copied into his commonplace book, perhaps a list of the works available at Chaise-Dieu,[100] contains an anthology of excerpts from Pliny, Valerius Maximus, and Macrobius.[101] This interest endured, for later the Pope wrote to the Bishop of Valence asking him to send copies of Cicero's works to the curia.[102] He also asked Petrarch to seek out Ciceronian manuscripts for him.[103] The scholar Luca Mannelli was commissioned to compile a dictionary of quotations from Seneca.[104] All this is evidence of some interest in classical literature, and certainly quotations from Seneca, Cicero, and Boethius feature in Clement's sermons. But this of itself does not make him a classical scholar. His enthusiasm for Cicero, for example, could well have been simply an adjunct to his literary or legal studies, while his quotations from Seneca are concerned with the attributes of imperial majesty.[105] And it is worth noting that his classical quotations are far outweighed by those from the Bible, and from Ambrose, Augustine, Gregory the Great, and Bernard. It is rather in his patronage that Clement can be seen to have helped the cause of classical learning. For example, he patronised Barlaam of Calabria, the 'Greek' bishop of Gerace, who taught Greek at the curia.[106] Among Barlaam's pupils was Petrarch, but there is no evidence that the Pope himself tried to learn it. Above all, Clement patronised Petrarch, and it was this bounty which held the poet to the city he professed to loathe – to 'Babylon'. Thanks to Clement, he enjoyed the revenues of several benefices, and at least twice was offered a bishopric.[107] He was also offered an apostolic secretaryship more

---

57, 134, 312, and 362 respectively; Maier, 1967, p. 255, n. 3 on Vat. Borg. 216; Loriquet, 1904, pp. 159–60, 180, on MSS Rheims 174–5 and 211; Baluze–Mollat, ii, p. 342, n. 4, adds MSS Paris, BN lat. 507 and 2032, and Vat. Lat. 3847. Several of Pierre's books went to enrich the papal library at Avignon: see Ehrle, pp. 226, 328, 345, 488, 490.

99 Vat. Borgh. 57: see Maier, 1952, pp. 75–6; Ehrle, p. 345, no. 748.

100 Maier, 1967, p. 309, n. 1.

101 Ibid.

102 Ehrle, p. 139.

103 Petrarch, *Ep. Fam.*, vii, 2, quoted by De Nolhac, 1907, i, p. 219, n. 2. Ehrle lists several volumes of Cicero in the 1375 inventory of the papal library: see pp. 539–40, 541–2. Compare also *Vita Ambrosii Traversarii*, p. 216.

104 See app. 1, no. 14 below.

105 See pp. 25–6 above.

106 The papal accounts record a payment to Barlaam 'in curia legenti grecum' on 7 August 1342: Schäfer, 1914, p. 198. On Petrarch and Barlaam see De Nolhac, 1892; Lo Parco, 1905.

107 Wilkins, 1955, pp. 8–24; 66. See Mollat, 1964, p. 259 for some of Petrarch's lurid descriptions of Avignon.

than once, probably in the hope that he would improve the literary style of the curia.[108] There has even been speculation that Petrarch was hoping to be offered a red hat in 1351, when he was mysteriously summoned back to Avignon from a visit to Italy by two cardinals.[109]

The attention of musicologists has been directed to Clement's patronage of musicians. Interestingly, two of the first payments he made after his coronation were to musicians, and several others feature in the papal accounts.[110] The Pope's most obvious patronage, however, was lavished upon Philippe de Vitry, who had been his contemporary at Paris, and later had held royal office under Charles IV and Philip VI of France. Philippe was notable for pioneering a new and secular style in music, now known as the *Ars nova*: in fact, the whole movement took its name from a treatise of that name which he wrote.[111] So sacrilegious did John XXII find the application of the new style to religious music that he issued an impassioned bull, *Docta sanctorum* (1324–5), in which he complained that sacred music was being pestered with 'notes of small value' (meaning semibreves and minims, which today would not be considered 'small'), that composers were truncating their melodies with hocket, depraving them with discants, and even stuffing them with upper parts lifted straight from secular song.[112] Singers were inebriating rather than soothing the ear, and they were accompanying their singing with lewd gestures which discouraged devotion.[113] Clement, however, seems to have winked at official opposition to the new style. Philippe wrote an ebullient motet to celebrate his election to the papacy. The piece is an example of a form which belongs to the tradition of secular rather than sacred music, and it displays several *Ars nova* characteristics.[114] Far from holding this against him, Clem-

---

[108] Wilkins, 1955, pp. 15–17; 22–4; 66–80.

[109] Ibid., pp. 63–80.

[110] Tomasello, p. 13.

[111] On *Ars nova* see Reese, 1941, pp. 331–59; Reaney, 1960; and Caldwell, 1978, pp. 159–80. For its historical context see Perroy, 1979.

[112] *Extrav. comm.*, III, ii, 1. For discussion, in addition to works listed at n. 111 above, see Hayburn, 1979, pp. 22ff.

[113] Ibid. An anonymous gloss on this passage, *Corpus Iuris Canonici*, ii (Lyons, 1572), states: '*Gestibus simulant*. Quod est turpe, et contra honestatem clericalem. In hoc quodammodo comparandi illis qui ludos theatrales in ecclesiis faciunt, vel ibi laruas induunt, ut suae insaniae ludibria exerceant'.

[114] Ed. Schrade, 1965, pp. 97–103. The tenor, instead of being taken from plainsong, appears to be freely composed, which is an *Ars nova* feature. I am grateful to my colleague David Chadd for examining the motet with me. For a translation see Tomasello, p. 15.

ent appointed Philippe as one of his commensal chaplains, and later, in 1351, to the bishopric of Meaux.[115] Although still in the service of Philip VI, and later that of his son John the Good, Philippe spent some of his time at Avignon, especially in the years 1342–3.[116] He may even have been chaplain to his friend Cardinal Guy de Boulogne.[117] It seems likely that it was he who advised Clement on appointments to the papal chapel. The Pope began a tradition of recruiting chanters from northern and central France, and these would almost certainly have been devotees of the new style.[118]

Privately Pierre Roger seems to have possessed the glimmerings of humanism, as is seen in his enlightened attitude to medical research and in the sheer breadth of his intellectual pre-occupations, which seem to anticipate those of the Renaissance polymaths. This is not, however, to suggest that he was a humanist scholar himself, far less a humanist pope. Many of his interests were traditional scholastic ones. Moreover, even in his youth he had appeared distinctly uneasy about novelty. In two Paris sermons he criticised his contemporaries for their interest in progressive and secular studies. They imitated the curiosity of Adam and Eve in their preference for unwholesome knowledge – for the new, rather than the old, the human, rather than the divine, the law of Justinian rather than the law of the Lord.[119] This does not sound like a humanist speaking.

Clement's real anticipation of the Renaissance popes lay in the encouragement he gave to a wide variety of scholars and artists through patronage. Indirectly this was to have consequences which the Pope himself could not have foreseen. Twentieth-century scholars have become aware of the importance of papal Avignon as a nursery for the development of a new humanistic, Franco-Italian culture, and as a clearing house for its transmission to other parts of Europe.[120] In painting, for example, Castelnuovo, Laclotte, and others regard Avignon as a meeting place for the artistic styles of Italy and the north. It then acted as a centre for the diffusion of artistic

---

[115] Coville, 1933, p. 523; Tomasello, p. 14.

[116] Coville, pp. 532–3; Tomasello, p. 14.

[117] Tomasello, p. 15.

[118] Hugho, 1977, pp. 334–5; Tomasello, p. 151. For biographies and places of origin see Tomasello, appendix, pp. 198–268.

[119] Pierre Roger, sermon 38, Ste-G. 240, fol. 120v. See also sermon 15, p. 474: 'Novitas enim parit discordiam, et ideo in rebus novis constituendis evidens debet esse utilitas, vel urgens necessitas'. In general see Smalley, 1975.

[120] Ullman, 1941; Simone, 1969, pp. 37–78.

styles and techniques to the rest of Europe, in particular to England, Bohemia, and Catalonia, and even on occasions back to Italy.[121] As the patron of Matteo Giovannetti and his *atelier* Clement obviously played a key role in this. Much the same is true of music. It has become clear that under Clement Avignon became a centre for the exchange of new musical ideas and compositions. Moreover, the French polyphonic *Ars nova* manuscripts which found their way to Ivrea and Apt are thought to have done so via Avignon.[122]

Through patronage, which established his court as the most brilliant in Europe, Clement tried to magnify the importance of Avignon. His aim to make the papal residence there appear permanent and legitimate, but without transferring the papal see from Rome, was closely linked with his policy of patronage. While he may not actually have referred to Avignon as *Nova Roma*, there are indications that he wanted it to appear as such. This emerges from his planning and decoration of the papal palace. The naming of the gate to the New Palace, that which bore his papal coat of arms, after the patron saints of Rome, Peter and Paul, clearly demonstrates this attitude. Then there is the question of the chapels. Whereas in Rome the popes had had the whole area of the city at their disposal for ceremonial purposes, at Avignon the whole of Rome, especially the basilicas, had in effect to be encompassed within the palace.[123] Clement's major contribution was the building of the Great Chapel of St Peter, which complemented the smaller one of St John. This meant that both the basilica of St Peter and that of St John Lateran were mirrored in arrangements at Avignon. This was accordingly reflected in papal ceremonial. St Peter's chapel was to become the place of the papal coronation. In Rome this was performed on the steps of the basilica: at Avignon before the door of the chapel.[124] Processions, which in Rome would have covered the area of the city between the Lateran and the Vatican, moved in Avignon between the two chapels of St John and St Peter.[125] Equally significant was Matteo Giovannetti's decoration of the chapel of St John on the theme of the lives of the Baptist and the Evangelist (see figure 13).

---

[121] Castelnuovo, 1962, pp. 10–21; Laclotte in Laclotte and Thiébaut, pp. 49–56; Enaud, 1963, pp. 170–1 and for further bibliography. For the influence on Bohemia, Harrison Thomson, 1950; Dvorák, 1901; Sharon, 1958, and on the Angevin court at Naples, Bologna, 1969, esp. pp. 298–305.
[122] Hugho, 1977, p. 335.
[123] Schimmelpfennig, 1980.
[124] Ibid., p. 318.
[125] Ibid.

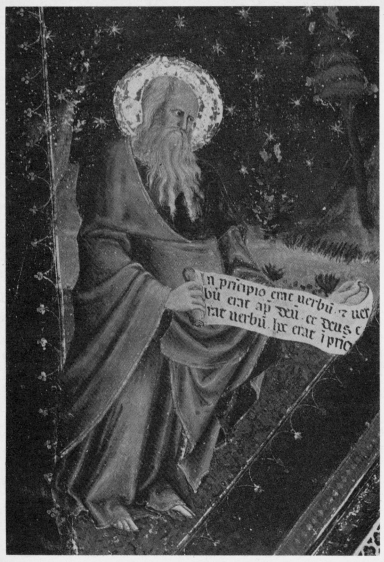

13 Matteo Giovannetti, fresco of St John the Evangelist, Chapel of St John,
Papal Palace (photo: Georges Gaud, 77950 Moisenay, France)

This was probably a deliberate imitation of the ancient decoration of St John Lateran, the pope's cathedral church, on the same theme.[126] Finally there is the question of the chapel of St Martial. Both Castelnuovo and Thiébaut have appreciated the political implications of the dedication as reflected in Giovannetti's frescoes.[127] It seems that Clement tried to build up the cult of the third-century saint and Bishop of Limoges (his own area) and link it with the papacy. Legend had it that the Saint had been a personal disciple of Christ, and he was therefore regarded as an Apostle. St Peter personally had sent him to Gaul, where he had evangelised Aquitaine (Limoges was then part of Aquitania prima). The legend and the miracles of the Saint were faithfully depicted by Giovannetti on the walls and ceiling of the chapel. Moreover, Clement decreed on 7 July 1343 that the feast of St Martial as one of the Apostles was to be celebrated throughout Aquitaine.[128] The Saint's mission to France seemed to give indirect apostolic sanction to the establishment of the papacy there. France itself had been favoured by St Peter: it had become a chosen land.

Clement had done what he could to establish *Nova Roma*, and the fact that he did not appoint a bishop of Avignon lends support to this policy. Nevertheless, he was on dangerous ground. If he broke the theoretical link with Old Rome by overtly becoming bishop of New Rome, he would break the all-important link with Peter and destroy the accumulated weight of tradition attached to the pope's role as bishop of Old Rome. He would also have been allowing his private *persona* to alter the nature of the papal office. On the highly sensitive issue of Old Rome, Clement would have to be as wary as he had been on New Rome. He would once again need to be like the Argus, the beast with a hundred eyes.

[126] Heck, 1980.
[127] Castelnuovo, 1981, pp. 404–5; Thiébaut, in Laclotte and Thiébaut, pp. 155–6. On St Martial see Duchesne, 1899, ii, pp. 104–17; and Wetterlöf, pp. 53–4.
[128] Déprez, no. 263.

Chapter 4

PROPRIISSIMA SEDES BEATI PETRI: THE PROBLEM OF OLD ROME

During the pontificate of Clement VI the city of Rome was to be the setting for ritual drama, for revolution, and for tragedy. The Romans were to witness the revolution of Cola di Rienzo in May 1347, the extraordinary pageantry of his actions, and his oratory, as 'Tribune of the People', the bathos of his fall in December of that year, the floods of 1345, the economic and social effects of the Black Death, followed by the earthquake of September 1349, which severely damaged St Peter's, St Paul's, the Lateran basilica, and Sta Maria Maggiore, the chaos produced by over 5,000 people a day descending on Rome the following year for the Jubilee celebrations,[1] with the tragic and occasionally bizarre scenes of starvation and mass hysteria which resulted – and all this occurred in a city constantly endangered by civil strife, as the Colonnas fought the Orsinis, the populace the nobility.

The real problem for the popes was that as bishops of Rome, rather than Avignon, they knew they ought to be there, but the dangers of Old Rome contrasted unfavourably with the attractions of New Rome. Petrarch saw the cardinals as fearful of being deprived of the pleasures of Beaune wine,[2] but the problem was at a far deeper level. Cola di Rienzo, who had visited Avignon in 1343 as part of a Roman embassy, identified it accurately. Some years later he reported that in consistory Clement had often recognised the Romans as his 'special flock' and had admitted his pastoral duty towards them, but that the excuse which he had proffered above all was that Rome under the tyrants was not a safe place for the pastors

---

[1] Baluze–Mollat, *Quinta Vita*, pp. 302–3. On the Jubilee see Rodocanachi, 1888, pp. 268–79; Gregorovius, 1898, vi, pt 7, pp. 320–7; Mollat, 1963; Schmidinger, 1978, pp. 327–9; 331–7, and for further literature.

[2] Petrarch, *Rerum Senilium*, bk ix, ep. 1, p. 845.

of the Church.[3] Cola then scornfully accused Clement of being the mercenary who fled when he saw the wolf coming, rather than a true pastor.[4] Conrad of Megenberg was convinced that the malice of the Romans had driven the papacy away from Rome.[5] Moreover, the fate of Clement's legate, Annibaldus de Ceccano, Cardinal-bishop of Tusculum, can have done little to allay papal fears. After a riot provoked by the unusual sight of the Cardinal's camel being exercised in the courtyard of the Lateran, Annibaldus, declaiming from the relative safety of a balcony, to avoid flying stones, pointed out that the people's behaviour would not encourage the Holy Father to return to live among them. 'In this City', he opined, 'he could be neither Lord nor Supreme Pontiff'.[6] Shortly afterwards an arrow pierced His Eminence's red hat while he was processing from St Peter's to the Lateran.[7] Clement had to grant his petition to be allowed to return to Naples, and it was on his way there that he died mysteriously, many said as the result of poisoning. His body was taken back to Rome, to St Peter's, and there interred 'but greenly, in hugger mugger'.[8]

Despite his natural reluctance Clement put forward a convincing practical case for returning to Rome when preaching to the Romans in 1343. Among other things he felt that it might heal the Greek Schism, check the advance of the infidel, and ensure that the lands of the Church in Italy were better governed – indeed, they might even be augmented.[9] Nothing daunted, however, he cloaked his less convincing case for remaining in Provence under an academic smokescreen – the proposition that a necessary cause should take precedence over a contingent one. Since he regarded setting a date for his departure for Rome as merely 'contingent', he refused to do so.[10]

Clement well appreciated the risks to the papal theory of govern-

---

[3] Cola di Rienzo, *Libellus*, p. 234.

[4] Ibid.

[5] Conrad of Megenberg, *Yconomica*, iii, 3, ch. 13, p. 404.

[6] *Historiae Romanae Fragmenta*, ch. 1, col. 484. On Annibaldus see Dykmans, 1973.

[7] Ibid., ch. 2, col. 486.

[8] Ibid., ch. 3, col. 490: 'In sepulcrum cadaver projecerunt. Nemo ipsum composuit. Quin immo negligenter adeo projectum fuit, ut facie ad terram versa ceciderit, eoque modo supinum remanserit'.

[9] Clement VI, sermon 14, Ste-G. 240, fols. 148r–9v.

[10] Ibid., fol. 150r: 'Sed dicet inflatus: "Si nunc non potes venire, assigna nobis diem adventus tui". Respondetur: dicunt logici quod . . . sic ex una necessaria et alia contingenti, semper sequitur conclusio contingens . . . Sic est modo in nostro proposito, quia quando erit dies illa in qua debeamus Romam accedere, ista est contingens, et ideo non possumus diem necessarium et determinatum assignare nostri adventus'.

ment if the link with Rome were to be broken. After all, Christians were used to thinking of themselves as members of the Roman Church, and to regarding their head as the Roman pontiff. A break with the city of Rome would have called into question the fundamental identity of Rome and Christianity on which the popes had built up so much of their system, for so complete a fusion had occurred in men's minds between the two that it was a simple matter to apply to the one concepts which had originally been applied to the other. In general, the early popes had appropriated a great deal of the administrative machinery of the Roman Empire for their own use, to say nothing of the profound influence which they had allowed Roman law to exert on their ecclesiology and their notion of sovereignty.[11] More specifically, it was useful to be able to apply many of the convenient myths which still endured about Rome to the Christian society. To emphasise its undying nature, for example, there was the idea of eternal Rome.[12] Above all, Roman myths could be used to foster the notion of universality. The popes themselves, as lords of Rome, could be seen as the successors of the Roman emperors, and therefore as heirs to their claims to be lords of the world. Rome itself was customarily referred to as the *communis patria*, the common fatherland of all mankind, which could easily be reinterpreted as all Christian mankind. John XXII and Benedict XII both adapted this idea when they referred to the Roman curia as the *communis patria*.[13] Then there was the idea that the Roman people were the representatives of the people of the Roman Empire: were they not, by the same token, the epitome of all Christians? And was not Rome itself the very centre, the nucleus, of the world? Because of their conditioning over many centuries to Roman ideas, because in effect those ideas had become part of the conventional wisdom, Western Christians could absorb them without difficulty in a Christian context. By jettisoning the link with Rome the papacy stood to lose much of the Roman theory which underpinned its own system: it might lose more than it would gain. The only wise thing to do was to seek a compromise solution which in no way limited the pope's universal powers, but which also allowed him to retain the advantages, and eschew the disadvantages, of the identity with Rome.

[11] Ullmann, 1975a, esp. pp. 71–7; Le Bras, 1949 and 1966.
[12] See Pratt, 1965.
[13] Raynaldus, v, ch. 53, p. 361. Baluze–Mollat, ii, n. 86, p. 483. For further examples and discussion see Wilks, 1963a, p. 35, n. 3; Kantorowicz, pp. 79, n. 89, 205, n. 35, and 217.

It is from this angle that Clement's concern to stress to the schismatic Armenians that the Catholic and apostolic Church was the same as the Roman Church can be appreciated. It emerged from the catechism he sent to test their faith. Apparently they had made an unsatisfactory reply to Benedict XII's similar question, in which they had implied that the Roman Church was not identical with the Catholic Church.[14] It was vital that the identity between Rome and the universal Church should be accepted by all Christians, and it needed to be spelt out especially to Eastern Christians, those who had no Roman conditioning on which to draw.

Underlying much of what Clement said about Rome was the assumption that he had contracted two marriages: the one in his capacity as vicar of Christ and representative of His mystical body, was to the universal Church: the other, in his capacity as bishop of the see of Rome, was to the localised church of Rome. He was married to his see in just the same way as any other bishop would be. Richard FitzRalph, Archbishop of Armagh, made the same point in a work partly dedicated to Clement when he observed that the pope underwent an election of twofold significance: he was elected both as *summus*, supreme bishop, and as *Romanus*, Roman bishop, simultaneously.[15] The crucial question was whether the marriage to the localised church of Rome was still in being. Clearly it was, for Clement alleged that his love for his bride and his wish to embrace her was what drew him to Rome.[16] He likened himself to Jacob, who had served Rachel's father for seven years so that he might marry her, but his love was so great that it seemed but a few days.[17]

---

[14] Tautu, no. 191, par. 693, p. 314.

[15] Richard FitzRalph, *Summa de Quaestionibus Armenorum*, bk viii, ch. 18, fols. 50r–v: 'idem legitime potest eligi duplici electione in romanum et in summum; ex quo sunt due dignitates distincte *quamvis annexe*. Et potest eligi in romanum et in summum unica electione'. For discussion see Wilks, 1963b, pp. 341–2. On FitzRalph and the Armenian question see Walsh, 1981a, esp. pp. 129–81.

[16] Clement VI, sermon 14 Ste-G. 240, fol. 148v: 'Sed sponsus non gaudet quia sponsam non habet, sed desiderat videre sponsam, et intuere uberes amplexus sponse . . . Sed ista est sponsa mea, videlicet Roma, ergo *desidero videre vos*': see Schmidinger, p. 346. Cf. the Clerk in the *Somnium Viridarii*, bk i, ch. 364, p. 222: 'Sponsa enim requisivit sponsum, clamat, requirit subsidium, postulat defensionem; cum qua conscientia poterit Papa denegare quin visitet et defendet eam? . . . Quarto dixi, quod debet rediri propter coniugii spiritualis vim et fidem compulsivam. Constat autem quod coniugium spirituale est contractum inter Romanum pontificem et ecclesiam Romanam, ratione cuius maior est unio inter ipsum et ipsam sponsam, quam inter virum et suam uxorem, cum ista unio sit spiritualis, illa vero carnalis'. For discussion and examples see Wilks, 1963a, pp. 39–40.

[17] Clement VI, sermon 14, Ste-G. 240, fol. 148v: 'Sed de hoc figuram habemus

The logical result of contracting two marriages was that the Pope became the head of two families. All Christians were the spiritual progeny of the Pope and the universal Church, but the people of Rome alone were the spiritual offspring of their bishop's marriage to the church of Rome. Sometimes Clement would contrast his care for one family with that of the other: as Pope or universal father he cared for all Christians, he wrote, but he held the people of the city within his inmost heart as the 'special sons' of himself and the Roman church.[18] The paternal theme also emerged at the opening of the 1343 discourse. The Romans had come to Avignon, he averred, to show their filial reverence, to seek paternal favour, and to express their boundless joy at his promotion to the Holy See. Clement's reply was 'just as a father rejoices in his son, so that son should rejoice in his father'.[19]

The subject of the Pope's two marriages was one about which Clement felt strongly. It is only in the light of this that we can interpret the accusations he made against the revolutionary Cola di Rienzo on at least two occasions. Cola was the son of a washerwoman and an innkeeper.[20] He had a gift for oratory, a taste for ceremonial, and a fertile imagination which was fired by the history and legends of Rome's former glory. He felt himself divinely inspired to liberate the city from the tyranny of the patrician families who ruled it, and to bring about a rebirth of the Roman Empire. As part of the Roman embassy of 1343, Clement had been sufficiently impressed with him to make him a notary. In May 1347, however, Cola fomented a popular revolution which brought him to power as 'Tribune of the People', although he ruled nominally in partnership with the papal legate. The Tribune professed to be the delegate of the people, but it soon became evident, as he became increasingly autocratic, that he had imperial aspirations. Matters came to a head in August 1347. On 1 August – significantly the anniversary of the day Octavius assumed the title of Augustus – Cola had himself knighted in an extraordinary ceremony, which was followed by a

---

Gen. xxix° [20] ubi dicitur quod ipsi Jacob servienti patris Rachelis, ut Rachelem haberet uxorem, septem annis, et videbantur sibi dies pauci pre amoris magnitudine': cf. Schmidinger, p. 346.

[18] Theiner, *Cod. Dip.*, no. 138, p. 140; and see also no. 143, p. 143; *MGH Const.*, viii, no. 376, p. 419. See also De Boüard, no. 40, p. 335.

[19] Clement VI, sermon 14, Ste-G. 240, fol. 147v: 'Respondetur: sicut pater letatur in filio, sic filius debet letari in patre': cf. Schmidinger, p. 345.

[20] On Cola di Rienzo see Burdach, 1913; Piur, 1931; Rodocanachi, 1888; Gregorovius, vi, pt 1, pp. 231–76; Origo, 1938; Cosenza, 1913; Wieder, 1978.

revolutionary proclamation. His coronation as Tribune, and another proclamation, followed a fortnight later. But his triumph was shortlived. The people soon became disillusioned with him, and in December he fell from power, partly as a result of his own cowardice. He fled from Rome, and after various adventures arrived in Prague, in 1350, where he was imprisoned by Charles IV, until persuaded by Clement to send the 'Tribune' to Avignon.

Clement's accusation against Cola was that he had not scrupled to blaspheme against the 'holy, catholic, and universal Church' by asserting that the universal Church and the city of Rome were the same – *prefatam Ecclesiam civitatemque Romanam idem esse asseruit.*[21] What really incensed the Pope was Cola's identification of the city of Rome with the universal Church, rather than with the localised church of Rome. He had confused Clement's two brides: he had made possession of the city of Rome a *sine qua non* for possession of universal authority, rather than *vice versa*. He had turned the city of Rome into the head of the Church and thus usurped the position of the papacy. His heresy was not, as has been assumed, to say that 'Church' and 'State' were one.[22] To Clement this would have constituted anything but blasphemy. For him there could be only one society, united, universal, and Christian, over which he wielded sovereignty in both spiritual and temporal matters, rather than two independent societies. Cola, as his letters and speeches as Tribune suggest, would have agreed that there was but one society: the point at issue was whether it was to be headed by Pope or Tribune. Implying his own headship of it Cola had gone to the lengths of summoning the rival imperial candidates, Louis of Bavaria and Charles IV, representatives of all the newly liberated Italian cities, and members of the Imperial College of Electors to convene at Rome for a new imperial election, and this after Clement had approved Charles as king of the Romans. No wonder Clement accused him of heresy and blasphemy.

Cola apart, Clement was worried about his two marriages. He was afraid that his opponents would argue that as pope he was the spouse of the universal Church and that he had no right to a *propria sedes*, his own particular see, as well.[23] After some particularly

---

[1] Letter to the Roman people, 3 December 1347, *MGH Const.*, viii, no. 376, p. 420. See also no. 517, p. 532, letter to Charles IV, 5 Feb. 1348.
[2] See, for example, Burdach, 1913, p. 101.
[3] Clement VI, sermon 14, Ste-G. 240, fol. 148v: 'videtur quod Roma non sit propria sedes papae. Probatur sic: sponsus universalis Ecclesie non habet pro-

tortuous reasoning he concluded that the term *proprium* could be used in more than one sense. It could mean either one's own, although not exclusively so, or it could mean one's own, exclusively. Individual churches belonged to the Roman Church, being subject to it, but each one had its own pastor and spouse as well – here he used *proprium* in the first sense. But the see of Rome was subject to none other than itself, and to the pope, and so it belonged to him in the fullest sense, that is, exclusively.[24] He later bestowed the significant title of *propriissima sedes beati Petri*, which made the same point.[25] One of his main arguments for wanting, or at least pretending to want, to go to Rome was for the 'appropriation', literally the taking possession of his see. After all, Rome was the *propria sedes* of the supreme pontiff and successor of St Peter, he observed: indeed, this was why he was called Roman pontiff, or Roman bishop.[26]

Despite Clement's insistence on his marriage to the church of Rome, he persisted in living at Avignon. This inevitably gave rise to contemporary criticisms on the theme of adultery and desertion. Men rushed to the defence of Rome as to that of a deserted bride, while Avignon, conversely, was condemned as a whore. Cola, for example, in an involved passage hoped that the Pope, who in order to look after the castle of Avignon had left his bride in a tavern, would leave the tavern, and with his groomsmen (presumably the cardinals) would hurry to return to his bride.[27] Peter Ceffons of Clairvaux, a Cistercian and a contemporary of Clement, addressed the Avignon clerics as a society of demons and adulterers of the bride

priam sedem; sed papa est sponsus universalis Ecclesie; ergo non habet propriam sedem, et sic, secundum istum modum Rome [*sic*] non est sua propria sedes'.

[24] Clement VI, sermon 14, Schmidinger, pp. 347–8: 'dicunt logici, quod proprium . . . dicitur duobus modis: primo modo, quando aliquid competit uni, non tamen competit illi soli . . . quia competit multis aliis. Secundo modo dicitur proprium quod sic competit uni, quod nulli alii competit . . . sic est in proposito nostro quia primo modo dicitur proprium, sed non dicitur proprie proprium; sed secundo modo dicitur proprium . . . tunc respondetur . . .: Alie ecclesie ab ecclesia Romana sic competunt pape, quod aliis pontificibus committuntur, quia quelibet cum hoc, quod est subiecta summo pontifici habet proprium pastorem et sponsum. Sed Romana sedes nulli alii competit, quam soli pape, et sic est sibi u maxime proprium, ergo cum illa sit michi maxime propria sedes'.

[25] Ibid., Ste-G. 240, fol. 149r; Schmidinger, p. 349.

[26] Ibid., Ste-G. 240, fol. 148v: 'movemur ex sedis appropriatione, quia Roma es propria sedes summi pontificis et successoris Petri. Unde vocatur Romanus pon tifex, Romanus episcopus. Ergo videtur quod debemus accedere Romam'. Cf Schmidinger, p. 347.

[27] Cola di Rienzo, *Libellus*, p. 261. For interpretation of this passage see Burdach 1913, pp. 48–9.

of Christ. This society had been designated by Christ as a great whore who fornicated with the kings of the earth.[28] The reference was, of course, to 'Babylon the great, the mother of harlots and abominations of the earth' described in the Apocalypse (xvii. 5). Petrarch added to this the previous verse, describing Avignon as the harlot 'arrayed in purple and scarlet colour, and decked with gold and precious stones and pearls, having a golden cup in her hand full of abominations and filthiness of her fornication'.[29] The comparison with Babylon signified more than the supposed life of luxury and promiscuity lived at Avignon, and was grounded directly on the marriage metaphor: Avignon had adulterously enticed the pope away from Rome, away from the bride of Christ.

In his 1343 discourse Clement answered the accusations about desertion and adultery directly. Returning to the theme of Jacob's marriage to Rachel, he explained that however much a bridegroom loves his bride he ought, when necessity demands it, to transfer to another. He reminded his audience of how Jacob was compelled to desert Rachel for Leah.[30] Not, of course, as he hastened to point out, that he was advocating a general policy of episcopal adultery and desertion. Far from it: only the pope, as spouse of the universal Church, was allowed to transfer himself from one see – one bride – to another. When the tempest had raged in the ocean, Peter alone had gone out on to the waves [Matthew, xiv. 29]. The other disciples had remained in the ship to show that the supreme pontiff, who occupied St Peter's position, ought to visit different areas to destroy evil among those committed to him, and to quell tempests. The other prelates had to remain in their own churches, those to which they had been specifically appointed.[31]

---

[28] Peter Ceffons, *Epistola Luciferi*, sec. B (ed. unfolioed): 'O societas gratissima demonibus . . . dum te Christus verificavit synagoga Sathanae et te designavit per meretricem magnam, quae fornicata est cum regibus terrae facta de matre noverca, de sponsa Christi adultera . . .' This work was formerly attributed to Nicholas Oresme, but is now thought to have been written by Peter: Trapp, 1957.

[29] Petrarch, *Liber Sine Nomine*, ep. 18, p. 230.

[30] Clement VI, sermon 14, Ste-G. 240, fol. 149v: 'Ergo quamvis sponsus sponsam diligat debet tamen cum oportunitas exigat, dimissa presentia sponse [*sic*], ad alia se transferre. Et de hoc habemus figuram Gen. xxx°, quod quamvis Patriarcha Jacob diligeret Rachelem, velut sponsam valde dilectam formosam et valde pulchram, oportuit tamen ipsum de beneplacito Rachelis descendere ad Lyam': cf. Schmidinger, p. 352.

[31] *Ibid.*, fol. 150r: 'Item tempestate in mari existente solus Petrus exivit ad fluctuationes maris. Mt. xiiii° [22–9]. Alii discipuli remanserunt in navi, ad denotandum quod Romanus pontifex, qui stat in loco beati Petri, debet ad diversas partes

For Clement it was not the pope who committed adultery: it was people like Cola di Rienzo who interfered with the Pope's marriage bonds to the *Ecclesia*. In his *Libellus*, the anti-papal composition addressed to Ernest Pardubitz, Archbishop of Prague, Cola defended himself against accusations made by Clement in a document which no longer survives. Apparently the Pope had called him adulterator of the sacred body of Christ.[32] This implies that he had either set himself up as pope or had created or threatened to create an anti-pope. Certainly Cola had usurped papal authority. Clement rightly described his summons to the imperial electors as 'subversive of the primacy of the *Ecclesia*'.[33] He also had no illusions that Cola's actions betokened his own imperial ambitions. He aspired to the height of Caesarean dignity, so he told Charles IV.[34] The Tribune had also encroached on Clement's powers of jurisdiction by attempting to judge between Louis of Hungary and Joanna of Naples on issues arising from the murder of Prince Andrew of Hungary.[35] According to a papal agent in Rome, Cochetus de Cochetis, Cola had also taken it upon himself to arbitrate in the Anglo-French conflict.[36]

Nevertheless, Cola tried vainly to maintain the illusion of recognition of papal authority. His declaration of August 1347 proclaimed that the sovereignty of the world had returned to the Roman people.[37] What this meant was that Cola himself had assumed it: he referred to the 'authority, power, and ancient jurisdiction, and power of arbitration granted to him by the people', and added as a bizarre afterthought, 'and lately by our lord the supreme pontiff',[38] not appearing to see the inconsistency. Absolute sovereignty could hardly have derived from two opposing sources, in effect from both 'above' and 'below'. Moreover, if the sovereignty of the world had

---

accedere, ut possit sibi commissarum omnium [mala] sedare et tollere tempestates. Alii vero prelati remanent velut in navi in propriis ecclesiis, quibus sunt ordinati et deputati'. The Latin of both Ste-G. 240 and Vat. Borg. 41, on which Schmidinger's edition is based, appears to be corrupt. MS Zwettl. Stifts-bibliothek Cod. 169 alone includes the word *mala*: Schmidinger, p. 352. See also Clement VI in Tautu, no. 26, par. 101. Cf., Bernard, *De Consideratione*, bk ii, viii, 16, p. 424 and Innocent III, Reg. ii, 200 (209), Hageneder, ii, p. 384. For further examples see Wilks, 1963a, p. 412, n. 3.

[32] Cola di Rienzo, *Libellus*, par. 20, p. 244.
[33] *MGH Const.*, viii, no. 376, p. 420.
[34] *MGH Const.*, viii, no. 390, p. 435.
[35] See Cola's letter to Clement, *Briefwechsel*, iii, no. 43, pp. 167–8.
[36] Cochetus de Cochetis, *Briefwechsel*, iv, Anhang 8, p. 24.
[37] Cola di Rienzo, Declaration of 1 Aug. 1347, *Briefwechsel*, iii, no. 27, pp. 101–2.
[38] Ibid.

returned to the Roman people, the implication was that the Pope had forfeited it by being away from Rome. Yet Cola also wrote to Clement referring to his existence both as head of the city and of the world.[39] On various occasions he declared that he would never do anything in derogation of the rights of the *Ecclesia*, notably in his declaration of sovereignty just after summoning the electors.[40] Clement was not deceived, and coldly pointed out the lack of consistency between the Tribune's words and deeds.[41] He would probably have been even more scathing if he could have seen the *Libellus*, where Cola compared himself to Christ.[42] It was not Cola's usurpation of papal authority which earned him the accusation of spiritual adultery. In all the letters Clement wrote, to his legate in Rome, to the Roman people, to Charles IV, and others about Cola's atrocities, there is no mention of it. What emerges, however, is that Cola was 'suspected of both schism and heresy'.[43] Schism was technically the crime of adhering to or creating a rival pope or a rival church. Did Cola create an anti-pope? Historians have been divided on this question.[44] Two chroniclers say that Cola summoned Clement to return to Rome when he summoned the electors, one of them, Matthew of Nuremberg, adding that he threatened that if Clement did not comply within a year, then he, Cola, would create another pope.[45] He must have known of the precedent of Louis of Bavaria's citation of John XXII and his creation of the anti-pope Nicholas V. There is, however, no other direct evidence that he summoned Clement. But our concern is with whether Clement, or anyone else, thought that he did. In the letters in which the accusation of schism appears the Pope says that Cola had summoned all those clergy remaining outside the city to return.[46] The bishop of Rome would surely have counted as a Roman cleric. Writing the day after the

---

[39] *Briefwechsel*, iii, no. 28, p. 106.

[40] Ibid., no. 27, p. 105.

[41] Clement VI to Bertrand de Déaulx, *Briefwechsel*, iv, no. 22: 'Licet itaque predictus Nicolaus omnia sub nostro et Ecclesie Romane nomine ac ad nostrum et ipsius Ecclesie honorem dicat se agere, quia *tamen non sunt consona verba factis*'.

[42] Cola di Rienzo, *Libellus*, pp. 250–1; 'sicut Christus xxxiii° sue etatis anno prostratis tyrannis inferni et libertatis spiritibus celum coronatus ascendit, sic et me tyrannorum Urbis sine ictu victorem et liberatorem unicum plebis sue, mee etatis anno consimili assumi voluit ad lauream tribunalem'.

[43] Clement VI to the Roman people, 3 December 1347, *MGH Const.*, viii, no. 376, p. 421; see also no. 517, p. 532.

[44] For a review of opinions see Burdach and Piur, *Briefwechsel*, i, pp. 188–9.

[45] *Vita Nicolai Laurentii*, ch. 26, col. 452; Matthew of Nuremberg, *Chronica*, ch. 86, p. 227.

[46] Clement VI, *MGH Const.*, viii, no. 376, p. 421; see also no. 517, p. 532.

summons, in defence of Cola, Cochetus did not believe that the Tribune wished to extend his power to include papal dominion, explaining that this was the opinion of the Romans.[47] This has usually been taken as a denial that Cola summoned Clement. Nevertheless, a few lines later, when describing Cola's antics, Cochetus opined that Cola had acted 'as if he were emperor, *and more than emperor*',[48] which seems to invalidate his earlier defence, given that papal power alone was above imperial. In the *Libellus* to Ernest, Cola specifically denied that he had arrogantly summoned Clement to return to Rome, but admitted that he had sent an embassy asking him to do so.[49] In a letter written a few months later to Ernest, Cola complained of his reception and imprisonment in Prague. He felt that the defenders of the faith in Prague would not have examined him if he had arrived at the head of two or three thousand horsemen, *even if I had created an anti-pope*.[50] It looks as if the subject was on Cola's by then disturbed mind, and that Clement had accused him both of summoning him to Rome and at least of threatening to create an anti-pope. It was this which merited the titles of schismatic and adulterator of the sacred body of Christ.

One of Clement's main reasons for wanting to preserve his marriage to his *propria sedes* may have been the realisation that if he did not have one, if he were not married to a particular see, then it could be argued that he was not a bishop. Despite the tendency in the fourteenth century to stress the jurisdictional powers of the pope rather than his sacramental powers, it was still vital that he should be consecrated bishop, and that he should be, in the words of FitzRalph, both *summus* and *Romanus*. Later in the century Wyclif was to demonstrate the danger of separating the two roles by asserting that the pope did not have to be bishop of Rome, or indeed a bishop at all. And this was to lead straight to his notion of lay headship of the Church.[51]

But did the pope necessarily have to be *summus* and *Romanus*? Why could he not, for example, be *summus* and *Avinionensis*? Clement had come perilously near that position by leaving the bishopric of

---

[47] Cochetus de Cochetis, *Briefwechsel*, iv, Anhang 8, p. 23.

[48] Ibid., p. 24.

[49] Cola di Rienzo, *Libellus*, p. 243.

[50] *Briefwechsel*, iii, no. 63, p. 350.

[51] Wyclif, *Tractatus de Potestate Pape*, ch. 10, p. 251: 'oportet necessario stare fidelem ubicumque migraverit; nec oportet nunc aliquam eius partem Romam vel Avinionam incolere vel esse presbiterum': cf. Wilks, 1963b, pp. 351–4. For earlier fourteenth-century views see Wilks, 1963a, pp. 392–6.

Avignon unfilled.[52] Despite this, he was convinced that he should be bishop of Rome rather than of anywhere else. Visiting different parts of his universal domain and transferring himself from one see to another, on however permanent a basis, was by no means the same thing as transferring the see itself. The minority opinion on this, in complete opposition to Clement, was that of Pierre de la Palu, who maintained that it was possible for the pope to change his see. He could appoint another bishop to Rome, and so could preside over all churches universally and none specially.[53] Peter himself had been without a special see when he had gone to Antioch: there was no reason why the pope should not follow his lead.[54] But it could be argued that Peter had then transferred his see from Antioch to Rome. If the Romans were now in rebellion, and another city in the world seemed more suitable and convenient for the government of the Church, then the pope could change his see, just as Peter had done, and just as the Emperor had translated the imperial seat to Constantinople – a somewhat dubious precedent since it made the pope follow the Emperor's lead.[55] If, however, the pope had not changed his see he was in the same position as an archbishop who could visit suffragan dioceses and stay in them for a time, but 'commonly' should remain in his own diocese.[56] A more representative view, and one in accord with Clement's, was that of Conrad of Megenberg, who held that although the pope presided over all churches universally, he presided over Rome specially, and he could not place another bishop there. Because the see of Rome had been chosen by divine command, it could not be changed by man and transferred to another place.[57] The most dramatic reaction to the suggestion that

---

[52] For discussion see above pp. 50–1.

[53] Pierre de la Palu, *Tractatus de Potestate Papae*, q. i, art. 3, p. 188: 'papa ex causa rationabili potest sedem suam mutare tripliciter. Primo modo, quod ponat Rome alium episcopum, et ipse presideat omnibus ecclesiis universaliter et nulli specialiter'. Pierre advanced an apparently conflicting view, however, in his *De Causa Immediata Ecclesiasticae Potestatis*: see Wilks, 1963a, p. 302.

[54] Ibid.: 'Sed Petrus usquequo venit Antiochiam fuit sine sede speciali, et ab illo tempore quo Antiochie Ignatium constituit quousque Rome sedit. Ergo et papa sic potest esse sine speciali sede'.

[55] Ibid., pp. 189–90.

[56] Ibid., p. 190: 'Sed utrum sede non mutata debeat alibi manere, dicendum quod sicut archiepiscopus potest visitare dioceses suffraganeorum et ad tempus manere, sed debet communiter in sua diocesi manere, ita etiam dicendum est de papa'.

[57] Conrad of Megenberg, *Yconomica*, iii, 3, ch. 1, p. 356: 'Dicitur eciam episcopus sive pontifex Romanus, quia licet summus pontifex omnibus ecclesiis presideat universaliter, tamen Romane ecclesie specialiter presidet, nec alius episcopus

the see of Rome could be changed is said to have come from John XXII. Petrarch recorded his reply to the tempting suggestion that he should translate the papacy from Rome to his native Cahors, and the Empire from Rome to Germany. Both of these transfers, John was assured, could be achieved without trouble, expense, or armed combat. John was appalled: he accused the speaker of being out of his mind, and trying to deceive him. For did he not realise that if this were to happen John and his successors would be mere bishops of Cahors and the emperor a mere German prefect? Whether he wished it or not, Rome would always be the head of everything: *velimus nolimus enim, rerum caput Roma erit.*[58]

Clement was not prepared to discuss the question of moving his see to Avignon: he was, however, prepared to answer those who thought that the Holy See should be at Jerusalem. Such suggestions were connected with the traditional idea that the centre of divine government should be located in the centre of the earth. It had a long biblical and classical pedigree. 'Thou mayest know that I am the Lord in the midst of the earth', God had said to Moses in Exodus, viii. 22; while representing pagan philosophy, Socrates had located the Delphic oracle in the navel of the earth. Related to this was the tripartite division of the globe into the three continents of Europe, Asia, and Africa. This had found expression in the tripartite or T-O maps which were common from the time of the Roman Empire to the fifteenth century.[59] According to a fourteenth-century chronicler the partitioning had been made after the Flood, when the three sons

Rome ponitur . . . Dicunt insuper quidam, quod, ex eo sedes summi pontificis Roma electa est ex divina iussione, per hominem mutari non possit, ut in alium locum transferatur'. One of the earliest to state this view was Guido de Baysio (d. 1313), *Rosarium*, p. 319: 'Ex hoc dicunt quidam, quod papa hodie suam sedem a Roma in alium locum mutare non posset, sive transferre, esset enim contra Domini iussionem, ut hic habetur'. Among other fourteenth-century writers see John of Athona, *ad Constit. Othonis*, p. 36: 'Hic queritur quod saepius est dubium an Papa suam sedem a Roma in alium locum transferre potest. Consuevit dici quod non, propter iussionem divinam: nam sedes Beati Petri primo fuit Antiochiam . . . quae postea iubente Domino Romam translata est'. See also Anon., *Somnium Viridarii*, bk i, ch. 364, p. 222; Alvarus Pelagius, *De Planctu Ecclesiae*, bk i, ch. 31, p. 35 (see Wilks, 1963a, p. 400, n. 1); Johannes Gaufredi, *ad Decretales*, V, xxxiii, 23, fol. 152v; Baldus de Ubaldis, *ad Decretales*, I, xxxiii, 5, fol. 131r.

[58] Petrarch, *Liber Sine Nomine*, ep. 17, pp. 224–5. It is doubtful if John XXII would have made such a crude separation of the 'two powers' as in this passage, which may indicate that Petrarch adapted the incident.

[59] The most obvious medieval examples are the Ebsdorf and the Hereford maps. On T-O maps in general see Bagrow, 1964, pp. 42–3 and George, 1969, pp. 28–9.

of Noah had divided the world among themselves.[60] By the fourteenth century it was accepted that anyone with claims to universal authority lived in the centre of the globe. A contemporary described how Cola di Rienzo, after his summons to the imperial electors, had triumphantly drawn his sword, and pointing to each of the three sections of the world in turn declaimed: 'This is mine, this is mine, this is mine!'[61] He was obviously in no doubt that Rome was the centre of the globe. Fourteenth-century chroniclers and cartographers differed on this. Although they accepted the tripartite division of the world they did not necessarily agree that Rome was its centre. Since many maps were made for crusading purposes it was more usual to find Jerusalem as the nucleus: sometimes Jerusalem and Rome were equidistant from the centre. Ranulf Higden's world map for his *Polychronicon* was symbolically shaped like a fish, the image for Christ, with Rome and Jerusalem equidistant from the centre.[62] Early Christians had regarded Jerusalem as the centre of a circle. Then, after the missions of St Paul, when the Faith had become Gentile, inhabitants of the West came to regard Rome as the centre of a circle, but Easterners saw Rome and Jerusalem as the centres of an ellipse.[63] Ranulf Higden's map reflects this.

If God Himself were located in the centre of the earth, it followed that His terrestrial vicar should also be. Innocent III, drawing on Psalm lxxiii [lxxiv] (12), referred to the Roman pontiff 'working our salvation in the midst of the earth'.[64] The problem was to decide where the middle was. In some cases nationalism prevailed over geography. The Milanese chronicler Galvaneus Flamma, a contemporary of Clement, neatly adapted the Greek doctrine of the mean to prove that Italy was *in medio* between north and south.[65] On

---

[60] Fra Paolino Minorita, *Prologus ad Mappam Mundi*, ed. R. Almagià, *Monumenta Cartographica Vaticana*, I (Vatican City, 1944), p. 4: 'Incipit prologus in mapa mundi ac trifaria orbis divisione. Sine mapa mundi ea que dicuntur de filiis ac filiis filiorum Noe et quae de iudeorum monarchiis ceterisque regnis atque provinciis, tam in divinis quam humanis scripturis non tam difficile quam impossibile dixerim ymaginari aut mente posse concepi'. Cf. Augustine's discussion on Genesis x and xi, *De Civitate Dei*, xvi, 3, pp. 501–4; see also xvi, 17, pp. 521–2.

[61] *Vita Nicolai Laurentii*, ch. 26, col. 452: 'Exinde evaginato ense aether per tres orbis partes percutiens, ait: *Hoc meum: hoc meum: hoc meum est!*'

[62] Bagrow, p. 47, for a reproduction of this.

[63] Chadwick, 1959. For Roman ideas of the city, particularly the concept of Rome as the *mundus*, see Storini Mazzolani, 1970.

[64] Innocent III, *Reg.*, ii, 193 (202), Hageneder, ii, p. 366. Clement himself referred to Christ 'working salvation in the midst of the earth': Déprez, no. 94, col. 9.

[65] Galvaneus Flamma, *Chronica Galvagnana*, ch. 202, p. 195: 'Cum ergo Ytalia sit in

the other hand, the Knight in the *Somnium Viridarii*, a work of French provenance, thought that France was the most convenient place in the world for the papacy to reside, because it was in the centre of the world; the map of the world actually showed Marseilles as the exact centrepoint, he added punctiliously.[66] Richard FitzRalph, in his *Summa de Erroribus Armenorum*, written when Clement was trying to bring the schismatics into the Roman Church, thought of Jerusalem as the centre of the globe, and therefore the most accessible place for the pope to live.[67] Wyclif, later in the century, was also to point to its central position and to argue the superiority of its claims over those of Rome – its greater antiquity, and greater holiness, due to the presence of Christ there.[68] Probably his real aim was simply to embarrass the papacy, for he knew full well that Jerusalem was in Islamic hands, and that the popes could not possibly have moved there.

Clement VI dealt directly with the claim that Jerusalem was the centre of Christendom by suggesting that Rome had become the new Jerusalem, rendering it unnecessary for the pope to go to old Jerusalem. He reasoned that if the pope had to go to Rome to worship the Apostles, because they could be worshipped only on ground wet with apostolic blood, then how much more pressing was the argument that he ought to go to Jerusalem: for here Christ had performed His miracles; here washed the feet of the disciples; here died for our redemption and for that of the whole human race:

medio inter aquillonem et meridiem . . . Ytalia in medio situata participat de utriusque extremitatis proprietate, quia secundum phylosophum medium sapit naturam suorum extremorum'.

[66] Anon., *Somnium Viridarii*, bk i, ch. 365, p. 226: 'Locus iste Franciae est eligibilior propter maiorem convenientiam, quam habet cum orbe: *quia in medio orbis*. Marsilia enim est in medio orbis situata, ut per mensuratores mappae mundi clarius est demonstratur. Forsan dici posset non improbabiliter, quod magis decet Romanum pontificem per orbem proficisci, quam Romae residere'.

[67] Richard FitzRalph, *Summa de Quaestionibus Armenorum*, bk vii, ch. 16, fol. 49r: 'Item ratio tua superior de facilitate accessus ad eum qui haberet precipue fidei surgentes quaestiones dissolvere [scil. papam] locum habet potius de Hierusalem de qua aut de circumstante sibi regione dicit Psalmista [lxxiii (lxxiv). 12]: *Deus enim rex noster ante secula operatus est salutem in medio terrae*, quam habet de Roma, que est in partibus occidentalibus Europe, cum inter omnes partes mundi ad medium terrae facilior sit generalis accessus'. For discussion on this see Wilks, 1963b, pp. 330ff. For further discussion on the connection of Rome with Jerusalem see Kantorowicz, 1957, p. 205, n. 35: Guido Vernani argued that the Jews should have presided over the world before Christ rather than the Romans because of their more central habitation: *De Reprobatione 'Monarchiae'*, pp. 135–6: 'Ego autem credo quod gens Iudeorum, et ratione situs terre que est in medio nostre habitabilis . . . magis de iure debebat principari gentibus quam Romani'.

[68] Wyclif, *de Potestate Pape*, ch. 8, pp. 166–7: see Wilks, 1963b, pp. 347–8.

therefore, he concluded, it seems that the pope ought to visit this place principally and not Rome.[69] Clement then went on to postulate something like a *translatio imperii*, a translation of empire, from Jerusalem to Rome. Christ had gone to Jerusalem because it was the chief city of the Israelites, and He had gone to save the House of Israel. But the Jews had rejected Christ, and so the disciples had been forced to turn to the Gentiles. The Pope then cited the words of Paul and Barnabas to the Jews [Luke, xix. 10]: 'It was necessary to preach the Word to you first, but seeing you reject it and judge yourselves unworthy of eternal life, behold we turn to the Gentiles'.[70] But he was not above adapting them for his own use. He attributed these words to St Peter. In view of Peter's position as the vicar of Christ, and the somewhat anomalous position of Paul in the medieval period,[71] it would be more telling if the translation appeared to be made by Peter. Jerusalem had been the principal city of the Jews, so Christ had gone there: Rome was the principal city of the Gentiles – one had only to look at Augustine's *De Civitate Dei* to know that. Divine rather than human inspiration had guided the Apostles to go there, to establish the see that was most peculiarly Peter's, *propriis-sima*, and to preach the Gospel of Christ universally from there.[72] Clement seemed to be saying that Christ Himself, in the person of His vicar, Peter, had moved His centre from Jerusalem to Rome, so that Jerusalem was absolved of all connections with Christ in so far as they related to papal primacy. Clement's idea was really a variation

---

[69] Clement VI, sermon 14, Ste-G. 240, fol. 149r: 'Non eis potest honorare per civitatem illam nisi supra terram sanguine sanctorum madidam. Ibi enim sunt corpora sanctorum Petri et Pauli, qui sunt nostre fidei principes et patroni. Est ibi Laurentius, Vincentius, Agnes, Cecilia, et sic de aliis. Sed arguitur contra, quia sic videtur quod deberet ire in Jherusalem et non Romam, quia in Jherusalem Christus fecit signa et mirabilia. Ibi lavit pedes discipulorum; ibi passus est; ibi sanguinem suum fudit pro nostra redemptione et pro salute generis humani. Ergo videtur quod debet visitare papa illa loca principaliter et non Romam'. Cf. Schmidinger, p. 349.

[70] Ibid.: 'Et quia in toto populo Israelitico principalior erat civitas Jherusalem, ideo venit, et ibi miracula fecit, et passus est in Jherusalem. Sed ut legitur Act. xiiiº [46] dixit Petrus Judeis: *Vobis oportebat primum loqui verbum Dei: sed quoniam repulistis illud, et indignos vos iudicatis eterne vite, ecce, convertimur ad gentes*'. Cf. Schmidinger, p. 349.

[71] On this see Battifol, 1938.

[72] Clement VI, sermon 14, fol. 149r: 'Et quia in populo toto gentilium, sive paganorum, civitas Romana principalior erat, ut apparet ex dictis beati Augustini a primo usque ad quintum *De Civitate Dei*, ideo non ordinatione humana sed divina inspiratione ordinatum est ut apostoli venirent Romam, et ibi esset pro-priissima sedes beati Petri, et ibi predicaretur universaliter verbum Christi'. Cf. Schmidinger, p. 349.

on Innocent III's *Per Venerabilem*, in which he had announced that the place which the Lord had chosen was known as the Apostolic see.[73] Arguments based on a divine transference of authority were stronger than the more usual ones based on the Donation of Constantine, by which Constantine had given imperial powers and rights in Rome to Silvester, for this made papal rights over the city dependent on the grant of a layman. Thus Clement's reasoning was an advance on that of Nicholas III in his bull *Fundamenta*, which Clement himself quoted.[74] Herman of Schildiz matched Clement's concern about the position of Rome *vis à vis* Jerusalem. Why, he wondered, should Rome, consecrated by the blood of Peter and Paul, be head of all the churches, rather than Jerusalem, consecrated by the blood of Christ? He concluded similarly to Clement, adding the point that Rome already enjoyed *principatus* over the whole world, which Jerusalem had never done.[75] What is interesting about this is that their views – Herman's more than Clement's – amount to a declaration that God was limited by the pre-eminence of Rome as the nucleus of the Gentile world. God was obliged to choose Rome as the centre of Christendom because of its position in the pagan world: it was already universal.

The divine transference of the see of St Peter from Jerusalem to Rome had great theoretical advantages. Not only could the popes translate all the ideology traditionally associated with the Roman Emperor and the Empire for their own Christian purposes, but they had also inherited the rich store of Jewish symbolism with which to strengthen their case. Besides petitioning Clement to return to Rome, the Romans had also requested that he should declare 1350 a jubilee year, which he did. The jubilee gave him and others a splendid opportunity to adapt Jewish ideas, and in so doing to provide answers to the questions of whether Rome could still be seen as the centre of Christendom, the Roman people as the epitome of all Christians, and Rome itself as the microcosm of the universal Church.

[73] *Decretales*, IV, xvii, 13. For Innocent, the moment when God had chosen Rome was when Peter had been turned back to the city by Christ's saying: 'Venio Romam iterum crucifigi'. This argument was used both by the publicists who wanted a return to Rome, who cited it as a precedent, and by those who did not, who stressed that it was a warning of what might become of the pope should he return. Cf. Cola di Rienzo, *Libellus*, p. 234; Anon., *Somnium Viridarii*, bk i, ch. 364, p. 222.

[74] Clement VI, sermon 14, Ste-G. 240, fol. 148r: *Sext.*, I, vi, 17. On the Donation see Huyghebaert, 1976.

[75] Herman of Schildiz, *Contra Hereticos*, ii, ch. 1, p. 60.

The jubilee was in origin an Old Testament ritual, and in his jubilee bull Clement made it plain that his own holy year of 1350 was proclaimed in emulation of the Mosaic law, as enshrined in Leviticus, xxv. 8–13.[76] In his Roman *collatio* he compared the Romans who had come to petition him to grant the celebration, to the people of Israel, those who had murmured against Moses and Aaron. The Romans were indeed murmuring against Clement for not returning to the city, and he therefore granted them the jubilee to 'stop the murmuring' of his peculiar people, the people of Israel–Rome.[77] The notion that Christians were the heirs of the Israelites was a traditional one, used elsewhere by Clement. Moreover, the jubilee, because it drew Christians from all over the world to Rome, was something of universal import. It seems reasonable to infer that Clement saw the Roman citizens as epitomising all Christians.[78] Nor would he have been alone in this. The idea had been demonstrated, albeit for different reasons, by Louis of Bavaria in 1328, when he had received his crown from the hands of the Romans, who represented all Christians.[79] Cola's declaration that the sovereignty of the world had returned to the Roman people, coupled with his earlier discovery of the *lex regia*, the bronze tablet which demonstrated that imperial authority had been bestowed on Vespasian by the Romans (a significant precedent), showed that his view of them was similar.[80] And it was precisely as the Tribune of the people of the city of Rome, the common fatherland of the whole world, that he claimed to wield universal authority.[81]

If the Romans were symbolic of all Christians, then it would be logical to find that Rome itself was still regarded as the nucleus, and, in a sense, the epitome, of the whole Church. Of course, the fact that

---

[76] Tautu, no. 155, par. 520: 'Nos autem attendentes, quod annis quinquagesimus in Lege Mosaica, quam non venit Dominus solvere, sed spiritualiter adimplere, iubilaeus remissionis'. Cf. Clement VI, sermon 8, MS Frankfurt, Stadtbibliothek 71, fol. 418r: 'Insuper legis Moysayce, quam salvator noster non venit solvere sed spiritualiter ad implere figura quinquagesima significari'. On the Old Testament Jubilee and for further bibliography see North, 1954.

[77] Tautu, no. 155, par. 520.

[78] See, for example, Clement VI, sermon 40, p. 159; Pierre Roger, sermon 15, p. 468. For discussion of its origins see Cerfaux, 1959, pp. 59–79.

[79] On the *Romani* as representing all Christians see Wilks, 1963a, pp. 122, 189ff.

[80] *Vita Nicolai Laurentii*, ch. 3, col. 406.

[81] See, for example, Cola's letter to Clement, in which he defended his claims to arbitrate in the Hungary–Naples dispute: *Briefwechsel*, iii, no. 43, p. 167: 'nuper ambassiatores regis Ungarie venerunt ad Urbem . . . postulantes . . . quod per me et populum Urbis, *patriae toti mundo communis*, de lugubri morte . . . Andree iustitia fieret'.

a jubilee had been proclaimed, which drew members of the universal Church to what many still regarded as 'the common fatherland of all believers', was an indication of this. Something which also suggests the symbolic significance of Rome was the ceremony of the holy gate.[82] This was the ceremonial opening of the golden gate of St Peter's by the pope, and also, possibly, that of the Lateran, which had been walled up since the previous jubilee. Its particular interest is that the ceremony was supposed to be prefigured in the east gate of the city of Jerusalem, which was opened only on the sabbath and on feast days. The idea of the opening of the gate had wide eschatological implications, the obvious one being that St Peter was opening the gate of Heaven to all those Christians who were saved. Thus Rome became the symbol of the Church Triumphant, the heavenly Jerusalem, which was itself the ideal of the terrestrial Church. The ritual is known to have been performed in the middle of the fifteenth century, and there is evidence for the existence of golden gates both at St Peter's and at the Lateran by this time. There is, however, some evidence that the ceremony may have been performed during Clement's jubilee year. The jurist Albericus de Rosate was in Rome in 1350. In the forged jubilee bull he preserved, Clement was made to relate how the night before he was to discuss in consistory whether to grant the Romans' petition for the jubilee year he had a vision. A 'reverend person' carrying two keys appeared to him and told him to open the door – *aperi ostium* – and through it to send forth the flame by which the whole world would be warmed and enlightened. The next day Clement celebrated the mass of the Virgin, and prayed that if the vision were good and genuine it might appear to him again that night, but that if it were false it might be entirely forgotten. Needless to say the vision reappeared.[83] Although the bull is spurious, its preservation by a contemporary shows that the idea of opening the door was current by the time of Clement VI.

A more reliable impression of the Pope's views on the position of Rome can be gleaned from his attitude to the Lateran basilica, his cathedral church. Of course, on the face of things, proclaiming a jubilee was a provocative action, for there were few things more calculated to advertise the Pope's desertion of his *propria sedes*. Indeed, one of the declared aims of the ceremonies was to focus

---

[82] On the ceremony of the golden gate see Thurston, 1900, pp. 28–54, 214–46, 405–10.
[83] Albericus de Rosate, *Dictionarium*, fol. 163v. On this see Thurston, pp. 34–6.

attention on the Roman church and to exalt its primacy, as Johannes Monachus had pointed out when glossing Boniface VIII's bull of 1300.[84] As if to make matters worse, Clement had added the Lateran basilica to those of St Peter and St Paul as a place which pilgrims had to visit in order to qualify for the jubilee indulgence.[85] He had even gone to the lengths of having the basilica restored 'most honourably and beautifully', as two of his biographers reported.[86] The Romans themselves were well aware of the central importance of the Lateran. Jean la Porte preserves the substance of their, now lost, petition of 1343 to Clement. They implored:

that it might please him to visit the city of Rome and the most holy church of the Lateran, which is the mother of all the churches of the city and the world, and his own principal and particular see, alas, for shame, deprived for so long of her occupant and denied the vision of her spouse.[87]

In the High Middle Ages the basilica had been thought to represent the New Temple of Jerusalem. It had been built by Constantine, and had been one of the first, possibly even the first, temple of the newly recognised Christian religion to be constructed. As such it had replaced the Old Temple of Jerusalem which had been destroyed. The Jews had prophesied that their temple was to be destroyed and rebuilt at the end of time – a prophecy grounded on the Old Testament, especially the Book of Daniel. But this had been subject to Christian adaptation, and the Old Temple came to symbolise the Incarnation, while its rebuilding was seen as the Resurrection. The Old Temple was the body of the earthly Christ, while the New Temple was the body of the risen Christ. Christ Himself had foretold that the Temple would be destroyed and that He would rebuild it in three days. By the Temple He had meant His own body [John, ii. 18–22]. Thus the Temple came to represent the mystical body of Christ, that is, the universal Church. The Old Testament symbolism of the Temple and the New Testament symbolism of the *Ecclesia* had merged. And both of these came to be applied to the Lateran basilica in its role as the New Temple. It became the coping-stone, the corner-stone; it was the stone, living and precious, which the builders rejected; it was the rock on which the Church was founded; and it was the stone hewn from the

---

[84] Johannes Monachus, *ad Extrav. Comm.*, V, ix, 1, col. 1424: 'intentum, qui est honor Dei et exaltatio fidei et primatus Ecclesie in Urbe existens'.
[85] Tautu, no. 155, par. 521.
[86] Baluze–Mollat, *Secunda Vita*, p. 271; *Tertia Vita*, pp. 287–8.
[87] *Tertia Vita*, p. 278.

mountain without hands, described in Daniel, ii. 34.[88] All these images were taken to apply both to Christ and to His Church, and all were used by Clement VI.[89] The Lateran basilica thus became the very epitome of the universal Church: it was its foundation and its life-giving nucleus.

Clement's view of the Lateran appears to correspond with this. In his jubilee bull he described how during the dedication ceremony of Constantine's basilica, performed by Pope Silvester, the famous *achiropiïton* of Christ, the 'painting executed without hands' had appeared miraculously over the papal throne and was seen by all the people of Rome.[90] The symbolic significance of this is great. A painting executed without hands can be associated with the stone hewn from the mountain without hands, which was generally taken to symbolise Christ and His virgin birth. A miraculous appearance of the Saviour immediately above the papal throne served to emphasise the fact that here was the seat of His vicar on earth, the pope. But Clement's most revealing remarks about the Lateran occurred in a letter to the Romans about the atrocities of Cola di Rienzo. After receiving the self-conceded office of 'Knight of the Holy Ghost', Cola had proceeded to a ritual immersion in the font of the Lateran basilica, the very one where Constantine had been baptised and cured of leprosy by Silvester. For this crime Clement hurled the anachronistic sounding title of 'paranoic' at him. Aptly he compared the fouling of the sacred font to the desecration of the Temple of Jerusalem at Belshazzar's feast. By immersing his sordid limbs, Cola had polluted the Temple of the Lord, that is, of Rome –

---

[88] For this see Ligota, 1956, esp. pp. 13–57.

[89] Clement VI, sermon 45, Ste-G. 240, fol. 342v: 'lapis excisus sine manibus est Christus natus de virgine . . . cuius regnum . . . non erit finis'; sermon 40, p. 150. Cf. Galvaneus Flamma, *Chronicon Maius*, ch. 570, p. 210: 'lapis, id est Christus, excisus de monte, id est, natus de virgine, sine manibus, id est sine virili semine, contrivit omnia imperia mundi'; *Chronica Galvagnana*, ch. 57, p. 167; Bartolus, *Super Constitutione ad Reprimendum*, p. 532. For Clement's use of the corner or coping-stone image see Tautu, no. 25, par. 98, no. 26, par. 101; Raynaldus, vi, ch. 46, p. 524. On the origins and history of the image see Ligota, pp. 35–57; Plumpe, 1943b; Ladner, 1942.

[90] Tautu, no. 155, par. 521. Writing at the end of the century Raoul de Presles recorded the same miraculous appearance of the painting and attested that it was still there in his own day: *Commentarium ad De Civitate Dei*, bk v, ch. 21 (ed. unfolioed): 'Laquelle eglise papa silvestre dedya solennelement et ou temps de sa dedicacio sapparut ou mur de lesglise une ymage painte en la fourme de nostre seigneur, laquelle ne fut point painte per home, mais par la grace du saint esperit. Et laquelle y est et a este ancores iusques au iour dhuy'. On Raoul de Presles see Decanter, 1954, and Lombard–Jourdan, 1981. On the painting see Hermanin, 1945, pp. 299ff.

templum Domini, quod est Rome.[91] And so we have a direct reference to the Lateran basilica as the New Temple of Jerusalem.

Clement's handling of the Roman question was masterly. In avoiding extreme solutions he had managed to loosen the tie with Rome a little, which had allowed him to press papal claims of universality to their limit. In so doing he had made himself less vulnerable to the attacks of those who claimed that papal power resided in the see as the representative of the universal Church, rather than in the papal office alone. In avoiding the total constriction which identity with Rome would have brought, Clement by no means severed the tie so completely that he became divorced from Rome, his bride. On the contrary, his overwhelming concern seems to have been to re-establish the position of the Roman see, his *propria sedes*, as the theoretical nucleus of the Christian world. This being so, there could be no risk of the pope being regarded as a mere bishop of Avignon, or worse still, as no bishop at all. In theoretical terms at least the dictates of the papal office had triumphed over the personal preferences of the man.

---

[91] *MGH Const.*, viii, no. 376, p. 420: 'Ipse quoque paraonicam [*sic*] pelvim . . . queve in venerabili Lateranensi basilica velut sacra res venerabiliter conservatur, originarie conditionis oblitus se contagiosum immundumque vitiis militare cingulum suscepturus immergens, quantum in se fuit, ausu damnabili prophanavit . . . Ille, inquam, *vasa templi Domini, quod fuit in Ierusalem*, sumendo pocula polluit; hic autem inmunda quelibet et sordida membra perfundens aqua fedavit *vas templi Domini, quod est Rome*'.

Chapter 5

CREATURAE NOSTRAE: POPE AND CARDINALS

'By ourselves we are not sufficient, and we therefore have to take men of truth into partnership with us – *ad consortium nostrum*',[1] Clement VI announced in consistory, thus highlighting a problem which was to bring in its train a host of others. The 'men of truth' were the cardinals, those who 'laboured with him and shared his burdens',[2] so he described them. And labour they certainly did. Clement's pontificate was one of immense difficulty, drama, and diplomatic activity. Recognising that despite his care for the whole crisis-ridden world he could not be ubiquitous,[3] Clement had to rely heavily on legates and nuncios. As such, the cardinals faced complex and dangerous situations: delicate negotiations in the Anglo-French war and that between Aragon and Majorca; the charged atmosphere in Rome after Cola di Rienzo's revolution; the celebrations of the jubilee in Rome in 1350, which led indirectly to the murder of Cardinal Annibaldus de Ceccano; the turmoil in Naples under Queen Joanna after her husband's murder; the controversial and difficult negotiations leading to the election of Charles of Moravia as king of the Romans in 1346 – in all these situations, and many more, legates or nuncios were involved. Small wonder that they sometimes pleaded to be allowed to return home to Avignon.[4]

At Avignon their labour was equally hard. Clement warned that at the curia the cardinals were expected to serve him day and night.[5]

[1] Clement VI, sermon 33, Ste-G. 240, fol. 527r.
[2] Déprez, no. 375: 'cardinales ipsi . . . nobiscum labores et onera partiuntur'.
[3] Theiner, *Cod. Dip.*, ii. no. 180, p. 182: 'etsi quaslibet partes Orbis nostre vigilancie creditas, quas personaliter visitare nequimus'.
[4] Annibaldus de Ceccano, not surprisingly, had asked to be allowed to return: see Dykmans, 1973, p. 263. Aimeric de Châtelus frequently petitioned to return from Sicily–Naples: see Cerasoli, no. 61, p. 239. In general see Guillemain, 1962, pp. 228–31.
[5] Clement VI, sermon 25, Ste-G. 240, fol. 452r: 'istam sanctam sedem, ubi habent servire Christo et eius vicario die et nocte'.

Paramount among their duties was attending consistory; and the more eventful a pontificate, the more frequent and contentious the discussions between pope and cardinals, the greater the number of royal visitors and official legations received in 'public' consistory. Consistory was also the supreme court of Christendom, and pope and cardinals together would sit in judgement, as they did on Joanna for Andrew of Hungary's murder (and, it seems, were totally disarmed by her). Cardinals might be called upon to sit on commissions to examine political or legal problems: for example, cardinals presided over several sessions of the 'conference of Avignon' in 1344, when Clement tried to arbitrate between England and France, and they examined the suitability of Charles for the kingship of the Romans. They would be asked for their opinions, often in writing, on matters such as heresy or the canonisation of saints, as they were in the case of the Breton St Yves. There was more routine business as well. At Avignon the papacy had become a highly centralised and bureaucratic institution. The increasing scope of the system of papal provisions and taxation is enough to show this. And more and more litigants were using the curia both as a court of appeal and of first instance. All this created work. The cardinals might hold high administrative offices such as that of Vice-Chancellor or Grand Penitentiary. They would also act as judges in their own courts or tribunals. In these and other roles they became indispensable to the practical running of the Christian society.[6]

Of course, such arduous roles did not go unrewarded, especially during Clement's pontificate. Apart from their allotted share in the revenues of the Church, Clement was noted for his unprecedented largesse to them.[7] The legislation *Licet in constitutione*, which he issued in 1351, at their request, to improve their creature comforts during conclaves was also typical of him.[8] And there were other sources of reward and profit: there were numerous gifts by which the cardinals' favour was procured, to say nothing of the political pensions paid to them by lay rulers.[9] The resulting grandeur of their lifestyles was illustrated not only by the 'incredible banquet' of 1343,

---

[6] See Mollat, 1951, pp. 22–112 and Mollat, 1964, pp. 497–500; Guillemain, 1962, pp. 196–7, 225–31.

[7] Clement had started his pontificate by giving more to the cardinals in customary election gifts than had any of his predecessors: see Baumgarten, 1908, p. 38. Studies of individual cardinals also testify to his generosity: see Zacour, 1960, pp. 14, 76; Dykmans, 1973, pp. 191ff.

[8] Raynaldus, vi, ch. 25, p. 550; Baluze-Mollat, *Prima Vita*, p. 210.

[9] Mollat, 1964, pp. 497–8.

but also by the fact that Innocent VI had to bring in measures to curb the extravagance of their households.[10] Their self-indulgence caused such scandal that St Bridget of Sweden delicately advised Clement to 'take the hammer' to them if they would not live more frugally, but only, of course, after he had curbed his own excesses.[11] By the year 1350 the Pope himself was in their debt to the tune of some 16,000 gold florins.[12] There is some evidence that by the following year even he was becoming a little impatient with them. In a sermon no longer extant, but reported by the chronicler Jean de Venette, Clement apparently castigated the cardinals and other prelates and curial officials who had tried to get the Mendicant Orders condemned, or at least prevented from preaching.[13] 'If the mendicants are silenced, what can you preach about?' Clement asked. 'If on humility, you yourselves are the proudest, the most self-important and pompous in the whole world . . . if on poverty, you are the most covetous and greedy – all the prebends and benefices in the world are not enough for you – if you preach about chastity . . . but on that we will say nothing, because God alone knows what each of you does'.

Both the personal and the official attitudes of Clement VI to his cardinals are of the greatest interest. In many ways the pontificate provides an overture to the Great Schism of 1378–1417, when there were to be two lines of popes, one at Avignon, the other at Rome. The responsibility of the cardinals for causing the crisis has gained considerable recognition.[14] It has been suggested that they acquired some of the attitudes and characteristics which occasioned the Schism during the Avignon period, especially during Clement's pontificate. For example, the origins of the 'French' character of the College, and the predominance of members from a particular line or district – the direct result of papal nepotism – have been laid at his door. This is fair comment. Among others he elevated to the College

[10] Zacour, 1975, pp. 343–55. On their extravagance see Mollat, 1964, pp. 503–15. On the banquet see above p. 52.

[11] Bridget of Sweden, *Revelationes*, bk iv, ch. 44, p. 251: 'Propterea Papa incipiat veram humilitatem in seipso . . . Deinde moderate disponat familiam suam . . . Ideo recipiat papa in manu malleum, et forficem, et flectat cardinales ad velle suum, non permittendo eos habere plura de vestibus, et familia, et de utensilibus, nisi quantum requirit necessitas, et vitae usus. Flectatque eos forfice, id est verbis lenibus, et consilio divino, paternaque charitate, qui si noluerint obedire, recipiat malleum, scilicet ostendendo eis severitatem suam . . .'

[12] Mollat, 1951, p. 74.

[13] Jean de Venette, *Continuatio Chronici*, 1351, p. 224. On the mendicant controversy see Walsh, 1981a, pp. 349–406; Coleman, 1984.

[14] In general see Ullmann, 1972a, pp. 4–8; Wilks, 1963a, p. 456; Guillemain, 1980, p. 28, and for what follows Bresc, 1980.

were his younger brother, Hugues Roger, who refused the papacy in 1362, and three of his nephews, the nineteen-year-old Pierre Roger (son of Guillaume Roger, his elder brother) the future Gregory XI, Guillaume de la Jugie (son of his sister Aliénor), and Nicholas de Besse (son of his sister Delphine). It was the French members of the College who were to take exception to the election of the Italian Urban VI in 1378, which was the immediate cause of the rift. The origin of the self-aquisitiveness of the cardinals, another contributory factor, has been seen as a result of their growing responsibilities, with attendant rewards. Consciousness of their vital role led them to assume greater powers and status than they possessed in strict theory. What has not been so readily recognised, however, is the importance of Clement's pontificate in the formation of opposing political ideas on the right relationship of pope and advisers, and the extent to which the Pope himself was responsible for a hardening and definition of the cardinals' views.

Clement's pontificate was marked by an unusual prologue: in 1342 the cardinals acted *sede vacante*, during the papal vacancy, in an emergency situation. Its epilogue was even more unusual: in 1352 they staged a *coup d'état* by drawing up an election capitulation (a practice to be imitated during the Schism and the subsequent conciliar period) designed to limit the authority of the next pope in their favour. Each of them swore to implement it should he be elected to the Holy See. If this had been successful it would have made a mockery of papal sovereignty, and would have destroyed the monarchic structure of the Christian society, substituting in its place the government of a few.

The background to this 'palace revolution' was the fourteenth-century reaction against absolutist forms of government, which opposed the traditional idea of a divinely appointed ruler answerable only to God. In part this was a result of a growing emphasis on the radical aspects of natural law, which stressed the innate abilities of the individual to take decisions through use solely of his natural reason. The popularity of Roman law maxims such as *quod omnes tangit ab omnibus tractari et approbari debet* – what touches all should be discussed and approved by all – was a reflection of this.[15] So also was the interest taken in Aristotle's works, which enshrined the idea that man is naturally a political animal.

[15] On the influence of this see the numerous contributions of Gaines Post reprinted in Gaines Post, 1964; see also Congar, 1958; Marongiu, 1968b; Wilks, 1972, pp. 253–4.

In his *Politics* Aristotle had described three types of constitution: monarchy, the rule of one good man; aristocracy, the rule of the few best men in the interests of all; and polity, an idealised type of democracy in which all the citizens, as equals, would rule and be ruled by turns. Each of these three constitutions might become perverted when the self-interest of the ruler or rulers came to predominate over the common interest, the good of the commonwealth. Thus monarchy was transformed into tyranny, aristocracy became oligarchy, and polity turned into democracy, which was in effect mob rule.[16]

One of the most important ways in which 'constitutional' ideas emerged was in the process for the appointment of both lay and ecclesiastical rulers. The conduct of this was an indication of the way in which a society was governed – by the one, the few, or the many. If a ruler was thought to be 'elected' by God, then he would have no need for the help of men in taking authoritative decisions. He would be God's representative on earth, and as such would be an absolute sovereign ruler. Such was the traditional system. If, however, the ruler was appointed through some form of election by men, then most likely such men would consider that they had retained a residual right to control him, forcing him to consult them on major decisions – *quod omnes tangit* – and to obtain their binding consent before taking action. And carried to extremes those who appointed and controlled a ruler might also claim to depose him.

In the fourteenth century there could be no question of popular government in the modern sense that rulers were democratically elected to represent the mass of the people. Such ideas were far in the future. Even allegedly extreme thinkers such as Marsilius and Ockham did not develop modern theories of popular representation,[17] although Ockham, discussing Aristotle's *Politics*, may be said to have laid the foundations when he pinpointed the impracticality of assembling every member of society in order to consent to the actions of government.[18] What happened in practice was that the

---

[16] Aristotle, *Politics*, bk iii, ch. 7.
[17] On Marsilius see Wilks, 1972. Ockham advanced the notion of popular consent as the basis for political obligation to the Emperor because imperial power had originally come from the people, but, once appointed, the Emperor needed no further consent to his actions: see McGrade, 1974, pp. 78–9, 104–91, 160–1.
[18] William of Ockham, III *Dialogus*, i, bk ii, ch. 19, p. 805: 'Quando autem pauci sufficiunt ad videndum perfecte, quid est agendum et quid omittendum, non expediat multitudinem convenire ad tractandum, sed melius est quod conveniant pauci, sufficientes tamen. Et ideo quando unus sufficit, non oportet convenire

leading members of a society would claim to be representing its members as a whole when they either elected a ruler or tried to limit him in the exercise of his power. Such claims had a less than secure foundation. But they were easier to justify within a secular than an ecclesiastical framework, for there they were less hampered by notions of divine transference of power. They were more speedily implemented in empire or kingdom, through electoral college or parliamentary institution,[19] than in provincial chapter or Sacred College:[20] metropolitan and pope were still thought to be chosen by God, despite the inconvenient mechanism of an election.

The logical answer to the succession problem in an absolutist system was for the sovereign to appoint his own successor (preferably placing the name under seal to be broken only on his death). Hobbes was to observe centuries later that 'There is no perfect form of government where the disposing of the succession is not in the present sovereign', and to warn of the imminent dissolution of society if there had to be a new choice.[21] This method was even more desirable in the case of the medieval papacy where the celibacy of the ruler precluded the possibility of a natural heir. Surprisingly, Augustinus Triumphus alone, writing early in the fourteenth century, suggested that the pope should 'elect' his own successor.[22] The only alternative to this was for an election to be held. But in such cases the electors, the cardinals, were regarded as the instruments of God, and their choice as the manifestation of the divine will. The effect was much the same as the biblical casting of lots. Herman of Schildiz expressed his confidence that the College of Cardinals was directed 'by God without error', more so than any other college. This was a neat combination of the notion of divine agency and the Roman law concept that a corporation – a *collegium* – could not err.[23] Conrad of Megenberg emphasised that although the cardinals were the electors of the pope, they did not confer apostolic authority upon him, except as tools or instruments. Both his power and his pontifical authority were immediately from God.[24] In the case of

multos'. See McGrade, 1974, pp. 108, 160–1. The passage under discussion is Aristotle, *Politics*, bk iii, ch. 8.

[19] For the growth of parliamentary institutions in the later medieval period see Clark, 1964; Marongiu, 1968a.

[20] For discussion on provincial chapters see Tierney, 1982a, pp. 26–7, and 83.

[21] Thomas Hobbes, *Leviathan*, pt 2, ch. 19, p. 127.

[22] Wilks, 1963a, pp. 467–9.

[23] Herman of Schildiz, *Tractatus contra Hereticos*, ii, ch. 7, p. 72. For further discussion of the cardinals as the instruments of God see Wilks, 1963a, pp. 460–1.

[24] Conrad of Megenberg, *Yconomica*, iii, 3, ch. 2, p. 365.

other appointments, since God Himself was present on earth in the person of His vicar, the pope, and could therefore communicate His will in such matters directly, there was in strict theory no need for elections, episcopal, imperial, or any other, although in practice these were held. By the time of Clement VI episcopal elections had in fact become a formality, since bishops were provided by the pope.[25] In terms of papal theory election meant simply that the pope, in his capacity as the vicar of Christ, marked out a man for office, and then delegated some of his own power to him on the understanding that it was to be exercised as the pope willed. In this case the pope himself was the divine agent in the election. So long as society remained the body of Christ, sacerdotally directed towards a goal of heavenly bliss, and the pope remained the vicar of Christ, such a theory remained appropriate. With the development of Aristotelian ideas about the nature and purpose of society and the way in which it should be governed, they became totally inadequate.

Given that the cardinals had become infected with the ideas of the *moderni* by 1352 there were two ways in which they might satisfy their hunger for power. They could range themselves on the side of the papal plenitude of power by trying to control its exercise. This involved the danger that they would do so in their own selfish interests and would thus become an oligarchy. Alternatively they could choose the aristocratic solution by which they would claim to represent the whole congregation of the faithful and stress their concern for the common good of all believers – Aristotle's 'few best men' ruling in the best interests of all members of society. In this instance they could have played an indispensable role as convenors and leaders of the general council, which would have left the laity a strictly limited part to play in conciliar proceedings. Clement's pontificate provides a foretaste of the solution the cardinals would adopt in 1378.

During Clement's pontificate the attitude of the cardinals was transformed from one of reason to one of rebellion. In the year 1342 their behaviour was still relatively restrained, despite the fact that they took full advantage of their canonical right to act *sede vacante*. They were concerned to forestall an invasion of Brittany by the English king during the early stages of the Hundred Years War.

---

[25] See Clement VI's letter to Edward III, 11 July 1342, Raynaldus, vi, chs. 55–9, where he tells the King that he has full authority to dispose of all churches and all ecclesiastical dignities, offices, and benefices.

During the period before Clement's election they explained to the belligerents that they were 'able to provide an opportune remedy' for the war situation.[26] Gregory X in his decree *Ubi periculum* (1274) had forbidden the cardinals to enter into negotiations other than those about the election, except in the direst emergency, and 'all and singular' had to agree on what constituted such an emergency.[27] But there was a loophole, for Gregory had legislated only for the duration of the conclave, rather than the whole period of the interregnum. It had been left to Clement V in *Ne Romani* (1311) to strengthen his predecessor's declaration and to add a definition that the papal plenitude of power did not lie with the College during a papal vacancy.[28] Canonists and publicists added their support to this,[29] and the cardinals' *sede vacante* powers were still being discussed during the pontificate of Clement VI. The canonist Lapus Tactus, for example, thought that the College could not absolve an excommunicant during a papal vacancy,[30] implying that it did not have the powers of binding and loosing inherent in the Petrine commission. Conrad of Megenberg went to some lengths to explain the position. During a papal vacancy the College of Cardinals was obviously the head of the Church, but it was a deficient and imperfect head. Although the *Ecclesia* was deprived of its vicar on the death of the pope, it was not deprived of Christ, its true principal, whose vicariate had been given to Peter and his apostolic successors. If the College possessed the vicariate of Christ, then the election of a new pope would be not only unnecessary, but also inexpedient.[31] The cardinals' action in 1342 might have implied that they considered the vicariate of Christ was theirs during a vacancy, but they did not express this, and so appeared to be acting within the letter of

---

[26] Déprez, 1903, pp. 66–7.

[27] *Sext.*, I, vi. 3.

[28] *Clem.*, I, iii, 2. For the circumstances in which *Ubi periculum* and *Ne Romani* were promulgated and the possible influence of Hostiensis on them see Watt, 1971, pp. 137–46.

[29] Alvarus Pelagius, *De Planctu Ecclesiae*, ch. 20, p. 33: '. . . vacante papatu, nullus succedit papae in iurisdictione, etiam cetus cardinalium, nisi in minimis . . .' For Johannes Andreae see Ullmann, 1976, no. 15, p. 20, n. 52. For Hostiensis see Tierney, 1955, pp. 72–5, 150–2, and, in general, pp. 183, 189, 208–11, 234–5. For a reappraisal of Hostiensis' views see Watt, 1971, pp. 131–7; 155–7 (where the gloss is edited).

[30] Lapus Tactus, *Commentaria super Clementinas, ad Clem.*, V, iii, 1, p. 232: 'Poterit ergo [scil. excommunicatus] absolvi a Papa vivente . . . et non a collegio cardinalium sede vacante . . .'

[31] Conrad of Megenberg, *Yconomica*, ii, 3, ch. 4, p. 104.

canon law. In any case, since almost 'all and singular' of them were Frenchmen, there can have been little doubt that the invasion of Brittany did indeed constitute the direst emergency.

By contrast there could be no justification in canon law for the episode of 1352 when the cardinals drew up their election capitulation. It was, rather, a direct violation of the law, for in *Ubi periculum* Gregory X had declared illegal 'all pacts, conventions, obligations, agreements, and intentions' entered into by oath or in any other way by the cardinal-electors. This need not necessarily imply that there were exact precedents for the electoral pact of 1352: so far this is the first one discovered in connection with a papal election. But there had been several capitulations in connection with both abbatial and episcopal elections before 1274.[32] It may be that Gregory realised that it was only a matter of time before what had been applied to other bishoprics would be applied to the bishopric of Rome. In any event, Innocent VI, once elected, was quick to condemn the 1352 pact as being 'in diminution of the plenitude of power', which it certainly was. His stand was supported by the lawyer Baldus de Ubaldis, who rightly regarded such agreements as being 'contrary to the liberty of the vicar of Christ'.[33]

The twelve clauses of the pact serve as an index of the issues at stake between Clement VI and his cardinals, and fall roughly into three groups.[34] Firstly, the cardinals' demands about appointment to the College: did they or the pope control entry to their ranks? Secondly, the clauses concerning their official, and above all, financial, privileges: did they have to sue to the pope for everything, or did they possess some things as of right? Finally, the clause demanding 'free judgement of affairs by deliberating and consenting'. This brought into focus the vexed issue of sovereignty, and as such provided a ground bass to the other clauses.

Much of the overt disagreement between Pope and College centred on the subject of the first group of clauses, election. The cardinals did not express their views on the papal election overtly:

[32] *Sext.*, I, vi. 3. On abbatial electoral pacts see Berlière, 1927, pp. 50–2; on episcopal electoral pacts see Oswald, 1933, esp. pp. 94–7, and app. 2, pp. 344–50 for the text of one.

[33] Innocent VI, *Solicitudo* [sic] *Pastoralis*, Gasnault-Laurent, no. 435, p. 137. Baldus de Ubaldis, *ad Decretales*, I, vi, 34, fol. 78r: 'Quid de papa qui iuravit ante quam eligeretur renunciare papatui ad beneplacitum cardinalium? Respondeo, non valet istud iuramentum, primo quia est contra libertatem vicarii Jesu Christi'.

[34] The clauses are reproduced in Innocent VI's *Solicitudo pastoralis*, Gasnault-Laurent, no. 435, pp. 137–8. For discussion see Mollat, 1951, pp. 100–5; Ullmann, 1976, no. 15, pp. 6–9; Pásztor, 1981, pp. 216–20.

they did not need to, for their action in drawing up the electoral pact spoke volumes. Clearly by the year 1352 they were beginning to espouse the notion of 'popular' election to the extent that they considered it their right to control the man they elected. From the papal standpoint, the election was in no way a popular one involving the delegation of power from 'below', with its corollary that the electors retained a residual right of control over the elect. Innocent's condemnation of the pact was enough to show this. The two views on the papal election were totally irreconcilable.

Equally divergent were those on the appointment of cardinals. Clement VI's view was quite unambiguous: he appointed them. The basic assumption in all that he preached on the subject was his own exalted position as Christ's earthly vicar. It was the power and 'incontrovertible preeminence' which he possessed in this capacity which enabled him to create cardinals, he explained in consistory.[35] By introducing a new cardinal into the College the Pope was 'communicating the radiance of his own clemency' to him.[36] To his nephew Nicholas de Besse, Clement emphasised that he had 'elected' him to his own society, declaring the while, 'he is a chosen vessel unto me' (Acts. ix. 15).[37] Another nephew, Guillaume de la Jugie, was reminded that the Pope had 'elected' him, not he the Pope (strictly true, since he had been appointed after Clement's own elevation),[38] and that his promotion was attributable to 'grace', meaning papal favour, rather than merit.[39]

Of course the Pope could consult others about whom to promote – not that he was bound to accept their suggestions, particularly those from outside the College. But Clement did reveal that the French royal house had played its part in shaping the College. Pierre

---

[35] Clement VI, sermon 4, Ste-G. 240, fol. 524r.

[36] Ibid., fol. 524v: 'Primo notatur ex parte assumentis potestas et eminentia irrefragabilis [*sic*], cum dicitur *assumpsi*. Unde hic inducitur papa, sicut ostendens et communicans radium sue clementie, inducendo admirationis stuporem'.

[37] Clement VI, sermon 33, Ste-G. 240, fol. 526v: 'Et ideo de isto dico quod legitur Actus ix [15] *Vas electionis michi iste est*. Ecce ergo hic. Ego elegi eum ad societatem nostram, quia vas est'.

[38] Clement VI, sermon 35, Ste-G. 240, fol. 244r: 'Dico . . . quia *vos*, de quo possumus dicere illud Joh. xv° [16]: *Non vos me elegistis, sed ego elegi vos, et posui vos ut eatis, et fructum afferatis, et fructus vester maneat.* Non inquit vos me elegistis, et ideo non potestis cum venerabilibus fratribus nostris cardinalibus similiter gloriari. Ipsi enim me elegerunt. Sed vos non me elegistis. Sed ego elegi vos'.

[39] Ibid., fol. 244v: 'ex parte moventis gratiam et amorem quia *vocati estis* I ad Thes. ii° [12]. Tamquam *pater filios* [11] *deprecantes vos et consolantes, testificati sumus ut ambuletis digne Deo qui vocavit vos in suum regnum et gloriam* [12], non ex meritis sed ex gratia'.

Bertrand the younger had been chosen partly to gratify the wishes of the French Queen;[40] while both King and Queen had petitioned for the appointment of Nicholas de Besse.[41] In 1350 Cardinal Gil Rigaud was promoted at the behest of King John the Good, and received his red hat at the royal court in Paris.[42] Similar requests from Edward III were greeted with less enthusiasm and no result.[43] Clement allowed the King to select two suitable candidates on the understanding that they would be promoted 'if the appointments seemed to be to the honour of God and the universal Church in the judgement of the cardinals'.[44]

On occasions like that it suited Clement to appear bound by consultations with his advisers, for none of them was Anglophile. Consultation appeared to be useful too when the Pope wanted to promote his nephews, although his remarks may well have been window dressing to disguise a *fait accompli*. His sermon about his nephew Nicholas, and Pierre Bertrand the younger, nephew of the celebrated lawyer, suggests that the cardinals were keen to accept Nicholas. Clement remarked casually that the previous day he had entered consistory thinking of Nicholas's promotion as something which would not occur, but at the petition of the whole College, without any disagreement, he had had to accept him. Some had even threatened to withhold their 'consent' to Pierre's appointment if the Pope would not agree.[45] Apparently the College had also obligingly

---

[40] Clement VI, sermon 4, Ste-G. 240, fol. 524v: 'Primo dico ex parte illustris regine Francie, que intercessit ferventer et specialiter determinando se ad istum episcopum Attrabatensis et per frequentes litteras et per solempnes ambaxiatores . . . Et vere sibi negare non possumus propter virtutem suam'. Perhaps what really prompted Clement was the memory that the Queen had granted him a substantial loan when he had been an archbishop: 'Et nobis magnum dedit subsidium cum essemus archiepiscopus et in minoribus constituti'(ibid). On his relationship with the Queen see Mollat, 1957.

[41] Clement VI, sermon 33, Ste-G. 240, fol. 527v: 'Et vere sponsus et sponsa, videlicet rex Francie et regina, sibi dicunt *veni*, quia pro ipso multum efficaciter scripserunt'.

[42] See Duchesne, 1660, ii, p. 542.

[43] Geoffrey le Baker, *Chronicon*, p. 111 [anno 1350]: 'rex scribens summo pontifici supplicavit quod aliquem clericum sui regni promoveret honori cardinalatus, asserens ipsum valde mirari quare ad illum sanctum ordinem nullum Anglicum a multis temporibus dignata est recipere curia Romana . . .'

[44] Ibid., p. 112.

[45] Clement VI, sermon 4, Ste-G. 240, fol. 525r: 'Vere dicimus in verbo veritatis quod heri de mane quomodo intravimus consistorium tantum cogitavimus de sua promotione, sicut de re que non est, sed ad petitionem totius collegii, nullo de collegio discordante, oportuit quod ipsum assumeremus. Et fuerunt cardinales qui dixerunt quod non consentirent in istum Attrabatensis [scil. Petrum Bertrandum] nisi nos assumeremus istum Nicolaum'.

put forward a unanimous request for the appointment of Clement's nineteen-year-old nephew Pierre Roger de Beaufort.[46]

The ceremonial order in use for the creation of cardinals provided for two sets of consultations between pope and cardinals.[47] The first took place in consistory and concerned the desirability of making new appointments, and the number to be made. The following day, Friday, the pope would consult each cardinal individually in his empty cathedral about whom to promote. When consistory re-assembled he would announce: 'Thanks be to God, we have the agreement about the people (to be promoted) of all the brethren, or almost all, or the major part', as the occasion demanded. The redactor added that nothing else was specifically explained about the agreement, and that the pope was immediately able to create cardinals.[48] The extent to which these consultations were binding is open to question. It was not spelt out that the pope had to obtain a majority of any sort, and even if this was implied, the term 'maior pars' was ambiguous: it could have meant a numerical majority, or, and this is more likely, it could have meant the consent of the wiser and senior members of the College.[49] In Clement's case this would have meant his own 'Limousin' party.

One of the cardinals' major complaints about Clement was that he appointed too many advisers. He had more promotions to his credit, or discredit, than any other Avignon pope in a comparable time.[50] When Benedict XII died he left nineteen cardinals; when Clement died the total was twenty-five or possibly twenty-six.[51] From

---

[46] Clement VI, sermon 47, Ste-G. 240, fol. 417r: 'ex eo solvitur intendente studiose cogitanti seriose unanimitatem collegii quod pro eo cum magna instantia concorditer supplicavit'.

[47] Dykmans, p. 241, considers that the order for the creation of new cardinals, included in the *Ceremonial of Jacques Stefaneschi*, was probably completed about 1328 under John XXII, and certainly during the lifetime of Stefaneschi, who died in June 1341. See also Schimmelpfennig, 1973, pp. 78–9; Tamburini, 1966, p. 141.

[48] Dykmans, ch. 116, §4, p. 475; ibid., § 10–13, p. 477.

[49] On the idea of the *valentior pars* as the true 'majority' see Wilks, 1963a, pp. 194–5.

[50] For the numbers created by other Avignon popes see Guillemain, 1962, p. 184, n. 7. John XXII alone exceeded Clement's total. In a pontificate lasting eight years longer than Clement's (1316–34) he created 28.

[51] Mollat, 1961, p. 101 gives 26 as the number, but 25 seems more likely. The cardinals summoned to the 1352 conclave seem to have been as follows: Cardinal-bishops Pierre Després, Talleyrand de Périgord, Bertrand de Déaulx, Etienne Aubert, Guillaume Court, Guy de Boulogne (probably absent from conclave); Cardinal-priests Pierre Bertrand de Colombier, Gil Albornoz, Pasteur de Sarrats, Raimond de Canillac, Guillaume de Aigrefeuille, Niccolò de Capocio, Pictavin de Montesquieu, Arnaud de Villemur, Pierre de Cros, Gil Rigaud, Jean de

17 December 1350, his last promotion ceremony, until the death of
Bertrand de Poujet, on 3 February 1352, the College had an unprecedented total of twenty-eight.[52] In less than a decade Clement had
created twenty-five cardinals – a number on which his biographers
comment, one adding that he would have created even more had he
lived longer.[53] In fact, he seems to have regarded twenty-five as the
ideal size for the College, and took a tactless delight in advertising
this large total.[54] Maybe he had practical reasons: no doubt he was
worried by the plague fatalities of 1348–9,[55] and perhaps he was
concerned at the amount of extra work he was having to impose on
his advisers and thought that more should share the burden. But
above all it seems likely that Clement regarded safety in numbers,
and that he realised that it would be more difficult for a large number
to be coordinated against the pope than a small one.

To an extent he was proved right. In December 1350 he promoted
twelve new cardinals, some at the request of King John of France.[56]
By promoting so many he seems to have fragmented the College,
aligning the more senior members, among whom were Etienne
Aubert, the future Innocent VI, and Elie de Talleyrand, against the
newer ones. Soon after the ceremony an undignified skirmish broke
out between the servants of the Pope's elder brother, Guillaume
Roger, and those of one of the new cardinals. After the cardinal's
house had been razed to the ground, and John the Good had acted as

Moulins, Hugues Roger; Cardinal-deacons Gailhard de la Mothe, Bernard de
Turre, Guillaume de la Jugie, Nicholas de Besse, Pierre Roger de Beaufort,
Rinaldo Orsini, Jean Duèsne de Carmaing. See Eubel, 1898, pp. 16–18; and
Wrigley, 1965a, pp. 450–2.

52 Those listed above and Ademar Robert (d. 1 December 1352), Guillaume d'Aure
(d. 3 December 1352), and Bertrand de Poujet (d. 3 February 1352). In less than a
week in December 1352 two cardinals and the Pope himself died.

53 Baluze-Mollat, *Secunda Vita*, p. 270; *Tertia Vita*, p. 286; Werner of Bonn, *Vita*,
p. 550.

54 Clement VI, sermon 47, Ste-G. 240, fol. 419v: 'Ut ista sedes sit sedes nostra in
cuius circuitu sunt xxiiii seniores sedentes, id est xxiiii cardinales qui nunc sunt,
non conputato legato, quia ergo iste numerus sic congruus est': cf. Apoc., iv. See
also sermon 42, Ste-G. 240, fol. 250v: 'Virtus etiam omnis in medio. Iste ergo
istum situm tam virtuosum in numero cardinalium, ad litteram tenet. Habet
enim xii super et xii post, et ipse recte in medio'.

55 Baluze-Mollat, *Tertia Vita*, p. 285 praises Clement for restoring the depleted
numbers of the College. The following 8 cardinals died in 1348–9: Hélie de
Nabinal, 5 January 1348; Imbert du Puy, 26 May 1348; Gozzo of Rimini, 10 June
1348; Pierre Bertrand, 23 June 1348; Giovanni Colonna, 3 July 1348; Pedro
Gomez da Barroso, 14 July 1348; Gaucelme de Jean Duèsne, 3 August 1348;
Aimeric de Châtelus, 7 January 1349.

56 Geoffrey le Baker, *Chronicon*, p. 112; Henry Taube, *Chronica*, p. 78. For details
see Eubel, 1898, p. 18.

peacemaker, the chronicler Henry Taube of Selbach concludes significantly that 'afterwards, dissension arose from various causes between the Pope and certain new cardinals'.[57] In a sense, however, Clement was building on existing divisions. There was, for example, the rivalry between Elie de Talleyrand and John de Commignes, which dated back to 1334.[58] This rivalry emerged in disagreements (reported by Villani) during a consistory held in April 1346, which discussed Charles of Moravia's appointment as king of the Romans, the murder of Andrew of Hungary, and Clement's decision not to receive the ambassadors of Andrew's avenging brother Louis. Talleyrand and the 'Limousin' party which he led supported the declared views of the Pope. Apparently John de Commignes accused Talleyrand of helping to plan the murder (he was related to the Neapolitan royal house and therefore had a personal interest in the affair). Bedlam ensued in consistory, with the result that all the cardinals then barricaded themselves into their houses. It was left to Clement to restore order.[59] The following year saw more friction over Neapolitan affairs after Louis had invaded Naples.[60] Concurrently there was the well-known rivalry between Talleyrand and his 'Limousin' party and Guy de Boulogne and his 'French' party, the indirect effects of which were to be felt right up to the eve of the Schism.[61]

It seems likely that the 'Limousin' party would have supported the Pope, sometimes successfully and sometimes not. There was, for example, disagreement over whether to send additional legates to Rome to help Bertrand de Déaulx after Cola di Rienzo's revolution. Clement's wish not to do so prevailed.[62] On the other hand, there are

---

[57] Henry Taube, *Chronica*, p. 78.

[58] Zacour, 1960, pp. 20–1.

[59] Ibid., pp. 25–6; Léonard, 1932, ii, pp. 13ff.

[60] Clement VI, letter to Bertrand de Déaulx, 1347, where the disagreements are outlined. MS Vatican, Instr. Misc. 1746: 'Nos cupientes imminentibus obviare periculis que temporum qualitas et negotiorum dispositio comminantur, cum fratribus nostris in consistorio super hiis que agenda forent circa hec consultationem frequenter habuimus, et quia consilia eorum convenire non poterant circa idem, sed sentiebant potius diversa diversi . . .' I am very grateful to Professor N. P. Zacour for generously supplying me with a transcript of this. For discussion of the circumstances surrounding its composition see Léonard, ii, pp. 13–14. The letter was never sent.

[61] Zacour, 1960, p. 37; Guillemain, 1980, pp. 23–4; Bresc, 1980, pp. 54–6.

[62] *Briefwechsel*, iv, no. 22, letter to Bertrand de Déaulx: 'maiori parti fratrum eorundem nostrorum videbatur omnino, ut ad obviandum tantis periculis . . . alios duos vel tres cardinales legatos statim ad Urbem mittere deberemus *quamvis nobis videretur contrariam*'.

letters to Hugh of Cyprus in which Clement explains that he is prevented by the cardinals from granting him the jubilee indulgence.[63]

Clement seems to have inherited a legacy of bitterness between pope and College from Benedict XII, which cannot have made things easy for him. Unlike his successor, Benedict was not only parsimonious, but he also refused to promote any of his relations or compatriots to the College. This meant that he could not rely on a solid body of support among the cardinals. The resulting lack of *rapport* is summed up by one of Benedict's biographers, who recorded that 'he believed all the lord cardinals were about to deceive him. He was rarely willing to receive their requests, and he distrusted them not a little'.[64] This attitude meant that Clement's nepotism was more noticeable than it might otherwise have been if Benedict had continued the favouritism shown by Clement V and John XXII.[65]

Predictably enough the cardinals' views on election differed from those of the Pope, and it is partly these views which stamp them as an oligarchy. As such, they appreciated the necessity of controlling their membership: they had to be self-perpetuating. The fourteenth-century French writer Nicholas Oresme, commenting on Aristotle's *Politics*, regarded this as the main criterion of an oligarchy, and obligingly specified the pope and cardinals as an example of an oligarchy in which election could be made only by the existing members.[66] The cardinals' capitulation accordingly demanded that no new creations should be made without the consent of a two-thirds majority. Equally important was the small size of the group. The first demand of the oligarchs was that their number should not exceed twenty, and that no new promotions should be made until

[63] Déprez-Mollat, nos. 2722, 2279.
[64] Baluze-Mollat, *Octava Vita Benedicti XII*, p. 236. For discussion see Pásztor, 1981, p. 217.
[65] Pásztor, p. 203.
[66] Nicholas Oresme, *Le Livre de Politiques d'Aristote*, bk iv, ch. 8, pp. 175–6: '[Text] Une autre espece de olygarchie est quant les princeys sunt tenus par gens qui sunt en tres grandes honorabletés et eslisent ceulz qui defaillent. [Gloss] . . . et se il sunt en nombre determiné, quant un de eulz est mort ou hors du princey, il eslisent un autre. Et se le nombre ne est determiné et il leur semble que il sunt peu, il eslisent autres avec eulz selon ce que bon le semble. Si comme le pape et les cardinalz esliroient cardinalz . . . [Text] Et se il les prennent et eslisent de aucuns determinés, ce est olygarchie'. For discussion see the introduction by Menut; Grignaschi, 1960; Quillet, 1977, pp. 123–60.

their existing total had shrunk to sixteen.[67] In the light of Clement's many appointments it is easy to see what provoked this clause.

The cardinals might have been expected to object to papal nepotism, but in fact they seemed happy to accommodate it. After all, as Oresme pointed out, nepotism was a hallmark of oligarchies.[68] In the circumstances they could hardly have objected, for of the twenty-five cardinals promoted by Clement, twenty-one were French (three Italian and one Spanish), and of these, ten, or possibly eleven, were related to Clement.[69] By contrast, of the nineteen members of the College in 1342, probably only four were related to previous popes, although Frenchmen predominated even then, there being fifteen of them, three Italians, and one Spaniard.[70] Clement was not the only Avignon pope to look after his own, but he certainly did it on an unprecedented scale. The only clause in the capitulation to touch upon the subject stated that the offices of rector of the lands or provinces of the *Ecclesia* and marshal of the Roman curia were not to be held by kinsmen of the pope. This may have been prompted by the failure of Clement's nephew Astorge de Durfort, rector of the Romagna, against the rebellious Visconti, partly through military incompetence, and partly through Clement's inability to supply him with enough money to pay his troops.[71]

The issue which followed naturally from election was that of control. Once elected, did the cardinals have legally defined rights, or were they wholly dependent upon the pope for favours? Clement was quite clear on this: he retained control. And, from a practical standpoint, it was easier to control men over whom he already had some kind of sway, like his nephews. This was the unacceptable face of nepotism. As Clement spelt out to one of them in consistory, an uncle has a sort of natural *imperium* over his nephew, especially over

---

[67] Gasnault-Laurent, no. 435, p. 138.

[68] Nicholas Oresme, *Le Livre de Politiques*, p. 176: 'Et malvese policie [olygarchie]; ce est assavoir quant tele eleccion est faicte par faveur et par acceptacion de personnes; pource qu'il sunt d'aucune compaignie ou aliance ou d'aucun office ou d'un certain lignage ou d'une especial partie de la region'.

[69] Clement's relations were as follows: Hugues Roger (brother), Pierre Roger de Beaufort (nephew), Nicholas de Besse (nephew), Guillaume de la Jugie (nephew), Pierre de Cros (cousin), Guillaume de Aigrefeuille (cousin), Bernard de Turre (relative by marriage), Gerard de la Garde (relative by marriage), Raimond de Canillac (relative by marriage), Aimeric de Châtelus (distant relative).

[70] Wrigley, 1982, pp. 63–81 for biographical details of the nineteen cardinals.

[71] Mollat, 1964, p. 217.

one whom he has adopted as his special son – *in peculiarem filium*.[72] The nephew, Guillaume de la Jugie, was tied to him by a natural bond.[73] He was, in biblical terms, 'bone of his bone and flesh of his flesh', with the convenient implication that Clement was Christ.[74] Nicholas de Besse was reminded of his upbringing at the papal court.[75] It was as if the Pope were playing on family ties, in effect using emotional blackmail, to create for himself a malleable college of advisers at a difficult time. His aim was to instil into them gratitude and dependence by magnifying the benefits he had conferred on seemingly unworthy recipients. He wanted to make it plain that they were his 'creatures', wholly dependent upon his will. As he spelt out to Guillaume, 'You are our work, our creature – *vos enim factura et creatura nostra*', and went on to remind him that all that he ever had or ever would have was due to the Pope. As if this were not bad enough, he added a rider that *factor habet imperare factura* – a maker has to control his handiwork, a creator to rule his creature.[76]

Being subject to the Pontiff's every whim did not suit the cardinals at all. They wanted to transform favours, *beneficia*, into prescriptive rights: hence the second group of clauses in the electoral pact dealt with their financial and other privileges. True, since the eighth century they had developed from an amorphous group of Roman clergy, who performed liturgical functions in the great basilicas, to a highly organised body, playing a vital role in the government of the Church.[77] But they had not managed to acquire much in writing to sanction this. There were the election decrees of Nicholas II (1059) and Alexander III (1179), Nicholas IV's financial legislation, and the conclave legislation of Gregory X, Clement V, and by 1352 of Clement VI himself. There was also the protection afforded them by Honorius III (1255), which categorised crimes against them as *lèse majesté*, as were crimes against the pope himself, with the inference that they were *pars corporis papae*, part of the body of the pope.[78] Yet

---

[72] Clement VI, sermon 35, Ste-G. 240, fol. 243r: 'Avunculus autem in re habet quoddam imperium in nepote, maxime quam sibi videtur in peculiarem filium adoptasse'.

[73] Ibid.

[74] Ibid., fol. 243r. Cf. Gen., ii. 23.

[75] Clement VI, sermon 33, Ste-G. 240, fol. 527r; sermon 4, Ste-G. 240, fol. 526r, Cf. above, p. 52, n. 48.

[76] Clement VI, sermon 35, Ste-G. 240, fol. 243r.

[77] For the earlier history of the Sacred College see Kuttner, 1945; Le Bras, 1964; pp. 340–8; Lefebvre, 1968; Klewitz, 1936; Fürst, 1967; Pásztor, 1981, pp. 199–203.

[78] This was incorporated by Boniface VIII into *Sext.*, V, ix, 5. For discussion see Ullmann, 1976, no. 5, p. 739, and 1978, no. 10, pp. 233–4.

there was no section in the official compilations of canon law which dealt with the cardinalate.[79] The electoral pact was an attempt to remedy such defects.

Some of the stipulations in this second group simply aimed to make theory and practice coincide, an aspect which prompted an anonymous glossator to remark that individual provisions of the compact were licit: there was nothing inherently bad in them. The illegality lay rather in their consequences.[80] Some of the financial clauses were confirmatory and were designed to safeguard the revenue of the College. For example, true to Nicholas IV's *Coelestis altitudo* (1289) the cardinals already received the half share of the Church's revenue which they were demanding.[81] They also expected to be consulted about a variety of papal actions, such as the levying of clerical taxation, concessions of tenths and subsidies to lay rulers, and of grants and alienations from the lands and possessions of the *Ecclesia* (whence much of their revenue derived). In fact, they were consulted on a number of these issues. Replying to a request of Alfonso of Portugal for a grant of tenths, for example, Clement said that the matter had been dealt with in consistory, as was customary – *sicut est de more*.[82] Other demands of the pact preserved the cardinals' privileges. For instance, a cardinal was not to be excommunicated or deprived of official privileges like attending consistory without the consent of a two-thirds majority of his colleagues. He was not to be imprisoned or deposed, nor his lands or possessions seized, even posthumously, without the unanimous consent of the whole College. In practice, the need for such exceptional action had not arisen since the time of Benedict XI (1303–4),[83] but had it done so there is no reason to think that Clement would not have discussed it with the College: indeed, most letters leaving the curia seemed to include a formula such as *de consilio fratrum nostrorum*, (according to the counsel of our brethren.) But there was nothing to say that the pope had to take counsel. This was what riled Innocent VI, the fact that the

---

[79] Watt, 1971, p. 127.
[80] Anon, *ad Sollicitudo pastoralis*: 'Scilicet illa in se licita sint, tamen quia a iure prohibita effecta sunt illicita, non quia in se mala sint, sed propter malum, quod inde sequi potest': quoted by Ullmann, 1976, no. 15, p. 34. See ibid., pp. 33–5 for discussion of the gloss.
[81] Nicholas IV, *Coelestis altitudo*, 18 July 1289: Potthast, 23010. On the revenues of the cardinals during the Avignon period see Mollat, 1951, pp. 61–72; 1964, pp. 478ff. On their rights and privileges in general see Fürst, 1967, pp. 111–15.
[82] Déprez-Mollat, no. 1410. See also ibid., no. 1922; Déprez, no. 1377; Theiner, *Mon. Pol.*, no. 605, p. 468 and no. 702, p. 532.
[83] Mollat, 1951, p. 102.

supreme pontiff, as he put it, was being told that he *had* to do certain things, that he was being coerced by man to adhere to certain rules and limits.[84] Here lay those illicit consequences divined by the glossator: here indeed lay the whole basic issue of sovereignty, and the right relationship between pope and cardinals.

The third group consists of those clauses in which the cardinals made their most basic demand – that for 'consent'. In fact, this underlies the whole capitulation, but the most dangerous clause was that which required the pope to allow them free judgement of affairs by 'deliberating and consenting'.[85] The all-embracing nature of 'affairs' gave them a limitless sphere of competence. Moreover, since the time of Hostiensis the word 'consent' had come to mean something which was both obligatory and binding, as opposed to the more inoffensive 'counsel', which featured in the letters of Clement and other pontiffs, and which did not have to be accepted.[86] Had the pope been limited by the cardinals' consent, he would have become a mere *primus inter pares*, if not the *ultimus inter pares*, and they, rather than he, would have wielded the papal plenitude of power. Conrad of Megenberg appreciated the problem when he pointed out that although the pope wrote *de fratrum nostrorum consilio*, even in constitutions which had not been discussed, as if he had taken the advice of the cardinals, in fact, the cardinals were at the same time assumed to be inferior to him. Conrad then quoted the conclave legislation of Clement V, *Ne Romani*, to show that papal authority came directly from God.[87]

Clement VI had a problem in defining the right relationship between pope and cardinals. On the one hand, he wanted to exalt his assistants so that they had sufficient power and status to perform the onerous and authoritative tasks he laid upon them. On the other hand, however much he raised them, he had to preserve his own plenitude of power inviolate. The balance between sublimation and abasement was a delicate one, and one which arguably Clement did not achieve.

There were two circumstances which seemed to warrant papal definition of the position of the cardinals, which gave Clement a chance to exalt them. The first was when they acted as legates or nuncios. In order to deal with the crises of the fourteenth century the

---

[84] Gasnault-Laurent, no. 435, p. 137.
[85] Ibid.
[86] Watt, 1971, pp. 135–6.
[87] Conrad of Megenberg, *Yconomica*, iii, 3, ch. 6, p. 370.

pope's representatives needed power. As Clement explained in consistory to Guy de Boulogne, a legate wielded both power and authority, and no one was superior to him save the pope himself.[88] The power of a *legatus a latere*, as Benedict XII had recognised, came literally from the side of the pope: he was *pars corporis papae*.[89] This meant that the office of legate had much the same qualities as the papal office itself, and Clement enumerated these to Cardinal Guy. The legate's office was one of 'sanctity and the most exalted power, of rectitude and unshakeable truth, of great plenitude and abundance, and of illustrious grandeur and nobility'.[90] To another cardinal, Guillaume Court, the Pope described the power of a legate as being of divine origin: it had derived immediately from Christ,[91] which, given Clement's role as Christ's vicar, was perfectly logical.

Plainly the legates were figures of immense power and prestige. While on legation they were used to living and acting as the pope himself, and were accorded all the ceremonial honours which would have been accorded to the Supreme Pontiff.[92] The sojourn of Annibaldus de Ceccano at the Lateran during the Jubilee year well exemplified this.[93] Small wonder if such experiences gave the cardinals delusions of grandeur, and if, when they returned to the curia, they resented, consciously or unconsciously, being deprived of their temporary 'papal' status.

The second occasion when Clement exalted the cardinals was on their election to the College, when the closeness of the partnership between the Pope and his 'men of truth' was underlined. For

---

[88] Clement VI, sermon 27, Ste-G. 240, fol. 441r: 'Ipse enim maior quocumque in legatione sua existente et potestate et auctoritate, et nullus eo superior nisi solus papa'.

[89] Benedict XII, Raynaldus vi, ch. 27, p. 111: 'dictum legatum, honorabile membrum Romanae ecclesiae, partemque corporis Romani pontificis et de latere ejus missum'. On the *legatus a latere* see Wasner, 1958. On the evolution of the different categories of representative, and in general, see Pacaut, 1955; Schmutz, 1972; and Sayers, 1971, esp. pp. 25–6. One of the reasons for appointing a nuncio as opposed to a legate was that legates did not enjoy their share of the cardinals' revenue *in absentia*, whereas nuncios did. This principle was included in the ceremonial order for the creation of legates and nuncios: see Dykmans, ch. 118, § 22–3, p. 500. For discussion see Kyer, 1978b, and for comparison of the papal legate with the legate of Roman law, Perrin, 1973.

[90] Clement VI, sermon 27, Ste-G. 240, fol. 441v.

[91] Clement VI, sermon 42, Ste-G. 240, fol. 250v: 'Potestas enim sue legationis non de terra, sed de celo duxit originem. Unde omnia potestas terrena de terra originatur; sed potestas ecclesiastica de celo a Christo inmediate derivatur'.

[92] Wasner, 1958, pp. 307ff.

[93] Dykmans, 1972, p. 263.

instance, they shared the papal habitation,[94] and Clement even allowed magnanimously, if inaccurately, that all that he had was theirs, and all that they had was his.[95] Pierre Bertrand the younger and Nicholas de Besse were welcomed into partnership with him and called *de miseria ad standum in latere nostro*.[96] They were raised from misery not just to a position *at* his side, but *in* it, as a *legatus a latere* would have been. Even humble cardinal-deacons like these two were part of the body of the pope.[97] So close was the union between Pope and College that they might even be said to have contracted a spiritual marriage. Clement explained that because they were accepted into partnership with him, the words of the Song of Solomon could be applied: 'My beloved is mine and I am his'.[98] These were the words habitually used to describe the marriage between Christ and His Church. Nicholas de Besse was invited to come with him so that he might rest in Jerusalem, by which Clement meant the Sacred College, and he continued by quoting Apocalypse, xxii, 17: '. . . and therefore come. And so the bridegroom calls the bride',[99] once again evoking the marriage metaphor. Although far-fetched, the idea was not completely illogical, given that the Sacred College enjoyed corporate legal status, and that marriage could not be contracted with a random group of individuals.

A much debated subject in the late-medieval period was the official standing of the cardinals in the ecclesiastical hierarchy. The College was composed of cardinal-bishops, cardinal-priests, and cardinal-deacons. But where did these stand, especially in relation to bishops? Was the office of cardinal of human or divine origin?

---

[94] Clement VI, sermon 27, Ste-G. 240, fol. 444r: 'Dicebam ultimo quam reddit eum conmendabiliter societas gaudiosa, quia reverti. Ut dicat illud Mt. xii° *Revertar in domum meam* . . .' Cf. Matt., xxi. 44.

[95] Clement VI, sermon 21, Ste-G. 240, fol. 445r: 'Unde isti sunt filii qui semper mecum sunt. Et omnia mea sua sunt, et omnia sua mea sunt sicut dicit Luce xv [31]'. [96] Clement VI, sermon 4, Ste-G. 240, fol. 535v.

[97] See, for example, John of Legnano, *De Censura Ecclesiastica*, fol. 309v: 'et haec sunt quatuor virtutes cardinales, quae debent esse in capite corporis mystici, scilicet in Romano Pontifice, et sicut sunt quatuor virtutes cardinales in quatuor partibus capitis, sed Cardinales sunt partes, non dico solum corporis, immo capitis, et sunt sedes illarum virtutum, vel esse debent'; also *De Fletu Ecclesiae*, p. 632; Paul of Liazariis, *ad Decretales*, I, v, 6, *Repetitionum . . . Iuris Canonici*, ii, fol. 223r: 'cardinales sunt pars capitis, ideo non iurant obedientiam papae'. For discussion and further examples see Tierney, 1955, esp. pp. 149ff, 211, n. 2, 233ff; Wilks, 1963a, p. 458, n. 1; Ullmann, 1972a, pp. 203–4; Leclercq, 1963, pp. 183–98; Alberigo, 1969, pp. 144ff. For the Roman law origins of the expression *pars corporis papae* see Ullmann, 1976, no. 15, p. 3, n. 4.

[98] Clement VI, sermon 4, Ste-G. 240, fol. 524r.

[99] Clement VI, sermon 33, Ste-G. 240, fol. 527v.

Ockham, not generally noted for his sympathy to cardinals, did at least appreciate their problem. He pointed out that the cardinals had been instituted by the pope 'voluntarily and at pleasure', and that there was no mention of their institution either by Christ or the Apostles. In fact, they did not feature at all, either in Holy Scripture or in the deeds of the Apostles.[100] Without apostolic descent it would be difficult to justify placing the cardinals at the summit of the ecclesiastical hierarchy, just below the pope himself. But by the fourteenth century some canonists and publicists were claiming that the cardinals were the heirs of the Apostles. The English Carmelite John Baconthorpe not only granted them apostolic succession, but also justified their hierarchical superiority by carefully distinguishing between sacramental and jurisdictional power. Although archbishops, bishops, and patriarchs were superior in terms of sacramental power, cardinals were greater by reason of papal jurisdiction – *ratione iurisdictionis papalis*.[101] The office of cardinal was thus a jurisdictional one and did not have to be matched by possession of sacramental power. This was also Clement's approach. In the first place he went some way to granting members of the College apostolic descent. Two of his biographers tell how during the ceremony in December 1350, when twelve cardinals were promoted, the Pope made the obvious apostolic comparison.[102] A less obvious one was made during his elevation sermon for the youthful Pierre Roger. The Pope had carefully changed the day to make it coincide with the octave of the Ascension, for normally cardinals were created only on Ember days.[103] This allowed him to

---

100 William of Ockham, I *Dialogus*, bk v, ch. 7, p. 477. For discussion of Ockham's views on the cardinals and further examples see Alberigo, 1969, pp. 141ff.

101 John Baconthorpe, *Quaestiones in Quatuor Libros Sententiarum*, q. x, art. iv, pp. 265–6: 'Licet Archiepiscopi, Episcopi et Patriarchae sunt maiores ratione ordinis Episcopalis, tamen Cardinales sunt maiores ratione iurisdictionis Papalis'. For discussion of John's views on the status and origins of the cardinalate see Ullmann, 1978, no. 10, pp. 232–4. Among other fourteenth-century writers to grant the cardinals apostolic status were Augustinus Triumphus, Aegidius Romanus, and, among the canonists, Johannes Monachus: see Tierney, 1955, pp. 183–4; Wilks, 1963a, p. 460, nn. 1 and 2; p. 464. For further discussion and for fifteenth-century examples see Leclercq, 1963, pp. 87ff; Alberigo, 1969, esp. pp. 92ff.

102 Baluze-Mollat, *Secunda Vita*, p. 270: 'assumpsit sibi XII quos vocavit apostolos'; *Tertia Vita*, p. 286. At the Council of Constance the apostolic number of twelve was proposed as the ideal total for the College. See Mollat, 1951, p. 107.

103 On this see Jordan, 1922, pp. 158–71. Clement himself admitted that he had made the change: sermon 47, Ste-G. 240, fols. 419r-v: 'Ex causa ergo illa congruentia solita observari ut fiat creatio in ordinibus mutari de consilio fratrum potuit'. See also ibid., fol. 419v: 'extra ordines istum creasti'.

use the text of Acts, i. 9: 'And while they beheld he was taken up'. He explained that this referred literally to the Apostles, but also, metaphorically, to 'our brothers', who succeeded to those Apostles.[104] Clearly he was not referring just to the cardinal-bishops because he went on to describe the supplications and approval which had preceded Pierre's promotion: these had been made *concorditer* – that is, with one mind. They reflected the *unanimitatem collegii*, the unanimity of the whole College,[105] and he nowhere singled out the cardinal-bishops in the sermon. Having thus granted all the cardinals apostolic descent, it followed for Clement, as for John Baconthorpe, that they took precedence over bishops. The superior angels in the celestial hierarchy are to the inferior as are cardinals to bishops and archbishops, so Clement told Nicholas de Besse.[106] He then went on to stress the jurisdictional character of the office by reminding him that the cardinals had to discuss arduous cases and keep secrets.[107]

So far Clement had given the cardinals the same sanction and a higher judicial status than the bishops. But this is by no means the same thing as granting them a share in the plenitude of power. The nearest Clement came to this was to state that cardinals were accepted not only in partial solicitude (the expression normally reserved for the bishops),[108] but in a certain measure into the plenitude of power itself.[109] And this was as far as he was prepared to go. He was prepared to accept the cardinals only in a certain measure – *quodam modo* – into the plenitude of power. It was merely a qualified acceptance. On the one hand they had immense power and status, appropriate to their functions, while on the other they must never forget their inferiority to the Pope. Clement summarised his position by misquoting from the Old Testament: 'The pillars of the earth are the Lord's, and I have set the world upon them'.[110] They were

---

[104] Ibid., fol. 416v.
[105] Ibid., fol. 417r.
[106] Clement VI, sermon 33, Ste-G. 240, fol. 528r: 'sicut se habuit [*sic*] angeli superiores assistentes et revelantes ad angelos inferiores: ita se habuit [*sic*] cardinales ad archiepiscopos et episcopos'.
[107] Ibid., 'quia cardinales habent discutere causas arduas et scire secreta'.
[108] On the history of this idea see Rivière, 1925.
[109] Clement VI, sermon 47, Ste-G. 240, fol. 416v: 'non solum assumuntur ad partem sollicitudinis, sed quodam modo in plenitudinem potestatis'. In the thirteenth century Hostiensis had thought that the cardinals shared the plenitude of power: see Watt, 1980, esp. pp. 105ff.
[110] Clement VI, sermon 47, Ste-G. 240, fol. 416v: 'Domini enim sunt cardines terre et posui super eos orbem. I Reg. ii [8]'. See also Theiner, *Mon. Pol.*, no. 585, p. 456: 'sanctae Romane ecclesie cardinales, quod dominus tamquam precipuas et sublimes ecclesie predicte columpnas', and Baluze-Mollat, *Tertia Vita*, p. 280,

indeed the giants who bowed in the presence of the vicar of Christ.[111] He never tired of reminding them that they were merely assistants.[112]

The trouble was that the cardinals were not prepared to bow to the vicar of Christ: they would not accept the subordinate role allotted to them. As oligarchs they considered that sovereignty should be shared between pope and cardinals. One means of achieving this would have been through the success of the electoral pact. Another was by engineering the election of a 'puppet' pope, preferably an outsider, who would owe everything to them, and who should therefore be tractable. It is highly significant that the election capitulation stated that the new pope was to be bound 'whether a cardinal or someone else',[113] as if its framers had envisaged the possibility of an outsider's being elected. It is in the light of this that the curious story of Jean Birel must be interpreted, and clearly this incident and the capitulation have to be taken in conjunction. Birel was not a cardinal: he was the prior–general of the Carthusians. He was put up as a papal candidate by one group of cardinals in 1352, but opposed by Elie de Talleyrand. Apparently Talleyrand persuaded the group to drop Birel's nomination because the Carthusian's known austerity would, as he termed it, 'set them back in their old condition',[114] meaning that he would reintroduce the spartan regime of Benedict XII.[115] He accordingly painted a grim picture of the loss of carnal and culinary delights which would result. Historians have

describing the promotion of Pierre Bertrand and Nicholas de Besse: 'duas in domo Domini pro firmiori substentatione fidei columpnas erexit'. For further examples and discussion see Wilks, 1963a, p. 457, n. 4; p. 461; Alberigo, 1969, pp. 89–90; Kuttner, 1945, pp. 176ff. For general discussion of this and related images see Greenhill, 1954, esp. pp. 337, 367–8.

[111] Clement VI, sermon 47, Ste-G. 240, fol. 416v: 'Isti enim sunt gigantes qui portant orbem, qui solum curvantur coram vicario Ihesu Christi. Job ix [13]'.
[112] Clement VI, sermon 4, Ste-G. 240, fol. 523r: 'Assumuntur ad officium et ad servicium'. See also sermon 47, Ste-G. 240, fol. 418v: 'Cardinales eliguntur ut Romani pontificis ministri et servitores, ut ipsius etiam corporaliter sustentatores'; ibid., fol. 416r: 'Unde qui ad istum statum assumuntur sicut assistentes summo ierarche in ecclesiastica ierarchia'. See also Clement's letter of December 1350 about the creation of new cardinals, Raynaldus, vi, ch. 47, p. 526: 'Inter quos, nimirum viros electos ex millibus, assumptos ad adiuvandum pontificem in gubernatione navis quae est Ecclesia', and Déprez, no. 726, p. 376.
[113] Gasnault-Laurent, no. 435, p. 135.
[114] *Brevis Historia Ordinis Carthusiensis*, quoted by Zacour, 1960, p. 21, where the conclave is examined.
[115] See the contemporary opinion of Galvaneus Flamma, *Opusculum de Rebus Gestis*, col. 1045: 'Hic [scil. Clemens] suorum predecessorum avaritias et crudelitates sua magna liberalitate obmutescere fecit'.

doubted the truth of the incident, largely because it is transmitted by a Carthusian source alone. But circumstances support its genuineness. Clement was mortally ill for at least a year before he died: his deathbed confession was actually made a year in advance of his death, that is, in December 1351, instead of December 1352.[116] This meant that the cardinals had ample time for stratagem. Moreover, if the affair is seen as part of the election-capitulation plan, then it becomes quite plausible.

The disunity which Henry Taube of Selbach underlined in describing the 'battle of Avignon' of 1350 also manifested itself over Birel. Ultimately it was this lack of unity which ensured the failure of the electoral pact. Certain cardinals, including Etienne Aubert (and it is Innocent VI who provides this evidence), had added an all-important proviso in swearing to the pact: 'if and inasmuch as this document proceeds *de iure*'.[117] Once elected pope, Etienne Aubert had neither compunction nor canonical difficulty in proving that the capitulation had proceeded anything but *de iure*, and in condemning and annulling it.

Some but not all of the blame for 1352 can be laid upon Clement. Undeniably he was autocratic, and the pontificate witnessed several disagreements between him and the cardinals. Besides being autocratic, he was probably over lavish in the amount both of power and possessions which he granted them, for the truism that 'revolution occurs when the position of inferiors is improving' surely applied in this case. On the other hand, there were contributory circumstances beyond Clement's control, such as the vastly increased amount of diplomatic work being undertaken by the curia, his own frequent indispositions, which must often have left the cardinals to act unsupervised, the difficult relationship with the College which he inherited, and the mounting social and economic tension. As Clement himself had realised, he could not cope with the problems of the mid-fourteenth century alone: he had to form a partnership with his men of truth. This being so, it is difficult to point to any major political issues in which they were not involved. In practice, when it came to taking decisions they must have acted not unlike a modern cabinet, with the pope as the equivalent of the prime minister. The realities of the situation must have contributed to the cardinals' conviction that they were really operating an oligarchic form of government with the pope as a *primus inter pares*. To this extent their

---

[116] Raynaldus, vi, ch. 38, p. 550.   [117] Gasnault-Laurent, no. 435, p. 136.

behaviour in 1352 was an explicable attempt to bring theory into line with practice.

Like many others, the cardinals were influenced by the half-formed ideas of the fourteenth century. They had taken advantage of the Achilles heel of the papal system, election, to experiment with concepts such as consent, participation, and a residual right of control over the ruler they deluded themselves into thinking they personally had elected. In the process they had emerged as oligarchs rather than as Aristotelian aristocrats. There was no question of their claiming to represent all Christians, no question of their summoning a General Council of the whole Church to pass judgement on an erring pope: they aimed at participation in papal authority for themselves alone. They were identified with the pope rather than the congregation of the faithful.

In adopting such a position in 1352 the cardinals provided a pointer to their attitude of 1378. Temporarily Innocent VI's decisive action, and perhaps Clement's attempts to fragment the College, coupled with the strength and consistency of traditional papal theory against ideas which were still in their infancy, had averted the crisis. But when a pope as overbearing as Boniface VIII or Clement VI again ascended the papal throne in the person of Urban VI the threat from the cardinals was to become a reality. The consequences of the resulting Schism and the conciliar movement were ultimately to destroy the medieval papacy as an institution of government. Once again in 1378 the cardinals ranged themselves on the side of the papacy rather than the congregation of the faithful. There would have been nothing to stop them from putting into practice the oft-advocated theory of summoning a General Council of the whole Church to depose an erring pope. Instead they decided to dethrone him themselves, at least by implication, by proceeding to a new election, which was thought to nullify the first.[118] By acting thus they had left the way clear for the laity to play its part in summoning a council and conducting its affairs. Not, of course, that this prevented the cardinals from trying to dominate the council once it had come into session.[119] But they were never to regain the theoretical ground they had lost in 1378. Perhaps it would not have been lost had their attitudes not become formed and hardened by their earlier experiences of conflict with the papal monarchy of Clement VI.

---

[118] For the views of Hostiensis that a second election nullified the first see Tierney, 1951.

[119] Ullmann, 1972a, p. 55.

Chapter 6

REGNUM GLORIOSUM: THE KINGDOM OF FRANCE

Pierre Roger's overwhelming love for his native France had been conditioned by his upbringing in Corrèze, and at the Abbey of Chaise-Dieu, his university days in Paris, and many years of devoted service to Charles IV and Philip VI. He was a man who set great store by personal loyalties to friends and relations, and in France he had a great many of both. In comparison, Pierre's acquaintance with England and its king was minimal. As Abbot of Fécamp, in Normandy, he had been the vassal of Edward III, and later, in 1331, he had met Edward when he did homage to him for lands attached to the archbishopric of Rouen.[1] He paid one brief, and frustrating, visit to England in 1328 as Philip's ambassador to demand Edward's homage for Aquitaine. He and his companion were subjected to an interminable wait, only to be denied access to Edward and to be told by Isabella, the Queen-Mother, that her son, born of a king, did not owe homage to the son of a count.[2]

Anglo-French relations grew progressively more strained from 1328 onwards until the outbreak of the Hundred Years War in 1337. Given his background, it is inconceivable that Pierre Roger, in his private capacity, could have been other than partial to France. The problem, however, arose when he became Clement VI, supposedly a new man. As pope he knew that the paternal aspect of his office laid upon him the 'care and solicitude' for all Christian peoples,[3] which should have excluded preference for one people over another. In practice this was difficult. In no other sphere of his duties was he to find it so hard to sublimate the desires of the man to the demands of the office, and to do so with so little success.

Accusations of Clement VI's partiality reverberated throughout Europe. The German chronicler Matthew of Nuremberg declared

---

[1] Déprez, 1902, p. 76, n. 2. [2] Ibid., p. 40.
[3] Tautu, no. 121, par. 383.

that 'himself a Frenchman, he fervently adhered to France' and that he and the King of France were of one heart – *unum cor erat*.[4] The Italian Matteo Villani described him as the 'great friend and protector of King Philip'.[5] The most damning indictments predictably came from the English themselves. Edward III's procurator drew up an appeal to a General Council of the whole Church against the judgement of Clement VI. The Pope had censured Edward for his adherence to Louis of Bavaria. In the document it was stated that 'the lord pope Clement VI . . . favours, encourages, listens to, and excuses Philip of Valois'.[6] But William of Ockham's accusation was the most damaging:

> The said lord Clement is schismatic because he creates schism between the kings of England and France, and favours one side, and provokes wars and strife between them.[7]

On the other hand, far from being the author of conflict, Clement enjoyed a reputation as a peacemaker, as chroniclers and biographers testify.[8] Conrad of Megenberg, replying directly to Ockham's charges, claimed that he had himself seen Clement sending out cardinals to conduct peace negotiations between the kings of France and England – something commented on also by his biographers. Yet even Conrad was constrained to admit Clement's partiality, excusing it somewhat feebly, and less than accurately, on the grounds that the Holy See had always adhered more to France than to other nations, so one read.[9]

In his role as Philip VI Valois' servant and a high-ranking French ecclesiastic Pierre Roger had had no reason to disguise his patriotism or his love for the French royal house. His biographers describe his love for Philip in extreme terms: he was joined to him with a bond of fervent love.[10] His affection for the Queen, Joan of Burgundy, who showed him many kindnesses, emerges both from letters and

---

[4] Matthew of Nuremberg, *Chronica*, ch. 69, p. 188.
[5] Matteo Villani, *Istorie Fiorentine*, bk iii, ch. 43, col. 186.
[6] MS BL Harley, 4763, fol. 4r. On the dating and circumstances of the appeal see Offler, 1939, pp. 624–5.
[7] William of Ockham, *De Electione Karoli IV*, p. 352.
[8] See above, ch. 1, p. 5, nn. 16 and 19.
[9] Conrad of Megenberg, *Tractatus*, p. 381. Cf. Baluze-Mollat, *Prima Vita*, pp. 247, 259; *Secunda Vita*, pp. 263–4; *Tertia Vita*, p. 276. Boniface VIII had favoured England in the Anglo-French arbitration of 1298: see Chaplais, 1951, p. 289. Benedict XII appears to have been neutral in the Hundred Years War until the formation of the Anglo-Bavarian alliance: see Jenkins, 1933, pp. 28–45.
[10] Baluze-Mollat, *Secunda Vita*, p. 263.

sermons.[11] Their son, who succeeded as John II, 'the Good', in 1350, was sufficiently close to Clement to visit him at Avignon during the first months of his reign. There he stood godfather to the Pope's infant niece, amid great baptismal celebrations.[12]

At Vincennes in 1329 Pierre Roger preached an *encomium* of the French kings, making it clear that they had always enjoyed a position of pre-eminence. This resulted partly from their own bounty, for the more a king gave to God, the more God would reward him, and the happier would he be. The French kings were therefore happier than all others.[13] Their pre-eminence sprang partly from the familiar legend that the French royal line, the noblest in the world, was descended from Priam, King of Troy, and the refugee Trojans, who had never paid tribute to the Roman Empire.[14] Moreover, they had always set an example to other kings as the most Christian, the most faithful, and the most generous.[15] He then went on to toy with the possibility that Philip might revoke all the gifts of his predecessors to the Church. If he did this, Pierre warned, then the emperor, always supposing there were one, would be able to revoke all that Constantine had given, and other kings would follow this example.[16] Pierre had in fact cut the emperor down to size and made him the equal, if not the inferior, of the king of France, something which provided a foretaste of his papal policy. He was also at pains to emphasise the special relationship which the French enjoyed with the papacy. Never since their conversion had the kings of France been known to have been heretical – to have wandered – he boasted, inaccurately in

---

[11] See n. 40, p. 106 above.

[12] Gasnault, 1964, p. 122.

[13] Pierre Roger, sermon 15, p. 461: 'Et ideo videbitur mihi quod quia inter caeteros Reges, Reges Franciae plura dederunt Deo, et Ecclesiae, et etiam Barones Regni, idcirco fuerunt super omnes alios foelices. Et quanto plura dederunt, tanto plura dedit eis Deus, sicut patuit de Clodovaeo, Carolo, sancto Ludovico, et aliis. Quanto enim aliquis plura dat Deo, tanto Deus plura sibi dat, cum ipsemet promiserit, *Date et dabitur vobis*: Luc. 6 [38]'. Augustine, *De Civitate Dei*, v, 24–5 had demonstrated that true happiness resulted from giving to God, but warned that this was no guarantee that God would reward the donor in this life. The Christian's aim should be happiness in the afterlife.

[14] Ibid., p. 471: 'Secundo, sanguinis nobilitas, quia a Priamo Rege Trojanorum, et successive a Carolo, et aliis Regibus tam inclitis descenderunt'. For further references to the 'Trojan theory' see Wilks, 1963a, p. 193, n. 2; Southern, 1970, pp. 189–93; Borchardt, 1971, pp. 32, 46, 200, 204, 223.

[15] Ibid., pp. 476–7: 'Advertat etiam vestra dominatio, si posset esse denigratio nominis, cum Reges semper fuerunt Christianissimi et fidelissimi, Deo et Ecclesiae, et semper dederunt exemplum aliis principibus dotandi et augendi ecclesias et libertates earum'.

[16] Ibid., p. 476.

view of Philip IV's behaviour to Boniface VIII.[17] In 1332, preaching at Avignon as Archbishop of Rouen in order to persuade John XXII to confer the leadership of the crusade on Philip, he returned to this theme. France and the papacy had stuck together through thick and thin, aiding each other with help, counsel, and favours. Consequently the popes had always applied the words of Hebrews, i. 5 to the French kings: 'I shall be to him a father; he shall be to me a son'.[18] These were the very words which Clement VI would apply to Charles IV some twenty years later. The following year, preaching on the same theme of mutual love, the Archbishop added a reminder that when the pope had been ejected from his see it had been the French king who had conducted him back,[19] the inference being that it was only through the help of the French kings that the Avignon popes would return to Rome. The obvious person to conduct the popes back would have been the emperor. The fact that there was no papally approved emperor at the time served to underline the point that the French king would make a most acceptable emperor.

As pope, Clement continued to favour Philip. The version of the Pope's otherwise standard coronation letter sent to the Valois included a unique paragraph reminding him of the Pope's love for

---

[17] Ibid., p. 471: 'Fidei inviolata sinceritas, quia nunquam legitur quod Reges Franciae, ex quo susceperunt fidem, ullo nunquam tempore a fide aberraverint'. Cf. Benedict XII, Raynaldus, vi, p. 119: 'reges Franciae nunquam dimiserint Ecclesiam memoratam'. Boniface VIII was prevented only by death from publishing the excommunication processes he had prepared against Philip IV the Fair: see Rivière, 1926, p. 91, n. 1. Innocent III had placed France under an interdict during the reign of Philip Augustus because the King had refused to be reconciled to his Danish wife.

[18] Pierre Roger, sermon 20, Ste-G. 240, fols. 296v–97r: 'Patet autem ex cronicis quanta fuit semper affectio corone Francie ad sanctam Romanam Ecclesiam et econtra sancte Romane Ecclesie ad coronam Francie. Unde tanta fuit affectio, tanta colligatio, tanta confederatio, tantus amor, que nunquam unus alteri defuit, quin adesset in omnibus prosperitatibus et adversitatibus et auxiliis et consiliis, gratiis, et favoribus oportunis. Unde semper dixit quilibet Romanus Pontifex specialiter inter ceteros reges Regi Francie illud Apostoli ad Hebr. primo [i. 5] *Ego ero illi in patrem et ipse erit michi in filium*'. On the crusade and Philip VI's deep commitment to it see Tyermann, 1985.

[19] Pierre Roger, sermon 2, Ste-G. 240, fol. 503r: 'Tanta enim fuit semper Ecclesie Romane ad regem Francie dilectio, et regum Francie ad Ecclesiam Romanam devotio, quod nunquam sibi mutuo in suis necessitatibus defuerunt. Unde et reges Francie et summum pontificem de sua sede eiectum ad eandem reduxerunt'. Probably the occasion referred to was when Pepin led an expedition against the Lombards in 754 on behalf of Pope Stephen III, after the Pope had crossed the Alps to seek the King's aid. Cf. Anon, *Somnium Viridarii*, bk ii, ch. 365, p. 225, where the author declared that the French had restored the popes to their see nine times. The French translator of the work echoes this: Anon, *Songe du Vergier*, bk i, ch. 363, p. 333. On this see Royer, 1969, pp. 141–52.

France and its King before his election, and assuring him that the 'plenitude of paternal affection' would continue and even be increased.[20] It did continue, for Clement never missed an opportunity to stress that the French house was the noblest in the world.[21] He reiterated its 'most Christian' status, and how 'its devotion had never declined to right nor left'.[22] At his coronation it was members of the French royal house, John Duke of Normandy and Duke Eudes of Burgundy, who performed the ceremony of *strator*, leading Clement's horse by the bridle, one on each side, a privilege usually reserved for the emperor.[23] When Clement appointed a king of the Fortune Islands, the office went to a princeling of the French royal house. When he appointed a captain-general of the crusade, the office went to a member of the French royal house. But when he appointed a king of the Romans, the office did not go to a member of the French royal house. Quite apart from the loss of prestige occasioned by the defeats of Crécy and Calais, Philip's persistent encroachments on ecclesiastical liberties were beginning to mar Franco-papal relations.[24] And there was the far more serious matter of Philip's determination to reconcile Louis of Bavaria with the Holy See.[25] But the idea of Philip's promotion to emperorship was very much in the air, and Clement did not trouble to disillusion him. He urged him to lead the crusade, and a draft petition of Humbert of Vienne for this honour contained a clause promising to serve under Philip should he decide to lead it.[26] Crusades had traditionally been led by the emperor. More significantly, the document by which Humbert appointed Philip of Orleans (the King's second son) his heir in 1343, contained a clause envisaging the possibility that France and the Empire might become united.[27] Clement kept Philip in the

---

[20] Déprez, no. 4.

[21] See, for example, sermon 10, on the Feast of St Louis, Bishop of Toulouse, Ste-G. 240, fol. 493r: 'Gloriosissimus vero Ludovicus habuit veram humilitatem a natura pariter et fortuna. A natura quia natus ex nobiliori genere mundi, de domo Francie; et in isto genere semper fuit vera nobilitas'.

[22] *MGH Const.*, viii, no. 652, p. 657.

[23] Baluze-Mollat, *Secunda Vita*, p. 263; *Tertia Vita*, p. 276. See also Déprez, 1902, p. 391.

[24] Mollat, 1960.

[25] Schwöbel, 1968, pp. 324–31, 475–8.

[26] Valbonnais, no. 205, p. 539: 'Item, est l'entente du dit Dauphin que en cas que le Roys de France voudroit passer la mer pour ceste euvre, que ledit Dauphin et sa compaignie seront dessous luy'.

[27] Ibid., no. 177, p. 459: '. . . le nom de Dalphin, ne les dittes armes, et ne sera ne puisse estre unis, ne ajousté ledit Dalphine au Royaume de France, *fors tant comme l'Empire y seroit unis*'. This treaty had been negotiated in the presence of Clement VI:

dark about his plans for the imperial election for as long as he could, and when he did enlighten him, barely a month beforehand, he felt constrained to apologise,[28] giving as his main reason 'certain negotiations' which Philip was having with Louis of Bavaria. Even after he had formally approved Charles as King of the Romans, Clement continued to favour Philip. In 1347, for example, he wrote to him reaffirming the faith he had in him, greater than that which he had in any other Christian king, and recalling the interdependence of the *Ecclesia* and Philip's predecessors.[29]

By the time Clement was elected pope he was already experienced in Anglo-French relations, having watched their deterioration from 1328 onwards. In this year the primary causes of the conflict were brought into focus.[30] On the death of the last Capetian without male issue Edward III advanced his unsuccessful claim to the throne of France. Philip VI's accession automatically raised the other issue, the anomalous status of the sovereign ruler of England as the feudal vassal, and by implication the inferior, of the sovereign ruler of France, because of the terms under which he held the Duchy of Aquitaine. The position was emphasised because liege homage had to be performed at the beginning of each reign. Pierre Roger's journey to England to demand the homage, and his subsequent one to Aquitaine to supervise confiscation of its revenues for Philip, marked the beginning of a long involvement in the conflict.

Clement expressed his longing for peace the moment he was appointed: indeed, his coronation letters stressed this longing.[31] As he later boasted to two of his cardinals, so determined had he been that he should not be thought lukewarm in this vital cause that he had written to the belligerent kings of France and England even before his coronation.[32] The survival of the letters he wrote as pope-elect evidence the truth of his boast. In these he emphasised his determination to labour for peace as his office demanded, and added that his natural desire for Anglo-French harmony had been increased with his elevation to the Holy See.[33]

see pp. 458; 462. The following year, 1344, John, Duke of Normandy, Philip's heir, was substituted for Philip of Orleans: see no. 196, pp. 526–7.

[28] *MGH Const.*, viii, no. 50, p. 73.
[29] Baluze-Mollat, iv, pp. 85–6.
[30] On the causes of the war see Le Patourel, 1958 and 1971; Palmer, 1971; Allmand, 1988, pp. 6–12.
[31] Déprez, no. 4.
[32] Ibid., no. 2726, letter of 14 August, 1346.
[33] See his letters of 10 May 1342 to Philip VI and his Queen, Déprez, 1903, pp. 73, 75.

The letters Clement wrote as pope also reverberate with his concern for peace. Within a fortnight of his coronation he had empowered two cardinal-nuncios, Pierre Després and Annibaldus de Ceccano, to negotiate a truce, and the letter he wrote to them enlarged on this concern. Christ had committed His special gift of peace to His vicar in the Church Militant so that it could be perpetuated. The Pope bore the office of *speculator*, or overseer, which enabled him to watch over his flock as a pastor, promoting those things which were conducive to peace and checking all those scandals by which the salvation of souls was so grievously impaired.[34] It was almost as if the Pope had a monopoly of peace as he had of power and authority.

The concept of peace was in fact closely linked with the Pope's special responsibility for the salvation of souls. By peace Clement seems to have meant the good order and harmony of the Christian society, without which it could not achieve its aim of salvation. Preaching in consistory on the return of Annibaldus de Ceccano and Etienne Aubert, who had imposed a truce after Edward's victory at Calais (August 1347), Clement elaborated on the Augustinian antithesis of the two cities, that of Jerusalem, signifying heaven, and that of Babylon, denoting hell. These two he applied to the opposing conditions of peace and war. Amid a cluster of contrasting statements he declared that Babylon, that is war, meant confusion, Jerusalem order; in Babylon was spoliation, in Jerusalem faithful possession; in Babylon was the bitter hatred caused by fighting, in Jerusalem mutual love; Babylon was ruled by diabolical tyranny, while Jerusalem was ruled by divine dominion, and so on. Finally, in Babylon was damnation, and in Jerusalem salvation,[35] by which he meant that only through the good order and harmony of the Church could salvation be achieved. War, he emphasised, was instigated by the devil, the ruler of Babylon.[36] Clement felt that as pope he was bound to seek peace by all possible means.

Did he do this? Before the question can be answered his personal ideas on the just war and its application to France, which so clearly influenced his later attitude, need to be examined. These emerge mainly from a *collatio* he preached on Ash Wednesday 1338 on the

---

[34] Déprez, no. 94.
[35] Clement VI, sermon 28, Ste-G. 240, fol. 449v. Cf. Augustine, *De Civitate Dei*, bk xvii, ch. 16, p. 581.
[36] Ibid., fol. 450r: 'Rex enim Babilonis dyabolus est et instigator bellice conmotionis dyabolus est'. Cf. *MGH Const.*, viii, no. 90, p. 115.

text of I Maccabees, iii. 58: 'Arm yourselves and be valiant, men, and be prepared for the morning, so that you may fight against the nations which are gathered together to destroy us and our holy place'.[37] In his role as military propagandist Pierre Roger told prospective recruits that mere possession of arms and the accoutrements of war would not make them soldiers: these things were allowed them to help them to be more practised in the defence of the *respublica*, and it was this defence which made them into soldiers.[38] What seemed to matter was the status and the intention of defending the realm. By the time this sermon was preached war was a certainty. Philip had confiscated Aquitaine, in reply to which Edward had presented his defiance to 'Philip of Valois, who calls himself King of France', and had formed an alliance with Louis of Bavaria.[39]

Pierre's criteria for waging war were based on those of Augustine. He concentrated especially on the need for justice and truth in the cause, and for malice and evil in the enemy, which necessitated invasion or resistance.[40] He was quite certain of the total injustice of the cause of Edward III and Louis of Bavaria. Louis had trumped the whole thing up by pretending that Philip held possessions which pertained by right to the Empire. But of course this was demonstrably false, since Philip held only what had belonged to his predecessors, predictably hailed as the most Christian, the most devoted, and the most just of all princes.[41] In any event, because of his manifold crimes, which were listed, Louis had been deprived of all imperial, royal, and ducal status.[42] This neatly invalidated the argument: they were no concern of Louis if he did not hold the imperial office. The only real cause Louis embraced, as Pierre well knew, was the money promised him by Edward III.[43]

The Archbishop of Rouen considered that war should be waged

---

[37] Sermon 1, Ste-G. 240, fols. 308v–14r. Mollat, 1928, p. 464, no. 1, dates the sermon at the end of 1339 or early 1340, but Ash Wednesday 1338, 25 February, seems preferable. Matthew of Nuremberg, *Chronica*, ch. 69, p. 188 states that it was preached before the kings of France and Bohemia, and van Werveke, 1901, p. 43, confirms that King John was at Avignon on that day.

[38] Pierre Roger, sermon 1, Ste-G. 240, fols. 310v–11r: 'Nec enim sunt milites propter hastiludia nec propter orneamenta [*sic*] sed illa eis permittuntur ut sint magis exercitati ad defensionem reipublice, pro qua debent militare'.

[39] Perroy, 1951, p. 93.

[40] Pierre Roger, sermon 1, Ste-G. 240, fol. 309r. Cf. Augustine, *Contra Faustum*, bk xxii, ch. 74, *CSEL*, xxv, p. 672.

[41] Ibid., fol. 311v.

[42] Ibid., fols. 313r–v.

[43] Ibid., fol. 311v.

only against the disobedient and rebellious.[44] Turning his attention to Edward, he therefore cast him in the role of the disobedient and rebellious vassal. This line of argument enabled him to concentrate on the feudal issue involved in the war and to ignore Edward's claim to the French throne, for French interests dictated that the conflict should be seen purely in feudal terms. These interests might well pose problems later for a pro-French pope, given Innocent III's celebrated declaration that he did not intend to judge *de feudo*, concerning a fief,[45] but at this stage the precedent did not bother Pierre Roger. He was convinced that Philip had every right in feudal terms to lay hands on the Duchy of Aquitaine.[46] In fact, Edward's harbouring of the recalcitrant French vassal Robert of Artois, who was *inter alia* suspected of poisoning his Aunt Matilda, had provoked the confiscation. Not, of course, that Philip wished to appropriate Edward's *dominium* of Aquitaine, so the Archbishop enlarged, but simply to impose justice in the way any lord might lay hands on his own feudal domain. The lordship of Aquitaine, in any case, belonged to Philip *de iure*: Edward, as a vassal, had only the use of it. Even if the French King had intervened without a just cause, his vassal would have had no grounds for action: the most that he could have done would have been to request that justice should be done to him, and Philip was prepared to deal justly with anyone. It was blatantly obvious that the French King had a just cause and his adversaries an unjust one.[47] And ultimately, as Pierre could not resist pointing out, no king with a just cause could fail. When a king knows that he is waging an unjust war he must expect his sin to be visited on his own head, but when justice is on his side he is fired by the thought of victory, and says with David, 'The Lord will help me, and I shall destroy my enemies'.[48] Such were the views of the future Clement VI. Unless they were to alter with the change in nature

---

[44] Ibid., fol. 309v.
[45] *Decretales*, II, i. 13.
[46] Pierre Roger, sermon 1, Ste-G. 240, fol. 311v.
[47] Ibid.: 'ordinavit ducatum Aquitanie ad manum suam realiter poni, non ad finem ipsum suo dominio appropriandi, sed sibi ad finem iustitiam faciendi, sicut domini consueverunt ponere manum in feudis suis. Quorum eciam habent de iure dominium directum, licet eciam vasalli habeant dominium utile . . . Et certe, domini, bene scitis, quod eciam si dominus ponat manum in feudo minus iuste, vasallus non debet propter hoc contra dominum rebellare, sed requirere quod iustitia sibi fiat, quam dominus rex paratus est facere cuicumque. Patet ergo quomodo dominus rex habet iustam causam et ipsi iniustam'.
[48] Ibid., fols. 311r–v. Cf. Ps. cxvii (cxviii). 7.

which elevation to the Holy See brought, he would surely find it difficult to fulfil his promise to work for peace.

Some disquiet seems to have been felt about Clement's impartiality right from the start. In announcing his election to the Plantagenet, the Sacred College found it necessary to reassure him that at such a critical time there could be no one less inclined to acts of partiality.[49] The untruth of this was soon manifested. In October 1342 Edward landed in Brittany to reinforce the English army already there. A French army was sent to defend the territory, under John of Normandy, who had so recently performed the service of *strator* for Clement. Before battle could be joined, however, Clement's nuncios, Annibaldus de Ceccano and Pierre Després, intervened and imposed the Truce of Malestroit (January 1343). Clement's delight and relief are evident from the jubilant *collatio* he preached on the nuncios' return to Avignon, on the appropriate theme of Ezechiel, i. 14: 'They went and returned with the appearance of a flash of lightning'. Clement admitted that he had thought it difficult, indeed, almost impossible, that peace could be imposed.[50] Clearly God, who alone could give peace, had helped them.[51] Their achievement was a matter of 'wonder and admiration'; and more in the same vein.[52] It seems likely that Clement's intervention had occurred at a time when the French would have lost the battle had it taken place. Soon after the truce Philip wrote confidently to Peter of Aragon about its terms, by which both kings were to send envoys to the Pope, 'who is indeed our friend'.[53] So far Clement had been so.

At the subsequent meeting of envoys, held at Avignon in 1344, Clement was supposed to be acting as the 'friend' both of Philip and of Edward III.[54] Writing to Philip in May 1344 he had stressed his intention to proceed 'not by our own authority, but by the power

---

[49] Letter of 8 May 1342, Rymer, *Foedera*, v, p. 311: 'credimus vestram serenitatem non potuisse pro nunc meliorem habere et minus intendentem ad actus partiales faciendum'.

[50] Clement VI, sermon 28, Ste-G. 240, fol. 62v.

[51] Ibid., fol. 62r. Cf. II Mach., xi. 10.

[52] Ibid., fol. 60r: 'Dico primo quod corda regum et aliorum omnem suo facto spectabili induxerunt in stupore et admirationem. Quis enim non stupeat, quis non miretur, qui audit exercitus regum ita fortes et terribiles . . . Certe stupendum est et mirandum'. On the truce see Poquet de Haut-Jussé, 1928, pp. 270–7.

[53] Miret y Sans, p. 69.

[54] For a full account see Déprez, 1925.

given to us by both parties'.[55] In other words, he was to act as a private person rather than as the embodiment of the papal office. This practice of arbitration, by which sovereign rulers submitted their disputes to a strictly impartial 'common friend' for adjudication, had become established by the late-medieval period. Its origins were in the Roman law practice of Compromise.[56] The 'friend' – usually the pope or a neighbouring prince – acted in his private capacity to show that he was not a superior judge: that way there could be no threat to the sovereignty of either of the belligerents. Clement chose this course almost certainly because by the fourteenth century there was no alternative. Innocent III had been able to declare in 1208 that 'it pertains most especially to us to recall those in discord to peace' – a view supported by Hostiensis[57] – and to act accordingly. By the end of the century, however, so sensitive had the whole issue of papal sovereignty in temporal affairs become that Philip IV and Edward I allowed Boniface VIII to arbitrate between them only in his private capacity.[58] By the Avignon period it seems unlikely that lay rulers would have accepted papal arbitration if it had been conducted out of the plenitude of power. Benedict XII's representatives, for example, negotiated between England and France 'not as judges or arbitrators, but as mediators and common friends'.[59] Edward III accordingly made great play of the fact that Clement would be acting not as a judge, but as a private person, and that he would preside 'unofficially and amicably' when he empowered his envoys.[60] It was as if the King were savouring it as a calculated attempt to deny papal supremacy. It is also possible that Clement would have relished the prospect of acting as Pierre Roger, for it was precisely in this role that he could be concerned with 'judging a fief'.

Once the conference started some doubt was cast on the sincerity of Clement's intentions to act unofficially by the fact that he conducted only one session alone.[61] The rest were presided over by

---

55 Déprez, no. 812.
56 For its use during the fourteenth century see Chaplais, 1951, esp. pp. 286–8; Gaudemet, 1961, esp. pp. 95–106. On the Roman law origins of the practice see Buckland, 1963, p. 532; Schulz, 1951, p. 564.
57 Innocent III, *PL*, 215, 1182, letter to citizens of Florence: Hostiensis, *ad Decretales*, II, i, 13, fol. 6v: 'Ad ecclesiam enim spectat pacem servare et facere observari'.
58 Gaudemet, p. 90.
59 Daumet, no. 644: Gaudemet, p. 95.
60 See his letters of 20 May 1343 and 29 August, Rymer, *Foedera*, v, pp. 366, 382.
61 John Offord [?], *Journal des conférences d'Avignon*, p. 251: 'venimus coram domino nostro papa solo sine aliquo cardinali sibi assistente'.

the Pope and six cardinals or just by two cardinals.[62] The cardinals' normal role was to assist the Pope in his official, not his private, capacity. In any case, it was virtually impossible to separate the 'unofficial' peace discussions from the other affair being thrashed out 'officially' by the Pope and the English envoys, that of papal provisions.

English anger about papal provisions had exploded in Commons' petitions to Parliament in both 1343 and 1344. Xenophobia apart, the English thought that money extorted from them by the curia was being used to finance their enemies. Edward III had therefore issued writs preventing the execution of papal mandates in England, and had blocked all appeals to the papacy.[63] Papal nuncios and collectors were more than likely to be arrested and imprisoned on arrival.[64] The discussions Clement was holding with the English on such matters formed an acrimonious sub-plot to the main drama of the peace conference. Often the sub-plot and its issues predominated.

Things started badly. The week the conference opened, an offensive letter from Edward to one of the cardinals about procurations, in which the cardinal was denied the normal courteous forms of address, was read out in consistory.[65] Early in November anti-papal edicts were stuck to the doors of Westminster Abbey and St Paul's: these were read out three times in consistory.[66] At this, Pope and cardinals determined to send ambassadors to England, with the threat that if they were molested, reprisals would be taken against the English envoys at Avignon.[67] A few days later Clement created one of the French envoys to the peace conference, Louis de la Cerda, a great-grandson of St Louis, Prince of the Fortune Islands, and authorised a crusade to enable him to conquer his still-pagan domain.[68] This favouritism was taken by the English as a deliberate insult. An anonymous chronicler, after noting Louis was one of

---

[62] Ibid., pp. 235, 237, 238, 240, 241, 245, 248, 250, 254.

[63] See the letter of one of the English envoys, probably Offord, to the Archbishop of Canterbury, in which he reported Clement's accusations against Edward, De Lettenhove, p. 216. In general see Mollat, 1964, pp. 431–4; Pantin, 1955, pp. 81–7.

[64] Mollat, 1964, p. 432.

[65] De Lettenhove, p. 226: 'en taunt que est dist en meysme le brief: "A toy Gaillard de La Mote", sauns plus cortoysement parler, et hier fust leu ledit brief en consistoire'.

[66] Ibid., p. 227.

[67] Ibid., p. 228.

[68] For Clement's authorisation see Zunzunegui, 1940–1, no. 16, p. 393. On Louis see Daumet, 1913.

Philip's ambassadors, commented that the future might reveal why Clement had taken such action. Would that it were to the honour of the English, whose love and prosperity the lord Pope 'inwardly did not desire'.[69] Even worse, Adam Murimuth reported English fears that Louis' expedition would be turned against them. The Prince, assisted by Philip VI and Clement, would invade the 'island of Great Britain', pretending that it was another of the Fortune Islands in rebellion against the Holy See.[70] This was not altogether far-fetched, for Edward III was well aware of the papacy's claim to possess all islands. John XXII had sent him a copy of Adrian IV's bull *Laudabiliter* (1155) by which the Pope had bestowed the 'island' of Ireland upon Henry II.[71] In 1342, almost certainly to insult the Pope, Edward himself had bestowed the Isle of Man on the Earl of Salisbury, granting him the title of king, despite the fact that the island had been a papal fief since 1219.[72]

In 1344 Anglo-papal relations were so tense that the discussions about papal provisions could not fail to be angry. One of the envoys, probably John Offord, Dean of Lincoln, described a heated session which took place in October 1344. Examining Edward's infringements of ecclesiastical liberties, the Pope warned that excommunication processes had already been prepared against him. Only the papal longing for peace had prevented their publication. Indeed, asserted Clement insincerely, if Philip had committed such atrocities he would have been excommunicated a long time ago.[73] In fact, Philip did later imitate Edward and infringe ecclesiastical liberties by confiscating all the goods, tithes, and ecclesiastical revenues of clergy not resident in France on 13 February 1347, which, among others, hit some of the cardinals. Although his actions offended the 'divine majesty', damaged the honour and status of the universal Church, and threatened Philip's good name and his salvation, there was no

---

[69] Adam Murimuth, *Continuatio Chronicarum*, pp. 242–3: 'Quare seu ad quem effectum hujusmodi fit creatio, nescitur adhuc, scietur autem postea; utinam ad honorem Anglicorum, quorum amorem vel prosperitatem idem dominus papa, ut creditur, intime non affectat'.

[70] Ibid., p. 163. For England's attitude to the papacy see Barnie, 1974, pp. 52–3.

[71] Theiner, *Mon. Hib.*, p. 201, no. 322: 'cum . . . Adrianus predecessor noster, sub certis modo et forma distinctis apertius in apostolicis literis indefactis . . . Henrico . . . dominium Hiberniae concessisset . . . tuae magnitudini mittimus inclusas': quoted by Weckmann, 1949, p. 61, n. 2; for discussion see pp. 48ff., and Watt, 1970, pp. 35–40.

[72] Geoffrey le Baker, *Chronicon*, p. 75. For confirmation of the island's status as a papal fief see *Liber Censuum*, xxix, letter of Reginald of Man to Honorius III.

[73] De Lettenhove, pp. 216–17.

question of excommunication. On the contrary, Clement's letter went on to recall, more in sorrow than in anger, his great affection for Philip and his kingdom.[74] This was a different attitude from that shown to Edward III in 1344. After his threat about excommunication, Clement moved on to a diatribe on the theme 'we are his superior, not he ours', during which he touched on the argument that England was a papal fief. He insisted on reading aloud all the correspondence between Innocent III and King John, which contained the terms on which John had surrendered England to the Holy See. The Dean commented a little unwisely that King John had had no right to prejudice his successors in this way, by surrendering England to the papacy and receiving it back as a fief, nor could he act contrary to the interests of the Crown. Clement lost his temper, *et incoepit aspere loqui* – and he began to speak roughly – wrote Offord.[75]

Against this inauspicious background it must have been difficult for the English to see Clement as a private and impartial mediator in their quarrel with France. Whatever his role, private or official, he was incapable of seeing things from any but the French viewpoint. French interests demanded that the conflict be seen in feudal terms; English interests that it should be seen in terms of Edward III's claim to the French throne, and according to Offord the conference opened with a clear statement of this intent:

Our petition concerns the kingdom and the crown of France, and we have no wish to ask for anything else, but we should like to listen to the ways for making peace which will be suggested to us, and to discuss them.[76]

This statement was to be repeated at intervals throughout the proceedings, and usually provoked the rejoinder from Clement that the English envoys had closed minds.[77] The French would not consent to the kingdom of France, nor the right to that kingdom, being included in any discussion or dispute. It therefore seemed best to Clement, 'that the petition concerning the kingdom should, as it were, sleep'.[78] Adam Murimuth's account of the proceedings is more pointed than Offord's. When the English nuncios petitioned for the kingdom of France and its crown, the Pope, 'taking the part of France, said . . .'[79] At one session with the cardinals, when the

---

[74] Baluze-Mollat, iv, p. 78.
[75] De Lettenhove, p. 218.
[76] Offord, *Journal des conférences*, p. 236.
[77] Ibid., pp. 237, 238, 256.
[78] Ibid., p. 237.
[79] Adam Murimuth, *Continuatio Chronicarum*, p. 247.

English tried again to raise the matter, they were reminded that war had erupted over Aquitaine long before Edward had assumed the title of King of France (in 1340).[80] The envoys replied that an embassy had been sent to advance Edward's hereditary claim before Philip's coronation.[81] Why, then, asked the cardinals, had Edward performed liege homage without mentioning his claim to the kingdom? This was a valid objection, and the English eagerly requested to be allowed to meet it 'publicly, wherever and whenever the Pope pleased'.[82] This reminded the cardinals of the papal veto on discussion of the subject, and they immediately clamped down on the English. Discussions about Aquitaine were no better because Pope and cardinals refused to countenance Philip's ceding it in full sovereignty to England. Even if Philip had agreed to it, the customs of the kingdom of France would not permit such an alienation, the cardinals explained.[83] It is interesting that they saw a sovereign ruler as subject to the 'customs' of his country, not to mention the possibility of the supreme pontiff, for whom they were acting, taking cognisance of them. It is even more interesting to recall that when Offord had made a similar point by suggesting that King John could not act contrary to the interests of the English Crown by granting England as a fief to the papacy, Clement had lost his temper. French customs were obviously far more binding than English. So much for the impartiality of the arbiter.

A great deal of bitterness had been generated by Clement's attitude, especially during 1344. It seems likely that it was in this year that Edward's appeal to a general council was drafted. Edward feared that in order to help France Clement would try to hinder his offensive by imposing canonical processes upon him for his previous adherence to Louis of Bavaria. He thought that Clement was not a fit judge of his conduct. He therefore offered, through his procurator, to submit to the correction of a general council of the Church. His procurator wrote as follows:

In these documents in the name of my lord, and since the Apostles should by right – *de iure* – be petitioned, I call upon and appeal to an audience of a

---

[80] *Journal des conférences*, p. 242.
[81] Ibid., p. 246. On the 1328 claim see Le Patourel, 1958, p. 175, n. 11; Déprez, 1902, pp. 35–6.
[82] *Journal des conférences*, p. 247.
[83] Ibid., pp. 243; 247–8. Pierre Roger himself at Vincennes had referred to the coronation oath which prevented the French kings from alienating the lands of the kingdom: sermon 15, pp. 456–7. See Martin, 1909, pp. 156–7; Riesenberg, 1956, p. 125.

general council of Holy Mother Church and to the Supreme Judge, who fails no one in His judgement, neither does He err.[84]

The implication was that the unerring judgement of God would be delivered by the council, which was tantamount to according it infallibility. Since the council appeared to be assuming an attribute which pertained especially to the Church in its corporate capacity, the inference was that the council, rather than the pope, represented the *Ecclesia universalis*. The whole thing was a blatant attempt to set the judgement of the council above that of the reigning pope, for it was not suggested that Clement was heretical and *ipso facto* deprived of his office. The somewhat ambiguous suggestion that an appeal to a general council constituted an appeal to the Apostles could be taken as a snub not only to the Pope, the successor of St Peter, but also to the bishops, the successors of the Apostles. Interestingly no suggestion was made as to who should summon the council. Many fourteenth-century writers thought that such a task should fall to the cardinals, even where appeals were made by lay rulers to the judgement of a council.[85] But of course in this case it would have been preposterous for a largely French College of Cardinals to have summoned a council to judge the pro-French sympathies of the Pope. Probably Edward himself would have summoned it, and the laity would have played a major role in its proceedings. In the event, the appeal was a piece of political bravado and was never published. But it stands as a graphic illustration of the lengths to which Clement's attitude could drive the English, quite apart from its interest as a foretaste of the later conciliar movement.

By the end of the conference it seems that even Clement himself recognised the difficulties his intransigence posed. Negotiations broke down after about three months' fruitless argument, not with the expected bang, but with a whimper. The English ambassadors needed to confer with Edward III before they could parley further, and the expectation was that they would later return to Avignon.[86] In writing to the English King the following year to try to persuade him to send his ambassadors back, Clement gave the significant promise that he would not be disposed more to one side than to the

---

[84] MS BL Harley, 4763, fol. 4r: 'Ad audienciam generalis concilii sancte matre [*sic*] Ecclesie iudicem que suppremum qui neminem fallit nec fallitur, in hiis scriptis nomine domini mei predicti provoco et appello, et apostolos quatenus de iure sunt petendi'.

[85] Tierney, 1955, pp. 77–80; Wilks, 1963a, p. 517, n. 3.

[86] *Journal des conférences*, p. 256.

other.[87] In 1348, still trying, the Pope wrote in the astonishing terms of *omnino partialitate cessante* – ceasing entirely from partiality.[88] It is extraordinary that an 'impartial' judge should have published such an overt admission of his bias.

One of the most damaging ways in which Clement's bias appeared was in the imposition of truces. There was a long history of discussion on the question of whether the pope could impose truces on warring kings, as evidenced, for example, in the dispute between Philip the Fair and Edward I. Clement obviously agreed with Innocent III on his capacity to do this. The English thought otherwise. The anonymous author of a memorandum on Edward's claim to the French throne was of the opinion that since war was a temporal affair, and the Pope had no jurisdiction in such matters, he had no right to impose truces.[89] This was written after the Truce of Malestroit. The Truce of Calais occasioned more criticism. Commenting on a somewhat obscure poem of John of Bridlington, John Erghome wrote of how the Pope had tried to deceive Edward in the negotiations before Calais fell, but the King had not been taken in by his documents. They were just another illustration that Clement 'always, inasmuch as he was able, was with the French against the English'.[90] Commenting on the truce which followed, another poet explained that in the Cornish language the word 'truce' meant 'sorrow', and this was exactly what it meant to the English, who felt that the agreement forced upon them by the Pope was an unjustified restraint upon Edward at the height of his triumphs.[91]

There were other practical manifestations of Clement's bias. The marriage alliances he tried to arrange for France were a means of securing allies for her, or at least of neutralising enemies. After the

---

[87] Déprez, no. 1844: 'non dirigendo, quoad hoc, affectum nostrum ad unam partem plus quam aliam, sed librando dumtaxat stateram veritatis et justitie, perquirere, tractare ac prosequi studebimus'.

[88] Ibid., no. 3742. See also no. 3812.

[89] Anon, *Mémoire sur les prétentions d'Edouard III à la couronne de France (1344)*, p. 263: 'Item cum dominus papa in temporalibus judicare non debeat, videtur quod, cum bellum licitum per principem sit indictum pro recuperatione juris sui temporalis, papa non potest treugas indicere'.

[90] John Erghome [?], 'Commentary on the *Vaticinium* of John of Bridlington', p. 164: 'Secundo ostendit auctor quod papa circa illud tempus voluit decepisse regem, cujus documentis rex non confidit. Pro quo est notandum quod papa Clemens semper in quantum potuit fuit cum Gallicis contra Anglicos, et induxit regem in quantum potuit per litteras et nuncios quod dimitteret bellum suum et vendicationem regni Franciae, in quo nullum jus habuit, nec justitiam . . .' On the events leading to the fall of Calais see Fowler, 1969, pp. 39–111.

[91] Anon, *On the Truce of 1347*, p. 57: 'Lingua Cornubica designat treuga dolores'.

death of Charles IV's wife in 1348 Clement suggested that he should marry a French princess.[92] John of Normandy was already married to Charles's sister. Clement also arranged a Franco-Castilian marriage alliance in order to outwit Edward III.[93] The Pope's skill in detaching the Flemings from their English alliance has long been recognised.[94] Then there were the considerable sums of money lent by both Pope and cardinals to Philip. Between 26 November 1345 and the end of February 1350 Clement and his family lent Philip 592,000 gold florins and 5,000 *écus*.[95] Loans from the Pope himself almost invariably coincided with a fresh burst of activity in the war.[96] There was also the question of tenths. Early in his pontificate Clement granted Philip *pro defensione regni*, for the defence of the kingdom, the tenths originally collected for the crusade under John XXII,[97] the very ones which he, as Pierre Roger, had failed to persuade Benedict XII to make over to Philip. This was done notwithstanding the fact that as Pierre Roger he had taken a solemn oath on Philip's behalf that the money would never be used for any purpose other than the crusade.[98] Perhaps Clement saw the conflict as the equivalent of holy war. In November 1344, while the conference of Avignon was in session, the Pope granted Philip a tenth for two years.[99] When Edward requested a similar grant in 1348, it was refused.[100]

Traditionally the only war of which the papacy could approve was the crusade, the holy war waged in defence of the universality of the Faith. Clement was determined to start a crusade, primarily to halt the Turkish advance in the Eastern Mediterranean. Holy war should have taken precedence over all other wars. The Pope accordingly pointed out to Edward III that holy wars were the only fitting ones for Christian kings and princes to pursue,[101] and he repeatedly urged him to make peace with Philip so that he might be free to go on the crusade.[102] Edward, for his part, took a perverse delight in reminding Clement at inopportune moments of how much he wanted peace so that he could go on the crusade. His nuncio did so on the breakdown of the negotiations at Avignon in 1344,[103] and Edward

[92] *MGH Const.*, viii, no. 652, p. 657.
[93] Mollat, 1953, col. 1146; Fowler, 1969, p. 92.
[94] Lucas, 1929, pp. 474–80.
[95] Faucon, 1879, p. 571.
[96] Ibid.
[97] Déprez, no. 914.
[98] Pierre Roger, sermon 2, Ste-G. 240, fols. 307r–v. On the tenths see Tyermann, 1985, p. 49.
[99] Déprez, no. 1250.
[100] Ibid., no. 3812.
[101] Ibid., no. 1582.
[102] Ibid., nos. 1326, 1462, 1590, 1844.
[103] *Journal des conférences*, p. 255.

repeated this sentiment in the defiant letter by which he informed Clement that he no longer considered himself bound by truces between the Valois and himself because of Philip's violation of past agreements.[104] Clement, however, did not believe him, and warned him that his pretence both at peace negotiations and about his intentions to crusade would earn him multiple damnation.[105] The Pope's attitude to Philip's crusading was different. Apart from the grant of 'crusading' tenths, Clement ordered that the crusading indulgences granted to other areas of Christendom should not run in France, by which he ensured that the best soldiers would remain to defend their fatherland.[106] Ultimately defence of France seemed to supersede even that of the universal Church. Clement never seems to have wavered in the conviction he had first expressed as Pierre Roger that France was engaged in a purely defensive, and therefore just, war. After Crécy, he wrote to Queen Joan in terms which suggested that her defeated husband had been the hero of the hour, praying God to 'remove altogether the harm from the blessed kingdom of France'.[107] But the most overt expression of his true feelings occurred in the letter of sympathy he wrote to the Duchess of Normandy on the death of her father, John of Bohemia, at the battle. John's last hours had been spent in a just war – *in iusto bello* – defending the kingdom of France.[108] He could hardly have been more explicit.

Clement's views had altered not a whit since he had delivered his *collatio* in 1338. Pinpointing the problem, he admitted that there could be no injuries to France, the country of his origin, which did not injure the Pope himself.[109] His deep personal patriotism found official expression in his policy on the canonisation of saints. He canonised the Breton priest St Yves at the request of Charles of Blois, Duke of Brittany, who not only went personally to Avignon to petition Clement about it, but also contributed to the cost of the

---

104 Rymer, *Foedera*, v, p. 453.
105 Déprez, no. 1844, pp. 21–2: 'Que quidem littere effectualiter continebant quod . . . ut posses sicut affectabas, in passagio transmarino nostri obsequiis intendere redemptoris. Ipse tamen, te per verba protrahens, nichil facere in effectu; sed pendentibus simulatis tractatibus, tibi procuraverat multa dampna'.
106 Déprez, no. 1704.
107 Déprez, no. 2790: 'plenius intellecto, qualiter rex ipse tanquam princeps magnanimus, fortis, constans et strenuus, paucis secum in conflictu remanentibus . . . laudabiliter et victoriose se gessit'; ibid: 'ut ipse, qui omnia . . . disponit et regit, noxia cuncta de regno Francie benedicto submoveat . . .'
108 Klicman, no. 721, p. 431.
109 Déprez, no. 2760.

proceedings. Charles was closely related to the Valois and to the Angevins.[110] In addition, Clement started the canonisation processes for Elzéar of Sabran (d. 1323) in December 1351. He had been the Count of Ariano and the associate of King Robert. He and his virgin wife, Dauphine, had divided their time between Provence and southern Italy.[111] The third saint about whom Clement legislated was Robert of Chaise-Dieu, the founder of his own abbey. He was already canonised, but Clement authorised the translation of his body to a new tomb (which was connected with the Pope's rebuilding of the church) and declared that the translation should be kept as an official festival.[112] He did much to promote the cult of St Robert and to encourage pilgrims to visit his tomb. It was in this connection that he commissioned Matteo Giovannetti to paint frescoes depicting scenes from the Saint's life on the walls of the church.[113] Clement's interest in the blessed seems to have had a distinctly personal, political, and local bias. The same attitude is evident in the dedication of his chapel at Avignon to his local Saint, St Martial, Bishop of Limoges,[114] and in the sermon he preached eulogising St Louis, Bishop of Toulouse, who happened to be Philip VI's uncle.[115]

In the last resort Clement could not separate the private person from the office of pope, and so he could not cease altogether from partiality. To that extent William of Ockham was correct. But on the basis that it is quite possible to favour one side and to desire peace simultaneously Clement's reputation as a lover of peace can be sustained. Conrad of Megenberg's *via media* was ultimately the right one: Clement as pope was peaceloving; as a Frenchman he was unashamedly partial.

[110] Vauchez, 1981, p. 93; Pocquet du Haut-Jussé, p. 290.
[111] Vauchez, p. 94.
[112] Van der Straeten, 1964, pp. 35–56. For Clement's bull see Déprez, no. 5064.
[113] Van der Straeten, 1964, pp. 40–1.
[114] See above, p. 73.
[115] See above, p. 126, n. 21.

Chapter 7

REX ROMANORUM:
THE WAY OF ADJUSTMENT

One of the greatest problems facing Clement VI in 1342 – arguably *the* greatest – was that of the Empire. There had been no papally approved emperor or king of the Romans (the office accorded to the emperor-elect before his coronation by the pope in Rome) since the death of Henry VII on 24 August 1313, nearly thirty years before. The pope, however, always needed an emperor or king of the Romans because he needed a supremely powerful lay ruler who would act as the defender of the Church – the *defensor Ecclesiae*, who would, in effect, perform the purely physical tasks which the supreme pontiff did not care to perform himself, especially those which involved the shedding of blood on the battlefield. Given this role, the emperor was expected to act as an obedient and dependent son to the pope.

Since the 'translation' of the Empire from Byzantium to the West, effected by the pope's crowning of Charlemagne in Rome on Christmas Day 800, the papacy had claimed to appoint and control the emperor and to invest him with his universal powers through coronation. By the fourteenth century, however, due to the growth of the lay spirit and nationalism, there was fierce opposition to the papal conception of emperorship. On the one hand, members of the Imperial College of Electors claimed that they empowered the king of the Romans solely through election, and that he had no need of papal approval, or even coronation, before starting to administer the Empire. On the other, there was a growing conviction, based on the historical precedents of ancient Rome, that the only people who could appoint the emperor were the citizens of Rome itself. This idea had been vividly enacted in the coronation of Louis of Bavaria as emperor in Rome in 1328 at the hands of the Roman people. During Clement's pontificate Cola di Rienzo was to draw on the same idea.

Louis of Bavaria was a living mockery of papal ideology. Elected in 1314 in opposition to Frederick the Handsome, Duke of Austria and head of the house of Habsburg, Louis had never been granted papal approval as king of the Romans, and was therefore regarded as a usurper. He had gathered a circle of provocative thinkers round him of the stature of Marsilius of Padua, John of Jandun, and William of Ockham, many of whom were associated with the breakaway wing of the Franciscan Order, the Spirituals. Louis' actions in Rome implemented some of their more advanced ideas. Not only did he have himself crowned emperor by the Romans, who represented all Christians, but he then deposed John XXII for heresy and for his permanent absence from Rome, appointing the Spiritual Franciscan Peter of Corbara as Nicholas V in his stead. Papal processes were imposed on the Bavarian, but a long series of embassies to the curia (one in which Pierre Roger himself took part) failed to effect his reconciliation.[1] In 1342 his existence still caused constant political unrest and divided loyalties in Germany, where he commanded a wide measure of support. Moreover, spiritual life was often frozen by repeated interdicts and excommunications. Clement VI's desire for a *defensor Ecclesiae* was partly dictated by the need for someone who would dislodge Louis for him.

By the fourteenth century suitable candidates for the imperial office were a rarity, for few, if any, lay rulers were prepared to play the part of the pope's obedient son. Clement's relationship with Philip VI, for example, cannot have been easy, for Clement must subconsciously have been aware that as Pierre Roger he had for years been the servant rather than the master of the French king. As pope he obviously found it difficult to reverse these roles, and this alone would have deterred him from selecting Philip as his candidate. His relationship with Charles, Margrave of Moravia, however, had been the seemingly ideal one of teacher to pupil. In his autobiography, thought to have been completed about 1350, Charles told of the grace with which he had been infused through listening to Pierre Roger preach, and how Pierre thereafter cherished him 'lovingly, and as a father', often instructing him in Holy Scripture.[2] Years later, in 1340, the Margrave visited Benedict XII on behalf of his father, John of Bohemia. He was received into the 'Cardinal of Rouen's'

---

[1] On Louis of Bavaria and the papacy see Müller, 1879–80; Offler, 1956a; Schwöbel, 1968; Schütz, 1973. For Pierre Roger's embassy of 1337 see Déprez, 1902, p. 147, n. 3. For Marsilius of Padua and John of Jandun as followers of Louis see Schmugge, 1966, pp. 30–8.
[2] *Vita Caroli*, ch. 3, p. 86.

house where, in the course of conversation, Pierre Roger suddenly prophesied that Charles would be *rex Romanorum*, king of the Romans, to which Charles rejoined, 'Before this you will be pope'.[3] These two somewhat unexpected truths were indeed 'prologues to the swelling act of the imperial theme', for in 1346 Clement was to engineer the election of Charles as *rex Romanorum* in opposition to Louis of Bavaria.

The apparent willingness of Charles of Moravia to agree to the conditions Clement imposed in return for his approval as king earned him the derision of contemporaries. Ockham reported on his reputation as the priests' king or mercenary – *regem clericorum seu stipendiarum ipsorum*.[4] Later historians accused him of devotion to his own kingdom of Bohemia at the expense of the Empire, echoing the famous verdict of Maximilian I that he was the 'father of Bohemia, arch-stepfather of the Empire'. Now, however, the view is emerging that Charles, far from being the pope's puppet, was a shrewd diplomat, a fitting match for the papacy, and that he did much to enhance the rights of the Empire.[5]

The Pope's difficulty in finding a suitable man to be emperor was compounded by a theoretical problem: by the fourteenth century the traditional conception of universal Roman emperorship was outmoded. The most vulnerable point in the theory of papal monarchy had always been that however exalted the pope's claims to universal authority, in practice he had no physical means of implementing them, not, that is, unless he could appoint a lay ruler to do this for him. Traditionally the emperor was regarded by the pope as his own specially appointed secular counterpart, who would use his physical *potestas*, or executive power, at the command of papal *auctoritas*. This traditional Roman distinction between authority and executive power had been applied to priesthood and laity respectively by Gelasius I in the fifth century, but it was still operative in the fourteenth. The salient point, one often misconstrued by later writers, was that both authority and power had to be exercised within the same society, for the executive power granted to the laity was always subject to the commands of the priesthood. This led to

---

[3] Ibid., ch. 14, p. 174.
[4] William of Ockham, *De Electione Karoli IV*, ch. 5, p. 358.
[5] For a summary of older views see Walsh, 1924, p. 23; Schneider, 1973. The most detailed work on the earlier part of Charles's reign is still Werunsky, 1880–92. The six-hundredth anniversary of the death of Charles IV in 1978 gave rise to a great deal of literature: for reviews see Walsh, 1980; Moraw, 1982. Of that literature see especially, Patze, ed., 1978; Seibt, 1978; Seibt, ed., 1978; Frey, 1978.

the important theoretical corollary that both aspects of that one society, the spiritual and the secular, were of the same territorial extent: Church and Empire were both universal. But by the fourteenth century the gap between theory and practice was vast. The *Ecclesia* itself never had in practice been universal: its universality was just a theoretical potentiality, a myth subscribed to by the popes and their supporting publicists and canonists. The *imperium*, the Empire, also had never really been universal in practice, any more than it had ever really coincided with the physical boundaries of Christendom. By the fourteenth century, such a coincidence was an increasingly remote possibility, given the growth of powerful, independent, sovereign states within the boundaries of the Christian society. Their rulers were unlikely to be obedient to the emperor, even if there were one.

What then could Clement do? There seemed to be three avenues open to him. The first was to do nothing about appointing an emperor. The second was to appoint and empower an emperor, assuming he could find one, using all the traditional ceremony and formulae. The third was the 'way of adjustment' by which he could strive to find some alternative solution, suited to fourteenth-century conditions, while still leaving the traditional theory seemingly intact. It was this avenue which Clement was to choose.

The first solution was dangerous, for without a visible ruler to exercise power over the *imperium* and to keep the concept of it alive, people might think that it had vanished. True, the pope himself claimed to be the true emperor, the *verus imperator*, and acted in certain matters during an imperial vacancy. Clement justified this on the basis that each thing returned to its origin. Imperial power was like the river described in Ecclesiastes, i. 7, which returned to its source only to flow outward again. This was why the pope acted as emperor during an imperial vacancy,[6] and there are examples of Clement doing so.[7] Such action was well founded in canon law and had the support of papal publicists.[8] Nevertheless, imperial power

---

[6] Clement VI, sermon 40, pp. 156–7.

[7] *MGH Const.*, viii, no. 35, p. 56; Riezler, nos. 2177a–d, pp. 787–8; Werunsky, no. 15, pp. 8–9; no. 43, p. 25; no. 90, p. 40; Déprez, no. 1013.

[8] *Clem.*, II, xi, 2, *Pastoralis cura*: 'nos tam ex superioritate, quam ad imperium non est dubium nos habere, quam ex potestate, in qua vacante imperatori succedimus'. Cf. Innocent IV, *ad Decretales*, II, ii, 9, fol. 82v: 'et inde est, quod in iure quod ab Ecclesia Romana tenet, succedit Papa imperio vacante'. See also Conrad of Megenberg, *Yconomica*, ii, 2, ch. 5, p. 49; Galvaneus Flamma, *Chronica Galvagnana*, ch. 189, pp. 187–8. For further discussion see Baethgen, 1920.

was not exercised as obviously as when there was an emperor. Clearly the Pope could not allow the *imperium*, as the secular aspect of the *Ecclesia*, to fade. It would mean that the already dubious identity of the two would be broken, and the *Ecclesia* would no longer be seen as an all-embracing community encompassing both temporal and spiritual affairs. Separation between the two aspects would in theory deprive the pope of his omnicompetence, and would limit the exercise of his authority to spiritual affairs alone.

The second solution was no better. To appoint an emperor and invest him with universal powers in the traditional way in the fourteenth century was totally unrealistic, even in theory, because the papacy itself had unwittingly damaged the concept of the universality of the Empire. It had failed to maintain the role of its secular counterpart as *dominus mundi*, lord of the world. The root of the trouble lay in two controversial, and ambiguous, pronouncements. The first of these, Innocent III's *Per Venerabilem*, contained the controversial words 'the king of France acknowledges no superior in temporal affairs', which appeared to deny the universal scope of the emperor's powers.[9] Unhappily the Pope did not make it clear that the words were merely a quotation from a letter written to him by the French King Philip II. Nor did he point out that since there was no crowned emperor at the time there was in practice no temporal superior other than the Pope to whom the King of France could turn when necessary. Innocent had intended neither a theoretical declaration that France was outside the territorial boundaries of the Empire, nor a *de facto* recognition of her manifest independence.

Even more damaging was Clement V's bull *Pastoralis cura* (1313),[10] which also appeared to enshrine the principle that the Empire had territorial limitations, and to sanction the territorial independence of the national sovereign rulers. During his Italian expedition of 1312 the Emperor Henry VII had cited Robert of Sicily–Naples on a charge of *lèse majesté*, for having organised resistance to him. The charge was framed on the basis that imperial power was *de iure* universal, and that Sicily was therefore subject to it. Sicily, however, was one of the Pope's *propria regna*, that is, an area administered directly by the pope in whatever way he chose,

---

[9] *Decretales*, IV, xvii, 13. For discussion see Tierney, 1962; Walther, 1976, pp. 14–19; 66ff.

[10] *MGH Const.*, iv, 1, no. 1166 [*Clem.*, II, xi, 2]. On the significance of the decree and the circumstances of its promulgation see Bowsky, 1960, pp. 178–92; Ullmann, 1965, pp. 195–9.

and exempted from the emperor's direct jurisdiction. This did not mean that such lands were not part of the universal *Ecclesia-imperium*, merely that the pope's administrative power over them was exercised differently. In this case, Robert held Sicily as a fief of the papacy. When he quite properly referred the matter to Clement V, the Pope responded with *Pastoralis cura*, in which he declared that Sicily was *extra districtum imperii*, outside the jurisdictional area of the Empire, and thus it did not pertain to the Emperor to judge King Robert.

This enactment had profound implications, perhaps more so than Clement V had intended. It is quite possible that he had meant to convey no more than the point that Sicily was outside the area of the Emperor's jurisdiction because it was a papal fief, rather than that it was outside the territorial boundaries of the *imperium*. This was not the interpretation generally put upon it. *Pastoralis cura* appeared to be an application of Roman law principles of jurisdiction, by which the territorial limits of a ruler's realm became the limits within which his law could be enforced. Clement V could thus be seen as limiting the area of imperial jurisdiction to the area where the emperor's power was effective, by the fourteenth century a relatively small one.

Reaction to this blunder was swift. By his edict *Ad Reprimendum* (1312), Henry VII hastened to reassert the universality of the Empire and the principle that the emperor could cite his subjects from anywhere.[11] During the reign of Clement VI this opinion appeared to be endorsed by Johannes Gaufredi, his ex-pupil. After asserting the universal jurisdiction of Christ, and therefore of His vicar, St Peter, John declared that the emperor was immediate lord of the whole world after Christ and His vicar. Innocent III's decretal *Per Venerabilem* was summarily dismissed as a *de facto* statement, and John concluded that the emperor was able to cite anyone to any part of the Empire.[12] On the other hand, the contemporary canonist Johannes Andreae, in glossing the words *districtum imperii*, was

---

[11] *MGH Const.*, iv, 2, no. 929, p. 965 [*Ad Reprimendum*]; see also no. 801, p. 802.

[12] Johannes Gaufredi, *Collectarius*, fol. 154r: 'Sed nulli est dubium quin Christus et Petrus ut eius vicarius fuerint domini universales totius mundi omnemque per consequens iurisdictionem habuerunt . . . et uniformiter eamque exercere in quacunque parte mundi potuerunt. Ergo et nunc ipsa redeunte ad ipsos quorum est sicut superioris domini ut est dictum. Et hoc sic confirmatur certum est quod de iure imperator in temporalibus est dominus immediatus post Christum, sicut et eius vicarius totius mundi . . . Nec obstat c. *per venerabilem* . . . cum dicit non recognoscit quasi de facto, ergo de iure secus. Nec dubitat aliquis quin de iure imperator posset trahere quemcunque ad quamcunque partem imperii sicut et rex ad quamlibet partem regni . . .'

struck by the inconsistency of the title *dominus mundi* and the evident reality of the situation, now sanctioned by Clement V, which denied him universal jurisdiction.[13]

Clement VI was sufficiently honest to admit publicly the problem of *Pastoralis cura*. Preaching in consistory he treated his audience to an unfamiliar rendering of Daniel's interpretation of Nebuchadnezzar's dream: the image fashioned of gold, silver, brass, iron, and clay. Instead of identifying the metals with the four earthly kingdoms of the Assyrians, the Medo-Persians, the Greeks, and the Romans, as was customary, Clement concentrated on the iron-and-clay feet of the image. As Daniel himself had explained, the fourth kingdom would be divided, and one part of it would be strong and the other brittle: and the Pope added ominously, just as we see literally today.[14] A few lines later he tackled the problem of the territorial extent of the *imperium*. It was, he announced, widely spread – indeed, no other temporal kingdom had limits so extensive.[15] But his use of the word 'limits' was a prelude to his next remark. According to the Roman lawyers, he explained, the emperor's *principatus* was unlimited, and he possessed all lands: he was the *dominus mundi*. 'But today, according to canon law, his *principatus* is limited', he admitted, and then referred specifically to *Pastoralis cura*.[16]

After this shattering admission Clement was left to pick up the pieces. But what was there left for him to do? There was no sense in appointing an emperor whose *imperium* would not be universal. To maintain the universality of the *Ecclesia* but to allow that of the *imperium* to diminish would be to deprive himself of his means of wielding administrative power over wide areas. Clearly the second

---

[13] Johannes Andreae, *Glossa Ordinaria ad Clem.*, II, xi, 2, col. 914: '*Districtum imperii.* Per hanc litteram et sequentes patet quod Imperator non distringit totum orbem, licet dicatur dominus mundi . . .'

[14] Clement VI, sermon 40, pp. 150–1. Cf. Daniel ii, 41–2. There is disagreement on whether the fourth kingdom should be identified with the Greek or the Roman Empire. Rowley, 1935, pp. 70ff. favours the 'Greek' view, whereas Young, 1949, pp. 275–9 favours the 'Roman'. For its use to illustrate the translation theory see Goez, 1958, pp. 366–77, and in general Southern, 1973, and Piaia, 1980.

[15] Clement VI, sermon 40, p. 151: 'Iste status [scil. imperatoris] est spatiose dilatatus. Nullum enim aliud regnum temporale est, quod non paucioribus limitibus coherceatur et quod habeat limites ita magnos'.

[16] Ibid.: 'Unde secundum legistas principatus eius est super omnem terram, et omnis [*sic*] terra est possessio eius, et ipse est dominus mundi; unde non habet ipse principatum limitatum, sed illimitatum secundum eos. Sed hodie secundum iura canonica principatus suus etiam limitatus est, sicut apparet *Extra de sent. et re iudic.* c. 'pastoralis' in Clem.'.

solution to the imperial problem would not work. The only one left was the 'way of adjustment', by which Clement tried to use that fragment of the theory of lay rulership which was undamaged, namely the kingship of the Romans. He tried to magnify the office of *rex Romanorum* at the expense of emperorship. In so doing he was adapting himself to a prevailing tendency, pandering to a current fashion for sovereign kingship. Clement chose to do this, firstly, by manipulating the election of an acceptable candidate by the German princes, and then, this much achieved, by using the ceremony of papal approbation, and in particular the *collatio* he preached, to demonstrate that he 'created' and empowered the king of the Romans.[17] He spared no efforts to underline the constitutive nature of the ceremony, and in so doing answered the challenge both of hostile publicists and of all those people who considered that they themselves empowered the king, in particular the electors and the Archbishop of Cologne.

Clement subscribed to the tradition that Gregory V had founded the Imperial College of Electors in the late tenth century,[18] which gave him justification, if he needed any, for controlling it. As Alvarus Pelagius had argued, imperial power came from papal power precisely because pope and *Ecclesia* had first empowered the electors.[19] When Charles was elected unanimously on 11 July 1346 at Rhense it was the reward of four years of intense papal diplomacy. Moreover, the presence of papal legates *a latere* confirmed Clement's interest in the affair.[20] Negotiations had been pursued with Charles and John of Bohemia, with Louis of Bavaria and his procurators, and with the electors. Agreements had been made and unmade, and much money had changed hands as support was purchased for Charles.[21] Archbishop Baldwin of Trier, the head of the Luxemburg house, and therefore a key figure, gave particular trouble by keeping

---

[17] For an analysis of the *collatio* see Patze, 1978, although he does not cover Clement's political theory. On the papal approbation theory see Feine, 1938. On the pope's right to 'create' the emperor see Ullmann, 1978, no. 2, pp. 89–108; Folz, 1969, pp. 75–89.

[18] Clement VI, sermon 40, p. 156. For other contemporary examples see Wilks, 1963a, pp. 247–8.

[19] Alvarus Pelagius, *De Planctu Ecclesiae*, bk i, ch. 37, p. 52. Cf. William of Sarzano, *De Potestate Summi Pontificis*, pp. 1063, 1068.

[20] Francis of Prague, *Cronica*, p. 442.

[21] See, for example, Matthew of Nuremberg, *Chronica*, ch. 71, p. 200; Henry of Herford, *Liber de rebus memorabilioribus*, p. 275. See also *MGH Const.* viii, nos. 55–8, pp. 78–88. For discussion see Werunsky, 1880, i, pp. 258ff.; Stengel, 1930, pp. 186–92; Speváček, 1971.

his options open.[22] His excommunication for consorting with Louis was lifted in November 1342.[23] But, as Stengel showed in 1930, he amended the draft of the procuration documents for his reconciliation with the papacy so as to leave the way open for a renewal of his relationship with Louis.[24] Despite this, Clement wrote to him in August 1343 stating that he wished to place a suitable man at the head of the *imperium*.[25] Even after this Baldwin produced an anti-papal commentary on a set of conditions Clement had tried to impose on Louis for his reconciliation in August 1344.[26] In this, Baldwin denied the pope's right to approve the imperial candidate.

During the four years, both John and Charles had visited Avignon. Charles stayed with Clement personally in 1344 and often engaged in secret discussions.[27] One result of these was the elevation of Prague to the status of an archbishopric.[28] On 7 April 1346 Clement deposed Henry of Virneberg, Archbishop of Mainz, for adhering to Louis, so depriving him of his electoral rights, and promoted the more pliable Gerlach of Nassau, appropriately the grandson of a *rex Romanorum*.[29] A fortnight later Charles and John were at Avignon, where Charles swore to abide by the harsh conditions Clement demanded of him as a *quid pro quo* for his election, one of which was to wage war on Louis.[30] The Pope was then in a position to write to the electors suggesting, though not ordering, the election of Charles.[31]

If Baldwin of Trier could keep his options open, so could Clement, for he was by no means certain of success, nor entirely confident of the material with which he had to work. As late as February 1344 Clement had to extract a renewed oath against Louis from John of Bohemia in his own and his son's name. Embarrassingly, Charles was then negotiating with Louis at Cheb, where he received a curt

---

[22] On Baldwin of Trier see Stengel, 1930 and 1960; Spevácek, 1971; Schubert, 1985, where further literature is given.

[23] Sauerland, no. 87, pp. 38–43.

[24] Stengel, 1930, pp. 186–92.

[25] Raynaldus, vi, ch. 59, pp. 329–30.

[26] Stengel, ii, no. 773, pp. 495–9.

[27] Henry of Diessenhoven, *Chronica*, p. 44. See also Beneš of Weitmil, *Cronica Ecclesie Pragensis*, p. 510.

[28] Klicman, no. 363, pp. 209–11.

[29] *MGH Const.*, viii, nos. 3, 4, pp. 4–6. Gerlach was the son of Count Gerlach of Nassau, who was the son of Adolf of Nassau, elected in 1292 to the kingship of the Romans.

[30] *MGH Const.*, viii, nos. 9–13, pp. 11–27 (for pre-election promises); and nos. 93–7, pp. 128–35 (for renewal before confirmation).

[31] Ibid., no. 19, pp. 40–1.

paternal order to desist.[32] Both John and Baldwin of Trier were still negotiating with Louis as late as March 1346.[33]

Meanwhile a series of embassies was dispatched to Clement by Louis to try to effect his reconciliation and his appointment as *rex Romanorum*. The procuration documents issued by him to his ambassadors were framed on the basis of notarial instruments written by papal officials and thus reflect the Pope's demands, as Offler has shown.[34] Louis, however, safeguarded his interests by a loophole clause empowering his procurators to alter the documents as necessary, and his true opinions were contained in a set of clandestine and contradictory instructions, which reveal his total lack of penitence.[35] Offler has demonstrated that until 1344 the procuration documents made provision for Louis' acceptance as *rex Romanorum*.[36] In support of this, in a *collatio* preached before John of Bohemia on 16 January 1344, Clement made a fleeting comparison of himself to Samuel after the people of Israel had requested him to give them a king – a subtle hint that he was still bearing Louis in mind as a possible king, and one probably delivered for John of Bohemia's benefit.[37] It seems likely that Clement was keeping John and Charles in suspense, for in a letter written to his nuncios at Avignon in November 1345, John was still unsure of his son's prospects. He urged them to let him know the Pope's intention about the destruction of the Bavarian as soon as possible. There was no more suitable and convenient way of destroying his power than the election of John's first-born son to the kingship of the Romans, he went on to point out.[38] At the time the Luxemburgers were diplomatically isolated, being opposed by a Polish-Wittelsbach-Hungarian coa-

---

[32] Beneš of Weitmil, *Cronica*, p. 510.

[33] *Vita Caroli*, ch. 19, p. 194.

[34] Offler, 1951, pp. 464–5. Offler's view seems preferable to that of Schwöbel, 1968: see Offler's review in *Erasmus*, XXI (1969), cols. 566–7.

[35] Offler, 1951, pp. 463, n. 3; 464, 479. A good example of such instructions is edited by Riezler, *Die literarischen Widersacher*, pp. 332–3. They refer to the second embassy to Clement of April 1344.

[36] Offler, 1951, p. 481, n. 2. See also Schwöbel, pp. 143–6. The conditions Clement sought to impose on Louis were similar to those he was to impose on Charles in 1346. Cf. the summaries of his demands of autumn 1343, Schwöbel, pp. 110–39, with Riezler, no. 2167, pp. 780–4, and cf. Gewold, *Defensio Ludovici IV*, pp. 173–8, with *MGH Const.*, viii, nos. 9–11, pp. 11–23.

[37] Clement VI, sermon 34, Ste-G. 240, fols. 359r–v: 'Idcirco sicut Samuel de preceptis Domini, qui filiis Israhel petentibus sibi dari regem, antequam concedetur, primo eis predixit, et contestatus est ius regni, I Reg. viii°; sic nos vobis predicere volumus ut attendatis et videatis quid offeratis . . .'

[38] *MGH Const.*, viii, no. 1, pp. 1–2.

lition.[39] John was even then discussing the renewal of a truce with the Wittelsbachs, and would probably have renewed it if Clement had not been prepared to promote Charles. It was largely due to Clement's efforts that when the Bohemians' truce with Poland also expired a state of cold war rather than open conflict ensued.[40] That John continued to parley with the Wittelsbachs until March may be an indication that Clement had overplayed his hand, thus frightening the Luxemburgers into the arms of the Bavarian. Alternatively, it could be simply that John too knew how to keep his options open. Nevertheless, on 13 April 1346 John and Charles were at Avignon to hear Clement publish his final processes against Louis,[41] and preach his vituperative piece on the theme *Hereticum hominem* against him.[42] The Pope could not resist one last game. He quoted two passages from letters of Ambrose to the Emperor Valentinian II. The first reads: 'What could be more honourable to the emperor than to be called a son of the *Ecclesia*? An emperor is within the Church and not above it. The good emperor seeks the help of the Church: he does not refute it'.[43] (Clement was to quote the same passage to Charles only seven months later.)[44] The second one, neatly adapted, reads: 'Do not trouble yourself, Emperor, to think that you have any imperial rights in divine matters. But if you wish to be emperor for a long time, be subject and obedient to Christ and his vicar'.[45] The final words were added by the Pope, and the quotation was not acknowledged. It is ironic to find Clement advising Louis on how to be a good emperor at this stage. It seems likely that it was meant as a warning to the Luxemburgers that Clement could still promote Louis as *rex Romanorum* if he wished.

The election of Charles was a diplomatic triumph for Clement.

---

[39] Ibid., pp. 1–2. On the anti-Bohemian coalition see Werunsky, 1880, i, pp. 388–9; Knoll, 1972, pp. 178–90, esp. p. 186.

[40] See Theiner, *Mon. Pol.*, nos. 632–3. For Clement's peacemaking efforts see Knoll, pp. 188–90.

[41] Raynaldus, vi, chs. 3–8, pp. 390–2.

[42] Clement VI, sermon 24, Ste-G. 240, fols. 374v–80r.

[43] Ibid., fol. 376v: 'Unde et Ambrosius in quadam epistola ad Valentinianum Imperatorem dicit: "Quid honorificentius Imperatori esse potest, quam ut filius Ecclesie esse dicatur?" [ep. 21, *Sermo contra Auxentium*, par. 36=*PL*, 16, 1018. Clement's rendering is a free one.] Et sic: "Imperator enim intra Ecclesiam et non supra Ecclesiam est. Bonus enim Imperator querit auxilium Ecclesie non refutat"'.

[44] Clement VI, sermon 40, p. 160.

[45] Sermon 24, Ste-G. 240, fol. 376v: 'Noli gravare, Imperator, ut putes te in ea que divina sunt imperiale aliquod ius habere. [Cf. ep. 20, par. 19=*PL*, 16, 999]. Sed si vis diu Imperator esse, Christo et eius vicario subditus et obediens esto'.

Nevertheless, there had been a danger that the princes would ignore the Pope's wishes and elect someone unsuitable. To forestall this, the Pope also controlled the choice of candidate by insisting that he should petition the Holy See for approval of his election, and also by demanding stringent oaths of obedience in return for granting such approval. If the elect refused to take the oaths, then he was plainly unfit for office. In Charles's case he would never have been elected, since the oaths had to be taken before his election, and then renewed before its confirmation. Clement also scrutinised his personal qualities during the 'approbation' sermon,[46] again to give himself a chance to reject the candidate in the event of the election plan misfiring. If this had happened, or indeed if the electors had failed to elect within the statutory time, then the papacy could, as in the case of an episcopal election, have provided its own 'opportune remedy', as Clement warned.[47]

The College of Electors was gaining power during the fourteenth century. Increasingly it was thought that the princes alone conferred power on the imperial candidate. German thinkers denied the necessity for papal approbation and asserted that election by the princes conferred administrative power on the elect, and that the only difference between the *rex Romanorum* and the crowned emperor was the name. The idea had started with the anonymous *Weistum* of 1252,[48] and had intensified during the heyday of Louis of Bavaria and his circle. It appeared especially in the manifestos issued in 1338 – in the Declaration of Rhense, issued by the princes themselves in July,[49] and in *Licet Iuris*, issued by Louis in August.[50] Above all, it was emphasised in *Fidem Catholicam* that

imperial power and authority is immediately from God alone and not from

---

[46] Clement VI, sermon 40, pp. 142–63.
[47] *MGH Const.*, viii no. 16, p. 31, where reference is made to this in the processes against Louis. See also the letters to the electors, no. 16, p. 32 and no. 101, p. 164. For the similar attitude adopted when episcopal electors had failed to reach a decision see Innocent III's decree (1215) in *Decretales*, I, vi, 41. Clement's attitude may be compared with Hostiensis, *ad Decretales*, I, vi, 34, fol. 6or: 'Electoribus igitur negligentibus imperatorem eligere, Papa eliget'; Baldus de Ubaldis, *ad Decretales*, I, vi, 34, fols. 78r–v: 'Ibi, admoniti et expectati, per hoc patet, quod electoribus imperatoris non est aliquis terminus ad eligendum praefixus a iure, sed papa bene potest statuere terminum, et post terminum supplere negligentiam electionariorum [*sic*]'.
[48] Zeumer, 'Ein Reichsweisthum', p. 406: 'Rex autem Romanorum ex quo electus est in concordia, eandem potestatem habet quam et imperator, nec dat ei inunctio imperialis nisi nomen'. Zeumer discovered the *Weistum* incorporated in the *Lectura* of Hostiensis. For further discussion see Mitteis, 1944, p. 216.
[49] Ed. Altmann and Bernheim, no. 34, p. 51.   [50] Ibid., no. 36, p. 52.

the pope, and . . . the emperor-elect is *rex Romanorum* from election alone, and has imperial authority, jurisdiction, and power even before he is anointed, consecrated, or crowned by the pope.[51]

In Clement's pontificate this view was strongly held by the publicist Lupold of Bebenberg[52] and by William of Ockham.[53]

The princes, like the College of Cardinals in the election of a pope, were regarded as the instruments of God in the election of the emperor.[54] It was logical that, like the cardinals, they should be regarded as a corporation, and one, moreover which 'represented' the Empire. This raised the question of whether they elected as a 'body', or as individuals. Canonistic opinion, as expressed by Hostiensis and Johannes Andreae, was that they elected as individuals, *tamquam ad singulares*.[55] Yet both Lupold of Bebenberg and Conrad of Megenberg later rejected this. Lupold argued cynically that men were so quarrelsome that nothing would ever get done if the electors could not adopt the majority principle. That they did so was an indication that they formed a *universitas*, a corporation, for the majority principle was one of the hallmarks of corporate status.[56] Moreover, their action was a representative one: it was deemed to be performed 'by the *universitas* of all the princes and the people subject to the kingdom and the Empire'.[57] The same opinion is implied by a chronicle account of Charles's election, which stated that he was elected 'by Gerlach of Mainz, Archchancellor of Germany, Baldwin

---

51 Ed. Becker: see p. 499. On the possible authorship of Bonagratia of Bergamo see Brampton, 1962. For analysis see Quillet, 1980.

52 Lupold of Bebenberg, *De Iure Regni et Imperii Romani*, ch. 7, p. 362: 'rex Romanorum post electionem a principibus vel a maiori parte ipsorum . . . habet eandem potestatem tam administrandi iura et bona regni, quam etiam exercendi alios actus qui de iure sunt Imperatori reservati: et hoc in provinciis et terris regno et imperio subiectis, quam habet post unctionem et coronationem imperialem factus postea Imperator'.

53 William of Ockham, *Octo Quaestiones de Potestate Papae*, q. iv, ch. 10, p. 155. For discussion of the use of Ockham's *Quaestio* iv by the anonymous author of the *Songe du Vergier* see Quillet, 1977, pp. 84–5. Offler, 1967, suggests that the *Octo Quaestiones* were posed by a member of Baldwin of Trier's entourage rather than by Louis of Bavaria. For Ockham's views on the imperial question see de Lagarde, iv, 1962; Bayley, 1949a, esp. pp. 206ff.; McGrade, 1974, pp. 104ff.

54 In the *Golden Bull*, issued by Charles in 1356, they are referred to in terms similar to those used to describe the College of Cardinals: see ch. 3, p. 56: 'velut columpne proceres sacrum edificium'; ch. 12, p. 68: 'solide bases imperii et columpne immobiles', ch. 31, p. 90: 'electores principes ipsius imperii columpne et latera'. Cf. p. 118, n. 110 above.

55 Hostiensis, *ad Decretales*, I, vi, 34, fol. 60v; Johannes Andreae, *ad Decretales*, I, vi, 34, fol. 108r.

56 Lupold of Bebenberg, *De Iure Regni et Imperii Romani*, ch. 6, pp. 357–8.

57 Ibid., ch. 6, p. 358. See also ch. 6, p. 357.

of Trier, Archchancellor of France, Walramus of Cologne, Arch-chancellor of Italy, by the King of Bohemia, the Chief Butler, and by Rudolf, Duke of Saxony, the Chief Marshal'.[58] The use of the electors' imperial chancery titles can be seen as an indication that the writer saw them as representing the different parts of the Empire, the *universitas* of the Roman people.

Obviously Clement VI's concern was to dispel such notions, and to reassert the pope's vital role in the appointment of the emperor. The electors were merely an *ad hoc* committee, called together at his instance to perform a particular duty. They did not enjoy corporate status, nor did they represent the Empire, and they therefore had no established powers. He had an opportunity to make the point during the election procedure, and again later when preaching. Given his involvement in every stage of the election process, it is likely that he influenced the form of the election decrees submitted by the electors to him, petitioning for approval of the election. Among the criteria for a 'canonical' and therefore acceptable election were that the elect had 'consented', and that he had petitioned for confirmation of the election: the similarity with the requirements for an episcopal election are no accident.[59] The election both of a bishop and a *rex Romanorum* highlighted the concept of representation. This was metaphorically expressed in the idea that the bishop was married, or spiritually united, to his see, and the *rex Romanorum*, or emperor-elect, to his *imperium*. Without consent no marriage was valid: indeed, in both canon and civil law what validated it was the mutual consent of the man and the woman.[60] In the late twelfth century the decretist Huguccio had seen the consent of the electors of a bishop as the answer to the consent of the episcopal candidate himself to his

---

[58] Michael of Leone, *Annotata Historica*, p. 470. Cf. *Golden Bull*, ch. 1 [8–12], pp. 49–50.

[59] See sermon 40, p. 163 where Clement expressed concern 'de electione dicti Karoli . . . concorditer celebrata per electores, *qui debuerunt et potuerunt et voluerunt electioni huiusmodi interesse, et de consensu per dictum Karolum . . . prestito, et de significatione tam per eum quam per electores* super electione huiusmodi nobis facta'. Cf. *MGH Const.*, viii, no. 159 where the election is referred to as 'canonical'. See also Beneš of Weitmil, *Cronica*, p. 513: 'Completo . . . sermone . . . papa . . . examinatio . . . processu et decreto eleccionis hujusmodi ipsam eleccionem canonice et de persona idonea celebratam . . . approbavit . . .' Benedict XII had also required that an imperial election should be 'canonical': see Raynaldus, vi, ch. 65, p. 189. For the similar criteria Clement required for a valid episcopal election see Tautu, no. 2, pars 4–6. For the influence of canon law on imperial election procedure see Hugelmann, 1909; Bayley, 1949b, pp. 206–7; Benson, 1968, esp. p. 356, n. 43.

[60] On consent as the validation of marriage see above p. 29, n. 48.

election. The electors' consent was equated with the solemn subscription, or underwriting, of each one to the decree which described and published the election. For purposes of the election, the electors represented the members, that is, the whole body of the church, and it was therefore the mutual consent of bishop and church which made the marriage binding.[61]

The same thing could be applied to imperial elections: hence one reason for the importance of the election decrees and Clement's interest in them. In all the fourteenth-century election decrees there is a close connection between the words 'consent' and 'approval'. Ater the election of both Henry VII (1308) and Louis of Bavaria (1314) the electors 'approved' the election, marking this by singing *Te Deum laudamus* (We praise thee, O God) at a nearby church. The elect himself, after suitable entreaties, consented, and the election was then published to the clergy and people,[62] presumably to ratify the whole business. After the election of Frederick of Austria (1314) the electors persuaded him to consent;[63] their own affirmation, however, was contained in their individual subscriptions to the election decree,[64] recalling Huguccio's remarks about electoral consent to an episcopal election. The electors then petitioned the pope to approve the election, as if this would set the seal on the marriage;[65] they made no attempt to publish the election to the people. Charles's electors by contrast each submitted an almost identical decree to Clement in which the usually brief reference to the consent of the candidate was magnified.[66] Moreover, there was no mention of the answering 'consent' or 'approval' by the electors. The most likely reason for both of these differences was that the pope who influenced the wording of the documents wanted to make it plain that the electors performed their duties as individuals. They were not themselves a corporation, and they therefore enjoyed no special role as the representatives of the body of the Empire. In support of this one elector obligingly described how the election had been published to 'a copious multitude of clergy and people' before the elect had consented to the election.[67] The publication had no legal standing

[61] Benson, 1968, pp. 122–33.
[62] The fuller decree is that for Louis, *MGH Const.*, v, no. 103, p. 102. For that for Henry see *MGH Const.*, iv, 1, no. 262, p. 230.
[63] *MGH Const.*, v, no. 95, p. 93.
[64] Ibid., p. 92.
[65] Ibid., p. 93. The pope was requested 'electionem huiusmodi canonicam de ipso a nobis factam solita clementia approbare'.
[66] *MGH Const.*, viii, nos. 63–6, pp. 93–9. See especially pp. 94, 95, 97, 99.
[67] Ibid., no. 63, p. 94.

because it was made to a mere multitude, a random and unrelated collection of individuals who, like the electors themselves, were in no way representative of the Empire as a whole.

By depriving the electors of their corporate status, and by the omission of the electoral consent from the election decrees, Clement wanted to make it plain that the electors did not function as one person in law, and that they had no role in empowering the king of the Romans. He did not, however, want to deny that Charles was married to the *imperium*, in the same way as any other king would be married to his realm. And in Charles's case the marital situation had an added dimension. The *imperium* was simply the secular aspect of the *Ecclesia*, and the one who represented the body of the Church was the pope himself. In a sense the spiritual union which took place was also that between the pope and the emperor. This was the *specialis coniunctio*, the 'special union', of which the canonists wrote.[68] This union was effected not through election by an *ad hoc* committee, but during the approbation ceremony itself. The point was made during the sermon, where Clement explicitly compared the relationship between the pope and the emperor-elect with matrimony. Legally, a marriage was not contracted unless it was publicly announced, but through confirmation it was seen to be ratified and contracted. Applying this to the imperial election Clement declared:

From election the marriage is not recognised unless it is announced; but by confirmation the marriage is seen to be established and ratified and contracted. But the pope has to approve the emperor-elect (*electum in imperatorem*), therefore his power originates from papal power.[69]

Seen from Clement's standpoint the election was almost irrelevant. It presented him with no more than a suggestion which could be accepted or rejected. In the solemn words of confirmation at the end of the sermon Clement himself 'nominated' Charles as 'king of the Romans, fit to be promoted afterwards into emperorship', in the sense that he elected or put him forward as a candidate, a use of the word current from the time of Innocent III.[70]

Conrad of Megenberg explained the papal position with some

---

[68] Innocent IV, *ad Decretales*, II, ii, 9, fol. 82v: 'Nam specialis coniunctio est inter papam et imperatorem, quia papa eum consecrat, et examinat, et est imperator eius advocatus, et iurat ei, et ab eo imperium tenet'. Cf. Hostiensis, *ad Decretales*, II, ii, 9, fol. 12v; Alvarus Pelagius, *De Planctu Ecclesiae*, bk i, ch. 44, p. 79.

[69] Clement VI, sermon 40, p. 156. Cf. Wilks, 1963a, p. 279.

[70] Ibid., p. 163. Cf. Innocent III, *RNI*, 62, p. 172: 'Ottonem reputamus et nominamus regem'. See Ullmann, 1976, no. 6, pp. 671ff.

charm. The election by the princes was no more than a necessary preamble to the papal confirmation of the emperor, for without the moisture of papal confirmation the imperial election could produce no flower.[71] Certainly Clement's concern during the approbation ceremony was to show that he propagated the flower, that he alone could empower the man he had chosen for office. In doing so he had to answer not only the general challenge from the College of Electors, but also more specific claims. On the one hand the clerical members of the College claimed that the coronation which one of them performed, usually at Aachen, was the true source of royal authority, while on the other a group of the princes claimed that what mattered was a somewhat bizarre ceremony performed after the election, when they elevated the elect on the high altar of St Bartholomew's church at Frankfurt.

A detail which often engages the attention of historians of papal, episcopal, and royal ceremonial is the exact moment at which the elect receives his power. This was usually marked by the use of the official title for the first time, without the suffix of *electus*, and sometimes also by the singing of the *Te Deum*. In Charles's case the sonority of the official words of confirmation must have underlined their constitutive character. The Pope received Charles as the special son of himself and the Roman Church, granted him grace and favour, named, announced, accepted, and declared him *rex Romanorum*, approved of his person, and pronounced him suitable and sufficient to receive the height of imperial dignity.[72] The suffix of *electus* had been used throughout the *collatio* until this moment. The official letter of approval, written later that day, correctly addressed Charles as 'king of the Romans fit to be promoted afterwards into emperorship'.[73] Clement's views also emerge from the forms of address he used to Charles, punctiliously addressing him as 'elect in the kingship of the Romans' in all letters written between his election and confirmation.[74] The papacy had followed this practice consistently from the time of Gregory X: in the correspondence which passed between him and Rudolf of Habsburg, before Rudolf's approbation, the Pope pointedly addressed him as King of the Romans elect;

---

[71] Conrad of Megenberg, *Yconomica*, ii, 2, ch. 9, pp. 59–60.

[72] Clement VI, sermon 40, p. 163.

[73] *MGH Const.*, viii, no. 102, p. 166.

[74] See for example ibid., no. 83, p. 110, the letter Clement wrote to congratulate Charles on his election, and no. 90, p. 116, dated 29 August 1346. See also no. 84, p. 111, to John of Bohemia, dated 30 July 1346, where Charles was referred to as 'elect in the kingship of the Romans'.

Rudolf equally pointedly replying as King of the Romans.[75] Writing nearly forty years later to Henry VII, Clement V was to cite this correspondence as a precedent.[76] Similarly, Boniface VIII had censured Albert of Habsburg for administering the lands of the *imperium* in parts of Germany, having received neither approval nor the name of king from the apostolic see.[77] Since Albert had condoned the deposition and murder of the previous king, Adolf of Nassau, Boniface displayed scant enthusiasm for his confirmation. When Albert eventually made reparation, the Pope announced that he who had been in 'a cloud of arrogance and ignorance' – a euphemism for one unyielding and totally blind to the papal viewpoint –was now devoted and ready to do all that was required of him.[78] John XXII, however, was the first pope to express this theory succinctly: 'Kings of the Romans do not exist until approbation, merely those elected into the kingship, and these are not to be had for kings, nor called kings'.[79] But despite this firm view, Clement VI was the first pope whose principles prevailed upon an imperial candidate: Charles IV adopted the title of *rex Romanorum* and numbered his regnal years from his approbation day, 6 November 1346, rather than from his German coronation or from his election.[80] This made little practical difference, except perhaps to add to the reputation of Charles as the papacy's puppet. But it made a theoretical impact, for Conrad of Megenberg was sufficiently struck to take it as an established practice, which it scarcely was after only one occurrence. He explained that the simple use of the title denoted that the candidate had been approved by his superior. The same was true of a bishop-elect, who also called himself prelate-elect of a particular church before his episcopal confirmation. Before confirmation the imperial candidate was just a 'hypothetical and conditional king'.[81]

---

[75] *MGH Const.*, iii, 1, no. 25, p. 27; no. 34, p. 32; no. 35, p. 33; no. 48, p. 42.

[76] *MGH Const.*, iii, 1, no. 455, pp. 398–9.

[77] *MGH Const.*, iv, 1, no. 109, p. 87.

[78] Ibid., no. 173, p. 140.

[79] *MGH Const.*, v, no. 792, p. 617.

[80] *MGH Const.*, viii, no. 70, p. 102; no. 73, p. 104; no. 75, p. 106; no. 88, p. 114 for letters between election and approbation (11 July–5 November 1346) and ibid., no. 110, p. 185; no. 111, p. 186 for letters between approbation and German coronation (6–26 November 1346). Also ibid., no. 342, p. 388 and no. 343, pp. 389–91 for letters of 24 November the following year, 1347, which are dated 'regnorum nostrorum anno *secundo*'. The chronicler Henry Taube of Selbach is wrong in saying that Charles numbered his regnal years from his first German coronation: *Chronica*, p. 98: 'Rex autem non ab hac coronacione [scil. secunda], set a prima annos regni sui scribit'.

[81] Conrad of Megenberg, *De translatione Romani Imperii*, ch. 17, p. 304: 'electus in

What marked the difference between the hypothetical and the true king was that the true king was entitled to administer the goods and lands of the *imperium*. Conrad had no doubt about this: 'The authority of administering is given to the Roman prince by the approbation of the pope and the Roman Church' he stated.[82] Again he supported Clement VI's opinion, which was that once granted papal grace and favour the king of the Romans had to exercise his right of administration. The pope administered the *imperium* only 'until an approved king or emperor' existed, explained Clement.[83] Benedict XII had thought the same.[84] Clement expected Charles to administer imperial territories in Italy immediately, as his promises demonstrate.[85] But above all, he had to destroy Louis of Bavaria: indeed, Clement reminded him of his pre-election promise to do this even before his confirmation.[86] If the king was expected to perform imperial duties he obviously needed the obedience which he would command as emperor. This entitlement too sprang from the day of his approval rather than his imperial coronation. The oaths which those excommunicated for consorting with Louis had to swear contained the promise: 'I will not obey or adhere to anyone as emperor unless he has first been approved by the Church'.[87]

The most direct and dramatic way in which Clement made known his views on kingship was during the approbation discourse; and it also gave him a splendid opportunity to indulge his passion for Old Testament symbolism. The whole sermon reverberated with com-

regem Romanorum, quamvis ab omnibus principibus electoribus vel a maiori parte, quamvis eciam coronatus ab archiepiscopis predictis, antequam confirmetur per sedem et approbetur, de iure non habet se scribere simpliciter *regem Romanorum*, sed cum addicione, scil. *electus in regem Romanorum* . . . Racio . . . est, quoniam electus ante confirmacionem suam tantum est rex ypotheticus et condicionalis, videlicet, si per papam fuerit approbatus, que condicio in omnibus electis per hanc addicionem *electus* connotatur. Sed per simplicem et kathegoricam tytuli posicionem connotatur esse confirmatum per superiorem. Unde nullus electorum in prelatum alicuius loci scribit se simpliciter eiusdem loci prelatum, sed pocius electum, antequam confirmetur'. Cf. *Yconomica*, ii, 2, ch. 2, pp. 80–1. On the titles and powers of the bishop-elect see Benson, 1968, pp. 90–149; 176–9.
[82] Conrad of Megenberg, *De translatione Romani Imperii*, ch. 16, p. 302. Cf. Alvarus Pelagius, *De Planctu Ecclesiae*, bk i, ch. 43, p. 77.
[83] Werunsky, no. 15, p. 9.
[84] Raynaldus, vi, ch. 65, p. 189.
[85] One of these promises obliged Charles to seek approval of his election 'que electus in regem Romanorum habet prosequi' before going to Italy to administer imperial territories, or sending his officials there. The promise also referred to those Charles would send to Tuscany and Lombardy 'pro terris et iuribus imperii gubernandis': *MGH Const.*, viii, no. 9, p. 15.
[86] *MGH Const.*, viii, no. 83, p. 111. For the pre-election promises see nos. 10–11.
[87] Ibid., no. 23, p. 44, and see also no. 26, p. 48; no. 378, p. 426.

parisons from Jewish history. The Gospels supplied no theory of divinely approved kingship, but the Old Testament, especially the Books of Kings, more than compensated. Indeed, Clement's whole theory of kingship could be epitomised by references to two Old Testament passages which occurred in the sermon: 'Not at the election of the people, but merely at their petition, Samuel, according to the counsel of God, gave them King Saul'[88] and his chosen text, 'Solomon shall sit upon my throne and reign for me'. He could not afford to rely simply on subtle changes in procedure or diplomatic document to drive home the point that the king of the Romans was given by God, through his terrestrial vicar, the pope. All power, as Paul's Epistle to the Romans had made clear, was of God, but in practice it could reach man only *mediante pontificali*, through the medium of the priesthood, explained Clement, supplying a careful gloss to Gratian's *Decretum*.[89] Bearing in mind that the prime function of the pope as vicar of Christ was to act as God on earth, this was the only logical way His power could reach the king. The whole thing was really a matter of history, for, as Clement instructed Charles, God had always wished that the kings of Israel – meaning their Christian heirs – should be approved or rejected by the ministry of the priests.[90] And approving or rejecting meant precisely that. The pope was not obliged to accept the choice of the electors: it rested entirely with him. After all, as Clement could not resist pointing out, there would have been nothing to prevent him from elevating the humblest of men to be king, as David, the least of the sons of Jesse, had been elevated over the people of Israel.[91] The grace

[88] Clement VI, sermon 40, p. 155, referring to I Reg., viii. 5, 6.

[89] Ibid., p. 151: 'Omnis enim potestas a Deo est, ad Rom. XIII [1]. Unde dicebat Iohannes papa LXXXXVI Di. c. 'si imperator' quod *habet imperator privilegia potestatis sue, que in administrandis legibus publicis divinitus consecutus est*, et subdit, quod *a Deo consecutus est propriam potestatem*, quod utique verum est sed *mediante pontificali*'. Cf. Gratian, X. XCVI, c. 11. The pope is in fact Gelasius I, not John, as Walter Ullmann kindly pointed out to me. Cf. also Guido Vernani, *De Potestate Summi Pontificis*, ch. 6, p. 66: 'Et potest, et debet ei legem imponere, ita quod omnis Imperii virtus *a Deo mediante authoritate Summi Pontificis* gubernatur'; and ch. 10, p. 73.

[90] Clement VI, sermon 40, p. 152.

[91] Ibid.: 'Samuel Saul reprobavit et David approbavit, sicut apparet I Reg. XV et XVI et quasi per totum, et etiam quoniam omnes filios Ysai reprobavit et solum David, qui erat minimus, approbavit, I Reg. XVI'. Cf. Guido Vernani, *De Potestate Summi Pontificis*, ch. 10, p. 75: 'Ecce manifeste patet, quod in populo Dei dignitas et potestas et ius regis, et iniunctio, seu consecratio ejus processit a Deo, mediante sacerdotio. Non solum autem Samuel Sacerdos Regem instituit Saulem, *sed etiam deposuit et destituit eum*, I Reg., xiii. Constituit etiam Deus Regem David per eundem Samuelem et inunxit eum, I Reg., xvi'.

and favour of imperial power, whether granted to king or to crowned emperor, was not a matter of right, it was a gift. You aspire to emperorship by a gift from the Lord, as Clement reminded Charles before the ceremony.[92] Royal power was a gift from God to the king, and the king himself was God's gift to the people. This was true in a special sense, for when the king was 'given' by God, through his vicar, he was not simply being appointed to a vacant office. Every time the pope instituted a king the Old Testament scene was re-enacted. To illustrate this, Clement quoted from Hugh of St Victor: the priesthood was instituted first, and then it instituted the royal *potestas* at God's command. The same thing still happened in the Church in Clement's own day, he explained. The priestly dignity consecrated the royal *potestas*, sanctioning it by benediction and – this was the salient point – forming it by institution. The spiritual power, as he went on to emphasise to Charles, instituted the temporal so that it might exist – *ut sit*; judged it in case it was not good, and consecrated it so that it might be good.[93]

The whole question of the consecration or coronation of the *rex Romanorum* was a difficult one. To have made his views on Roman kingship completely unambiguous Clement should have crowned the king of the Romans himself. As he admitted during his sermon, the kings of Israel had been the only ones to be anointed,[94] and logically their Christian heirs should also have been. But to have crowned the king himself would have made public Clement's reluctance to create an emperor, which would have been diplomatically unwise. Moreover, it would have made an already difficult relationship with Walramus, the Archbishop of Cologne, a well-nigh impossible one. Indeed, he would probably never have got Walramus to agree to elect Charles at all if he had let fall the merest hint of such a plan. The problem was that Walramus, like his predecessors, but unlike the rest of the German princes, considered that he created the *rex Romanorum* through the coronation he performed, usually at Aachen. In Charles's case, the ceremony

---

92 *MGH Const.*, viii, no. 32, pp. 53–4.
93 Clement VI, sermon 40, p. 154. Cf. Hugh of St Victor, *De Sacramentis Christianae Fidei*, bk ii, pt 2, ch. 4: *PL*, 176, 418.
94 Clement VI, sermon 40, pp. 152–3: 'Et ideo dicit Augustinus super Ps. XLIIII, quod reges soli Israel inungebantur, quod habebant immediate ordinem ad [*sic*] Christum, a quo dependet omnis unctio. Merito ergo, quia istud imperium catholicum est et unctionem recipit promovendus ad ipsum debet approbari per summum sacerdotem'. Cf. Augustine, *Enar. in Ps.*, xliv, 19: *CSEL*, 10 (1), p. 507.

actually had to be performed at Bonn, because Aachen was still in the hands of Louis of Bavaria's adherents, and its citizens refused to admit him for the ceremony. But this did not alter the principle. Nothing daunted, Walramus wrote to various cities notifying them of Charles's coronation, and describing how he had himself anointed, consecrated, and crowned the 'elect'. In consequence of this coronation the citizens were ordered to obey Charles as the true king of the Romans, which implied that his right of administering the *imperium*, like his royal title, had been imparted to him through coronation.[95] He was in no doubt that the ceremony was indeed the coronation of the *rex Romanorum* and, to judge from the contemporary chronicle accounts of Charles's Bonn coronation, this opinion was widespread.[96]

Clement had to find a subtle way of demolishing Cologne's pretensions. One thing he could, and did, do was to make the approbation ceremony appear constitutive and as much like a coronation as possible. This was one of several reasons for choosing the basic enthronement text for his sermon. He also took an unexpected interest in the German ceremony, as his correspondence shows. He wrote to the disloyal citizens of both Aachen and Cologne urging them to admit Charles for his coronation, promising eternal blessings if they obeyed, and threatening renewed excommunications and interdicts if they refused,[97] for both cities had been penalised for adherence to Louis. Archbishop Baldwin of Trier was issued with two sets of documents, enabling him to ban or absolve as the occasion demanded.[98] When the ceremony took place, at Bonn, the Pope's enthusiasm was such that he wrote to congratulate Charles immediately he had been notified of it.[99]

Clement could afford to be lavish in his congratulations: he had just scored a diplomatic triumph. He had achieved a reversal of the

---

[95] *MGH Const.*, viii, no. 338, p. 383. On the 'German' coronation and the role of the Archbishop of Cologne see Krammer, 1913, esp. pp. 221–6; Goldringer, 1957.

[96] See, for example, Henry of Diessenhoven, *Chronica*, p. 54: 'Approbacione vero facta et Karolo transmissa per papam, *ipse Karolus coronatus fuit in regem Romanorum*'. Cf. Beneš of Weitmil, *Cronica ecclesie Pragensis*, p. 514; Francis of Prague, *Cronica*, p. 442, and Henry Taube, *Chronica*, p. 66. See also Baluze–Mollat, *Prima Vita*, p. 246, where the biographer refers to Frankfurt and Aachen as the places 'ubi consueverunt fieri tam electio *quam coronatio regum Romanorum*'.

[97] *MGH Const.*, viii, no. 20, p. 42, and no. 89, pp. 114–15.

[98] Ibid., nos. 24–5, pp. 45–7.

[99] Ibid., no. 158, pp. 243–4. The letter was dated 6 January 1347; the coronation had taken place on 26 November 1346.

normal order in which the elect received his confirmation and his crown. Previous German rulers had been crowned as soon as possible after election, and a description of the 'German' coronation usually featured as an ingredient of the election decrees.[100] But Charles's election decrees contained no such description: he received the Pope's grace and favour on 6 November 1346, before his crown, which was bestowed on 26 November. That this was more than coincidence is borne out by a letter Clement wrote to the citizens of Aachen, asking that they would grant entry to their city to the elected candidate for his coronation, and making it clear that he would already have received the grace and communion of the Holy See – *gratiam et communionem obtinentem sedis eiusdem*.[101] It is interesting that Clement did not commit himself on what sort of coronation it was: he offered no opinion on whether it was that of a *rex Romanorum* or a merely German king. As so often, Clement's achievement was not lost on the perceptive Conrad of Megenberg, who seized on 'approbation before coronation' as the correct order of events. Papal approval alone conferred the right to administer the *regnum* or *imperium*, and for this reason neither the Aachen coronation (Charles had in fact been crowned a second time, in 1349, at Aachen), nor the similar one at Milan, which in any event could not take place without papal consent, could confer any rights. Charles of Moravia, after all, had enjoyed administrative power over the *imperium* before he had been crowned at Aachen, or indeed anywhere else – clearly this was a reference to the Bonn ceremony.[102] Thus

---

[100] Adolf of Nassau was elected on 5 May 1292, crowned on 24 June 1292, and probably approved in May 1295. Albert of Austria was elected on 27 July 1298 (for the second time), crowned on 24 August 1298, and approved on 30 April 1303. Frederick of Austria was elected on 19 October 1314, crowned on 25 November 1314, and not approved. Louis of Bavaria was elected on 19–20 October 1314 and crowned on 25 November. Henry VII was elected on 27 November 1308, crowned on 6 January 1309, and approved on 26 July 1309.

[101] *MGH Const.*, viii, no. 20, p. 42.

[102] Conrad of Megenberg, *De translatione Romani Imperii*, ch. 16, p. 302: 'coronaciones et uncciones due, quarum una regi Romanorum Aquisgrani per archiepiscopum Coloniensem impenditur, et alia unccio et coronacio que per archiepiscopum Mediolanensem in villa Modycensi . . . impenditur, non dant uncto et coronato auctoritatem amministrandi iura et bona regni, et imperii Romani . . . Auctoritas amministrandi datur principi Romano per approbacionem papa et ecclesie Romane . . . Ergo non datur illi per dictas coronaciones, quia *debito ordine procedendi approbacio ecclesie plerumque sequitur coronaciones easdem, et aliquando ex manifesto consensu summi pontificis precedit eas, sicut nuper patuit in Karolo rege Bohemie*, qui cum tempore Ludwici quarti Romani imperatoris eligeretur . . . mox Clemens papa sextus consensit in eandem eleccionem . . . Unde dictus Karolus poterat amministrare bona et iura imperii antequam cor-

Conrad cited the example of Charles's coronation with the assurance of one drawing on established precedent, which it was not.

The imperial election apart, Walramus of Cologne's delusions of grandeur were rivalled by those of some of the lay princes, although during Clement's pontificate not those who had been concerned in the 1346 election. After the death of Louis of Bavaria, an anti-king, Günther of Schwarzburg, was illegally elected. Because he had no chance of being crowned either by the Archbishop of Cologne, or his rival of Mainz, who occasionally in the past had performed such ceremonies, the princes made use of the ceremony of enthronement, or *elevatio*, of the candidate on the high altar of St Bartholomew's, Frankfurt.[103] Louis of Bavaria had been so enthroned, and probably Henry VII before him, so that although Günther was not enthroned until 1349, Clement VI would already have been aware of the inherent threat to the papacy posed by such a ritual. The full significance of it emerges from the elevation order preserved by Baldmar, canon of Frankfurt. In coronation orders the enthronement was the moment when the ruler, fully invested with his powers, was seen to take possession of his realm, something which reflected Roman law principles.[104] The elevation order emulated this, and several other points of contemporary coronation orders. It did not refer to the candidate as king until after the elevation and the singing of the *Te Deum*: then it announced: 'The psalm being finished, the *king* descends from the altar'.[105]

An indication of the creative significance of the ceremony came from Günther himself in the extraordinary edict he issued confirming *Licet Iuris*. He proceeded to annul all papal processes against Louis of Bavaria, 'since the pope, according to all divine and human law, ought to be subject to the emperor'.[106] This remark shows the extremes to which opposition theories could be pushed, and it is the

onaretur Aquisgrani vel alibi'. See also *Yconomica*, ii, 2, ch. 16, pp. 80–1, where Conrad states that to regard the coronations as confirmation of the king-elect would be to deny papal authority, unless you say that they are coronations of a German king or that of a king of some other kingdom which is part of the Empire. You might alternatively say that they are hypothetical or conditional – the condition being that the pope has to confirm them, in which case they are subordinate and defective, being entirely dependent upon the hands of the pope.

[103] On the ceremony see Rieger, 1885; Krammer, 1905.

[104] See Schulz, 1951, pp. 282ff.

[105] *MGH Const.*, ix, no. 13, p. 13. A similar order was preserved by John Latomus, *Acta aliquot vetustiora in Civitate Frankofurtensi . . . collecta*: see p. 413. Although Latomus was not a contemporary witness, historians have found no cause to doubt him: see Grotefend, 1884, i, p. 88.

[106] Goldast, *Collectio Constitutionum*, iii, no. 284, p. 414.

more astonishing when one recalls that Günther was not even emperor at the time: he admitted to confirming Louis' edict on the basis of his election as king of the Romans. In effect, he was saying that the pope ought to be subject to the king of the Romans, for he dated the document, uncrowned as he was, in the first year of his reign. The decisive point, however, was that he felt himself able to legislate because his election had been 'approved and confirmed' by all the clerics and people. The meaning of confirmation had been attached to enthronement since Carolingian times – the enthronement prayer of the Order of Seven Forms, for example, had stated that the ruler was 'confirmed' in the throne, and this was repeated by later coronation orders.[107] By stating that his election had been 'confirmed' Günther can only have been referring to the St Bartholomew's ritual. Interestingly, after Günther's death, the electors were to confirm their acceptance of Charles as king with a similar 'elevation' ceremony.[108] Again Clement's choice of the basic enthronement text 'Solomon shall sit upon my throne', acquires meaning, and during the sermon he made it plain that he alone was responsible for 'enthroning' and for 'confirming' the king in office. He was, as he stressed, lifting Charles high above all nations and peoples:[109] he was enthroning him, he said, that very day.[110]

The enthronement aspect by no means exhausts the significance of the Solomon text. What mattered most to Clement was that Solomon – Charles – was to sit upon his throne and rule for him, and this point was frequently reiterated. As he himself admitted, he had not the slightest intention of renouncing the throne himself. 'He shall rule for me when he reigns for my honour and that of my see: when he reigns on my behalf he will totally direct his rule to the honour of God and the Holy See', the Pontiff declared.[111] In

---

[107] Vogel and Elze, *Pontificale Romano-Germanicum*, ordo lxii, ap. 2, p. 261. On the 'Order of Seven Forms' see Ullmann, 1969, pp. 103ff, esp. p. 107.

[108] John Latomus, *Acta*, p. 415 says that at Frankfurt Charles 'ab omnibus electoribus concorditer est electus, inductus et exaltatus'. Janson, 1880, p. 110, first demonstrated that Charles was not, in fact, re-elected.

[109] Clement VI, sermon 40, p. 151: 'Faciam te excelsiorem cunctis gentibus [Deut., xxxvi. 19] . . . Posuit solium eius super omnes principes [Esther, iii. 1]'.

[110] Ibid., p. 146: 'et Salomon filius Bersabee sublimatus est, dicente David ipsi Bersabee: "Vivit Dominus, quia, sicut iuravi tibi, Salomon filius tuus regnabit post me, *et ipse sedebit super solium meum pro me, sic faciam hodie*" [III Reg., i, 5] . . . Iste ergo filius tuus *sedebit super istud solium* et regnabit; et *hoc faciam sibi hodie ipsum approbando et electionem eius confirmando*'. Clement also appeared to equate enthronement with confirmation here.

[111] Ibid., pp. 151–2: 'Sed quare dicit: "pro me"? numquid dimittam sibi istam kathedram et istam sedem? Certe non intendo. Sed *pro me* regnabit, quando *pro*

counselling Charles to pay attention to the pope as to an exemplar, Clement cited the well-worn explanation by St Bernard of the two swords (Luke, xxii. 38), which represented temporal and spiritual power, with the reminder that the temporal sword always had to be exercised at the sacerdotal command.[112] Charles was given no chance to forget that he had to wield the pope's executive power rather than his own, and that he had to do so as a totally obedient and subservient son.[113] To demonstrate such closeness Clement accordingly implied the idea of procreation: Charles was received as the special son of Pope and *Ecclesia*: 'I shall be to him a father, he shall be to me a son, and I shall establish the throne of his kingdom over Israel', declaimed the Pope, once more resorting to Old Testament phraseology.[114]

Clement considered that the relationship between pope and *rex Romanorum* was as close as that between pope and emperor. It is not easy to disentangle his views on Roman kingship from those on emperorship, but then he had his reasons for blurring the distinction. He tried to make it appear that promotion to emperorship was semi-automatic once Charles was an approved king of the Romans. Like Innocent III, he regarded the elevation to emperorship as a two-stage process: the elect was promoted first to the summit of royal, and then of imperial, excellence and domination,[115] he explained, trying to make it look as if one followed naturally from the other. The promises extorted from Charles before election were couched in terms of 'if I shall be elected'.[116] On renewal, before confirmation, 'if I shall be approved' was substituted,[117] but when they were renewed

---

honore meo et istius sedis regnabit; quando *pro me* regnabit, quando suum regimen ad honorem Dei et istius sancte sedis totaliter ordinabit'.

[112] Ibid., pp. 155–6. See Bernard, *De Consideratione*, iv, 3, p. 454. Cf. Alvarus Pelagius, *De Planctu Ecclesiae*, bk i, ch. 37, p. 53: 'Item dominus est mundi [scil. imperator] quantum ad executionem gladii temporalis, quo regulariter Papa non utitur, licet ab eo sit'; Galvaneus Flamma, *Chronica Galvagnana*, ch. 108, p. 180: 'Eodem modo est de imperio, id est de universali dominio totius mundi, quia sumus [*sic*] pontifex est imperator quantum ad auctoritatem et executionem, quam non exercet, imperator quantum ad executionem immediatam, quam exercet, licet sit auctoritas delegata per papam'; and ch. 110, p. 184; Herman of Schildiz, *Contra Hereticos*, ii, ch. 12, pp. 91–2.

[113] Clement VI, sermon 40, p. 153: 'papa habet actum preceptivum, quia regulare. Imperator enim habet sequi preceptum sue moderationis vel ordinationis . . . Unde imperator habet ad eum attendere, sicut ad exemplar'.

[114] Ibid., p. 152: I Par., xxii. 10.

[115] Ibid., p. 144: 'Collocatur gloriose, quia assumitur ad fastigium regalis et tandem imperialis excellentie et dominationis'. Cf. p. 149. On Innocent III see Ullmann, 1976, no. 6, p. 666.

[116] *MGH Const.*, viii, nos. 9–13, pp. 11–27.   [117] Ibid., nos. 93–7, pp. 128–35.

after this ceremony they were unconditional: Charles promised that he would not enter the city of Rome before his appointed coronation day, and that he would leave that same day.[118] The wording of the document made it appear that the point at issue once Charles had been approved was no longer 'if' he went to Rome, but merely 'when', for he had been approved not just as *rex Romanorum*, but as 'king of the Romans, fit to be promoted afterwards into emperorship'.[119]

In fact, Clement had not the slightest intention of crowning Charles. It suited his 'way of adjustment' to have a king of the Romans rather than an emperor. It also allowed him to use the imperial insignia as a bargaining counter to try to ensure that 'Solomon' really would rule for the honour of the Holy See. When, in 1351, the King sent his ambassadors to petition for the diadem Clement was evasive. Writing to the Guelf cities he explained that he did not think he could refuse Charles's request outright, if only because it might drive him into the arms of the Ghibelline Archbishop of Milan, 'the enemy of God and of His Holy Church'. He had therefore, he explained, underlined the dangers of undertaking an expedition to Italy at that time.[120]

But there were other reasons. By the year 1351 it had become clear that Charles was not the obedient son for whom Clement had hoped. Relations between them had cooled considerably since 1346. The rift had started when, after the death of his first wife, Charles had married Anna of the Palatinate in 1349. Clement had strongly advised him to marry a French princess. To make matters worse, Anna was a Wittelsbach, and the marriage was a deliberate violation of the oath Charles had taken in April 1346 not to marry a relation or descendant of Louis of Bavaria without the special licence of the Holy See. For Charles the marriage was a political one designed to win him the support of Anna's father, Rudolf, Elector of the Palatinate.[121] After the ailing Günther of Schwarzburg had been induced to resign his claims to the kingship of the Romans, Charles came to terms with him and the Wittelsbachs, including Louis of Brandenburg, son of Louis of Bavaria, and with Henry of Mainz, at Eltville. The chronicler Henry Taube notes that Charles's proposed

[118] Ibid., no. 149, pp. 234–6.
[119] Clement VI, sermon 40, p. 163.
[120] Raynaldus, vi, ch. 30, p. 544.
[121] On all this see Werunsky, ii, p. 164. Seibt, 1978, pp. 161–2. For Charles's promise to Clement see *MGH Const.*, viii, no. 12, p. 25, and for Clement's letter to Charles urging a French marriage, see no. 652, p. 657.

embassy to Clement to inform him of the *rapprochement* with Louis
was not destined to take effect.[122] It was after Eltville that the
ceremony of 'elevation' took place at Frankfurt, followed by a
second coronation as *rex Romanorum*, this time at Aachen.[123] Needless to say, Clement ignored these.

The picture which emerges of Charles is certainly not that of a
Pfaffenkönig, a 'priests' king'. It suited him initially to fall in with
Clement's plans, and those of his father, for without the Pope he
would not have been elected as *rex Romanorum*. Once he had the full
support of the Wittelsbachs, and there was no opposition to him in
Germany, the situation he really wanted, he could afford to dispense
with Clement's goodwill up to a point, bearing in mind that he did
not have the imperial crown. His submitting to a second coronation,
correct in all its details from the point of view of the princes, was a
clear indication of his true views: their ideas were more important to
him than those of the Pope. Eugen Hillenbrand has suggested that
the Aachen coronation marked the transformation of the former
rebel against the *Reich* into the defender of its rights. Charles's *Vita*
was completed about this time and published as a propaganda
document to present an image of the peace-loving monarch, devoted
to justice and the good of the *imperium*.[124]

Charles was crowned in Rome on Easter Day 1355, but the
ceremony was a phantom one. Innocent VI was not there, and far
from making a triumphal entry into the city, Charles entered
covertly at night by a back gate.[125] Once he had the crown, and
Clement VI was dead, Charles allowed his true opinions to be
published in the *Golden Bull* of 1356. In this he stated that the king of
the Romans elect should confirm all the rights and privileges of the
prince electors before he started to administer the *imperium*.[126] In
other words, he was denying the necessity for papal approbation,
and asserting that election by the princes conferred administrative
power on the elect – precisely the view of the princes themselves.

Clement's initial reservations about the loyalty of the Luxem-

[122] Henry Taube of Selbach, *Chronica*, p. 96: 'Hiis et aliis pactis interpositis Karolus
et Ludwicus predicti facti sunt amici, ac super huiusmodi composicionis negocio
Karolus sollempnem ambassatam proponit dirigere ad dominum Clementem
papam: set hoc legacio nullum sorciebatur effectum'.

[123] Ibid., p. 97. Matthew of Nuremberg, *Chronica*, ch. 120, p. 278. For the elevation
see p. 165 above.

[124] Hillenbrand, 1978, p. 72.

[125] See Jean la Porte Annonay, *Liber de coronatione*, ch. 39, p. 77; chs. 47–51, pp.
85–90.

[126] *Golden Bull*, ch. 2, iv, p. 55.

burgers had been well founded. As a traditional *defensor Ecclesiae* Charles was less than ideal. Nor was his *de facto* political power anything like universal. Charles was really just another national sovereign ruler, more concerned with his own affairs than those of the papacy. In Eastern Europe he must have looked no more than part of a triumvirate, of which Louis of Hungary and Casimir of Poland were the other members. Obviously there would have to be further theoretical adjustments to the traditional theory. Clement's aim therefore seems to have been to try to bring about a state of equality and balance among the lay rulers of Christendom, so that he could call on any of them to perform imperial functions, such as leading crusades against the infidel. Simultaneously, he tried to create or to strengthen close political or personal relationships with as many of them as possible. His policies emerged in two ways: firstly, through his efforts at international diplomacy, and, secondly, through the ceremonies connected with the appointment of kings or the investiture of papal vassals with their fiefs.

Clement's activities as a peacemaker did not all stem wholly from his love of peace *per se*. Underlying them was his desire to maintain a political balance among the national sovereign states of Europe, as in the case of Poland and Bohemia. His partiality for France in the Hundred Years War sprang partly from the fear that Edward III would have been excessively powerful had he succeeded in his claim to the throne of France. Clement's aim was to foster the notion that the rulers of France and the *regnum Romanorum* were brothers and equals. Initially his efforts were directed to John of Normandy, Philip's heir, rather than to Philip himself. Even before Charles's election John had sworn that he would be a true and 'legal' friend to his 'brother' Charles, anachronistically referred to as *rex Romanorum*.[127] (Charles was in fact John's brother-in-law.) It would have suited Clement if Charles's second wife, like the first, had been a French princess. But the most telling indication of Clement's encouragement of the equality of the *rex Romanorum* and the French ruler occurred in Charles's pre-election promises. He was required to submit all disputes with France to immediate papal arbitration, the inference being that the Pope regarded both kings as having no superior in temporal affairs.[128] They were thus equals. Again,

---

[127] *MGH Const.*, viii, no. 42, p. 69. See also no. 128, p. 308. John's promise of 4 August 1347.

[128] Ibid., no. 11, pp. 21–3. See the remark of Peter the Chanter cited by Gaines Post, 1964, p. 463, n. 101: 'Sed si pares non habentes superiores ut rex Francorum et

Clement was playing on a theme current in fourteenth-century France, and one which he had himself aired at Vincennes in 1329.[129] The problem during his pontificate was to maintain this equilibrium by preventing either monarch from becoming too powerful. He was uneasy about the agreement between Humbert, Dauphin of Vienne, and Philip, by which the Dauphin's territory was to be ceded to the house of Valois should he die heirless.[130] When Humbert's wife died childless Clement urged him to remarry a 'suitable woman, from whom, by God's gift, he might receive many children'.[131]

Clement's policy towards Poland was in some ways similar. In 1349, when lasting peace had been established between Poland and Bohemia, Clement refused Charles's request to release Breslau from dependence on the Polish primatial see of Gnesen, and to subject it to the newly created see of Prague.[132] It is as if he wanted to strengthen the position of Casimir of Poland (quite apart from the fact that in 1349 Charles was *persona non grata*). Poland had once been a fief of the papacy, and Clement was anxious to revitalise the 'feudal' nexus between himself and its king. He habitually referred to it as 'pertaining immediately to the Roman Church' or as subject to it *censuale*, that is, for a *census*;[133] and the king did indeed pay an annual *census* or feudal rent.

The papacy found it convenient to adapt the feudal system to its own use when administering its *propria regna* – its own particular kingdoms. Apart from anything else, its terminology would have been readily understood by lay rulers and was a good deal more palatable than the authoritarian phrases usually employed by the papacy in dealing with subordinate officials. The popes therefore granted out their *propria regna* to lay rulers as 'feudal' fiefs,[134] and these rulers accordingly became 'vassal' kings, taking the customary oaths of liege homage and fealty to their lord, the pope. Part of the aim of the feudal system was to emphasise the personal relationship which existed between lord and man. This was exactly what the pope wanted to do, and the oaths of the vassal king, like that of the

imperator bellent periculum est. Ad papam enim recurrendum esset, ut ad maiorem'.
[129] See p. 124 above.
[130] Valbonnais, no. 177, pp. 458–62; no. 196, pp. 526–7.
[131] Valbonnais, no. 240, pp. 602–3: cf. De Pétigny, 1839–40, p. 281.
[132] Theiner, *Mon. Pol.*, no. 695, pp. 528–9.
[133] See ibid., no. 605, p. 468; no. 702, p. 532; no. 713, p. 539. On Poland as a fief of the papacy see Knoll, 1972, p. 194; Vlasto, 1970, pp. 133ff.
[134] See Jordan, 1932, which deals with the period from Gregory I to Innocent III. See also Ullmann, 1970, pp. 331ff.

feudal vassal, had to be renewed on the accession of each pope and on the succession of each vassal to the fief.[135] Just as in the case of the *rex Romanorum*, Clement wanted to stress his close ties with these dependent rulers – they, like Charles, became the 'special sons' of the papacy.[136] But the oath taken was quite different from that of the *rex Romanorum* to the pope. As Lupold of Bebenberg emphasised, this was in no way an oath of homage taken by a feudal vassal to his lord: it was, rather, an oath to defend faithfully the pope and the Church.[137]

Feudalism did provide a convenient veneer, but the device could not be extended too far, and the pope had to be selective in using it as a method of controlling national sovereign rulers. The difficulty was that feudalism implied a contractual relationship between lord and man, which involved rights and duties on both sides – indeed, it might even be taken to imply some degree of equality between them – whereas what the pope wanted was total obedience from subordinate rulers, as he did from the *rex Romanorum*. This aspect was well demonstrated in the case of Joanna of Naples. Clement had gone to some lengths to separate the oath of fealty (24 August 1344) from the ceremony of homage and investiture (28 August 1344) to make the point that the vassal had to be submissive before she could be invested with the fief. As a final reminder of her inferior status Clement ordered an innovation: the vassal was made to kneel to perform the homage. Joanna protested violently at the time and again later in writing to Clement. But Clement was unmoved.[138]

The feudal system also gave Clement an alternative way of expressing his theories on the creation of kings. In the case of Louis de la Cerda, King of the Fortune Islands, he was investing a vassal with a new fief. In the case of Andrew of Hungary and Louis of Taranto, to both of whom he granted a royal title, he was partly making use of his 'feudal' right to approve the marriage of a woman vassal, for both were successive husbands of Joanna. It was on such occasions, however, that the similarity with the king of the Romans really became marked. There could be considerable delay between

---

[135] See, for example, Clement's letter granting the Fortune Islands to Louis de la Cerda, where these conditions are set out: Raynaldus, vi, ch. 44, p. 360; and for the oath taken by Joanna of Naples see ch. 25, p. 354.

[136] See, for example, letters to Andrew of Hungary, Joanna's husband, Raynaldus, vi, ch. 46, p. 413; to Casimir of Poland, Theiner, *Mon. Pol.*, no. 538; to Alfonso of Castile, Raynaldus vi, ch. 52, p. 364.

[137] Lupold of Bebenberg, *De Iure Regni et Imperii Romani*, ch. 9, p. 368.

[138] On all this see Léonard, i, pp. 353–66; St Clair Baddeley, 1897, pp. 322–9.

granting the royal title and bestowing the crown, so that the crown could be used as a bargaining counter in much the same way as the imperial crown was with Charles. When writing to his irate brother, Clement justified the delay in crowning Andrew of Hungary with the sharp reminder that royal coronations were a matter of grace and favour rather than of right,[139] again recalling the creation of the king of the Romans, rather than the rights of a vassal.

In fact, there was little difference between the way a vassal king and a *rex Romanorum* or emperor was created. All were created out of the papal plenitude of power. As in the case of the king of the Romans,[140] the Pope granted the royal title by making what was clearly intended to be a constitutive declaration in consistory. Writing to the Archbishop of Braga, Clement described how he had created Louis of Taranto King of Naples. With the advice of the cardinals he had 'marked out' – *insignivimus* – Louis by the 'denomination and honour' of a royal title, and he had accordingly 'wished, ordained, and decreed' that he should be called by that title.[141] A similar ceremony had obviously taken place for Andrew.[142] The Pope elected or 'nominated' kings in precisely the same way as he elected or nominated the king of the Romans. He marked them out from other men. And to them, as to the Roman king, he had plenty to say about the suitability of the man he had chosen.[143]

The impression that Clement wanted to blur the distinction between the two types of king is strengthened by an analysis of the powers he granted. Louis de la Cerda, for example, was an obscure ruler of a yet more obscure, and still pagan, territory. Yet despite this, Clement created him, in the words of his sermon text, 'prince over a great people' [Num., xiv. 12]. Louis was granted *merum et mixtum imperium* – both absolute and limited power – and full

---

[139] Raynaldus vi, ch. 55, p. 416: 'asserentes quod coronatio magis ex gratia, quam justitia, dependebat'.

[140] See p. 158 above.

[141] Déprez, no. 5147.

[142] Cerasoli, no. 23, p. 32, Clement to Joanna: 'Super eo vero quod quia in consistorio nostro dum prefatum Regem *insignivimus* Regali titulo, ipsumque tamquam virum tuum coronati et inungi tecum . . . ordinavimus'.

[143] On the suitability of Andrew see Clement's letter to Joanna, Cerasoli, no. 31, p. 30. The real panegyric was to come in the sermon which Clement preached after the murder (sermon 48), where the Pope compared it to the Passion of Christ, not entirely to Christ's advantage: see Wood, 1975, pp. 165–6. See Léonard, i, p. 257 for conflicting interpretations of his character. The suitability of Louis de la Cerda was discussed when Clement created him Prince of the Fortune Islands: see sermon 45, Ste-G. 240, fols. 338r–v, and sermon 12, BN, lat. 3293, fols. 297r–99v.

temporal jurisdiction over his new domain, which meant that within the kingdom he recognised no temporal superior, save the pope himself.[144] At one point in the *collatio* Clement broke into a thoroughly imperial quotation from the *proemium* to Justinian's *Institutes*: 'Imperial majesty must be adorned not only with arms, but with law'.[145] No effort was spared to glorify the position of this very minor ruler: to make him feel that he was quasi-imperial. And perhaps in return Louis might be induced to perform some imperial tasks for Clement.

The power of an emperor, a *rex Romanorum*, or a vassal king was held in trust for the papacy, and the moment the trustee proved disobedient his power could be withdrawn. So long as Saul obeyed Samuel he prospered and did well, but the moment he disobeyed he was dethroned, so Clement reminded Charles, adding that there were precedents in more recent history – the processes of Innocent IV against Frederick II (1245) were an example.[146] Clement's approbation sermon for Charles reverberated with references to the translation of empires and kingdoms and the deposition of lay rulers. Exactly the same was true of his sermons for Louis de la Cerda, where the same comparisons were used. So long as biblical rulers had been faithful to God and obedient to his precepts they had prospered, but once they became unfaithful they had suffered numberless misfortunes and the kingdom had been transferred to another.[147] In Louis' case Clement was also able to underline the point in feudal terms. He explained that a vassal acted against his lord

---

[144] Raynaldus vi, ch. 39, p. 359, where Clement granted Louis 'merum et mistum [*sic*] imperium et jurisdictionem omnimodam temporalem'. *Merum et mixtum imperium* implied that the ruler was normally limited by law, but that in exceptional circumstances he had the power to act above it: see Wilks, 1963a, p. 208. See also Gilmore, 1941, pp. 19–127; Perrin, 1972 and 1973.

[145] Clement VI, sermon 12, BN, lat. 3293, fol. 298v: 'Et ideo dicit ille in primo [Proem] *Institute*: Imperatores maiestatem non solum armis decoratam, sed etiam legibus oportet esse armatam, et utrumque tempus'.

[146] Clement VI, sermon 40, p. 153. On the translation theory in general see Goez, 1958, and for Innocent IV and Frederick see esp. pp. 171–3.

[147] Clement VI, sermon 12, BN, lat. 3293, fol. 297r: 'Ad litteram enim sicut vassalus se habens infidelitatem erga dominum suum meretur perdere et subditos suos et fidelitatem eorum. Unde in toto libro Regum quamdiu reges servaverunt fidelitatem Deo, obediendo eis mandatis ipsum colendo et adorando, tamdiu regnum eorum fuerunt prosperatum. Sed quam cito infideliter agebant erga dominum, et multa infortunia patiebantur, et regnum ad alios transferebatur'. On the *rex inutilis* see Peters, 1970, esp. pp. 135–69 where the deposition of Sancho II of Portugal by Innocent IV is discussed. Cf. also Conrad of Megenberg, *De Translatione Romani Imperii*, ch. 113, pp. 296–7: 'Item consimili racione probabo omnia regna christiane religionis per papam posse in alios, quam in suos iam possessores transferri. Quia cum papa iure divino transtulerit

by not according him the honour and the services due to him, by entering into agreements with his adversary, and by handing over to the adversary the castle he held of his lord. He acted against the Lord God by not rendering Him due service, by entering into pacts with the devil, by having no regard for the Lord, but instead for Beelzebub, prince of devils. Such men, warned Clement, are reproached and censured by the Lord, and the kingdom is transferred.[148]

Clement had been forced to adopt a way of adjustment. He could not have left the imperial office vacant, nor could he have created an emperor in the traditional mould, in view of the damage done to both the practical and the theoretical universality of the emperor's powers. He showed both intelligence and diplomatic expertise in his solution, which was to use that part of the theory which was still undamaged – the kingship of the Romans – and then to make other rulers resemble that king as closely as possible. There had been no extended discussion on whether the *regnum Romanorum* was universal or not: most of the argument had centred on whether the king of the Romans and the emperor were the same. Conrad of Megenberg, in stating that they were, had also suggested that the *regnum* and *imperium* were of the same territorial extent,[149] although wisely he did not discuss what this was. The fact that the office was attached to a people, the Romans, who symbolised all Christians, rather than to a defined territory, could be taken to imply that it was universal, at least in theory. In effect, Clement had performed a volte-face, and had arrived at the same view as that of his opponents, who declared that the distinction between the *regnum* and the *imperium Romanorum* was merely a verbal one:[150] the office and the powers were the same.

imperium, ita poterit transferre alia regna, cum precepta iuris divini omnes ligent': Alvarus Pelagius, *De Planctu Ecclesiae*, bk i, ch. 13, p. 30.

[148] Clement VI, sermon 12, BN, Lat. 3293, fol. 298r: 'Et videte quod vassalus infideliter agit erga dominum ei honorem et servicium debitum non impendendo, fedus cum adversario iniendo, et ei castrum quod tenet a domino tradendo. Et sic recte infideliter agit erga Dominum, qui ei debitum servicium non impendit, qui cum demone fedus inivit . . . non consulentes Dominum sed Belzebub, principem demoniorum . . . Et ideo tales a Domino reprehenduntur et arguuntur et regnum eorum transferetur'.

[149] Conrad of Megenberg, *De Translatione Romani Imperii*, ch. 14, p. 298: 'Ad omnes enim regiones et provincias se regnum Romanorum extendit, ad quas se imperium Romanorum extendit'.

[150] William of Ockham, *Octo Quaestiones de Potestate Papae*, q. iv, ch. 2, p. 127, where he summarises German opinion: 'Alia est opinio quae videtur fuisse opinio principum Germanie . . . quod inter regem Romanorum et imperatorem seu regnum Romanorum et imperium solummodo est verbalis distinctio, ut sint diversorum nominum, sed eiusdem officii et potestatis'.

But there was always the vital difference that for the opposition thinkers the electors conferred the imperial powers, while for Clement the supreme pontiff alone could 'elect' and empower and enthrone the candidate through the all-important and creative ceremony of papal approbation.

Chapter 8

'OUTSIDE THE CHURCH THERE IS NO SALVATION'

The greatest gap between theory and fact in the papal scheme of things was that, despite their claims to wield sovereignty over a universal society, the popes recognised that in practice the Church Militant was not, and never had been, universal in extent. There were considerable areas of the world, and various groups of people – schismatics, heretics, infidels, and Jews – outside it. Clement VI, like his predecessors, wanted to make theory and practice coincide as nearly as possible: he wanted to make the Church Militant truly universal. He wanted to convert the infidel, to unite the schismatics with the Roman Church, and to bring all heretics and unbelievers to an acknowledgement of the true Faith and into obedience to the Roman pontiff.

The situation Clement inherited in 1342 was extremely threatening. Through the advance of the infidel, the danger was that Christian territories instead of being extended would actually be diminished. In lamenting this only four months before his election Pierre Roger described the *Ecclesia* as harrowingly thin and drawn as a result of the attacks of the infidel, and warned that she would grow worse unless a 'timely remedy' were to be applied.[1] Of the different infidel groups the Turks presented the greatest danger. They occupied Egypt, Syria, and Asia Minor, although not Cilician Armenia, and by Clement's time they had reached the Bosporus, opposite Constantinople, and threatened to advance further. Clement himself voiced the fear that they would soon reach Naples if they were not checked.[2] And he had no illusions about their aims. Writing to the Hospitallers in 1344, he declared that the 'ferocious and abominable Turks' aimed at the shedding of Christian blood and the

---

[1] Pierre Roger, sermon 43, Ste-G. 240, fol. 396v.
[2] Clement VI, sermon 14, Ste-G. 240, fol. 149v: 'nisi Turcorum potentie resistentiam apponamus [non] dubium est quin veniant Neapolim'.

'extinction of the name of Christianity'. He went on to deplore the fate of the Christian inhabitants of 'Romania' and the surrounding areas who were being 'invaded, molested, captured, and otherwise afflicted more cruelly and incessantly than ever'.[3] Elsewhere he lamented that over 30,000 people had been forced to deny Christ and to worship the treacherous Mahomet.[4] The name 'Romania' had been applied to the Latin Empire of Constantinople by the leaders of the Fourth Crusade when they had established it in 1204. It embraced an area from Crete and Rhodes in the south, to Durazzo in the northwest, and Constantinople in the northeast. Despite the Greek reconquest of Constantinople in 1261, several areas of 'Romania' remained in Western hands – southern Greece (Morea), Athens, Negroponte, Crete, Rhodes, and many of the Aegean and Adriatic islands.[5] In 1342 one of the most urgent needs was the defence of these areas against the Turkish advance, and against constant acts of piracy, many of them launched from Smyrna (Asia Minor). The plight of Cilician Armenia, sandwiched as it was between the Mamelukes of Syria and Egypt and the Turks of Asia Minor, was also a problem for the papacy, the more so because of the dubious orthodoxy of the Armenians and their catholicos, or patriarch, who adhered to the Greek rather than the Roman Church. The Byzantine Schism had been re-established when Constantinople had been recaptured by the Greeks, and the papacy ardently desired the reunion of the two Churches under papal headship. Added to all this, there was the perennial problem of the Holy Land in infidel hands. Nor were the Pope's problems limited to the Eastern Mediterranean. There was also the threat posed to Eastern Europe by the Tartars, especially to Poland and Hungary, and that to Christian Spain by the Saracens of Granada. Indeed, there was even danger within the geographical boundaries of Christendom caused by heretics and schismatics, in particular by Louis of Bavaria and his circle, who threatened papal authority and the unity of the Church.

Not all of those 'outside' the Church necessarily presented a physical danger. There were, for example, several pagan areas of the

---

[3] Déprez. no. 711.

[4] Clement VI, sermon 14, Ste-G. 240, fol. 149v: 'et dicimus cum cordis anxietate non modica, quia iam ultra xxx^{ta} milia hominem a modicis temporibus citra ipsi Turci conpulerunt ad negandum Christum et ad adorandum perfidum Machometum'.

[5] The definition of 'Romania' is debated: see, for example, Thiriet, 1959, pp. 3–4, and Wolff, 1948, esp. p. 34. The definition adopted here is that given by Housley, 1986, p. 10.

14 Map of the Levant in the mid-fourteenth century

known world which had yet to be claimed for the Roman Church.
There were also the Jews who, as a minority group, were rather
persecuted than persecutors. But these too had to be brought within
the *Ecclesia* if it were to achieve universality.

179

The only means of dealing with most of those 'outside' the Church was the crusade, the holy war. Originally the crusade had been a 'general passage', an expedition on a large scale for the recovery of the Holy Land. Gradually, however, holy war came to be applied to a much broader spectrum, both theoretically and physically. By Clement's time any war which defended or protected Christian territories against infidels, schismatics, or heretics might be given the status of a crusade, as might any military expedition to recover or even to acquire lands for Christendom.[6] Expeditions could be mounted for a specified time and with limited aims, as was Clement's Latin League of 1344, and could still be declared as holy war.[7] What was unchanging, of course, was the pope's sole competence to declare such war. This was partly because of its universal nature (and it could be argued that even an expedition with a limited aim was concerned with the realisation of the Church's universality). It was also, as Pierre Roger had reminded John XXII in 1333, because the pope alone could authorise the necessary crusading vows.[8] This was a view supported by the canonists.[9] In the fourteenth century expeditions on a relatively small scale were granted the status of holy war and the necessary vows, with attendant indulgences and privileges, authorised by the pope. In some cases national rulers might gain considerably, either through the acquisition of lands, or through the help granted them in defending their own territories, or in financial terms. Clement sometimes found it convenient to harness particularist ambitions to the universal cause of extending the Faith. Thus Louis de la Cerda found himself empowered to lead a fully authorised crusade to take possession of his newly enfeoffed, but as yet unconquered, territory of the Fortune Islands.[10] Casimir of Poland was granted tenths to help him in his war against the pagan Lithuanians, which would conveniently extend his own territories.[11] Alfonso XI of Castile's siege of Algeciras against the Saracens was accorded the status of

[6] Housley, pp. 3–6.
[7] Ibid., pp. 121–2.
[8] Pierre Roger, sermon 2, Ste-G. 240, fol. 299v: 'Est enim negotium istud vestrum specialiter . . . ex potestatis plenitudine, quia nullus alius potest passagium generale indicere: nullus alius obligatos ex voto universaliter per totum mundum potest ad transfretandum compellere. Ergo vestrum est discernere'.
[9] See Villey, 1955, pp. 569–80; Russell, 1975, pp. 115–16, 123–5, 200–1. On crusading indulgences see Brundage, 1969, pp. 68–114.
[10] See p. 133, n. 68 above. Clement also seems to have authorised an expedition in 1351: see Zunzunegui, 1940–1, app. no. 16, p. 397. See also Vincke, 1942.
[11] Theiner, *Mon. Pol.* no. 702, p. 532.

holy war, and the King was granted tenths on the clergy and a loan of some 20,000 florins by Clement.[12] Alfonso's success would obviously contribute greatly to the defence of Christian Castile against attacks from Granada as well as enhancing his own authority.

Clement's attitude to those 'outside' the Christian society sprang from his role as the 'vicar of Him who wishes that all shall be saved and that none shall perish', as he described himself. He was convinced that 'outside' the Church was neither grace nor salvation.[13] To underline the perils in store for such people he used some of the traditional metaphors for the Church, coupled with Augustinian antitheses. Inside the sheepfold was safety: outside prowled voracious beasts, ready to devour the flock.[14] All those within Noah's Ark would be saved, while those outside would perish in the flood.[15] 'Outside' denoted 'outer darkness' and 'wailing and gnashing of teeth' in contrast to the safety and light 'within'.[16]

Clement's concern was for salvation, both of individual souls and of the Christian society as a whole. The Byzantine schismatics, for example, could expect no salvation because they had de-*via*-ted and needed to be brought back to the 'right way' – 'ad *viam* rectam' – which led to eternal salvation.[17] Alvarus Pelagius a few years earlier had warned that even a martyr for the name of Christ could not be saved if he were schismatic.[18] But schism also presented the greatest possible danger to the universal Church. In the case of Eastern heretics it was tantamount to setting up an alternative society.[19] In

[12] Déprez, no. 225; Déprez-Mollat, no. 308. For discussion see Housley, pp. 60–1.
[13] *MGH Const.* viii, no. 23, p. 44: 'nos, qui vices illius in terris licet immeriti gerimus, qui omnes querit salvos fieri et neminem vult perire, cupientes eos [hereticos et schismaticos] ad sancte Dei ecclesie unitatem, extra quam non est alicui gratia neque salus, reduci'. See also Theiner, *Cod. Dip.*, no. 220, p. 227; Tautu, no. 60, par. 198; no. 120, par. 379. Cf. I Tim., ii. 4.
[14] Tautu, no. 120, par. 379.
[15] See, for example, *MGH Const.*, viii, no. 24, p. 43; Tautu, no. 25, par. 98; no. 26, par. 104; no. 28, par. 108. Cf. Cyprian, ep. 73, 21 [*PL* 3, 1123]. For further examples see Wilks, 1966, p. 492, n. 3.
[16] Clement VI, sermon 5, p. 134. Cf. Matt., viii. 12.
[17] Tautu, no. 28, par. 108. Cf. no. 29, par. 112. John XXII had described his duty as exercising the rod of correction on those who deviated from the right way: Tangl, *Die päpstlichen Kanzleiordnungen*, p. 92: 'in eos qui a recto deviant virgam correctionis exercens'.
[18] Alvarus Pelagius, *De Planctu Ecclesiae*, bk i, ch. 23, p. 33: 'extra unam ecclesiam militantem et eius oboedientiam nullus salvatur, etiam martyr pro Christo nomine, si sit in schismate constitutus'. Cf. Augustine, ep. 108, *CSEL* 34, p. 62: 'eos qui extra unitatem, etiamsi pro illo nomine moriantur, occidi posse, non posse coronari'.
[19] See, for example, Tautu, no. 26, par. 102 where Clement complains that: 'Quae quidem Graecorum populus provide non attendens, aliam sibi confinxit

the case of Louis of Bavaria it was an even more heinous crime, for Louis had set up an anti-pope and anti-cardinals. This was the equivalent of 'rending the seamless garment of Christ': it was 'placing two heads on one body', Clement declared while preaching against him.[20] It was 'dividing Christ Himself', which meant killing Him: it was the unparalleled crime of 'Christicide'.[21]

Schism was closely related to heresy – indeed, the Pope considered that schism could hardly exist without heresy,[22] and if the equation of heresy with disobedience and treason is recalled this is perfectly logical. Traditionally heretics were placed 'outside' the Church by sentence of excommunication. This literally, as Clement explained, separated them from the communion of the faithful.[23] While agreeing with the traditional view, he had his own variation. He considered that heretics by the mere fact of being so were already *de facto* outside.[24] The text of a *collatio* against Louis was an adaptation of Apocalypse, xi. 2: 'The court [a metaphor for heretic] which is without the temple, cast out and measure it not'. This led the Pope to an investigation of how a heretic could be cast out if he were already outside. Among other things, he was outside through the maliciousness of his own iniquity, for, as the Pope admonished, sins divide from God and from the *Ecclesia*, His spouse. Such a one would be cast out *de iure* when he was publicly anathematised and his crimes published.[25] The man who held and persisted in condemned views was also separated and outside *de facto*. This situation became *de iure* when he was condemned as a heretic and relieved of the cares of secular office, or, if he had none, when a crusade was preached

ecclesiam, cum sit unica tantummodo . . . et ab Apostolicae Sedis unitate recessit nec constitutionem Domini nec Petri magisterium imitatur'.

[20] Clement VI, sermon 24, Ste-G. 240, fol. 376v: 'Quarto ratione scismatis, sicut enim satis ipse volens dividere tunicam Domini inconsutilem, constituens in uno corpore duo capita; constituit antipapam et anticardinales'.

[21] Ibid.: 'Unde iste Christum dividunt. I ad Cor. i [13]: *Divisus est Christus*. Quasi dicat sicut Christicida est qui Christum dividit; sic qui dividit eius sponsam sanctam matrem Ecclesiam'.

[22] Ibid.: 'Scisma autem sine heresi vix est'.

[23] Clement VI, sermon 5, p. 131: 'Excommunicatio enim separat a fidelium communione'.

[24] Ibid.: 'Tamen michi videtur quod aliquantulum altius et subtilius contemplanti occurrit, quod aliquid quod est foris, potest foras eici, ymmo foras eicitur de facto, tribus modis'.

[25] Ibid.: 'Videtur enim michi, quod aliquis est foris ecclesiam quandoque per maliciam inique operationis. Peccata enim divident a Deo et ab ecclesia sponsa sua . . . Modo videtur michi, quod qui est foris per maliciam inique operationis, foras eicitur quando publice anathematizatur et eius perversitas propalatur'.

against him and the necessary indulgences granted.[26] Heretics were those who had descended to the level of the beasts outside the sheepfold by giving rein to their unregenerate and bestial nature, which was supposed to have been shed in baptism. Louis was therefore described as 'a rabid dog, a devouring wolf, a fetid he-goat, and a cunning serpent'.[27] He was also seen as a microcosm of society. He had within himself no foundation of faith: he was himself 'subverted' and would in turn subvert the whole structure of the Church.[28] To illustrate this danger the Pope resorted again to corporate images. Since patristic times, health had been associated with salvation and disease with sin, and Christ had been seen as the divine physician.[29] Louis was therefore depicted as a leper and a foul cancer whose contagion would spread over the whole body. He was a 'putrid and infected member'.[30] Amputation, or excommunication, was a last resort. The Church always tried to persuade a heretic to recant, so that he could be 'reincorporated'.[31] But ultimately the health of the whole body was more important than that of a single limb. In dealing with Louis, Clement compared himself and Benedict XII to good doctors who had tried to cure his sickness by lenient

---

[26] Ibid., p. 132: 'Tercio, qui est foris per adherenciam et pertinaciam dampnate assertionis, foras eicitur quando sentencialiter sicut hereticus condempnatur et curie seculari relinquitur vel, si haberi non potest, contra eum indulgentia conceditur et crux predicatur'.

[27] Clement VI, sermon 24, Ste-G. 240, fol. 379v: 'Et videtur michi quod iste est devitandus: . . . sicut canis rabidus; sicut lupus rapidus; sicut hircus fetidus; sicut serpens callidus'; ibid., fol. 377v: 'Dico . . . quod est in eo lupina rapacitas consumptiva'.

[28] Ibid., fol. 379v: 'Dicitur quod subversus est qui eiusmodi est. Ad litteram enim, sicut domus non habens fundamentum subvertitur et evertitur, et ideo vitatur; sic qui non habet fundamentum fidei subvertitur, et evertitur; sicut iste non habet. Et ideo subversus est . . . Cogitabam enim quod iste subversus est et subversor'.

[29] See Arbesmann, 1954, pp. 23–5.

[30] Clement VI, sermon 24, Ste-G. 240, fol. 374v: 'vitatur aliquid propter contagium, sicut morbus contagiosus vitatur ab aliis. Unde Numerosum v° [2–3] *Precipe filiis Israel, ut eiiciant de castris omnem leprosum . . . ne contaminent ea cum habitaverint vobiscum* . . . hereticus est contagiosus ad inficiendum. Suo morbo enim inficit'; see also fol. 375r. Raynaldus vi, ch. 63, p. 329, to Baldwin of Trier: 'eiusdem Ecclesiae, a qua velut membrum putridum separatus fore dignoscitur'; ch. 17, p. 381, to Louis of Hungary: 'prefatus Ludovicus sic extra communionem fidelium . . . tamquam putridum et infectum membrum extiterit', and ch. 18, p. 382, to Philip VI of France.

[31] Tautu, no. 87, par. 308: 'reincorporatus oboedientiae Sanctae Romanae Ecclesiae'. Cf. Benedict XII, Raynaldus vi, ch. 1, p. 23: 'disponeret se reincorporari unitati sanctae matris Ecclesiae'.

means. It was only when the patient grew worse that the knife had to be applied.[32]

In addition to imposing canonical processes against the heretical and schismatic Louis, Clement had tried to deal with him in practical terms through the appointment of Charles of Moravia as king of the Romans. Solving the problems posed by the schismatics and heretics in the East, however, was even more difficult, if only because they were inseparable from the infidel problem. Both the Byzantines and the Armenians expected the papacy to furnish them with military aid against the Turks. But the Pope needed to ensure their loyalty to Rome and their recognition of papal authority before committing any resources. To aid them without this would have been tantamount to condoning schism. In the case of Armenia, Clement's negotiations were a continuation of those of Benedict XII. Benedict had sent a detailed questionnaire to the schismatics in an attempt to enforce both doctrinal orthodoxy, and, above all, the recognition of papal primacy. Clement's Armenian catechism was a further instalment, since their replies to Benedict had been unsatisfactory.[33] In the final analysis, lack of internal unity and the Pope's lack of military resources to assist them against the Turks made reunion impossible.

Clement's initial achievement was the formation of a naval league, known as the Holy League, to defend the Latin strongholds of the Levant. The idea was not original: a naval league against the Turks (in which the Greeks had participated) had been formed in 1334, during John XXII's pontificate, and had achieved limited success. Benedict XII's efforts to revive it had come to nothing, but in 1341 an embassy sent by Hugh IV of Cyprus and Hélion of Villeneuve, Grand Master of the Hospitallers, had implored the Pope's aid against the Turks. The idea of forming the League was therefore being discussed at the time of Clement's accession. One of the reasons for Cardinal Guillaume Court's legation to Italy during the early months of the reign was to persuade the Venetians to join the League. His success gave Clement the opportunity to preach an exultant *collatio* when he returned to Avignon in 1343.[34] The League was accordingly composed of papal forces, Venice, the Knights Hospitaller, and Cyprus. Together these captured the key port of

---

[32] Clement VI, sermon 5, p. 142: 'Unde noster predecessor et nos voluimus sibi facere sicut facit bonus medicus, ut primo revocaremus eum lenibus, scilicet exhortationibus et monitionibus; sed quia infirmitas non curatur sed gravatur, oportet membrum illud eicere et resecare'.

[33] Tautu, *Acta Benedicti XII*, no. 59, pp. 160–229.

[34] Clement VI, sermon 42.

Smyrna (Izmir) on 28 October 1344, which was hailed as a great triumph, and which generated a good deal of popular support for the crusading movement throughout Europe.[35] But the Turks retaliated, killing the three commanders of the League. Clement was then faced with the tasks of providing reinforcements to strengthen the tenuous hold on Smyrna and of finding new leaders. This was not easy at the time, because the Hundred Years War absorbed the energies and resources of the French and English kings, and there was no emperor or king of the Romans. Clement tried to reason with Edward III that it was better to slake his aggression on the enemies of the Christian Faith than upon Philip VI, but to no avail.[36] The lack of suitable and willing leaders accounts for Clement's choice of the militarily inept Humbert of Vienne, who led an undistinguished expedition to Smyrna in 1345. He fought one inconclusive battle, and in 1347 was allowed to wend his inglorious way home.[37] Further crusades were prevented by the combined effects of plague and economic decline (of which the crash of some of the Italian banks was just one manifestation). When Clement did try to reconstitute the League in 1351 the war of Aragon and Venice against Genoa in the Levant precluded success.[38]

The Greeks were as much threatened by the Turks as the Latins, especially since they had reached the Bosporus. Byzantium stood to gain from any action the West might take against their common enemy, but there is no record of any Greek participation in the Holy League, perhaps because of the confusion caused by the civil war then raging in Constantinople. Nevertheless, the Greeks, like the Armenians, often requested military aid against the Turks, proferring the reunion of the Byzantine church with Rome as a bargaining counter. This allowed the papacy to press its advantage by demanding reunion first, trailing the prospect of armed assistance before them as a *quid pro quo*.[39] In fact, during Clement's pontificate, neither

[35] Housley, 1986, pp. 146–9. On the League and the Smyrna campaign see ibid., pp. 32–4; 120–2; 251–4, and app. 1. See also Gay, 1904, pp. 32–54; Atiya, 1938, pp. 239–301; Geanakoplos, 1975, pp. 59–61. On the crusade in general in the fourteenth century in addition see De Vries, 1964; Luttrell, 1965; Hazard, ed., 1975; Muldoon, 1979a and 1979b.

[36] Déprez, no. 1844, p. 26, to Edward III: 'O fili predilectissime, utinam! intra precordia regia revolves diligenter, quanta sue salutis merita, quanteque laudis preconium . . . acquires . . . si, reformata cum eodem rege pace . . . ad prosequendum Dei negotium . . . te . . . exerceres adversus hostes fidei catholice vires tuas'.

[37] On Humbert see Faure, 1907, in addition to works listed at n. 35 above.

[38] See Duvergé, 1939.

[39] See Gay, pp. 94–118; Nicol, 1969; Loernertz, 1953; Geanakoplos, 1975, pp. 57ff.

side could have given the other what it wanted. The papacy did not have the resources: the schismatics were not sufficiently united internally to have been able to impose union on their clergy and people. But it suited all parties to keep negotiations alive. Interestingly, Byzantine embassies were sent to Avignon in 1343, when Clement was intent on the formation of the League, and in 1348, at a time when he may have been planning a full-scale crusade – a *passagium generale* – to the Holy Land.[40] If the Greeks were not directly involved in the League or in Humbert's crusade, the Latin presence in the Levant afforded the opportunity for contact with them. The papal registers show that Clement used Humbert's expedition to pursue negotiations with the Byzantine Empress Anne, a Latin princess who ruled as regent for her son, John V Paleologus.[41] Moreover, when John Cantacuzenus, hitherto a persecutor of the Latins in Constantinople, seized the throne from Anne and her son in 1347, he arrived at the capital to find Humbert's ambassador already there, presumably ready to discuss the union question. As it suited Cantacuzenus, for political reasons, to take up the cause, he dispatched an embassy to Avignon the next year.[42] Clement sent two bishops to Constantinople in 1350.[43] Negotiations foundered, however, for many reasons. Quite apart from the undercurrent of political and theological strife in the city, which made any sort of unity impossible, the Greeks insisted on the calling of an ecumenical council to thrash out theological differences.[44] This was not a scheme calculated to appeal to the Pope, who was himself responsible for defining doctrine as Christ's earthly vicar, and would not have cared to have his definitions subjected to conciliar scrutiny.

Humbert of Vienne was, on the face of things, not the ideal leader for a crusade. Apart from his military incompetence, he was under ecclesiastical censure for a quarrel with his archbishop. Indeed, both Pope and cardinals seem to have had initial reservations about him.[45]

[40] See nn. 70–1 below.
[41] See Déprez, nos. 2580, 2582, 2595. For discussion see Gay, pp. 94–6, Geanakoplos, pp. 61–2; Gill, 1979, pp. 205–7; Housley, pp. 255–6.
[42] Gay, p. 96; Gill, pp. 64–5; Nicol, 1968, pp. 66–7, and 1972, pp. 241–2.
[43] Déprez-Mollat, nos. 2131–7.
[44] John Cantacuzenus, *Historiae*, bk iv, ch. 9, pp. 61–2. For discussion see Nicol, 1969, pp. 82–6.
[45] Humbert Pilati, *Memorabilia*, Valbonnais, no. 284, p. 677: 'fecit tractari . . . ut sibi daretur Capitaneatus Generalis passagii pro eundo in Turquiam, *et licet D. nostro papae et D. cardinalibus displiceret* ultra modum obtinuit'. On Humbert's

But he did have some things to recommend him. He had signed away his estates and title to the house of Valois by a treaty which was to become effective if he should remain heirless – a distinct possibility, given the delicate state of his wife's health. While Clement had his reservations about the agreement,[46] it did mean that Humbert's territorial ambitions were lukewarm. Among the conditions Clement was able to impose, despite the Dauphin's contrary request, was that the Holy See was not bound to give him anything by virtue of his leadership of the crusade.[47] Humbert was also refreshingly respectful to the papacy. He had provided a foretaste of this in 1335 when Louis of Bavaria had offered him the crown of Dauphiné, only to be rebuffed with the reply that Humbert would not accept it unless Louis were first crowned emperor by the pope. In the document he carefully excused himself for using the word *imperator*, explaining that he intended absolutely no recognition of Louis as emperor to be inferred from this.[48] The same attitude to the papacy is discernible in the petition Humbert sent to Clement requesting the leadership of the crusade. He recognised Clement as Christ's representative on earth, and 'offered and presented his body and his followers' to the Pope to be 'used for his honour and his service'.[49] Clement would have found it hard to reject one whose attitude was in such stark contrast to that of most of his contemporaries. Nor was Humbert's offer idly made, for throughout the expedition he referred all decisions to Clement.[50] The delays which this occasioned probably contributed materially to the failure of the venture.

Predictably the Pope's attitude to the office of captain-general was similar to his views on the king of the Romans and other lay rulers. Like the king of the Romans, Humbert was expected to petition for his office, and then to swear obedience to the Pope, underlining his total dependence upon him.[51] When Clement 'elevated' Humbert to

---

contemporary reputation see Faure, pp. 540–2, and see further Gay, p. 77; Housley, pp. 34–5; 254–7.

[46] See p. 171 above.

[47] Valbonnais, no. 208, p. 543: 'Par haec autem nolumus nos, vel sedem praedictam ad dandum aliud tibi ratione Capitaneatus et Ducatus hujusmodi quoquomodo adstringi'. See also Déprez, no. 4218. Cf. Housley, p. 254.

[48] Valbonnais, no. 50, p. 281.

[49] Ibid., no. 205, p. 539.

[50] Faure, p. 540, considers that in naming Humbert captain-general Clement was really appointing himself to command the expedition. See also Gay, pp. 75–7; Housley, pp. 255–6.

[51] Clement VI, sermon 16, Ste-G. 240, fol. 521v: 'Et quia inter ceteros principes reperi instantem sepius, supplicationem humilius, optantem ardentius, offeren-

office he staged a splendid ceremony, during which he preached what amounted to an approbation *collatio*. A fourteenth-century scribe who copied it was so overwhelmed by the magnificence of the occasion that he wrongly, but understandably, described it as a 'sermon on the *coronation* and mission of the Dauphin'.[52] Much of the sermon was taken up with eulogising Humbert in order to emphasise his suitability for office.[53] As in the case of Charles of Moravia and Louis de la Cerda, Clement also tried to impress the exalted character of the office upon the recipient, referring to his 'glorious uplifting' and resorting, as so often, to Old Testament terminology. Humbert was being made a 'leader in Israel', in the words of his sermon text: 'Whilst he fulfilled the Word, he was made leader in Israel'.[54]

Almost certainly the Pope made one of his resounding consistory declarations, later incorporated into the bull of appointment, to drive home the point that he alone instituted the office of captain-general and empowered its holder. Clement 'created, appointed, and ordained' him 'captain-general of the holy and apostolic see and leader of the Christian army against the Turks by apostolic authority'.[55] Significantly, too, the Pope seems to have changed Humbert's name. He explained that Humbert was being promoted 'on account of his name and title – as Ymbert, the Dauphin'. He then divided the name 'Ymbert' into its constituent parts – *ymber*, that is, rain, and *thus*, that is, incense.[56] Leaving aside the somewhat tedious variations which followed on the theme of rain and incense, the analysis of the name Ymbert acquires meaning when it is borne in mind that the Dauphin's name was actually *Hum*bert: this was Clement's way of emphasising the change. As might be expected, it was reflected in the diplomatic practice of the curia: Clement addressed him as 'Humbert' before his appointment, and as 'Ymbert' thereafter.[57] The Dauphin's vanity was touched. His

tem liberalius, dilectum filium Imbertus'. Cf. the bull of appointment, Valbonnais, no. 208, p. 543, and also for reference to the oath taken.
52 BN lat. 3293, fol. 297r.
53 Sermon 16, Ste-G. 240, fols. 521r–3v. See also the bull of appointment, Valbonnais, no. 208, p. 543.
54 Clement VI, sermon 16, Ste-G. 240, fol. 523r. Cf. I Mach., ii. 55.
55 Valbonnais, no. 208, p. 543.
56 Clement VI, sermon 16, Ste-G. 240, fol. 523r.
57 Cf. Déprez, no. 1398, letter of 15 January 1345: 'Dilecto filio nobili viro Humberto Dalphino Viennensi' with the greeting of the bull of appointment: Valbonnais, no. 208, p. 542: 'Nobilo viro Imberto Dalphino Viennensi Capitaneo Generali'.

secretary, Pilati, reported that a few days later the captain-general, in the presence of his chancellor and others, ordered that in future his name was to be written with a capital 'Y', so that it would be written as 'Ymbert'.[58] He had left behind him his private *persona*, Humbert, and had been reborn as a new man, totally identified with his new office. He had changed his name in precisely the same way as the pope himself did – to show that a miraculous transformation had taken place.

In making use of Humbert, Clement was having to accept second best in the absence of a more powerful lay prince. Humbert's inferior status may explain the lengths to which Clement went to exalt him. The sources give no indication that when John XXII had declared a crusade in 1333 and appointed Philip VI its leader there had been a comparable ceremony. Indeed, Philip had not attended consistory, sending instead his procurators, of whom Pierre Roger had been one.[59]

Clement hoped to extend papal *imperium* through Humbert's expedition, and indeed this was an aim of a good many crusades, although it was not always overtly declared. The acquisition or recovery of lands in infidel or pagan hands did in practice bring new areas under papal authority. This might have the effect of boosting the pope's waning prestige in the West and counterbalancing the erosion of Christian territories in the East by the Turks. Clement therefore wrote to Humbert after the capture of Smyrna stating that he hoped to acquire many other infidel territories in the surrounding region and to spread the Christian Faith.[60] In supporting Casimir of Poland's war against the Lithuanians his hope was that not only would the King's success extend Poland – one of the Pope's *propria regna*, as he hastened to point out[61] – but that it might also add another papal fief: Clement openly declared his intention of granting Kiejstut, co-prince of Lithuania, a royal crown and title once he was converted to Christianity.[62] When Algeciras fell to Alfonso XI after a long siege in the spring of 1344, Clement was jubilant. In a

---

[58] Humbert Pilati, *Memorabilia*, Valbonnais, no. 284, p. 677.
[59] See the bull by which John XXII declared the crusade and conferred its leadership on Philip: Raynaldus, v, chs. 3–6, pp. 545–7. See also Baluze-Mollat, *Quinta Vita Joannis XXII*, p. 174.
[60] See Clement's letter to Humbert of January 1345, written after the capture of Smyrna, Déprez, no. 1397: 'sperans . . . acquirere multas alias terras infidelium circumposite regionis cultumque fidei catholice . . . dilatare'.
[61] Theiner, *Mon. Pol.* no. 702, p. 532.
[62] Raynaldus, vi, ch. 24, p. 497.

congratulatory letter to the victor he described the triumph as being 'for the exaltation and spreading of the Faith'.[63] More importantly, amid tremendous celebrations at Avignon, the Pope solemnly elevated the 'temple', recently purged and consecrated to the Virgin by the Archbishop of Toledo, to the status of a cathedral church. In the *collatio* preached on the occasion, on the text 'By the blessing of the just shall the city be exalted (Prov., xi. 11)' he described how the former town had become a city, 'a priestly and royal city'[64] – how it was 'newly raised into cityship'. By its transformation into a cathedral city it had acquired a new form, and the old one had been expelled, Clement explained.[65] And to highlight this theme of renewal, to show that the city had in effect been reborn as a true city, it was given a new name, the 'City of the Green Isle' – *nunc vero civitatem Insulae Viridis*, he wrote.[66] The city cast off its old nature and acquired a new one in the same way as Humbert (Ymbert) did on becoming captain-general of the crusade, or Pierre Roger on becoming Clement VI, for that matter. True, the city's new name did not stick, but this does not detract from the Pope's efforts to leave his mark upon it, to show that it had come within the sphere of priestly *imperium*. To Louis de la Cerda, Clement was more direct in admitting the connection between papal *imperium* and the extension of the Faith than he was to the others. Extending the one was the same thing as extending the other: 'the glorious and abundant extension of the Faith in this instance agrees with the glorious and abundant extension of our *imperium*',[67] he declared.

In strict theory, the extension of papal *imperium* might not have been regarded as a valid criterion for the 'just' and therefore 'holy' war. But there were subtle ways of rationalising it. Augustine and Aquinas had both stipulated that a just war had to avenge some wrong, such as the restoration of something which had been seized unjustly.[68] In some cases, therefore, Clement made it appear that the wars he authorised were for the recovery of once-Christian ter-

---

[63] Déprez, no. 981.

[64] Clement VI, sermon 6, Ste-G. 240, fol. 551v: 'Deo cooperante, cepit in civitatem erigere ut amodo dicatur civitas sacerdotalis et regia'. Cf. I Peter, ii. 9.

[65] Ibid.: 'Et istud videmus satis in formis naturalibus, quandoque enim forma nova acquiritur et precedens expellitur'.

[66] Raynaldus, vi, 1344, ch. 52, p. 364. See also Déprez, no. 981: 'ac subsequenter villam de Algezira predictam in civitatem, que vocatur Insula viridis . . . insignitam'.

[67] Clement VI, sermon 45, Ste-G. 240, fol. 337v.

[68] Thomas Aquinas, *Summa Theologiae*, IIa, iiae, q. 40, art. i, p. 1267. On Augustine see Markus, 1983, and in general Russell, 1975.

ritory. There are hints that he would have liked Humbert's expedition to go to Jerusalem,[69] and that, after its failure, he was planning a separate expedition to go there.[70] There could be no doubt that this had been unjustly seized. In a letter the Pope wrote of the recovery of the Holy Land – *recuperatio* – and referred to it as 'the inheritance of Christ'.[71] Preaching before John XXII, Pierre Roger had urged all the faithful to fight for its recovery. Christ had bought the Holy Land with His own blood, which meant that all Christians ought to try to effect its restoration to Him, the more so because it had been lost through no fault of Christ's, but through the iniquities of Christians themselves. It was only fitting that the land should be restored to Christ by a Christian army.[72] Algeciras, of course, did not need such justification: its recovery was part of the *Reconquista* which had been going on for centuries.[73] In any case, both Humbert's expedition and the siege of Algeciras could have been justified on the grounds that they were defensive wars.

It was more difficult to justify obscure territories like the Fortune Islands as in need of reconquest. Yet even here Clement managed to find some evidence of their once-Christian status. He cited a letter of Augustine, which proved that there had once been Christian monks and abbots on one of the islands.[74] There was not a shadow of doubt that they ranked, in the words of Simon Maccabeus, as 'the inheritance of our fathers which our enemies had wrongfully in their

---

[69] One of the texts Clement used in sermon 16 was the lamentation of Mathatias the priest, I Mach., ii, 7: 'Woe to me, wherefore was I born to see this misery of my people and of the holy city when it was delivered into the hands of the enemy', and, comparing himself with Mathatias, he referred to Jerusalem 'in manibus spurcidorum Agarenorum' (Ste-G. 240, fol. 521v). A Genoese chronicler thought that Humbert's expedition was bound for Jerusalem: Georgius Stella, *Annales Genuenses*, col. 1086: 'Ibant scil. Delphinus et alii Hierosolymam ad sacrosanctum Jesu Dei nostri sepulchrum'. Cf. Gay, p. 64.

[70] See Clement's bull of 17 March 1348 to all the faithful, Déprez-Mollat, no. 1605. The Black Death prevented the plan from being fulfilled. See Gay, pp. 85–6; Housley, p. 32.

[71] Déprez-Mollat, no. 1605.

[72] Pierre Roger, sermon 2, Ste-G. 240, fol. 301v: 'Sed certum est quod Christus terram illam sanctam proprii corporis sanguine comperavit . . . Ergo merito quilibet Christianus debet conari ut Christo restituatur, et maxime quia Christus eam perdidit non propter factum suum, sed propter peccata nostra, scilicet Christianorum . . . Sicut propter peccata nostra Christus eam perdidit, sic per virtutis exercitium debet sibi per Christianos restitui atque reddi'.

[73] On this see Lomax, 1978.

[74] Clement VI, sermon 45, Ste-G. 240, fol. 340r: 'de istis insulis, specialiter de Capraria, legitur expresse quod ibi fuerat Christiani monachi et abbates valde sancti. Unde beatus Augustinus scribit epistolam ad Eudoxium, Abbatem Insule Caprarie'. Cf. Augustine, ep. 48, *CSEL*, 33, pp. 137–40.

possession a certain time', and that 'we, having opportunity, claim the inheritance of our fathers'.[75] Clement also used what has been termed the 'omni-insular' doctrine, by which the papacy claimed to possess all islands.[76] The foundation of this claim was the Donation of Constantine, by which the Emperor had granted possession of all islands to Pope Silvester.[77] Clement cited the example of Boniface VIII, who had granted the islands of Djerba and Kerkennah to Roger de Loria in 1295,[78] although this was an unhappy precedent since Roger had been no more successful in conquering and converting his kingdom than Louis was to be.[79]

It would have been possible to justify expeditions to the Holy Land, Granada, or the Fortune Islands simply because they were possessed by infidels. The classic discussion on the position of infidels during the late-medieval period was that of Innocent IV. Clement followed him only up to a point. Innocent had accorded the pope universal jurisdiction by right, but had realised that in practice it would not be recognised. All men were the sheep of Christ by creation, he explained, although not all were of the fold.[80] He considered that the lordship of infidels was not of itself evil, and that the pope therefore had no *prima facie* cause to destroy it: it was held without sin.[81] Starting from his premiss of the universality of papal jurisdiction, Clement explained that the whole world had once been Christian. Using Paul's words to the Romans, he emphasised that when Christ had sent forth his followers to preach, the sound of their voices had gone out into all lands. And this meant that there was

---

75 Ibid., fol. 340r. I Mach., xv. 34.
76 See Weckmann, 1949.
77 *Donation of Constantine*, pp. 84–5.
78 Clement VI, sermon 45, Ste-G. 240, fol. 339r: 'Videtur . . . michi quod istam potestem habeam . . . a concessione facta per Constantinum, qui dimisit Silvestro et eius successoribus totum imperium occidentis, sicut apparet in epistola Constantini, in qua etiam sit expressa mentio de insulis. Unde et dominus Bonifacius papa viii Rogerio de Loria quasdam alias infeudavit'.
79 For the bull of provision for the first bishop of the Canary Islands – all that Clement achieved there – see Eubel, 1892, pp. 237–40.
80 Innocent IV, *ad Decretales*, III, xxxiv, 8: 'Omnes autem tam fideles quam infideles oves sunt Christi per creationem, licet non sint de ovili Ecclesie. Et sic per predicta apparet, quod Papa super omnes habet iurisdictionem et potestatem de iure, licet non de facto'. Cf. John of Legnano, *De Principatu*, p. 443 and ibid, p. 444; Alvarus Pelagius, *De Planctu Ecclesiae*, bk i, ch. 37, p. 54 and also ch. 13, p. 30; ch. 37, pp. 45–6; Galvaneus Flamma, *Chronica Galvagnana*, ch. 184, p. 185; ch. 196, p. 191. For discussion on papal jurisdiction over infidels see Ullmann, 1949, pp. 115–36; Wilks, 1963a, pp. 423ff.; Muldoon, 1979a, pp. 3–28.
81 Innocent IV, *ad Decretales*, III, xxxiv, 8, fol. 176v. Cf. Aquinas, *Summa Theologiae*, IIa, iiae, q. x. art. 1, p. 1131.

literally no corner of the world where they had not been heard. Everywhere had once been Christian, and of course infidels could have no rights in lands which had once been sanctified.[82] Clement concluded that infidels could have no rights anywhere in the world, and that they merited attack simply *ratione infidelitatis*, 'by reason of infidelity'.[83]

There were two aspects to the discussion, the lordship of infidels over Christians and that of infidels over infidels. On the first he supported Innocent IV, and Aquinas, whom he cited, that infidel lordship over Christians should be destroyed.[84] But he gave their view his own peculiar slant by taking the opportunity to air once again his favourite metaphor of the ruler who was married to his people. He thought that if a man remained in infidelity he deserved to lose the rights he had over a faithful wife. The same thing applied to the dominion of an infidel lord over a faithful servant. The inference seemed to be that the marriage thought to have taken place between a ruler and his people was valid only if both parties were Christian.[85] The question of 'mixed' marriages was one which captured the attention of contemporary canonists.[86]

---

[82] Clement VI, sermon 45, Ste-G. 240, fol. 337v: 'Qui quando misit apostolos non solum misit ad unam provinciam, sed ad universam terram . . . Et de quibus dicitur in Ps. et deducit Apostolus ad Romanos x [18] *In omnem terram exivit sonus eorum et in fines orbis terrae verba eorum*', and ibid., fol. 340r: 'Prima ratio est quia terre iste quandoque fuerunt Christianorum et ideo non possunt ibi infideles ius habere. Quod autem quandoque fuerunt Christianorum videtur ex ratione generali pro auctoritatibus supra allegatis, scilicet *in omnem terram* . . . Unde Apostolus . . . reputat valde falsum quod sit aliqua pars que non audierit vocem Apostolorum et discipulorum. Unde dicit sed dicens numquid non audierunt. Hoc quidem *in omnem terram*, etc.'.

[83] Ibid., fol. 341r: 'Quarta ratio est generaliter ratione fidelitatis. Forte enim infideles ratione infidelitatis merentur perdere omnem dominium, et possunt cogi ad suscipiendum fidem vel dimittendum terras quas possident'.

[84] Ibid., fol. 341v: 'Sed prosequendo de aliis infidelibus Thomas clare in secunda secunde q. x in corpore questionis dicit quod per sententiam vel ordinationem Ecclesie, auctoritatem Dei habentis dominium vel prelatio infidelium super infideles tolli potest, quia infideles merito sue infidelitatis merentur potestatem amittere super fideles qui transferuntur in filios Dei'. Cf. Aquinas, *Summa Theologiae*, IIa, iiae, q. x, art. 10, p. 1138.

[85] Ibid., fol. 341v: 'Videtur enim esse tam de iure divino quam de iure positivo, maior inseparabilitas et maior coniunctio in matrimonio inter virum et uxorem quam inter dominum et servum. Sed ex merito infidelitatis aliquis manens in infidelitate sua comperare facto fideli meretur perdere ius quod habet super fidelem ratione dicti matrimonii. Ut patet per Apostolorum I ad Cor. vii° et extra *de divorciis* [*Decretales*, IV, xix]'.

[86] For example, Albericus de Rosate, *Dictionarium*, p. 147: 'Quid iuris sit de matrimonio infidelium que contrahunt cum Christianis? Dico secundum omnes quod nullum est ipso iure . . .' This was based on the maxim 'Matrimonium non

Clement pretended to be more dubious about the lordship of infidels over infidels, but his conclusion was plain enough: the *Ecclesia* could use the plenitude of power to order its destruction whenever this was expedient.[87] It was not necessarily always expedient. In the case of the Tartars, Clement's initial reaction was tolerant, even friendly, to judge from his letter to Djani-beg, Khan of the Crimea. This was because the Khan's predecessors had allowed Christian preachers into their territories and had protected them.[88] No doubt the Pope hoped that the Khan would emulate his forbears, and so foster a peaceable extension of papal *imperium*. Infidel lordship would become Christian lordship. It was only later in the pontificate, when the Tartars attacked the Christian kingdoms of Poland and Hungary, that the Pope declared a crusade against them.[89] But ultimately, as Clement warned, all non-Christian lordship merited the use of force, because all true dominion was based on virtue, and there was no virtue among infidels, merely its shadow: true dominion among them was thus impossible.[90] This was comparable with the radical view of the publicist Aegidius Romanus, advanced in 1302, that infidels could have no true and just possession, dominion, or power, but only 'by usurpation and with injustice'.[91] Clement's view was an advance on Innocent IV's idea of the sinless nature of infidel jurisdiction. Among canonists, it was more like that of Hostiensis.[92] It was also similar to that adopted by several fourteenth-century writers that 'outside the *Ecclesia* there is no *imperium*'.[93]

tenet propter disparitatem cultus'. For discussion of marriage between infidels and Christians see Esmein, 1929, i, pp. 242–59; Ullmann, 1949, pp. 59–66; Noonan, 1972, esp. pp. 263–4, 342–7; Muldoon, 1975, esp. pp. 139–40.

[87] Clement VI, sermon 45, Ste-G. 240, fols. 341v–2r: 'Sed maius dubium est de dominio infidelis super infidelem. Sed hic tango aliqua conferendo. Et videtur quod per auctoritatem seu sententiam Ecclesie, que plenam potestatem habet, potest iuste statui et ordinari quod tale dominium ab eis tollatur sive in una regione sive in omnibus sicut ei visum fuerit expedire'.

[88] Raynaldus, vi, chs. 21–2, p. 316.

[89] Theiner, *Mon. Pol.*, no. 713, p. 539.

[90] Clement VI, sermon 45, Ste-G. 240, fol. 343r: 'nullum dominium debet esse sine virtute. In infidelibus autem nulla est virtus, sed ymago virtutis solum. Ergo nec verum dominium cum *sine fide impossibile sit placere Deo.* ad Hebr. xi° [6]'.

[91] Aegidius Romanus, *De Ecclesiastica Potestate*, bk ii, ch. 11, p. 96. For discussion see Villey, pp. 570–4.

[92] Hostiensis, *ad Decretales*, III, xxxiv, 8, fol. 128v: 'Mihi tamen videtur quod in adventum Christi omnis honor et omnis principatus et omne dominium et iurisdictio de iure et ex causa iusta . . . omni infideli subtracta fuerit et ad fideles translata'.

[93] Anon., *Songe du Vergier*, bk i, ch. 155, p. 316, where the clerk summarises the arguments of Innocent IV and Hostiensis, deciding in favour of the latter:

On the related question of the forcible conversion of infidels, Clement was again more extreme than Innocent IV. Innocent thought that infidels should not be compelled to embrace Christianity, but merely to admit Christian preachers. It was only in cases where they were blatantly infringing natural law that the pope could step in to punish them, although Innocent did not commit himself on what form that punishment should take. In practice, as he had to admit, it could be shown that the majority of infidels were breaking natural law by worshipping idols rather than the one God, the creator, which justified papal intervention.[94] Innocent at least allowed the possibility that some infidels might not be infringing natural law; Clement VI did not. As sinners against natural law, infidels must be compelled by the pope, the prince of monarchs, whose duty it was to coerce his subjects to live according to right reason, he declared.[95] The compulsion of infidels to live according to right reason was a euphemism for their forcible conversion to Christianity, so that they would live according to divine law. Clement reached this conclusion again largely through arguments based on universality. He described to Louis de la Cerda how men are infused with the spirit of the creator. They are made in the image of Christ. If the things which are Caesar's, because they bear his image, must be rendered to Caesar, then how much more should things belonging to God and bearing His image be rendered to Him. This could happen only through the Faith.[96] Employing the familiar imagery of the Book of Daniel, the Pope observed that the fifth kingdom was given to the Christian people, and that it had to crush all infidel kingdoms. Christendom had to fill the whole earth like the

'Parquoy il samble que, par l'avenement de Iesuchrist, toute seignourie et juridiction si fust ostee dez Mescreans et transportee es Crestians'. See also Galvaneus Flamma, *Chronica Galvagnana*, ch. 196, p. 191: 'imperium non est nec esse potuit extra ecclesiam, id est apud aliquem ydolatrem vel hereticum'; Guido Vernani, *De Potestate Summi Pontificis*, p. 58. For discussion see Muldoon, 1966, esp. pp. 578–9 on Hostiensis, and 1979a, pp. 15ff.

[94] Innocent IV, *ad Decretales*, III, xxxiv, 8, fol. 176v.

[95] Clement VI, sermon 45, Ste-G. 240, fol. 340r: 'ratio est quia isti peccant contra legem nature. Peccantes autem contra legem nature puniendi sunt per principem monarchie sicut est papa ad quem pertinet subditos cohercere ut vivant secundum rectam rationem'.

[96] Ibid, fol. 343r: 'Unde anima in quolibet a Deo creando infunditur, et infundendo creatur. Ergo magis cogendus est quilibet ad reddendum Deo que Dei sunt quam ad reddendum Cesari que Cesaris sunt. Sed aliquis cogendus est ad reddendum Cesari que Cesaris sunt, ergo cogendus est magis ad reddendum Deo que Dei sunt. Unde Christus quia in numismate erat ymago Cesaris mandaverit reddi Cesari. Mt. xxii [21]. Cum ergo in anima cuiuslibet hominis sit ymago Christi, debet cogi ut reddat eam Christo, quod non potest nisi per fidem'.

great mountain of the prophecy. On this basis, kings who forced infidels to embrace Christianity were to be lauded: indeed, the Pope himself ought to use force against them.[97] But was this right? After all, as Clement realised, pagans should come voluntarily to the Faith. And there was no reference in Scripture to the compulsion of infidels.[98] But, as so often with Clement, it was the spirit rather than the letter of Scripture which counted, and this seemed to indicate that the Church must realise its universal potential on earth. To make this point he drew on Romans, xi. 25–6: 'Blindness in part is happened to Israel, until the fullness of the Gentiles be come in. And so all Israel shall be saved'.[99] Israel in this case signified the universal Church, and blindness, as was usual in papal writing, signified unbelievers and heretics. Clement was convinced that the fullness of the Gentiles should have been converted at the coming of Christ, but as this had clearly not happened they would now have to be compelled, assuming that they would not come in voluntarily.[100] By forcing them it was as if the Pope were helping the fulfilment of a divine prophecy. Nor did it conflict with basic Christian ideas, since it had been advocated by Augustine.[101]

Clement's attitude to the final group of 'outsiders', the Jews, was different from that to infidels. Traditionally, from the time of Gregory I onward, the papacy's attitude had been one of tolerance, although it was often limited tolerance.[102] Innocent III, for example, had protected the Jews in his *Constitutio pro Judaeis*, itself partly a repetition of earlier legislation, but he had added a saving clause to the effect that protection would apply only to those Jews who did not plot against the Faith.[103] The Fourth Lateran Council of 1215 had imposed the wearing of distinctive clothing upon the Jews.[104] John XXII initially protected them from the fanatical Pastoreaux, but later appeared to condone their banishment from papal ter-

---

[97] Ibid., fols. 342v–3r. Cf. Dan., ii. 34.

[98] Ibid., fol. 339v: 'Cum iste non possit habere dictas insulas sine bello, quomodo possumus iuste sibi dare et indicere talibus infidelibus iustum bellum, maxime cum infideles non sint cogendi ad fidem, sed voluntarie venire debent? . . . Iterum non placent Deo coacta servicia. Iterum non legimus aliquod in sacra scriptura fuisse coactum'.

[99] Ibid., fol. 343r.

[100] Ibid.

[101] On Augustine's attitude to coercion see Markus, 1970, pp. 133–53; Brown, 1964.

[102] See in general Bardinet, 1880; Synan, 1965; Grayzel, 1966.

[103] Grayzel, pt 2, no. 5, p. 92. See his comments on the indebtedness of Innocent to earlier popes at pp. 76–8.

[104] See Cutler, 1970.

ritories by assisting the foundation of chapels dedicated to the Virgin on the sites of former synagogues.[105] To guard the purity of the Faith he renewed the proscriptions of the Talmud issued by Clement IV and Honorius IV.[106]

In the year 1348 the Jews were accused, not for the first time, of poisoning the wells and fountains and so causing the Black Death. Thousands were massacred, and the murders were supplemented by Jewish suicides and politic conversions to Christianity.[107] Clement issued a bull protecting the Jews and their property on 4 July 1348,[108] and this was followed by a tougher one on 26 September.[109] By the following spring the papal orders had taken effect, perhaps because of their cogent logic that since the plague did not spare the Jews themselves, and since it raged in areas where there were no Jews, they could hardly have caused the disease.[110] A few months later, however, the massacres started again with renewed ferocity, inspired by the bands of heretical Flagellants who swept Europe. These thought that they could appease the wrath of God, which had dealt mankind the punishment of plague, through their revoltingly spectacular penance of public flagellation. For good measure, they also demanded the extermination of the Jews, in the belief that God willed it.[111] Through invective and flagellation they would whip up the people's emotions and then lead them forth to murder. Clement VI condemned them in October 1349.[112]

Clement's attitude, as evidenced by his three bulls, was one of tolerance towards the people of Israel. His main accusation against the Flagellants was that under pretence of piety they had let loose the works of impiety. They had cruelly shed the blood of the Jews, whom 'Christian piety receives and sustains and does not allow to be harmed'.[113] Certainly Clement had sustained them the previous

---

[105] See John's letter to the Archbishop of Narbonne, 19 June 1320, Coulon, no. 1104; and see no. 1284 describing the foundation of the chapel at Bédarrides, 4 September 1321. For discussion of John's attitude see Synan, pp. 129–31.
[106] Raynaldus, v, ch. 24, pp. 137–8.
[107] Baluze-Mollat, *Prima Vita*, pp. 251–2; *Sexta Vita*, p. 306. On the accusations see Guerchberg, 1965, and on these and the massacres see Bardinet, p. 19, and Synan, pp. 132–3.
[108] Raynaldus, vi, ch. 33, p. 477.
[109] Déprez, no. 3966.
[110] Ibid.
[111] Baluze-Mollat, *Prima Vita*, pp. 251–2; *Sexta Vita*, pp. 306–7. For the belief that they were performing God's will see Fredericq, 1903, p. 691. In general see Cohn, 1962, pp. 124–48.
[112] Raynaldus, vi, ch. 21, p. 495.
[113] Ibid.

year. He had condemned the Jewish massacres in the strongest possible terms, threatening excommunication to any who harmed them. He had protected their property and had ordered Christians to submit any quarrels they had with Jews to due process of law.[114] Much of this repeated the *Constitutio pro Judaeis*. There could scarcely have been a greater contrast than with Clement's attitude to infidels. The question of forcible conversion was equally divergent. Clement did admit to hating the faithlessness of the Jews, who obdurately refused to recognise the hidden meaning of their own scriptures and prophets, and to accept the Faith and salvation.[115] Nevertheless, again echoing the *Constitutio*, Clement forbade Christians to force unwilling Jews to baptism, though they were to accept 'without calumny' any who came voluntarily. He added that those who were compelled to be baptised were not believed to possess the true Faith.[116] The contrast scarcely needs underlining.

Why did Clement tolerate the Jews? Since we lack any sermon of his on the subject it is not an easy question to answer. In his personal capacity as Pierre Roger he seems to have been interested in Jewish culture. His copying of the Hebrew alphabet into his commonplace book at Paris indicates this, as does the dedication of one, and probably two, works to Clement at Avignon by the astronomer Leo Judaeus, the Rabbi Levi ben Gerson, which Clement then had translated from Hebrew into Latin.[117] The destruction of the Jews would have brought the Pope no personal advantage. Nor would it have brought financial gain, for, as Renouard has shown, there is no evidence that the Avignon popes were in their debt.[118] There was also no territorial or political advantage, for the Jews lived in minority groups in Gentile domains, to which they presented no physical threat. There was no practical reason to persecute them.

There may, however, have been theoretical reasons for tolerating them. The traditional reason was that of Augustine, namely that they bore witness to the truth of the Faith, more especially since they possessed the writings in which the coming of Christ was prophesied.[119] Innocent III had endorsed this in his introduction to the

---

[114] Ibid., ch. 33, p. 477 and Déprez, no. 3966.

[115] Déprez, no. 3966.

[116] Raynaldus, vi, ch. 33, p. 477, 4 July 1348. Cf. John Baconthorpe, *Quaestiones in Quatuor Libros Sententiarum* q. xii, art. 1, p. 270: 'An Judaei ad fidem alliciendi sint? Ubi nota quod ad Baptismum est necessarius consensus, ideo nullus dicitur ad Baptismum compelli'. For discussion see Ullmann, 1978, no. 10, p. 236.

[117] See above pp. 65–6.   [118] Renouard, 1941, p. 106, n. 58.

[119] Augustine, *Enarratio in Psalmum lviii*, CC, xxxix, p. 744.

Constitutio, and although Clement did not repeat it, his remarks about the Jews' refusal to recognise the meaning of the Prophets, also noted by Innocent, may be a shorthand formula for a familiar idea. Clement's friend Jean de Fayt, a master in theology at Paris, had cited it in the sermon he preached to persuade Clement to condemn the Flagellants, above all for their massacre of the Jews.[120]

The sole reason the Pope gave for protecting the chosen people was that they were precisely that, for Christ had issued from them.[121] This, however, is a drastic abbreviation of his views. From Clement's political *collationes* and letters there emerges a close identification between the people of Israel and the Christian people. Charles IV had become the prototype of Solomon, and Clement had 'established the throne of his kingdom over Israel'.[122] Humbert of Vienne was, in the words of Maccabees, made a 'leader in Israel'.[123] Then there was the identification of Rome with Jerusalem, and the comparison Clement made between his cathedral church of the Lateran and the Temple of Jerusalem – *templum Domini quod est Rome*, signifying that for him the Temple of Jerusalem was the prototype of the Lateran.[124]

The people of Israel had become the prototype of the Christian people. In one sermon before John XXII, Pierre Roger had explained that the Holy Land belonged to Christians by right of succession, for God had promised it to Abraham and his seed for ever, and Christians were the heirs of Abraham.[125] The canonist John Calderinus in discussing the Petrine commission saw Abraham as the prototype of the pope. When God had promoted Abraham He had changed his name from Abram to Abraham to show that he had become the father of many nations. The same thing was true of the pope, who was also the father of many nations.[126]

[120] Jean de Fayt, *Sermones*, p. 705. On Clement and Jean de Fayt see app. 1, nos. 6–8.
[121] Déprez, no. 3966.
[122] I Paral., xxii. 10. Clement VI, sermon 40, p. 152. See above pp. 166–7.
[123] Clement VI, sermon 16, Ste-G. 240, fol. 521v.
[124] See above pp. 94–5.
[125] Pierre Roger, sermon 2, Ste-G. 240, fols. 300v–1r: 'Primo quidem ratione successionis. Terra enim sancta dicitur terra promissionis. Fuit enim Gen. xii° [7] promissa semini Abrahe . . . Et ad Gal. iii° [16] *Abrahae dictae sunt promissiones et semini eius. Non dicit in seminibus, quasi in multis, sed quasi in uno, et semini tuo qui est Christus.* Patet ergo quomodo illa terra iure successionis debetur Christianis'.
[126] Johannes Calderinus, *Commentaria ad Decretales, Proemium*, ii, fol. 2r: 'hoc fuisse signatum in veteri testamento, Gen., xvii [5] ubi Deus promovens Abraam mutavit sibi nomen dicens: *Eris pater multarum gentium. Nec ultra vocabit nomen tuum Abram, sed appellaberis Abraham, quia patrem multarum gentium constituti te.* Quod optime convenit pape, quod pater est multarum gentium'. For discussion

For Clement VI the *Ecclesia* itself was a continuation of the synagogue, and the advent of Christ had effected a transformation rather than a break. Before the birth of Christ the synagogue had been limited to one people, in one land, Judea, he told Louis de la Cerda. But now the Church was universally diffused throughout all lands.[127] In the New Testament God did not speak just to the people of Israel through the Prophets: He spoke to the whole world through the Son whom He had constituted the heir of all things.[128]

Ultimately Clement saw Christ Himself as the essential link between Jew and Gentile. He was the mean between them, connecting and including both. As he explained, echoing the sermons of Innocent III, Christ had liked to perform all His actions *in medio*. He had been born in between two animals, the ox and the ass, denoting respectively Gentiles and Jews.[129] Christ always wished to be *in medio* so that He might, like the biblical corner-stone, unite two things equally, that is, the Gentiles and the Jews.[130] Shortly before his elevation to the papacy, Clement declared that just as the ox and the ass had tarried at the manger, and Christ had offered food to both, so today both peoples were fed and refreshed in the manger of the Church.[131]

On the question of the 'outsiders' there was no conflict between Clement's official and his unofficial attitudes, except in so far as he allowed Philip VI to discourage his soldiers from going on the crusade, which would have left France unprotected against the English.[132] The Pope's aim was to bring all those outside the Faith into obedience to the Roman see. Heretics were a threat to the internal structure of the Church. Schismatics either divided the

and further examples of Abraham as the prototype of the pope see Wilks, 1963a, pp. 538–40.

127 Clement VI, sermon 45, Ste-G. 240, fol. 337v.

128 Ibid.: 'Et propter hoc in novo testamento non est Deus solum locutus filiis Israhel in prophetis, sed locutus est toti mundo in filio quem constituit heredem universorum'.

129 Clement VI, sermon 46, Ste-G. 240, fol. 413r: 'Et ideo videtur michi quod quasi omnia facta sua voluit facere in medio. In medio duorum animalium bovis et asini, id est in medio populo gentilis et iudei nasci. Per bovem enim . . . populus Israheliticus . . . per asinum autem . . . populus gentilis'. Cf. Innocent III, *PL*, 217, 509.

130 Ibid.: 'Voluit sicut lapis angularis [Ps. cxvii (cxviii).22] in medio poni ut coniungeret utrumque pariter: iudeorum scilicet et gentilium'. Cf. Innocent III, *PL*, 217, 811.

131 Pierre Roger, sermon 43, Ste-G. 240, fol. 395v: 'Et sicut ista duo animalia in presepi iacebant et ambobus alimentum commune ihesus prebobat, sic uterque populus in presepi hodie ecclesie pascitur et reficitur'.

132 See above, p. 140, n. 106. Cf. Housley, pp. 86–7.

Church from within, or set up an alternative society outside it: they presented either an internal threat to the papal plenitude of power, or a violation of the universality of that power. Both of these groups merited persecution. Infidels were a threat to existing Christians, and they occupied territory to which they had no right. They too were a denial of the universality of papal *imperium*, especially when seen in the context of the fulfilment of Old Testament prophecies about Christendom filling the whole earth. Infidel lordship had to be destroyed and the fullness of the Gentiles brought in, if necessary by force. But the Jews were a different case. Clement could scarcely have fulfilled his role as the vicar of Christ, the corner-stone who had joined Jew and Gentile to make them one, if he had persecuted the people of Israel. Ultimately it was only when the Christian society on earth had achieved both internal harmony, through obedience to the Roman pontiff, and universality, through the inclusion of all peoples, that it would truly mirror the Church Triumphant. Only then could the heavenly Jerusalem descend to earth and the forces of Babylon finally be overcome.

Chapter 9

CONCLUSION

Clement VI died on St Nicholas's Day 1352 (6 December). Almost a year to the day before this – on 7 December 1351 – he had made his deathbed confession. In it he recognised, as he had done more than once in consistory,[1] that as a man he was both sinful and fallible. He had, he wrote, lived as a sinner among sinners. His main worry was that in preaching, disputing, or lecturing, 'through a slip of the tongue', *ex lapsu lingue*, he might have uttered something contrary to the truth and the Faith. He submitted all his faults for correction to the authority of the Apostolic See.[2] There could hardly have been a clearer separation between the person and the office.[3]

How successful had Pierre Roger's transformation from human being to terrestrial god been, allowing for the odd *lapsus lingue*? Did Clement VI allow his private passions or prejudices to alter the nature of the papal office? Was he a 'Renaissance' pope in the sense that his personality dominated the office? The answer to such questions must be 'no'. In the first place, Clement worked entirely within the accepted framework of a corporate Christian society, the *corpus Christi mysticum*, which was in theory universal and unique. Indeed, he did everything he could towards the realisation in practice of the theoretical universality of the Church Militant on earth, both through his crusading policies and through his encouragement of the conversion of those on the geographical borders of Christendom. He also lost no opportunity to stress the universality of care he had assumed for all Christians. This preoccupation with universality

---

[1] Clement VI, sermon 31, Ste-G. 240, fol. 435r. See p. 66, n. 88 above. See also sermon 34, Ste-G. 240, fol. 359r.
[2] Déprez, no. 5138.
[3] This attitude was supported by Guido Terreni, *Quaestio de Magisterio Infallibili Romani Pontificis*, p. 27: 'Summus pontifex, etsi, ut est persona singularis, possit in se errare, tamen propter communitatem fidelium, et universalitatem Ecclesie . . . non permittit eum determinare aliquid contra fidem'. The Clerk in the *Songe du Vergier*, ii, ch. 154, p. 129, was later to dwell on the pope's capacity to sin *conme honme privé* [sic].

meant that there was no question of his jettisoning his universal responsibilities in order to embroil himself in local politics, as the Renaissance popes were later to do in Italy. His insistence on remaining bishop of Rome coupled with his avoidance of being seen as a mere bishop of Avignon is sufficient testimony of this.

Inseparable from Clement's efforts to realise the universality of the Christian society were those to uphold papal sovereignty against seemingly overwhelming odds. In practice the nature of society was changing gradually but irreversibly from a united and universal body orientated to a Christian purpose to a collection of independent national sovereign states, whose rulers considered that they owed subjection to no one. This, and the development of the lay spirit, of new and secular values, leading to demands for participation and consent in matters of government, caused the role of the pope as a divine and omnipotent ruler to be challenged as never before. In his expressions of the theory of papal monarchy Clement was thoroughly traditional. But, given that he wanted to express it at all, he could hardly have been otherwise. He was often reiterating theories which had reached their fullest expression over a century earlier. Moreover, in dealing with concepts such as sovereignty and universality he was dealing with absolutes: nothing can be added to them or subtracted from them. If, however, there was an opportunity to extend theories which supported them to their limits, then Clement would do so, sometimes appearing to compete with the canonists and papal publicists. Thus his remark that he possessed Rome because he possessed the world, rather than the world because he possessed Rome, brought his views into line with the publicists. The same was true of his opinions on infallibility, which, given his identification with the Holy Ghost, the spirit of truth, which prevented him from erring in matters of faith, were more like those of Guido Terreni than John XXII. His conviction that infidels merited destruction simply because they were such was an advance on that of Innocent IV and was voiced in order to help Clement extend the Faith, and with it his own *imperium*.

Arguably there were occasions when the Pope's efforts to stress his role as a mortal god went too far. This was so in his relations with his advisers, the cardinals – so much so that it drove them to stage a palace revolution in 1352. By the drawing up of their electoral pact they tried to limit the pope in the exercise of his plenitude of power and to transform the government of the Church from a monarchy to an oligarchy. But Clement's situation was difficult: however much he stressed his omnipotence in theory, in practice, particularly in the tumultuous conditions of the fourteenth century, it could not be implemented without help. Force of circumstances meant that the cardinals had to be given extensive powers, responsibilities, and resources, which not merely stimulated their appetites for more, but made them doubly resentful when the Pope treated them as his 'creatures'. True, he might on occasions have been a bit more tactful with them. But it is difficult to see how he could have 'shared' sovereignty with them without changing the nature of the papal monarchy, given both the indivisibility and inalienability of sovereignty.

Clement had embraced all the traditional ideas of the papal-hierocratic theory on sovereignty. There were, however, one or two sensitive areas where he did allow his private passions and prejudices to influence him, circumstances where he did not manage to separate the person from the office. This was blatantly so in the case of France, where his love of his native land rendered him incapable of impartial mediation in Anglo-French conflicts. It also led him to protestations about his lack of bias which were less than sincere. His love for France also led to his refusal to set a date for returning the papacy to Rome, and again to a certain lack of sincerity in his public declarations about it. Nevertheless, he made sure that his attitude did no damage to the theory of the successorship of St Peter. It could even be argued that he had strengthened it by freeing it from the limitation of being tied to a particular place. The only accusation that can be made against Clement is that in one particular respect he had allowed the private man to predominate over his fulfilment of the demands of the office.

Clement cannot be called a Renaissance or humanist pope. But it is undeniable that he lived like an extravagant secular prince. This, and his generous patronage of scholars and artists, to say nothing of his nepotism, do make him appear superficially as the forerunner of the Renaissance popes of the late fifteenth century. But Clement was providing no more than a foretaste of things to come. He was in a sense harnessing the scholarly interests which were an inherent part of Pierre Roger – as evidenced by his early writings – as well as his natural generosity, to the service of the office. In building up Avignon as the intellectual and cultural hub of the Christian world he was trying to compensate for the cultural heritage, and therefore the prestige, which had been lost by leaving Rome.

Clement's attitude to his monarchic role was inflexible, but this did not mean that he did not occasionally bend to the extent of taking account of opposition theories and making at least some effort to answer them, provided that the answers were within the limits of the accepted theory. He seemed especially concerned to answer the questions posed in connection with his absence from Rome. He made it plain that it was essential for the pope to have a *propria sedes*, and that this still had to be the see of Rome. He also provided a subtle answer to malicious suggestions that Jerusalem was a more fitting nucleus for Christendom than was Rome. Above all, he met the attacks of those who claimed that by being away from Rome the pope had broken the link with St Peter, and in so doing had forfeited his possession of the plenitude of power. Clement had succeeded directly to the universal jurisdictional powers of Christ Himself in the same way as Peter had done. He was Peter's successor regardless of any connection with Rome. The same concern to answer his opponents was apparent during the course of the appointment of the king of the Romans, although here it was less patent. For example, his methods of meeting the claim of the electoral princes to create the *rex Romanorum* was to build up the ceremony of papal approbation in such a way as to make it plain that he alone created the king. He also made careful changes in the format of the election decrees, which deprived the princes of all claim to elect as representatives of the people of the *imperium*: they formed nothing more than an *ad hoc* committee summoned to perform an occasional duty. Clement also showed himself more than a match for the Archbishop of Cologne in the way in which he contrived that Charles should receive confirmation of his election, which entitled him to administer the Empire, before the Archbishop had had a chance to crown him, thus depriving the prelate of all claim to a creative role in the procedure.

The only real adjustment Clement made – and it was adjustment rather than change – was in connection with the imperial office, and this was made from necessity rather than choice. He had to find some way of rendering *Pastoralis cura* harmless, while retaining the advantages which the papacy derived from having a subordinate lay official with universal powers. There was little point in creating an emperor whose power would be no more universal in theory than in practice. But the theory of the *rex Romanorum* appeared to be unscathed and therefore serviceable. Clement accordingly tried to build up the status of the king of the Romans to compensate for the lack of a more traditional *dominus mundi*. But in using Charles he was using a man who was really no more than one of a group of national sovereign rulers, and whose effective power was no greater than theirs. He was unlikely, and ultimately unwilling, to be much practical help to Clement in wielding his executive power. The Pope therefore turned to those regional sovereigns with whom he had some personal tie in the hope that they would do this for him. In so doing, he magnified their status so that they appeared equal to the king of the Romans. Balance and equilibrium were his leitmotifs.

In some ways the sheer conservatism of Clement's thought, as identified by Guillemain, may cause surprise. There can be no doubt of his great intelligence, his academic distinction, his political experience and expertise, and his lively awareness of the contemporary world, as shown by his scientific and humanistic interests and friends. And yet none of this seems to be reflected in his papal sermons and letters. Why such rigid conservatism in such an intelligent man? Why did he make relatively little attempt to come to terms with contemporary problems? It is virtually impossible to place Clement in his fourteenth-century context by referring to his writings. There is little indication that he was writing after the radical challenges of men like Marsilius and Ockham, or that he was the contemporary of Petrarch, or Cola, writing in the high summer of the early humanist movement. His lack of innovation can be explained partly on the basis that there was nothing new he could say. The papal-hierocratic theory had reached its climax long before Clement's pontificate: there was really nothing left to be said. The minor adjustments he did make show that without damaging the nature of the papal office there was really no answer to the new ideas – except to raise old ones to ever greater heights. The air of unreality of papal theory in the conditions of the fourteenth century, and the vast and ever-increasing chasm between theory and practice, cannot have escaped Clement. But to have made radical changes in papal theory would have been to allow the person to dominate the office. Ultimately the extent of Clement's conservatism was a measure of the considerable extent to which he did manage to identify himself with his office. Perhaps, too, it was a measure of his political wisdom and experience – an indication that he was indeed 'prudent and farseeing like the Argus', the beast with a hundred eyes.

Appendix 1

LIST OF WORKS DEDICATED TO OR COMMISSIONED BY CLEMENT VI (PIERRE ROGER)

1 Bartholomew of Urbino, *Milleloquium Ambrosianum*. Commissioned by Clement VI.

2 Bartholomew of Urbino, *Milleloquium D. Aurelii Augustini*. Commissioned by Clement VI and has dedicatory letter to him.

3 Bartholomew of Urbino, *De Romani Pontificis Christi Vicarii Auctoritate*. Unfortunately not extant. For references to it see Ossinger, 1768, p. 211, and Perrini, 1929, i, p. 204, n. 7. Peebles, 1954, pp. 555–6, contends that the work influenced Clement in granting Bartholomew the see of Urbino.

4 Bernard Gui, *Legenda Sancti Thomae de Aquino*. Dedicated to Pierre Roger. See Laurent, 1931, p. 161, n. 1 on this and for further bibliography. See also Thomas, 1921, p. 162.

5 Guido Terreni, *Summa de Heresibus et earum confutationibus*. Dedicated to Pierre Roger, see dedicatory letter, fol. 1r.

6 Jean de Fayt, *Tabula Moralium Aristoteles*. Commissioned by Clement VI: see Hauréau, 1892, v, p. 72. See also Huyghebaert, 1967. Mangeart, 1860, p. 374, MS 383 (400) edits an extract showing that John used Walter Burley's *Commentary on Aristotle's 'Ethics'* (see below no. 18).

7 Jean de Fayt, *Tabula Sermonum Augustini*. MS Paris BN latin 2032 (fourteenth century, written by Hugo of Paris, clerk of the diocese of Rodez) has an initial with a portrait of Clement. See also Dvorák, 1901, p. 77.

8 Jean de Fayt, *Tabula super Boetium de Consolatione*. Extant in MSS BN latins 2074, 14603, and Valenciennes 383 (400). The extract edited by Mangeart, 1860, implies that it was written before Jean became abbot of St Bavon (April 1350, provided by Clement). Probably commissioned by Clement.

9 Jean de Murs, Astronomical Calendar. The incipit to MS BM Sloane 3124, fol. 2r, states that it was 'arranged by Master John de Muris and several other experts in astrology at the mandate of the lord pope Clement VI in the fifth year [of his pontificate] with a Canon': quoted by Thorndike, 1934, p. 317.

10 Jean de Murs, Prognostications based on planetary conjunctions of 8 June 1357 and 20 October 1365. Despite the fact that this work referred to a period after Clement's death, it appears to have been written for him as a prophetic warning of future events: see Thorndike, 1934, pp. 318–19.

11 Jean de Murs and Firman de Beauval, Treatise on Calendar Reform.

Commissioned by Clement in connection with his efforts to reform the calendar, see above p. 66. The work was written in 1344–5 and contains a dedicatory letter to Clement. See Thorndike, 1934, p. 269, n. 4, for list of manuscripts.

12 Levi ben Gerson, *De Instrumento Secretorum Revelatore*. Translated into Latin by Peter of Alexandria. Translation commissioned by Clement in 1342: see Thorndike, 1934, p. 309.

13 Levi ben Gerson, Treatise on the conjunction of 1345, translated into Latin by Peter of Alexandria. Thorndike, 1934, p. 310 says it was 'not improbably intended for Clement VI': for list of manuscripts see p. 310, n. 62.

14 Luca Mannelli, *Tabulatio et Expositio Senecae*. Commissioned by Clement and written 1347–52: see Käppeli, 1948, pp. 437–64.

15 Nicholas Rosselli, *Tractatus de Jurisdictione Ecclesiae super Regnum Apuliae et Siciliae*. See app. 2, no. 2, below.

16 Richard FitzRalph, *De Pauperie Salvatoris*. Commissioned by Clement VI (see dedication letter, pp. 273–4) but presented to his successor, Innocent VI: see Walsh, 1981a, pp. 365–6.

17 Richard FitzRalph, *Summa de Quaestionibus Armenorum*. On this see Walsh, 1981a, pp. 129–81, esp. p. 130, n. 3 on the dedication copy.

18 Walter Burley, Commentary on Aristotle's *Ethics*. The dedicatory letter of the Commentary on the *Politics* implies that this work was also dedicated to Clement, but there is no extant dedicatory manuscript or known correspondence about it: Maier, 1964, p. 99. The fact that it was used by Jean de Fayt for his *Tabula Moralium Aristoteles* argues that there was a copy of this work at Avignon, which was almost certainly the dedication copy.

19 Walter Burley, Commentary on the *Politics* of Aristotle. This was 'rededicated' to Clement in 1342 after having been written originally for Richard Bentworth, Bishop of London, then Richard de Bury, Bishop of Durham. The dedicatory letter to Clement is found in MS Vat. Borghese 129, which was presented to Clement on 23 November 1343 and bears his portrait. For an edition of the letter and discussion of the manuscript see Maier, 1964. On the commentary see Harrison Thomson, 1947, pp. 557–78; Martin, 1951; and Daly, 1964 and 1969. Cf. app. 2, no. 8, below.

20 William de Mirica, Commentary on the *Physiognomy* of Aristotle. A dedicatory letter to Clement is extant in MS Oxford, Bodleian Library, Canon. Misc. 350: see Thorndike, 1934, p. 527, n. 9.

Appendix 2

PORTRAITS OF CLEMENT VI

1 MS BN latin 2120, fol. 1r – miniature in initial letter of dedication letter of Bartholomew of Urbino, *Milleloquium D. Aurelii Augustini* [reproduced as frontispiece to this work]. Lauer, 1940, p. 328, describes the manuscript as 'XIVe siècle. Écriture et décoration italiennes'.

2 MS Vat. Archiv. Armadio, 35, vol. 70 – miniature in initial of dedication letter of Nicholas Rosselli, *Tractatus de Jurisdictione Ecclesiae super Regnum Apuliae et Siciliae*: see Mann, 1928, p. 139, n. 2. Cf. app. 1, no. 15, above.

3 Portrait in initial letter of *Unigenitus Dei Filius* (28 January 1343), reproduced in F. Garapoli, *Anno Jubilaei Romae* (Rome, 1929): cited by Mann, p. 139, n. 2. Unfortunately Garapoli's work is not available to me.

4 Matteo Giovannetti of Viterbo – portrait painted in 1344. The portrait, although now lost, was seen in the seventeenth century by Ludovico Suarez, who mentioned it in a letter to Cardinal Barberini of 1 August 1638: see Castelnuovo, 1959, p. 48, n. 16.

5 Matteo Giovannetti of Viterbo – figure of Clement VI kneeling at the foot of the Cross in Crucifixion scene in the Chapel of St Martial at the Papal Palace: see Laclotte and Thiébaut, 1983, p. 165. The figure is barely recognisable.

6 Matteo Giovannetti of Viterbo (?) – portrait of Pope receiving a book from John the Good, preserved by Roger de Gaignières: see Kahr, 1966, pp. 3–16, where this attribution is made, and p. 73 for reproduction.

7 Andrea di Cione Orgagna (1308–68). Reference in Vasari, *Le Vite*, ii, p. 221, to a portrait in Sta Croce, Florence, which was described as in profile and 'ritratto di naturale'. Cf. Mann, p. 130, n. 1.

8 MS Vat. Borghese 129 – dedication copy of Burley's Commentary on Aristotle's *Politics*: see app. 1, no. 19. The miniature shows Burley presenting the book to Clement.

9 MS Paris BN latin 2032 – dedication copy of Jean de Fayt's *Tabula Sermonum Augustini*: see app. 1, no. 7. The miniature is in the initial letter 'C', fol. 1r, and the folio has a decorated margin with the arms of Clement VI in the other three corners.

10 Madrid, Biblioteca de Palacia, Cod. 149 (fourteenth century). Dedication copy of Luca Mannelli, *Tabulatio . . . Senecae*. The miniature shows Clement being presented with the text. For reproduction see Käppelli, 1948, p. 252. See app. 1, no. 14.

11 *RV* 187, fol. 29v, no. 169, *de curia*. The bull, which is one to Chaise-Dieu, authorising the foundation of eight chapels, is decorated with a miniature of the Pope, wearing his triple tiara, and signing the document with one finger of his right hand: see Déprez, no. 3975, p. 494, n. 1.

Appendix 3

CLEMENT VI (PIERRE ROGER): LIST OF SERMONS AND *COLLATIONES* REFERRED TO IN THE TEXT

1 Accingimini et estote filii potentes et estote parati in mane ut pugnetis adversus nationes has quae convenerunt nos disperdere et sancta nostra. I Mach., iii. 58: Ste-G. 240, fols. 308r–14r

Pierre Roger, Ash Wednesday *collatio* (25 February 1338)

2 A me decretum est ut unicuique placuerit in regno meo de populo Israel . . . Et fuerunt verba ista ad litteram dicta Esdrae scribae quando post destructionem Jerusalem [cf. I Esdr., vi. 11ff.]: Ste-G. 240, fols. 289v–305r: 494v–505v

Pierre Roger, crusading sermon (16 July 1333)

3 Ascendit super omnes caelos ut adimplet omnia. Ad Ephes., iv. 10: Ste-G. 240, fols. 88r–95r

Pierre Roger, Ascension Day sermon (21 May 1327)

4 Assumpsi michi duas virgas. Zach., xi. 7: Ste-G. 240, fols. 523r–26r

Clement VI, *collatio* on the elevation of Pierre Bertrand and Nicholas de Besse (19 May 1344)

5 Atrium quod est foris ejice foras. Apoc., xi. 2: ed. Offler, 1955

Clement VI, *collatio* on the publication of processes against Louis of Bavaria (Maundy Thursday, 10 April 1343)

6 Benedictione iustorum exaltabitur civitas. Prov., xi. 11: Ste-G. 240, fols. 511r–53r

Clement VI, *collatio* on the elevation of Prague, Algeciras, and another city (30 April 1344)

7 Benyamin adolescens in mentis excessu. Ps., lxvii (lxviii). 28: ed. Ubald d'Alençon, 1911

Pierre Roger, St Francis' Day sermon

8 Clemens et pius omnipotens Deus misericordiarum pater: MS Frankfurt, 71, fols. 417r–21r

Clement VI, sermon on the jubilee year

9 Convertet[que] Deus spiritum regis in mansuetudinem. Esther, xv.11: Ste-G. 240, fols. 458r–63r

Clement VI, *collatio* on the reconciliation of Giovanni Visconti of Milan (1352)

10 Corona fratrum quasi plantatio cedri. Ecclesiasticus, i.13: Ste-G. 240, fols. 487v–95v

Clement VI, sermon on the Feast of St Louis, Bishop of Toulouse

11 Cum iudicatur exeat condemnatus et oratio eius fiat ad peccatum: fiant dies eius pauci et episcoporum eius accipiat alter. Ps., cviii (cvix).7–8: ed. Schunk, ii, pp. 352–75

Clement VI, *collatio* on the deposition of Henry, Archbishop of Mainz (7 April 1346)

12 Data est ei corona. Apoc., vi.2: BN latin, 3293, fols. 297r–99v, and ed. Martinez, 1966

Clement VI, coronation *collatio* for Louis of the Fortune Islands (28 November 1344)

13 De radice colubri egredietur regulus. Isa., xiv.29: Ste-G. 240, fols. 542v–45v

Clement VI, *collatio* during processes against Giovanni Visconti of Milan (1350)

14 Desidero [enim] vos videre: ut impertiar vobis aliquid gratie spiritualis ad confirmandos vos; id est simul consolari in vobis per eam que est invicem fidem vestram atque meam. Ad Rom., i.11–12: Ste-G. 240, fols. 147v–53r; Vat. Borghese 41, fols. 7v–14v, ed. Schmidinger, pp. 323–65

Clement VI, reply to the Romans (27 January 1343)

15 Deum timete, regem honorificate. I Pet., ii.17: ed. Durand de Maillane, *Les Libertez de l'Église Gallicane*, pp. 460–79

Pierre Roger, Vincennes discourse (22 December 1329)

16 Dum implevit verbum factus est dux in Israel. I Mach., ii.55: Ste-G. 240, fols. 521r–23v; BN latin, 3293, fols. 279v–82r

Clement VI, *collatio* on the creation of Humbert of Vienne as Captain-general (? 26 May 1345)

17 Ecce rex tuus venit tibi mansuetus. Mt., xxi.5: Ste-G. 240, fols. 101v–08v

Clement VI, Advent sermon (3 December 1346)

18 Et iste bonus est nuntius. II Reg., xviii.26: Ste-G. 240, fols. 68r–70r

Clement VI, *collatio* on the return of Cardinal Bernard d'Albi from Aragon (10 September 1343)

19 Exulta et lauda habitatio Sion quia magnus in medio tui sanctus Israel. Is., xii.6: Ste-G. 240, fols. 26r–41v; extracts ed. Perarnau, 1981, pp. 119–23

Clement VI, second sermon on the canonisation of St Yves (19 May 1347)

20 Faciem firmavit ut iret in Ierusalem et misit nuntios. Luc., ix.5: Ste-G. 240, fols. 290v–98v

Pierre Roger, crusading sermon (19 February 1332)

21 Fecit in domo sancti cherubim duos. II Par., iii.10: Ste-G. 240, fols. 444v–49r

Clement VI, *collatio* on the creation of Elie de Talleyrand and Bertrand de Déaulx as Cardinal Bishops (4 November 1348)

22 Filius noster iste protervus et contumax est monita nostra audire contemnit. Deut., xxi.20: ed. Schunk, ii, pp. 332–40

Clement VI, *collatio* on the suspension from office of Henry, Archbishop of Mainz (15 October 1344)

23 Heloy, Heloy. Marc., xv.34: Ste-G. 240, fols. 528r–42v; extracts in *Acta Sanctorum*, May, iv (Antwerp, 1886), pp. 578–9; Baluze–Mollat, ii, pp. 341, 359

Clement VI, first sermon on the canonisation of St Yves (18 May 1347)

24 Hereticum hominem post unam et secundam correptionem devita sciens quia subversus est qui eiusmodi est. Ad Titum, iii.10–11: Ste-G. 240, fols. 374v–80r, ed. Schunk, ii, pp. 332–40

Clement VI, *collatio* during processes against Louis of Bavaria (Maundy Thursday, 13 April 1346)

25 Hii sunt viri qui ascenderunt de captivitate quam transtulerat Nabuchonosor rex Babylonis in Babylonem et reversi sunt in Ierusalem. I Esdr., ii.1: Ste-G. 240, fols. 449r–54r

Clement VI, *collatio* on the return of Annibaldus de Ceccano and Etienne Aubert from France (1347–8)

26 Hoc sentite in vobis quod est in Christo Iesu. Ad Phil., ii.5: Ste-G. 240, fols. 562r–67v

Pierre Roger, university sermon for Palm Sunday

27 Homo quidam nobilis abiit in regionem longinquam accipere sibi regnum et reverti. Luc.,xix.12: Ste-G. 240, fols. 440v–44v

Clement VI, *collatio* on the return of Guy de Boulogne from Hungary and Lombardy (7 June 1350)

28 Ibant et revertebantur in similitudinem fulguris coruscantis. Ezech., i.14: Ste-G. 240, fols. 60r–63r

Clement VI, *collatio* on the return of Pierre Després and Annibaldus de Ceccano from France (January 1343)

29 Impius cum in profundum venerit peccatorum, contemnit: sed sequitur eum ignominia et opprobrium. Prov., xviii.3: Eichstätt, Staatliche Bibliothek, 698, fols. 494r–95r, ed. Offler, 1974

Clement VI, *collatio* during processes against Louis of Bavaria (11 July 1343)

30 Impleti sunt dies purgationis Mariae, Luc., ii.22: Ste-G. 240, fols. 169v–76v

Pierre Roger, Purification sermon (2 February 1330)

31 Legatus [autem] fidelis, sanitas. Prov., xiii.17: Ste-G. 240, fols. 434v–40r

Clement VI, *collatio* on the return of Bertrand de Déaulx from Italy (17 November 1348)

32 Lex clemencie in lingua eius. Prov., xxxi.26: Vat. Lat., 2541, fols. 233v–36r

Clement VI, sermon on Pope Clement I

33 Loquere tu [nobis] et audiemus. Exod., xx.19: Ste-G. 240, fols. 525v–28r

Clement VI, *collatio* on the creation of Nicholas de Besse as cardinal (1 June 1344)

34 Nolite errare. Deus non irridetur que enim seminaverit homo hec et metet. Ad Gal., vi.7: Ste-G. 240, fols. 359r–60v; Klosterneuburg, Stiftsbibliothek, 204, fols. 135v–38r; extracts in Höfler, 1868, pp. 22–3

Clement VI, *collatio* for Louis of Bavaria's procurators (16 January 1344)

35 Obsecro vos ego vinctus in Domino ut digne ambuletis vocatione qua vocati estis. Ad Ephes., iv.11: Ste-G. 240, fols. 242v–44v

Clement VI, *collatio* on the arrival of Cardinal Guillaume de la Jugie (12 October 1342)

36 Omnis multitudo sanctorum est et cum ipsis est dominus. Num., xvi.3: Ste-G. 240, fols. 49v–51v

Pierre Roger (?), All Saints' Day sermon

37 Principes populorum congregati sunt cum Deo Abraham. Ps., xlvi (xlvii).10: Ste-G. 240, fols. 117v–26r

Pierre Roger, sermon on St Peter and St Paul's Day (29 June 1339)

38 Quis putas puer iste erit. Luc., i.66: Ste-G. 240, fols. 117v–26r

Pierre Roger, St John the Baptist's Day sermon (24 June 1333)

39 Reges eorum ministrabunt. Isa., lx.10: Klosterneuburg, Stiftsbibliothek, 204, fols. 165r–72r, ed. Walch, 1760, pp. 47–71

Clement VI, Epiphany sermon on clerical vices

40 Salomon sedebit super solium meum et ipse regnabit pro me, illique precipiam, ut sit dux super Israel. III Reg., i.35: *MGH Const.*, viii, no. 100, pp. 142–63

Clement VI, *collatio* on the approbation of Charles of Bohemia as King of the Romans (6 November 1346)

41 Sic currite ut comprehendatis. I ad Cor., ix.24: Oxford, Jesus College, 36, fols. 74r–78r

Pierre Roger, Septuagesima sermon (8 February 1327)

42 Sicut frigus nivis in die messis ita legatus fidelis ei qui misit eum. Prov., xxv.13: Ste-G. 240, fols. 247v–51r

Clement VI, *collatio* on the return of Cardinal Guillaume Court from Italy (30 October 1343)

43 Signum magnum apparuit in celo. Apoc., xii.1: Ste-G. 240, fols. 387v–97v

Pierre Roger, Epiphany sermon (6 January 1342)

44 Sol illuminans per omnia respexit. Eccli., xlii.16: fols. 139r–47v

Pierre Roger, university sermon for St Augustine's Day

45 Te faciam principem super gentem magnam. Num., xiiii.12: Ste-G. 240, fols. 336v–43v, ed. Martinez, 1964

Clement VI, *collatio* on the creation of Louis de la Cerda as Prince of the Fortune Islands (15 November 1344)

46 Vestitutum erat veste aspersa sanguine et vocabitur nomen eius verbum Dei. Apoc., xix.13: Ste-G. 240, fols. 408r–16r

Clement VI, sermon on the Feast of the Circumcision (undated)

47 Videntibus illis elevatus est. Act., i.9: Ste-G. 240, fols. 416r–20v

Clement VI, *collatio* on the creation of Pierre Roger de Beaufort as Cardinal (5 June 1348)

48 Vox sanguinis fratris tui Abel clamat ad me de terra. Gen., iv.10: Ste-G. 240, fols. 361r–67r

Clement VI, *collatio* against the murderers of Andrew of Hungary (1 February 1346)

BIBLIOGRAPHY

I ORIGINAL SOURCES

(A) MANUSCRIPTS: CLEMENT VI (PIERRE ROGER)

Sermons and *Collationes*
Frankfurt, Stadtbibliothek, 71, fols. 417r–21r
Klosterneuburg, Stiftsbibliothek, 82
Klosterneuburg, Stiftsbibliothek, 204
Oxford, Jesus College, 36, fols. 74r–78r
Paris, Bibliothèque Sainte-Geneviève, 240
Paris, Bibliothèque Nationale, latin 3293
Vatican City, Biblioteca Apostolica Vaticana, Vat. Borghese 41, fols. 7v–14v
Vatican City, Biblioteca Apostolica Vaticana, Vat. Lat., 2541, fols. 233v–36r

Other works
Brussels, Bibliothèque Royale Albert Iᵉʳ, 359 (11437–40), fols. 25r–67v (Pierre
    Roger, Postill on *Quia quorundam mentes*) Vatican City, Biblioteca Apost-
    olica, Vat. Borghese 247 (Pierre Roger, 'Commonplace manuscript')

OTHER WRITERS
Graz, Universitätsbibliothek, 348, fols. 80r–87r (Paul Koëlner, *Treatise on
    Preaching*)
London, British Library, Harley 4763, fols. 3r–5r (Edward III's appeal to a
    general council)
Oxford, Bodleian Library, Laud Misc., 432, fols. 120r–263r (Paul Koëlner,
    Treatise on Preaching)
Paris, Bibliothèque Nationale, latin 3294, fols. 206v–7v (Jean de Cardaillac,
    Sermones)
Paris, Bibliothèque Nationale, latin 2120, fol. 1r (Bartholomew of Urbino,
    Milleloquium Sancti Augustini)

216

Bibliography

(B) PRINTED EDITIONS: ANONYMOUS WORKS

Anon., *Commentarium in Unam Sanctam*, ed. P. de Lapparent, 'L'Oeuvre politique de François de Meyronnes', *Archives d'histoire doctrinale et littéraire du moyen âge*, XII (1940–2), pp. 126–51

Anon., *Commentarius super erroribus Joannis de Poliaco*, Raynaldus v, chs. 22–30, pp. 165–9

Anon., *Mémoire sur les prétensions de Edouard III à la couronne de France (1344)*, ed. K. de Lettenhove, *Oeuvres de Froissart*, XVIII, Brussels, 1874, pp. 256–72

Anon., *On the Truce of 1347*, ed. T. Wright, *Political Poems and Songs*, RS, XIV, I (London, 1859), pp. 53–8

Anon., *De Potestate Ecclesiae*, ed. J. Leclercq, 'Textes contemporains de Dante sur les sujets qu'il a traités', *Studi Medievali*, ser. 3, VI, 2 (1965), pp. 507–17

Anon., *Reply to Petrarch's 'Apologia'*, ed. H. Cochin, 'Le Grande Controverse de Rome et d'Avignon au XIVe siècle', *Études Italiennes*, II (1920), pp. 89–94

Anon., *Sodom Fair: or the Market of the Man of Sin . . . with the Life of Clement the Sixth and blasphamous [sic] Bull which he published for the Year of Jubele, 1350*, London, 1688

Anon., *Somnium Viridarii de Iurisdictione Regia et Sacerdotalis*, ed. M. Goldast, *Monarchia Sancti Romani Imperii* (Hanover, 1612), i, pp. 58–229, reprinted and ed. F. Chatillon and M. Schnerb-Lièvre, *Revue du Moyen Âge Latin*, XXII (1966), 58–229

Anon., *Le Songe du Vergier*, ed. M. Schnerb-Lièvre, 2 vols., Paris, 1982

AUTHORS

Aegidius Romanus, *De Ecclesiastica Potestate*, ed. R. Scholz, Weimar, 1929

Albericus de Rosate, *Dictionarium Iuris tam Civilis quam Canonici*, Venice, 1601

Alvarus Pelagius, *Collirium Adversus Hereses*, ed. R. Scholz, *Unbekannte kirchenpolitische Streitschriften aus der Zeit Ludwigs des Bayern, 1327–54*, Rome, 1911–14, ii, pp. 491–514
  De Planctu Ecclesiae, ed. E. T. Rocaberti, *Bibliotheca Maxima Pontificia*, iii, Rome, 1698, pp. 23–266

Aristotle, *The Politics of Aristotle*, tr. and ed. E. Barker, Oxford, 1946

Augustine, *Contra Faustum Manichaeum*, CSEL, xxv, Prague, Vienna, and Leipzig, 1891
  De Civitate Dei, CC, xlvii–xlviii, Turnhout, 1955
  Tractatus in Ioannis Evangelium, CC, xxxvi, Turnhout, 1954

Baldus de Ubaldis, *Commentaria super Tribus Prioribus Libris Decretalium*, Venice, 1595

Bartholomew of Urbino, *Milleloquium Ambrosianum*, Lyons, 1556
  Milleloquium D. Aurelii Augustini, Lyons, 1555

Bartolus of Sassoferrato, *Commentaria ad Digestum*, Basle, 1562

Bernard of Clairvaux, *De Consideratione*, ed. J. Leclercq and H. M. Rochais, *Sancti Bernardi Opera*, iii, Rome, 1963, pp. 393–493

Bridget of Sweden, *Revelationes*, ed. C. Durato, Antwerp, 1611

Cicero, *De Officiis*, Loeb Classical Library, XXX, London and Cambridge, Mass., 1968

Bibliography

Cola di Rienzo, *Commentary on Dante's Monarchia*, ed. P. G. Ricci, 'Il commento di Cola di Rienzo alla *Monarchia* di Dante', *Studi Medievali*, series 3, VI, 2 (1965), pp. 679–708

Libellus contra Scismata et Errores, Scriptus ad Archiepiscopum Pragensem, eds. K. Burdach and P. Piur, *Briefwechsel*, iii, pp. 231–78

Conrad of Megenberg, *De Translatione Romani Imperii*, ed. R. Scholz, *Unbekannte kirchenpolitische Streitschriften*, ii, pp. 249–345

Tractatus contra Wilhelmum Occam, ed. R. Scholz, *Unbekannte kirchenpolitische Streitschriften*, ii, pp. 346–91

Yconomica, ed. S. Kruger, *MGH SsM*, iii, 5 (Stuttgart, 1971–7)

Cyprian, *De Ecclesiae Catholicae Unitate*, ed. M. Bévenot, Oxford, 1971

Francis Petrarch, *Liber Sine Nomine*, ed. P. Piur, *Petrarcas 'Buch ohne Namen' und die päpstliche Kurie*, Halle, 1925, pp. 161–238

Opera Omnia, Basle, 1581

François de Meyronnes–Pierre Roger, *Disputatio*, ed. J. Barbet, Paris, 1961

Galvaneus Flamma, *Chronica Galvagnana*, ed. V. Hunecke, 'Die kirchen-politischen Exkurse in den Chroniken des Galvaneus Flamma, O.P. (1283–ca. 1344). Einleitung und Edition', *Deutsches Archiv*, XXV (1969), pp. 166–97

Chronicon Maius, ed. V. Hunecke, *Deutsches Archiv*, XXV (1969), pp. 198–208

Guido de Baysio, *Rosarium seu in Decretorum Commentaria*, Venice, 1601

Guido Terreni, *Quaestio de Magisterio Infallibili Romani Pontificis*, ed. B. F. M. Xiberta, *Opuscula et Textus*, ii, Münster–in–Westfalen, 1926

Summa de Heresibus et Earum Confutationibus, Paris, 1528

Guido Vernani, *De Potestate Summi Pontificis*, Bologna, 1756

De Reprobatione 'Monarchiae' Composita a Dante, ed. T. Käppeli, 'Der Dante-gegner Guido Vernani, O.P., von Rimini', *QF*, XXVIII (1937–8), pp. 123–46

Herman of Schildiz, *Tractatus contra Haereticos*, ed. A. Zumkeller, Würzburg, 1970

Hostiensis, *Commentaria in Quinque Decretalium Libros*, Venice, 1581

Innocent IV, *Commentaria in Quinque Libros Decretalium*, Venice, 1578

Jean de Fayt, *Sermones*, ed. P. Fredericq, 'Deux sermons inédits de Jean de Fayt sur les Flagellants (5 octobre 1349) et sur le Grand Schisme d'Occident (1378)', *Bulletin de l'académie royale de Belgique*, classe des lettres, Brussels, 1903, pp. 688–718

Johannes Andreae, *Commentaria ad Decretales*, Venice, 1581

Glossa Ordinaria ad Clementinas, in *Corpus Iuris Canonici*, ii, Lyons, 1572, cols. 793–1102.

Glossa Ordinaria ad Sext., in *Corpus Iuris Canonici*, ii, Lyons, 1572, cols. 1–792

Johannes Calderinus, *Commentaria ad Decretales*, in *Repetitionum in Universas fere Iuris Canonici*, ed. L. A. Giunta, ii, iii, iv, Venice, 1587

Johannes Gaufredi, *Collectarius Iuris*, Lyons, 1514

Johannes Monachus, *Glossa Ordinaria ad Extravagantes Communes*, V, ix, 1, in *Corpus Iuris Canonici*, ii, Lyons, 1572

John Baconthorpe, *Quaestiones in Quatuor Libros Sententiarum et Quodlibetales*, Cremona, 1618, Gregg reprint, 1969

Bibliography

John Erghome [?], 'Commentary on the *Vaticinium* of John of Bridlington', ed. T. Wright, *Political Poems and Songs*, RS XIV, 1, London, 1859, pp. 123–215

John of Athona, *Commentaria ad Constitutiones Othonis*, Oxford, 1679
Commentaria ad Constitutiones Ottobuoni, Oxford, 1679

John of Hesdin, *Invectiva contra Fr. Petrarcham*, ed. E. Cocchia, 'Magistri Johannis de Hysdinio *Invectiva contra Fr. Petrarcham et Fr. Petrarchae contra cuiusdam Galli Calumnias Apologia*. Revisione Critica del Testo con Introduzione, Storica e Commento', *Atti della Reale Accademia di Archeologia, Lettere e Belle Arti*, n.s., VII, Naples, 1920, pp. 112–39

John of Legnano, *De Censura Ecclesiastica, Tractatus Universi Iuris*, xiv, Venice, 1584
De Fletu Ecclesiae, ed. O. Raynaldus, *Annales Ecclesiastici*, vii, Lucca, 1752, pp. 631–57
De Principatu, ed. G. Ermini, 'Un ignoto trattato *De Principatu* di Giovanni da Legnano', *Studi di Storia e diritto in onore di Carlo Calisse*, iii, Milan, 1940, pp. 423–46

John of Roquetaillade, *Vade Mecum in Tribulacione*, ed. E. Brown, *Appendix ad Fasciculum Rerum Expetendarum et Fugiendarum ab Orthuino Gratio editum Coloniae MCXXXV*, ii, London, 1690, pp. 496–507

John Wyclif, *Tractatus de Blasphemia*, ed. M. H. Dziewicki, Wyclif Society, London, 1893
Tractatus de Potestate Pape, ed. J. Loserth, Wyclif Society, London, 1907
Trialogus, ed. G. Lechler, Oxford, 1869

Lambertus Guerrici de Hoyo, *Liber de Commendatione Johannis XXII*, ed. R. Scholz, *Unbekannte kirchenpolitische Streitschriften*, ii, pp. 154–68

Lapus Tactus, *Commentaria super Clementinas*, Rome, 1589

Louis Sanctus of Beringen, *Tractatus de Pestilentia*, ed. A. Welkenhuysen, 'La Peste en Avignon (1348) décrit per un témoin oculaire, Louis Sanctus de Beringen', in *Pascua Medievalia: Studies voor Dr J. M. de Smet*, Louvain, 1983, pp. 452–90

Lupold of Bebenberg, *De Iure Regni et Imperii Romani*, ed. S. Schardius, *De Iurisdictione, Auctoritate et Praeeminentia Imperiali ac Potestate Ecclesiastica*, Basle, 1566, pp. 328–409

Nicholas Oresme, *Le Livre de Politiques d'Aristote*, ed. A. D. Menut, Philadelphia, 1970

Nicholas Rosselli, *Tractatus de Jurisdictione Ecclesiae super Regnum Apuliae et Siciliae*, S. Baluzius, *Miscellanea*, ed. J. Mansi, i, Lucca, 1761, pp. 468–73.

Fra Paolina Minorita, *Prologus ad Mappam Mundi*, ed. R. Almagia, *Monumenta Cartographica Vaticana*, i, Vatican City, 1944

Paul of Liazariis, *Commentaria ad Decretales*, in *Repetitionum in Universas fere Iuris Canonici*, ed. L. A. Giunta, ii–iv, Venice, 1587

Peter Ceffons, *Epistola Luciferi ad prelatos Ecclesie*, Magdeburg, 1549

Petrarch, Francis, *see* Francis Petrarch

Philip de Mornay du Plessis, *The Mystery of Iniquity*, 'Englished' by S. Lennard, London, 1612

Pierre de la Palu, *Tractatus de Potestate Papae*, ed. P. T. Stella, Zurich, 1966

Bibliography

Raoul de Presles, *Commentarium ad 'De Civitate Dei'*, Abbeville, 1486

Richard FitzRalph, *De Pauperie Salvatoris*, bks i–iv, ed. R. L. Poole in John Wyclif, *De Dominio Divino*, Wyclif Society, London, 1890, pp. 257–546

Summa de Quaestionibus Armenorum, Paris, 1511

Seneca, *De Clementia*, in *Moral Essays*, ed. J. W. Basore, i, pp. 356–449, Loeb Classical Library, CCXIV, London and Cambridge, Mass., 1970

Thomas Aquinas, *Quaestiones Quodlibetales*, ed. R. Spiazzi, 8th edition, Turin and Rome, 1949

Opera Omnia, Rome, 1822ff.

Summa Theologiae, Editiones Paulinae, Rome 1962

Thomas Hobbes, *Leviathan*, ed. M. Oakeshott, Oxford, 1960

Ugolinus de Celle, *Tractatus de Electione et Coronatione Regis Romanorum*, ed. E. E. Stengel, *Nova Alamanniae*, i, no. 123, pp. 71–9

Walter Burley, *Epistola Dedicatoria ad Commentarium in VIII Libros Politicorum Aristotelis*, ed. A. Maier, 'Zu Walter Burleys Politik-Kommentar', *Ausgehendes Mittelalter gesammelte Aufsätze zur Geistesgeschichte des 14 Jahrhunderts*, i, Rome, 1964, pp. 83–9

William of Monte Lauduno, *Commentaria ad Clementinas*, in *Repetitionum in Universas fere Iuris Canonici*, ed. L. A. Giunta, vi, Venice, 1587

William of Ockham, *Dialogus*, ed. M. Goldast, *Monarchia Sancti Romani Imperii*, Frankfurt, 1612, ii, pp. 398–976

De Electione Karoli IV in Conrad of Megenberg, *Tractatus Contra Wilhelmum Occam*, ed. R. Scholz, *Unbekannte kirchenpolitische Streitschriften*, ii, pp. 346–63

De Imperatorem et Pontificum Potestate, ed. Scholz, *Unbekannte kirchenpolitische Streitschriften*, ii, pp. 453–80

Octo Quaestiones de Potestate Papae, ed. J. G. Sikes, *Opera Politica*, i, Manchester, 1940, pp. 1–221

William of Sarzano, *Tractatus de Potestate Summi Pontificis*, ed. R. del Ponte, *Studi Medievali*, series 3, XII, 1971, pp. 1020–94

Wyclif, John, *see* John Wyclif

NARRATIVE SOURCES

Adam Murimuth, *Continuatio Chronicarum*, ed. E. M. Thompson, *RS*, XCIII, London, 1874

Aegidius li Muisis, *De Domino Papa Clemente Sexto, Corpus Chronicorum Flandriae*, ed. J. J. de Smet, ii, Brussels, 1841, pp. 308–12

Baluzius, S., *Vitae Paparum Avenionensium*, ed. G. Mollat, 4 vols., Paris, 1914–27

Bartolomeo Platina, *Liber de Vita Christi ac Omnium Pontificum*, ed. G. Gaida, *RIS*, iii, pt 1, Città di Castello, 1913–32, pp. 272–5

Beneš of Weitmil, *Cronica Ecclesiae Pragensis*, ed. J. Emler, *FRB*, iv, Prague, 1884, pp. 459–548

Biblia Sacra iuxta Vulgatam Clementinam, third edn, Madrid, 1959

Breve Chronicon Clerici anonymi, ed. J. J. de Smet, *Recueil des Chroniques de Flandres*, iii, Brussels, 1856

Bibliography

Charles IV, *Vita Caroli Quarti*, ed. E. Hillenbrand, *Die Autobiographie Karls IV. Einführung, Übersetzung und Kommentar*, Stuttgart, 1979

Chronique parisienne anonyme, ed. A. Hellot, *Mémoires de la Société de l'histoire de Paris*, xi, Paris, 1885

Francis of Prague, *Cronica*, ed. J. Emler, *FRB*, iv, Prague, 1884, pp. 347–456

Galvaneus Flamma, *Opusculum de Rebus Gestis ab Azone Luchino et Joanne Vicecomitibus ab ann. 1328 usque ad ann. 1342*, ed. L. A. Muratori, *RIS*, xii, Milan, 1728, cols. 997–1050

Geoffrey le Baker, *Chronicon*, ed. E. M. Thompson, Oxford, 1889

Georgius Stella, *Annales Genuenses*, ed. L. A. Muratori, *RIS*, xvii, Milan, 1730, cols. 952–1318

Giorgio Vasari, *Le Vite*, eds. R. Bettarini and P. Barochi, 11 vols., Florence, 1979–

Giovanni Villani, *Istorie Fiorentine*, ed. L. A. Muratori, *RIS*, xiii, Milan, 1728, cols. 9–1002

Henry of Diessenhoven, *Chronica*, ed. J. F. Böhmer, *FRG*, iv, Stuttgart, 1868, pp. 16–126

Vita Joannis XXII=*Quinta Vita Joannis XXII*, Baluze–Mollat, i, pp. 172–7

Henry of Herford, *Liber de Rebus Memorabilioribus*, ed. A. Potthast, Göttingen, 1859

Henry Taube of Selbach, *Chronica*, ed. H. Bresslau, *MGH*, *SRG*, n.s., i, 1924

Historiae Romanae Fragmenta, ed. L. A. Muratori, *Antiquitates Italicae Medii Aevi*, iii, Milan, 1740, cols. 251–548

Jean de Venette, *Continuatio Chronici Guillelmi de Nangiaco*, ed. H. Géraud, *Société de l'histoire de France*, clix, Paris, 1843

Jean la Porte Annonay, *Liber de Coronatione Karoli IV Imperatoris*, ed. R. G. Salomon, *MGH*, *SRGUS*, xxxv, 1913

John Cantacuzenus, *Historiae*, ed. L. Schopen, 3 vols., *Corpus Scriptorum Historiae Byzantinae*, Bonn, 1828–32

John Latomus, *Acta Aliquot Vetustiora in Civitate Frankofurtensi . . . Collecta*, ed. J. F. Böhmer, *FRG*, iv, Stuttgart, 1868

John of Victring, *Liber Certarum Historiarum*, ed. F. Schneider, ii, *MGH*, *SRGUS*, xxxv, 1909–10

Matthew of Nuremberg, *Chronica*, ed. A. Hofmeister, *MGH*, *SRG*, n.s., iv, 1955

Matteo Villani, *Istorie Fiorentine*, ed. L. A. Muratori, *RIS*, xiv, Milan, 1729, cols. 9–728

Michael of Leone of Würzburg, *Annotata Historica*, ed. J. F. Böhmer, *FRG*, i, Stuttgart, 1843, pp. 451–79

Peter of Herenthals, *Vita Clementis VI*, Baluze–Mollat, i, pp. 298–303

Thomas Burton, *Chronica Monasterii de Melsa*, ed. E. A. Bond, *RS*, XLIII, London, 1866–8

Thomas Walsingham, *Historia Anglicana*, ed. H. T. Riley, *RS*, XXVIII, London, 1863

Vasari, Georgio, *see* Georgio Vasari

Vita Ambrosii Traversari, ed. L. Mehus, Florence, 1759

Bibliography

Vita Nicolai Laurentii, ed. L. A. Muratori, *Antiquitates Italicae Medii Aevi*, iii, Milan, 1740, cols. 399–480

Werner of Bonn, *Vita Clementis VI*, Baluze–Mollat, i, pp. 543–50

DOCUMENTS

Albanès, J.-H. and Chevalier, U., *Gallia Christiana Novissima: Histoire des Archevêches et abbayes de France*, vii, Paris, 1920

Altmann, W. and Bernheim, E., eds., *Ausgewählte Urkunden zur Erläuterung der Verfassungsgeschichte Deutschlands im Mittelalter*, Berlin, 1904

Baluzius, S., *Miscellanea novo ordine digesta*, ed. J. D. Mansi, 4 vols., Lucca, 1761–4

Becker, H. J., ed., 'Das Mandat *Fidem Catholicam* Ludwigs des Bayern von 1338', *Deutsches Archiv*, XXVI (1970), pp. 496–512

Benedict XII, *Acta Benedicti XII (1334–1342)*, ed. A. L. Tautu, Pontificia Commissio ad Redigendum Codicem Iuris Canonici Orientalis, Fontes, series 3, viii, Vatican City, 1958

Benoît XII. Lettres closes, patentes et curiales se rapportant à la France, ed. G. Daumet, Paris, 1899–1920

Benoît XII. Lettres closes et patentes intéressantes les pays autres que la France, ed. J.-M. Vidal, Paris, 1913

Burdach, K. and Piur, P., eds. *Briefwechsel des Cola di Rienzo*, 5 parts = *Vom Mittelalter zur Reformation*, Bd. ii, Berlin, 1912–29

Cerasoli, F., ed., 'Clemente VI e Giovanna I di Napoli. Documenti inediti dell'Archivio Vaticano', *Archivio storico per le provincie napoletane*, XXI (1896), pp. 3–41, 227–264, 427–75, 667–707; XXII (1897), pp. 3–46

Charles IV, *Bulla Aurea Karoli IV. Imperatoris Anno MCCCLVI Promulgata [Golden Bull]*, ed. W. D. Fritz, *MGH Fontes Iuris Germanici Antiqui in Usum Scholarum*, Weimar, 1972

Clement VI, *Acta Clementis VI*, ed. L. Klicman, *Monumenta Vaticana Res Gestas Bohemiae Illustrantia*, i, Prague, 1903

Acta Clementis Papae VI (1342–52), ed. A. L. Tautu, Pontificia Commissio ad Redigendum Codicem Iuris Canonici Orientalis, Fontes, series 3, ix, Vatican City, 1960

Lettres closes, patentes et curiales intéressant les pays autres que la France, eds. E. Déprez and G. Mollat, Paris, 1960–1

Lettres closes, patentes et curiales se rapportant à la France, eds. E. Déprez, J. Glénisson, and G. Mollat, Paris, 1901–61

Corpus Iuris Canonici, 2 vols., Lyons, 1572

Das Constitutum Constantini, ed. H. Fuhrmann, *MGH, Fontes Iuris Germanici Antiqui in Usum Scholarum*, x, Hanover, 1968

De Boüard, A., *Le régime politique et les institutions de Rome au moyen-âge, 1252–1347* = *BEFAR*, CXVIII, Paris, 1920, pièces justificatives, pp. 275–340

De Lettenhove, K., ed., 'Lettres des ambassadeurs anglais envoyés à Avignon (septembre–novembre 1344)', *Oeuvres de Froissart*, xviii, Brussels, 1874, pp. 202–35

Denifle, H. and Chatelain, A., eds., *Chartularium Universitatis Parisiensis*, ii, Paris, 1894

Bibliography

Donation of Constantine, see *Das Constitutum Constantini*

Duchesne, L., *Fastes Episcopaux de l'ancienne Gaule*, ii, Paris, 1899

Durand de Maillane, *Les Libertez de l'église gallicane prouvées et commentées*, iii, Paris and Lyons, 1771

Dykmans, N., ed., *Le Cérémonial papal de la fin du Moyen Age à la Renaissance*, ii, *De Rome en Avignon ou le Cérémonial de Jacques Stefaneschi*, Brussels and Rome, 1981

Friedberg, Ae., ed., *Corpus Iuris Canonici*, 2 vols., Leipzig, 1879

Gattico, J. B., ed., *Acta Selecta Caeremoniarum Sanctae Romanae Ecclesiae*, i, Rome, 1753

Gewold, C., ed., *Defensio Ludovici IV Imperatoris contra Bzovium*, Ingoldstadt, 1618

Goldast, M., ed., *Collectio Constitutionum Imperialium*, iii, Offenbach, 1610

Golden Bull, see Charles IV

Gregory VII, *Dictatus Papae*, ed. E. Caspar, *MGH Epistolae Selectae*, ii, 1, Berlin, 1920, pp. 201–8

Gregory XI, *Lettres secrètes et curiales relatives à la France*, eds. L. Mirot, H. Jassemin, *et al.*, Paris, 1935–57

Innocent III, *Opera Omnia*, ed. J. P. Migne, *PL* 214–17

   Regestum Innocenti III Papae super Negotio Romani Imperii, ed. F. Kempf = *Miscellanea Historiae Pontificiae*, xii, Rome, 1947

   Die Register Innocenz' III, eds. O. Hageneder and A. Haidacher, Graz, Vienna, and Cologne, 1965–

Innocent VI, *Lettres secrètes et curiales*, eds. P. Gasnault and M.-H. Laurent, Paris, 1959–68

John XXII, *Lettres secrètes et curiales . . . relatives à la France*, eds. A. Coulon and S. Clémencet, Paris, 1900–62

John Offord [?], *Journal des conférences d'Avignon*, ed. K. de Lettenhove, *Oeuvres de Froissart*, XVIII, Brussels, 1874, pp. 235–56

Kühn, M., ed., *MGH Leges*, IV, *Const.*, ix, Weimar, 1974

Le Liber Censuum de l'église Romaine, eds. P. Fabre and L. Duchesne, Paris, 1910

Miret y Sans, J., ed., 'Lettres closes des premiers Valois', *Le Moyen Age*, XXIX (1917), pp. 53–88

Pfeffel, C. F., *Recherches historiques concernant les droits du pape sur la ville et l'état d'Avignon*, Avignon, 1768

Potthast, A. F., ed., *Regesta Pontificum Romanorum*, 2 vols., Berlin, 1874–5

Raynaldus, O., *Annales Ecclesiastici*, iv–vii, Lucca, 1749–52

Repetitionum in Universas fere Iuris Canonici Partes . . ., ed. L. A. Giunta, 6 vols., Venice, 1587

Riezler, S., *Die literarischen Widersacher der Päpste zur Zeit Ludwig des Baiers*, Leipzig, 1874

Rymer, T., *Foedera*, v, London, 1708

Sauerland, H. V., ed., *Urkunden und Regesten zur Geschichte der Rheinlands aus dem Vatikanischen Archiv*, iii, Bonn, 1905

Schäfer, K. H., *Die Ausgaben der apostolischen Kammer unter Benedikt XII, Klemens VI und Innocenz VI (1335–1362)*, Paderborn, 1914

Bibliography

Schimmelpfennig, B., ed., *Die Zeremonienbücher der römischen Kirche im Mittelalter*, Tübingen, 1973

Schrade, L., ed., *Polyphonic Music of the Fourteenth Century*, Monaco, 1965

Schunk, J. P., ed., *Beyträge zur Mainzer Geschichte mit Urkunden*, Mainz and Frankfurt, 3 vols., 1788–9

Schwalm, I., ed., *MGH, Leges* IV, *Const.*, iii, Hanover and Leipzig, 1904–6

MGH, Leges, IV, *Const.*, iv, 1, Hanover and Leipzig, 1906

MGH, Leges, IV, *Const.*, v, Hanover and Leipzig, 1909–13

Stengel, E. E., ed., *Nova Alamanniae. Urkunden, Briefe und andere Quellen zur deutschen Geschichte des 14. Jahrhunderts*, Berlin, 1921–30

Tamburini, F., ed., *Le Cérémonial apostolique avant Innocent VIII*, Rome, 1966

Tangl, M., *Die päpstlichen Kanzleiordnungen (1200–1500)*, Innsbruck, 1894

Theiner, A., ed., *Codex Diplomaticus Dominii Temporalis Sanctae Sedis*, ii, Rome, 1862

Vetera Monumenta Historica Hungariam Sacram Illustrantia, i, Rome, 1859

Vetera Monumenta Poloniae et Lithuaniae Historiam Illustrantia, i, Rome, 1860

Valbonnais, J. P. Moret de Bourchenu de, ed., *Mémoires pour servir à l'histoire de Dauphiné*, Paris, 1711

Viard, J., ed., 'La Messe pour la peste', *BEC*, XLI (1900), pp. 334–8

Vogel, C. and Elze, R., eds., *Pontificale Romano-Germanicum, Studi e Testi*, CCXVI (1963)

Walch, C., *Monimenta Medii Aevi ex Bibliotheca Regia Hanoverana*, I, fasc. 4, Göttingen, 1760

Weiland, L., ed., *MGH, Leges*, IV, *Const.*, ii, Hanover, 1896

Werunsky, E., ed., *Excerpta ex Registris Clementis VI et Innocentis VI*, Innsbruck, 1885

Zeumer, K., ed., 'Ein Reichsweisthum über die Wirkungen der Königswahl aus dem Jahre 1252', *Neues Archiv*, XXX (1905), pp. 405–15

Zeumer, K. and Salomon, R., eds., *MGH, Leges*, IV, *Const.*, viii, Hanover and Leipzig, 1910–26

II SECONDARY WORKS

Adcock, F. E., 1964, *Roman Political Ideas and Practice*, Michigan, 1964

Adnès, P., 1971, 'Indulgences', *DS*, VII, 2, Paris, 1971, cols. 1713–14

Alberigo, G., 1969, *Cardinalato e Collegialità*, Florence, 1969

Allmand, C., 1988, *The Hundred Years War: England and France at War c.1300–c.1450*, Cambridge, 1988

Altaner, B., and Stuiber, A., 1966, *Patrologie*, seventh edn, Freiburg, Basle, and Vienna, 1966

Arbesmann, R., 1954, 'The concept of *Christus-Medicus* in St Augustine', *Traditio*, X (1954), pp. 1–28

Atiya, A. S., 1938, *The Crusade in the Later Middle Ages*, London, 1938

Baethgen, F., 1920, 'Der Anspruch des Papsttums auf das Reichsvikariat. Untersuchungen zur Theorie und Praxis der *potestas indirecta in temporalibus*', *ZSSR, Kan. Abt.*, XLI (1920), pp. 168–268

Bibliography

Bagrow, L., 1964, *History of Cartography*, second edn, rev. R.A. Skelton, London, 1964

Barbet, J., 1961, Introduction to *François de Meyronnes–Pierre Roger: 'Disputatio'*, Paris, 1961, pp. 11–35

Bardinet, L., 1880, 'Condition civile des Juifs du Comtat Venaissin pendant le séjour des papes à Avignon, 1309–76', *Revue historique*, XII (1880), pp. 1–47

Barnie, J., 1974, *War in Medieval Society. Social Values and the Hundred Years War, 1337–99*, London, 1974

Bataillon, L.J., 1980, 'Approaches to the study of medieval sermons', *Leeds Studies in English*, n.s., XI (1980), pp. 19–35

Battifol, P., 1938, *Cathedra Petri = Unam Sanctam*, iv, Paris, 1938

Baudry, L., 1949, *Guillaume d'Occam. Sa vie, ses oeuvres, ses idées sociales et politiques*, Paris, 1949

Baumgarten, P.M., 1908, 'Wahlgeschenke der Päpste an das heilige Kollegium', *Römische Quartalschrift für Christliche Alterthumskunde und für Kirchengeschichte*, XXII (1908), pp. 36–55

Bayley, C., 1949a, 'Pivotal concepts in the political philosophy of William of Ockham', *JHI*, X (1949), pp. 199–218

1949b, *The Formation of the German College of Electors in the Mid-Thirteenth Century*, Toronto, 1949

Becker, H.-J., 1970, 'Das Mandat *Fidem Catholicam* Ludwigs des Bayern von 1338', *Deutsches Archiv*, XXVI (1970), pp. 454–512

Benson, R. L., 1967, '*Plenitudo potestatis*: evolution of a formula from Gregory IV to Gratian', *Studia Gratiana*, XIV = *Collectanea Stefan Kuttner*, iv, Bologna, 1967, pp. 195–217

1968, *The Bishop-Elect: a Study in Medieval Ecclesiastical Office*, Princeton, 1968

Benzing, J., 1965, *Lutherbibliographie*, Baden-Baden, 1965

Berlière, U., 1927, *Les Elections abbatiales au moyen âge = Académie royale de Belgique, classe des lettres et des sciences morales et politiques. Mémoires*, n.s. XX, Brussels, 1927

Bévenot, M., 1971, Introduction to Cyprian, *De Lapsis* and *De Ecclesiae Catholicae Unitate*, Oxford, 1971

Bignami-Odier, J., 1952, *Études sur Jean de Roquetaillade*, Paris, 1952

1981, 'Jean de Roquetaillade, théologien, polémiste, alchemiste', *HLF*, XLI (1981), pp. 75–104

Biscaro, G., 1927, 'Le relazioni dei Visconti di Milano con la Chiesa: Giovanni e Luchino – Clemente VI', *Archivo Storico Lombardo*, LIV (1927), pp. 44–95

Bock, F., 1941, *Einführung in das Registerwesen des Avignonesischen Papsttums*, QF, XXXI, Rome, 1941

Bolgar, R.R., 1954, *The Classical Heritage and its Beneficiaries*, Cambridge, 1954

Bologna, F., 1969, *I pittori alla corte angioina di Napoli, 1266–1414*, Rome, 1969

Borchardt, F., 1971, *German Antiquity in Renaissance Myth*, London, 1971

Bowsky, W., 1960, *Henry VII in Italy*, Nebraska, 1960

Bibliography

Boyle, L.E., 1972, *A Survey of the Vatican Archives and its Medieval Holdings = Subsidia Mediaevalia*, i, Toronto, 1972

Brampton, C.K., 1962, 'Ockham, Bonagratia and the Emperor Louis IV', *Medium Aevum*, XXXI (1962), pp. 81–7

Bresc, H., 1980, 'La Genèse du Schisme: les partis cardinalices et leurs ambitions dynastiques', *Genèse et débuts*, pp. 45–57

Brown, E.R., 1981, 'Death and the human body in the later middle ages: the legislation of Boniface VIII on the division of the corpse', *Viator*, XII (1981), pp. 221–70

Brown, P.R., 1964, 'Saint Augustine's attitude to religious coercion', *Journal of Roman Studies*, LIV (1964), pp. 107–16

Brundage, J.A., 1969, *Medieval Canon Law and the Crusader*, Madison, Milwaukee, and London, 1969

Buckland, W.W., 1963, *A Textbook of Roman Law from Augustus to Justinian*, third edn, Cambridge, 1963

Buisson, L., 1958, *'Potestas und Caritas': die päpstliche Gewalt im Spätmittelalter = Forschungen zur kirchlichen Rechtsgeschichte und zum Kirchenrecht*, ii, Cologne, 1958

Bulst, N., 1979, 'Der Schwarze Tod: Demographische wirtschafts-und kulturgeschichtliche Aspekte der Pestkatastrophe von 1347–1352', *Saeculum*, XXX (1979), pp. 45–67

Burckhardt, J., 1878, *The Civilization of the Renaissance in Italy*, tr. S.G.C. Middlemore, 2 vols., London, 1878

Burdach, K., 1913, *Rienzo und die geistige Wandlung seiner Zeit=Briefwechsel*, i, Berlin, 1913

Burdach, K. and Piur, P., 1929, *Kommentar zum Briefswechsel des Cola di Rienzo=Briefwechsel*, v, Berlin, 1929

Burnham, P.E., 1978, 'The patronage of Clement VI', *History Today*, XXVII (1978), pp. 372–81

Caldwell, J., 1978, *Medieval Music*, London, 1978

Campana, A., 1946, 'The origin of the word "humanist"', *JWCI*, IX (1946), pp. 60–73

Campbell, A.M., 1931, *The Black Death and Men of Learning*, New York, 1931

Canning, J.P., 1980, 'The corporation in the thought of the Italian jurists', *History of Political Thought*, I (1980), pp. 9–32

Canning, J.P., 1987, *The Political Thought of Baldus de Ubaldis*, Cambridge, 1987

Caplan, H., 1970, *Of Eloquence. Studies in Ancient and Medieval Rhetoric*, Cornell, 1970

Castelnuovo, E., 1959, 'Avignone rievocata', *Paragone*, X (1959), pp. 28–51

1962, *Un pittore italiano alla corte di Avignone. Matteo Giovannetti e la pittura in Provenza del secolo XIV*, Turin, 1962

1981, 'Avignone e la nuova pittura artisti pubblico committenti', *Aspetti culturali della società Italiana nel periodo del papata avignonese=Convegno del Centro di Studi sulla spiritualità medievale università degli studi di Perugia*, XIX (1981), pp. 389–414

Bibliography

Cazelles, R., 1958, *La Société politique et la crise de la royauté sous Philippe de Valois*, Paris, 1958

Cerfaux, L., 1959, *The Church in the Theology of St Paul*, tr. G. Webb and A. Walker, New York, Edinburgh, and London, 1959

Cerfaux, L. and Tondriau, J., 1957, *Un Concurrent du Christianisme. Le culte des souverains dans la civilisation Gréco-Romaine*, Tournai, 1957

Chadwick, H., 1959, *The Circle and the Ellipse: Rival Concepts of Authority in the Early Church*, inaugural lecture, Oxford, 1959

Chaplais, P., 1951, 'Règlement des conflits internationaux au XIVe siècle (1293–1377)', *Le Moyen Age*, LVII (1951), pp. 269–302

Charland, Th.-M., 1936, '*Artes Praedicandi': contribution à l'histoire de la rhétorique au moyen âge*, Paris and Ottawa, 1936

Charlesworth, M.P., 1937, 'The virtues of a Roman emperor: propaganda and the creation of belief', *PBA*, XXIII (1937), pp. 105–33

Chavasse, C., 1940, *The Bride of Christ: An Enquiry into the Nuptial Element in Early Christianity*, London, 1940

Cheyette, F.L., ed., 1968, *Lordship and Community in Medieval Europe*, New York, 1968

Clarke, M.V., 1964, *Medieval Representation and Consent*, New York, 1964

Cohn, N., 1962, *The Pursuit of the Millennium*, London, 1962

Coleman, J., 1984, 'FitzRalph's antimendicant "proposicio" (1350) and the politics of the papal court at Avignon', *JEH*, XXXV (1984), pp. 415–40

Congar, Y.M.-J., 1958, '*Quod omnes tangit, ab omnibus tractari et approbari debet*', *Revue historique de droit français et étranger*, series 4, XXXVI (1958), pp. 210–54

1961, 'Aspects ecclésiologiques de la querelle entre mendiants et séculiers dans la seconde moitié du XIIIe siècle et le début du XIVe', *Archives d'histoire doctrinale et littéraire du moyen âge*, XXXVI (1961), pp. 35–151

Cosenza, M.E., 1913, *Francesco Petrarca and the Revolution of Cola di Rienzo*, Chicago, 1913

Coville, A., 1933, 'Philippe de Vitri, notes biographiques', *Romania*, LIX (1933), pp. 520–47

1938a, 'Écrits contemporains sur le peste de 1348 à 1350', *HLF*, XXXVI (1938), pp. 325–89

1938a, 'Gilles li Muisis, Abbé de Saint Martin de Tournai. Chroniqueur et moraliste', *HLF*, XXXVI (1938), pp. 250–324

Cutler, A., 1970, 'Innocent III and the distinctive clothing of Jews and Muslims', *Studies in Medieval Culture*, iii, Michigan, 1970, pp. 92–116

Daly, L.J., 1964, 'Walter Burley and John Wyclif', in *Mélanges E. Tisserant*, iv = *Studi e Testi*, CCXXXIV (1964), pp. 163–84

1969, 'Some notes on Walter Burley's Commentary on the *Politics*', in *Essays in Medieval History Presented to Bertie Wilkinson*, eds. T.A. Sanquist and M.P. Powicke, Toronto, 1969, pp. 270–81

Daumet, G., 1913, 'Louis de la Cerda ou d'Espagne', *Bulletin Hispanique*, XV (1913), pp. 38–67

Bibliography

De Boüard, A., 1920, *Le Régime politique et les institutions de Rome au moyen âge, 1252–1347* = *BEFAR*, CXVIII, Paris, 1920

Decanter, J., 1954, 'La Muse de Raoul de Presles', *Positions des thèses, École nationale des chartes* (1954), pp. 37–41

De Lagarde, G., 1962–3, *La Naissance de l'esprit laïque au déclin du moyen âge*, iv: *Guillaume d'Ockham. Défense de l'Empire*, Paris, 1962; v: *Guillaume d'Ockham: critique des structures ecclésiasiales*, Paris, 1963

De Loye, G., 1974, 'Réception du Pape Clément VI par les Cardinaux Hannibal Ceccano et Pedro Gomez à Gentilly et Montfavet, 30 avril–1 mai 1343 (ou 1348)', *Actes du Congrès International Francesco Petrarca*, Avignon, 1974, pp. 331–53

De Lubac, H., 1949, *Corpus Mysticum: l'eucharistie et l'église au moyen âge*, second edn, Paris, 1948

Demaitre, L., 1975, 'Theory and practice in medical education at the University of Montpellier in the thirteenth and fourteenth centuries', *Journal of the History of Medicine*, XXX (1975), pp. 103–32

De Nolhac, P., 1892, 'Petrarque et Barlaam', *Revue des Études Grecques*, V (1892), pp. 94–9

   1907, *Pétrarque et l'humanisme*, Paris, 1907

De Pétigny, J., 1839–40, 'Notice historique et biographique sur Jacques Brunier, chancelier d'Humbert II, dauphin de Viennois', *BEC*, I (1839–40), pp. 263–87

Déprez, E., 1899, 'Une Tentative de reforme du calendrier sous Clément VI. Jean de Murs et la Chronique de Jean de Venette', *Mélanges*, XIX (1899), pp. 131–43

   1900, 'Les Funérailles de Clément VI et d'Innocent VI, d'après les comptes de la cour pontificale', *Mélanges*, XX (1900), pp. 235–50

   1902, *Les Préliminaires de la Guerre de Cent Ans. La papauté, la France, et l'Angleterre*, Paris, 1902

   1903, 'La Guerre de Cent Ans à la mort de Benoît XII: L'intervention des cardinaux avant le conclave et du Pape Clément VI avant son couronnement', *Revue Historique*, LXXXVII (1903), pp. 58–76

   1925, 'La Conférence d'Avignon (1344): l'arbitrage pontificale entre la France et l'Angleterre', in *Essays presented to T.F. Tout*, eds. A.G. Little and F.M. Powicke, Manchester, 1925, pp. 301–20

De Vries, W., 1964, 'Die Päpste von Avignon und der christliche Osten', *Orientalia Christiana Periodica*, XXX (1964), pp. 85–128

Douie, D., 1932, *The Nature and Effect of the Heresy of the Fraticelli*, Manchester, 1932

Duchesne, F., 1660, *Histoire de tous les cardinaux françois*, Paris, 1660

Duvergé, S., 1939, 'Le Rôle de la papauté dans la guerre de l'Aragon contre Gênes (1351–56)', *Mélanges*, L (1939), pp. 221–49

Dvořák, M., 1901, 'Die Illuminatoren des Johann von Neumarkt', *Jahrbuch der Kunstsammlungen des allerhöchsten Kaiserhauses*, XXII (1901), pp. 35–126

Dykmans, M., 1973, *Le Cardinal Annibal de Ceccano (c.1282–1350). Étude biographique et testament de 17 Juin 1348* = *Bulletin de l'Institut Historique Belge de Rome*, XLIII (1973), pp. 145–315

Edwards, M.V., 1984, 'The Luther Quincentennial', *JEH*, XXXV (1984), pp. 597–613

Ehrhardt, E., 1953, 'Das *Corpus Christi* und die Korporation im spätrömischen Recht', *ZSSR, Rom. Abt.*, LXX (1953), pp. 299–347

Ehrle, F., 1890, *Historia Bibliotecae Romanorum Pontificum*, Rome, 1890

Eichmann, E., 1951, *Weihe und Krönung des Papstes im Mittelalter*, Munich, 1951

Enaud, F., 1963, 'Simone Martini à Avignon', *Les Monuments historiques de la France*, numéro special (1963)

Engelmann, E., 1886, *Der Anspruch der Päpste auf Konfirmation und Approbation bei den deutschen Königswahlen*, Breslau, 1886

Esmein, J.P.H., 1929, *Le Mariage en droit canonique*, second edn, 2 vols., Paris, 1929

Eubel, C., 1892, 'Der erste Bischof der Canarischen Inseln', *Römische Quartalschrift für Christliche Alterthumskunde und für Kirchengeschichte*, VI (1892), pp. 237–40

1898, *Hierarchia Catholica Medii Aevi*, I, Monasterium, 1898

Faucon, M., 1879, 'Prêts faits aux rois de France par Clément VI, Innocent VI et le comte de Beaufort (1345–60)', *BEC*, XL (1879), pp. 570–8

1904, *Notice sur la construction de l'église de la Chaise-Dieu*, Paris, 1904

Faure, C., 1907, 'Le Dauphin Humbert II à Venise et en Orient (1345–47)', *Mélanges*, XVII (1907), pp. 509–62

Fayard, A., 1962, 'Le Tombeau de Clément VI à la Chaise-Dieu', *Almanach de Brioude*, XLII (1962), pp. 39–82

Feine, H.E., 1938, 'Die Approbation der Luxemburgischen Kaiser in ihren Rechtsformen an der Kurie', *ZSSR, Kan. Abt.*, XXVII (1938), pp. 364–97

Ferguson, W.K., 1948, *The Renaissance in Historical Thought*, Cambridge, Mass., 1948

Fife, R.H., 1957, *The Revolt of Martin Luther*, New York, 1957

Folz, R., 1969, *The Concept of Empire in Western Europe from the Fifth to the Fourteenth Century*, tr. S.A. Ogilvie, London, 1969

Foreville, R., 1974, 'Jubilé', in *DS*, VII (1974), cols. 1478–87

Fournier, P., 1938a, 'Pierre de la Palu, théologien et canoniste', *HLF*, XXXVII (1938), pp. 39–84

1938b, 'Pierre Roger (Clément VI)', *HLF*, XXXVII (1938), pp. 209–38

1938c, 'Jean Gaufredi, auteur du *Collectaire*', *HLF*, XXXVII (1938), pp. 522–31

Fowler, K., 1969, *The King's Lieutenant: Henry of Grosmont, First Duke of Lancaster, 1310–61*, London, 1969

Fowler, K., ed., 1971, *The Hundred Years War*, London, 1971

Fredericq, P., 1903, 'Deux sermons inédits de Jean de Fayt sur les Flagellants et sur le Grand Schisme d'Occident', *Bulletin de l'Academie royale de Belgique*, classe des lettres, Brussels, 1903, pp. 688–718

Frey, B., 1978, '*Pater Bohemiae – Vitricus Imperii*'. *Kaiser Karl IV. in der Geschichtsschreibung*, Bern, Frankfurt-am-Main, and Las Vegas, 1978

Fürst, C.G., 1967, '*Cardinalis*', *Prolegomena zu einer Rechtsgeschichte des römischen Kardinalskollegiums*, Munich, 1967

Bibliography

Gagnière, S., 1985, *Le Palais des papes d'Avignon*, Avignon, 1985

Gasnault, P., 1964, 'Comment s'appelait l'architecte du palais des papes d'Avignon, Jean de Loubières ou Jean de Louvres?' *Bulletin de la Société Nationale des Antiquaires de France*, 1964, pp. 118–27

Gaudemet, J., 1961, 'Le Rôle de la papauté dans la règlement des conflits entre états aux xiiie et xive siècles', *Recueils de la Société Jean Bodin*, XV (1961) pp. 79–106

Gaussin, P.-R., 1962, *L'Abbaye de la Chaise-Dieu (1043–1518). L'Abbaye en Auvergne et son rayonnement dans le Chrétienté*, Paris, 1962

Gay, J., 1904, *Le Pape Clément VI et les affaires d'Orient*, Paris, 1904

Geanakoplos, D., 1975, 'Byzantium and the Crusades, 1261–1354', in Hazard, iii, 1975, pp. 27–68

George, W., 1969, *Animals and Maps*, London, 1969

Gierke, O., 1927, *Political Theories of the Middle Age*, tr. F.W. Maitland, Cambridge, 1927

Gill, J., 1979, *Byzantium and the Papacy*, New Jersey, 1979

Gillet, P., 1927, *La Personalité juridique en droit ecclésiastique*, Malines, 1927

Gillmann, F., 1912, 'Romanus Pontifex iure omnia in scrinio pectoris sui cervetur habere', *Archiv für katholisches Kirchenrecht*, XCII (1912), pp. 3–17
1915, '*Dominus Deus noster papa?*', *Archiv für katholisches Kirchenrecht*, XCV (1915), pp. 266–82

Gilmore, M.P., 1941, *Argument from Roman Law in Political Thought*, Cambridge, Mass., 1941

Goez, W., 1958, *Translatio Imperii*, Tübingen, 1958

Goldringer, W., 1957, 'Das Zeremoniell der deutschen Königskrönung seit dem späten Mittelalter', *Mitteilungen des oberösterreichischen Landesarchiv*, V (1957), pp. 91–111

Gounot, R., 1962, 'Note technique sur le dessin du tombeau de Clément VI', *Almanach de Brioude*, XLII (1962), pp. 78–80

Grayzel, S., 1966, *The Church and the Jews in the Thirteenth Century*, rev. edn, New York, 1966

Greenhill, E.S., 1954, 'The child in the tree: a study of the cosmological tree in Christian tradition', *Traditio*, X (1954), pp. 323–71

Gregorovius, F., 1898, *History of the City of Rome in the Middle Ages*, tr. A. Hamilton, vi, 1, London, 1898

Grignaschi, M., 1960, 'Nicholas Oresme et son commentaire à la *Politique* d'Aristote', *Album Helen Maud Cam*, Louvain, 1960, i, pp. 97–152

Grotefend, H., 1884, *Quellen zur Frankfurter Geschichte*, 2 vols., Frankfurt, 1884

Guerchberg, S., 1965, 'The controversy over the alleged sowers of the Black Death in the contemporary treatises on plague', in Thrupp, 1965, pp. 208–24

Guillemain, B., 1962, *La Cour pontificale d'Avignon (1309–76): étude d'une société* = *BEFAR*, CCI, Paris, 1962
1980, 'Cardinaux et société curiale aux origines de la double election de 1378', in *Genèse et débuts*, pp. 19–30
1982, 'Clemente VI', *Dizionario Biografico degli Italiani*, XXVI, Rome, 1982, pp. 215–22

Bibliography

Hale, J.R., Highfield, R., and Smalley, B., eds., 1965, *Europe in the Late Middle Ages*, London, 1965

Harrison Thomson, S., 1947, 'Walter Burley's Commentary on the *Politics* of Aristotle', in *Mélanges Auguste Pelzer*, Louvain, 1947, pp. 557–78

1950, 'Learning at the court of Charles IV', *Speculum*, XXV (1950), pp. 1–20

Hauréau, B., 1892, *Notices et extraits de quelques manuscrits latins de la Bibliothèque Nationale*, v, Paris, 1892

Hayburn, R.F., 1979, *Papal Legislation on Sacred Music, 95 AD to 1977 AD*, Minnesota, 1979

Hazard, H.W., ed., 1975, *A History of the Crusades*, iii. *The Fourteenth and Fifteenth Centuries*, Wisconsin, 1975

Heck, C., 1980, 'La Chapelle du consistoire et les crucifixions dans la peinture murale Avignonnaise du XIVe siècle: le renouvellement d'un thème d'origine romaine du service de l'affirmation de la légitimité pontificale', in *Genèse et débuts*, pp. 431–43

Heft, J., 1982, 'John XXII and papal infallibility: Brian Tierney's thesis reconsidered', *Journal of Ecumenical Studies*, XIX (1982), pp. 759–80

Hermanin, F., 1945, *L'Arte in Roma dal secolo VIII al XIV*, Bologna, 1945

Heyen, H.J., ed., 1985, *Balduin von Luxemburg, Erzbischof von Trier, Kurfürst des Reiches, 1285–1354*, Trier, 1985

Hillenbrand, E., 1978, 'Die Autobiographie Karls IV. Entstehung und Funktion', in Patze, ed., 1978a, pp. 39–72

1979, *Vita Caroli Quarti. Die Autobiographie Karls IV. Einführung, Übersetzung und Kommentar*, Stuttgart, 1979

Höfler, C., 1868, *Aus Avignon*, Prague, 1868

Housley, N., 1986, *The Avignon Papacy and the Crusades, 1305–1378*, Oxford, 1986

Huber, K.A., 1978, 'Clemens VI. (Pierre Roger)', in Seibt, ed., 1978, pp. 99–110

Hugelmann, K.G., 1909, *Die deutsche Königswahl im 'Corpus Iuris Canonici'* = *Untersuchungen zur deutschen Staats- und Rechtsgeschichte*, XCVIII, Breslau, 1909

Hugho, N., 1977, 'Les Livres liturgiques de la Chaise-Dieu', *RB*, LXXXVII (1977), pp. 62–96, 289–348

Huyghebaert, N.-N., 1967, 'John Bernier de Fayt', *DHGE*, XVI (1967), cols. 780–2

1976, 'La Donation de Constantin ramenée à ses véritables dimensions: à propos de deux publications récentes', *RHE*, LXXI (1976), pp. 45–69

Jacob, E.F., 1956, 'John of Roquetaillade', *BJRL*, XXXIX (1956), pp. 75–96

James, E.O., 1959, *The Cult of the Mother-Goddess: an Archaeological and Documentary Survey*, London, 1959

Janson, K., 1880, *Das Königtum Günthers von Schwarzburg*, Leipzig, 1880

Jenkins, H., 1933, *Papal Efforts for Peace under Benedict XII*, Philadelphia, 1933

Jordan, E., 1922, 'Le Sacré Collège au moyen âge', *Revue des cours et conférences*, XXIII (1922), pp. 158–71

Bibliography

Jordan, K., 1932, 'Das Eindringen des Lehnswesens in das Rechtsleben der römischen Kurie', *Archiv für Urkundenforschung*, XII (1932), pp. 13–110

Joyce, G.H., 1949, *Christian Marriage: An Historical and Doctrinal Study*, second edn, London, 1949

Käppeli, T., 1936, *Le Procès contra Thomas Waleys*, O.P., Rome, 1936

    1948, 'Luca Mannelli (†1362) e la sua *Tabulatio* e *Expositio Senecae*', *AFP*, XVIII (1948), pp. 237–64

Kahr, M., 1966, 'Jean le Bon in Avignon', *Paragone*, CXCVII (1966), pp. 3–16

Kantorowicz, E.H., 1957, *The King's Two Bodies: A Study in Medieval Political Theology*, Princeton, 1957

Kelley, F.E., 1987, 'Ockham: Avignon, before and after', in *From Ockham to Wyclif*, eds. A. Hudson and M. Wilks = *SCH*, subsidia 5 (Oxford, 1987), pp. 1–18

Kemp, E.W., 1948, *Canonization and Authority in the Western Church*, Oxford, 1948

Klewitz, H.W., 1936, 'Die Entstehung des Kardinals-kollegiums', *ZSSR, Kan. Abt.*, XXV (1936), pp. 115–221

    1941, 'Die Krönung des Papstes', *ZSSR, Kan. Abt.*, XXX (1941), pp. 96–129

Knoll, P.W., 1972, *The Rise of the Polish Monarchy*, Chicago and London, 1972

Krämer, F., 1956, 'Ueber die Anfänge und Beweggründe der Papst-namenänderungen im Mittelalter', *Römische Quartalschrift*, LI (1956), pp. 148–88

Krammer, M., 1905, *Wahl und Einsetzung des deutschen Königs im Verhältnis zu einander*, Weimar, 1905

    1913, *Das Kurfürstenkolleg von seinen Anfängen bis zum Zusammenschluss im Renser Kurverein des Jahres 1338*, Weimar, 1913

Kristeller, P.O., 1961, *Renaissance Thought. The Classic Scholastic and Humanist Strains*, New York, 1961

Kuttner, S., 1938, 'La Réserve papale du droit de canonisation', *Revue historique de droit français et étranger*, XVII (1938), pp. 172–228

    1945, '*Cardinalis*: the history of a canonical concept', *Traditio*, III (1945), pp. 129–214

Kuttner, S. and Ryan, J.J., eds., 1965, *Proceedings of the Second International Congress of Medieval Canon Law*, Vatican City, 1965

Kyer, C.I., 1978a, 'A misplaced quaternion of letters of Benedict XII', *AHP*, XVI (1978), pp. 337–40

    1978b, '*Legatus* and *nuntius* as used to denote papal envoys, 1245–1378', *Medieval Studies*, XL (1978), pp. 473–7

Labande, L.-H., 1925, *Le Palais des papes et les monuments d'Avignon au XIVe siècle*, 2 vols., Marseilles, 1925

Laclotte, M., 1960, *L'École d'Avignon*, Paris, 1960

Laclotte, M. and Thiébaut, D., 1983, *L'École d'Avignon*, Flammarion, 1983

Ladner, G.B., 1942, 'Symbolism of the biblical corner-stone', *Medieval Studies*, IV (1942), pp. 43–60

Lambert, M.D., 1961, *Franciscan Poverty: the Doctrine of the Absolute Poverty of Christ and the Apostles in the Franciscan Order, 1210–1323*, London, 1961

Bibliography

1977, *Medieval Heresy. Popular Movements from Bogomil to Hus*, London, 1977

Lauer, P., 1940, *Catalogue général des manuscrits latins*, ii, Paris, 1940

Laurent, M.H., 1931, 'Pierre Roger et Thomas d'Aquin', *Revue Thomiste*, XXXVI (1931), pp. 157–73

Lea, H.C., 1896, *A History of Auricular Confession and Indulgences*, London, 1896

Lear, F.S., 1965, 'The idea of majesty in Roman political thought', in *Treason in Roman and Germanic Law: Collected Papers*, Austin, Texas, 1965

Le Bras, G., 1949, 'Le Droit romain au service de la domination pontificale', *Revue historique de droit français et étranger*, XXVII (1949), pp. 376–98

1964, *Institutions ecclésiastiques de la Chrétienté médiévale*, Paris, 1964

1966, 'L'Église médiévale au service du droit romain', *Revue historique de droit français et étranger*, XLIV (1966), pp. 193–209

Leclercq, J., 1963, 'Paris corporis papae. Le sacré collège dans l'ecclésiologie médiévale', in *L'Homme devant Dieu. Mélanges offerts au Père Henri de Lubac*, ii, Lyons and Paris, 1963, pp. 183–98

Lefebvre, C., 1968, 'Les Origines et le rôle du cardinalat au moyen âge', *Apollinaris*, XLI (1968), pp. 59–70

Leff, G., 1957, *Bradwardine and the Pelagians*, Oxford, 1957

1967, *Heresy in the Later Middle Ages*, 2 vols., Manchester, 1967

Lenzenweger, J., 1983, 'Clemens VI.', *Lexikon des Mittelalters*, ii, Munich and Zurich, 1983, cols. 2143–4

Léonard, E.G., 1932, *La Jeunesse de Jeanne Iere, reine de Naples, comtesse de Provence*, 2 vols., Monaco and Paris, 1932

Le Patourel, J., 1958, 'Edward III and the kingdom of France', *History*, XLIII (1958), pp. 173–89

1971, 'The origins of the war', in Fowler, ed., 1971, pp. 28–50

Ligota, C.R., 1956, *Petrus, Petra, Ecclesia Lateranensis: a Study in the Symbolic Aspects of Papal Authority in Their Bearing on the Investiture Contest*, unpublished doctoral dissertation, Cambridge, 1956

Little, A.G. and Powicke, F.M., eds., 1925, *Essays Presented to T.F. Tout*, Manchester, 1925

Loenertz, R.J., 1953, 'Ambassadeurs grecs auprès du Pape Clément VI (1348)', *Orientalia Christiana Periodica*, XIX (1953), pp. 178–96

Lomax, D., 1978, *The Reconquest of Spain*, London, 1978

Lombard-Jourdan, A., 1981, 'A propos de Raoul de Presles. Documents sur l'homme', *BEC*, CXXXIX (1981), pp. 191–207

Lo Parco, F., 1905, *Petrarca e Barlaam*, Reggio Calabria, 1905

Loriquet, H., 1904, *Catalogue général des manuscrits des bibliothèques publiques de France*, xxxviii, Paris, 1904

Lucas, H.S., 1929, *The Low Countries and the Hundred Years War*, Michigan, 1929

Ludat, H., and Schwinges, R.C., eds., 1982, *Politik, Gesellschaft, Geschichts-schreibung. Giessener Festgabe für Frantisek Graus zum 60. Geburtstag*, Cologne and Vienna, 1982

Luscombe, D.E., 1980, 'Conceptions of hierarchy before the thirteenth century', in Zimmermann, ed., 1980, i, pp. 1–19

Luttrell, A., 1965, 'The crusade in the fourteenth century', in Hale, Highfield, and Smalley, 1965, pp. 122–54

Bibliography

McGrade, A.S., 1974, *The Political Thought of William of Ockham*, Cambridge, 1974

Maier, A., 1952, *Codices Burghesiani Bibliothecae Vaticanae = Studi e Testi*, CLXX, Vatican City, 1952

1964, 'Zu Walter Burleys Politik-Kommentar', *Ausgehendes Mittelalter gesammelte Aufsätze zur Geistesgeschichte des 14. Jahrhunderts*, i, Rome, 1964, pp. 93–9

1967, 'Der literarische Nachlass des Petrus Rogerii (Clement VI) in der Borghesiana', *Ausgehendes Mittelalter, gesammelte Aufsätze zur Geistesgeschichte des 14. Jahrhunderts*, ii, Rome, 1967, pp. 255–315; 503–17

Mangeart, J., 1860, *Catalogue des manuscrits de la Bibliothèque de Valenciennes*, Paris, 1860

Mann, H.K., 1928, *Tombs and Portraits of the Popes of the Middle Ages*, London, 1928

Markus, R.A., 1970, *Saeculum: History and Society in the Theology of St Augustine*, Cambridge, 1970

1983, 'St Augustine's views on the "just war"', *SCH*, XX (1983), pp. 1–13

Marongiu, A., 1968a, *Medieval Parliaments: A Comparative Study*, tr. S.J. Woolf, London, 1968

1968b, 'The theory of democracy and consent in the fourteenth century' in Cheyette, ed., 1968, pp. 404–21

Martin, C., 1951, 'Some medieval commentaries on Aristotle's *Politics*', *History*, XXXVI (1951), pp. 29–44

Martin, O., 1909, *L'Assemblée de Vincennes de 1329 et ses conséquences*, Paris, 1909

Martindale, A., 1967, *Gothic Art*, London, 1967

1988, *Simone Martini, Complete Edition*, Oxford, 1988

Martinez, M.G., 1964, 'Sermón de Clemente VI Papa acerca de la otorgación del Reino de Canarias a Luis de España, 1344', *Revista de Historia*, XXIX (1964), pp. 88–111

1966, 'Segundo sermón de Clemente VI Papa, en ocasión de la coronación de Luis de España como Principe de las Islas Canarias', *Revista de Historia*, XXX (1966), pp. 164–71

Mersch, E., 1951, *Le Corps mystique du Christ*, third edn, Paris, 1951

Michaud-Quantin, P., 1970, *'Universitas': expressions du mouvement communautaire dans le moyen-âge Latin*, Paris, 1970

Miethke, J., 1969, *Ockhams Weg zur Sozialphilosophie*, Berlin, 1969

1978, 'Geschichtsprozess und zeitgenössisches Bewusstein. – Die Theorie des monarchischen Papats im hohen und späteren Mittelalter', *Historische Zeitschrift*, CCXXVI (1978), pp. 564–99

1980, 'Zur Bedeutung der Ekklesiologie für die politische Theorie im späteren Mittelalter', in Zimmermann, ed., 1980, pp. 369–88

Mitteis, H., 1944, *Die deutschen Königswahl, ihre Rechtsgrundlagen bis zur goldenen Bulle*, second edn, Brunn, 1944

Mollat, G., 1917, *Étude critique sur les 'Vitae Paparum Avenionensium'*, Paris, 1917

Bibliography

1928, 'L'Oeuvre oratoire de Clément VI', *Archives d'histoire doctrinale et littéraire du moyen âge*, III (1928), pp. 239–74

1951, 'Contribution à l'histoire du sacré collège de Clément V à Eugène IV', *RHE*, XLVI (1951), pp. 22–112, 566–94

1953, 'Clément VI', *DHGE*, XII, Paris, 1953, cols. 1129–62

1956–7, 'Correspondence de Clément VI par cédules', *Bullettino dell'Archivio paleografico*, n.s., II–III (1956–7), pt 2, pp. 175–8

1957, 'Clément VI et Jeanne de Bourgogne, reine de France', *Comptes Rendus des séances de l'Académie des Inscriptions et Belles Lettres* (1957), pp. 412–19

1960, 'Le Saint-Siège et la France sous le pontificat de Clément VI', *RHE*, LV (1960), pp. 5–21

1961, 'Clément VI et la vicomtesse de Turenne', *Mélanges*, LXXIII (1961), pp. 375–89

1963, 'Le Jubilé de 1350', *Journal des Savants* (1963), pp. 191–5

1964, *Les Papes d'Avignon 1305–78*, tenth edn, Paris, 1964

1974, 'Jean de Cardaillac, prélat, orateur et diplomat', *HLF*, XL (1974), pp. 187–210

Moraw, P., 1982, 'Kaiser Karl IV, 1378–1978: Ertrag und Konsequenzen eines Gedenkjahres', in Ludat and Schwinges, eds., 1982, pp. 224–318

Muldoon, J., 1966, '*Extra ecclesiam non est imperium*: the canonists and the legitimacy of secular power', *Studia Gratiana*, IX (1966), pp. 551–80

1975, 'Missionaries and the marriage of infidels', *The Jurist*, XXXV (1975), pp. 124–41

1979a, *Popes, Lawyers and Infidels: The Church and the Non-Christian World 1250–1530*, Philadelphia, 1979

1979b, 'The Avignon papacy and the frontiers of Christendom: the evidence of Vatican Register 62', *AHP*, XVII (1979), pp. 125–95

Müller, C., 1879–80, *Der Kampf Ludwigs des Baiern mit der römischen Kurie*, Tübingen, 1879–80

Musée des Beaux-Arts de Dijon, 1971, *Les Pleurants dans l'art du moyen âge en Europe*, Dijon, 1971

Nabuco, J., 1966, Introduction to F. Tamburini, ed., *Le Cérémonial apostolique avant Innocent VIII*, Rome, 1966

Nicol, D.M., 1968, *The Byzantine Family of Kantakousenos (Cantacuzenus) ca. 1100–1460*, Washington, D.C., 1968

1969, 'Byzantine requests for an oecumenical council in the fourteenth century', *Annuarium Historiae Conciliorum*, I (1969), pp. 69–95

1972, *The Last Centuries of Byzantium, 1216–1453*, London, 1972

Noonan, J.T., 1972, *Power to Dissolve: Lawyers and Marriages in the Courts of the Roman Curia*, Harvard, 1972

North, R., 1954, *Sociology of the Biblical Jubilee*, Rome, 1954

Offler, H.S., 1939, 'England and Germany at the beginning of the Hundred Years War', *EHR*, LIV (1939), pp. 608–31

1951, 'Uber die Prokuratorien Ludwigs des Bayern für die römische Kurie', *Deutsches Archiv*, VIII (1951), pp. 461–87

1955, 'A political *collatio* of Pope Clement VI, O.S.B.', *RB*, LXV (1955), pp. 126–44

Bibliography

1956a, 'Empire and papacy; the last struggle', *TRHS*, series 5, VI (1956), pp. 21–47

1956b, Introduction to *Tractatus contra Ioannem, Guillelmi de Ockham, Opera Politica*, iii, Manchester, 1956, pp. 20–8

1967, 'The origins of Ockham's *Octo Quaestiones*', *EHR*, LXXXII (1967), pp. 323–32

1974, 'An interpolated *collatio* of Pope Clement VI, O.S.B.', *RB*, LXXXIV (1974), pp. 111–25

Opitz, G., 1938–9, 'Über Registrierung von Sekretbriefen (Studien zu den Sekretregistern Clement VI)', *QF*, XXIX (1938–9), pp. 89–134

Origo, I., 1938, *Tribune of Rome. A Biography of Cola di Rienzo*, London, 1938

Ossinger, J.F., 1768, *Bibliotheca Augustiniana*, Ingoldstadt, 1768

Oswald, J., 1933, *Das alte Passauer Domkapitel bis zum dreizehnten Jahrhundert und sein Wahlkapitulationswesen*, Munich, 1933

Pacaut, M., 1955, 'Les Légats d'Alexandre III (1159–81)', *RHE*, L (1955), pp. 821–38

Pächt, O., 1943, 'A Giottesque episode in English medieval art', *JWCI*, VI (1943), pp. 51–70

Palmer, J., 1971, 'The war aims of the protagonists and the negotiations for peace', in Fowler, 1971, pp. 51–74

Pantin, W.A., 1955, *The English Church in the Fourteenth Century*, Cambridge, 1955

Pásztor, E., 1981, 'Funzione politico-culturale di una struttura della chiesa: il cardinalato', *Aspetti culturali della società italiana nel periodo del papato Avignonese*, Todi, 1981, pp. 216–20

Patze, H., 1978, 'Die Konsistorialrede Papst Clemens' VI. anlässlich der Wahl Karls IV.', in Patze, ed., 1978, pp. 1–37

Patze, H., ed., 1978, *Kaiser Karl IV, 1316–1378. Forschungen über Kaiser und Reich*, Göttingen, 1978

Paulus, N., 1913, 'Das Jubiläum vom Jahre 1350', *Theologie und Glaube*, V (1913), pp. 532–41

1923, *Geschichte des Ablasses am Ausgang des Mittelalters*, Paderborn, 1923

Peebles, B.M., 1954, 'The verse embellishments of the *Milleloquium Sancti Augustini*', *Traditio*, X (1954), pp. 555–66

Peghaire, J., 1932, 'L'Axiome *Bonum est diffusivum sui* dans le néoplatonisme et le thomisme', *Revue de l'université d'Ottawa*, section spéciale, i (1932), pp. 5*–30*

Pélissier, A., 1951, *Clément VI, le magnifique, premier pape limousin, 1342–52*, Brive, 1951

Perarnau, J., 1980, 'La butlla de canonització de Sant Iu (16 de juny de 1347) i les altres de tema Franciscà del Vat. Lat. 6672', *Estudios Franciscanos*, LXXXI (1980), pp. 355–70

1981, 'El sermó de Climent VIè amb la fórmula de canonització de Sant Iu', *Estudios Franciscanos*, LXXXII (1981), pp. 117–23

Perrin, J.W., 1972, 'Azo, Roman Law and Sovereign European States' in *Studia Gratiana*, XV=*Post Scripta: Essays on Medieval Law and the Emergence of the European State in Honor of Gaines Post*, Bologna, 1972, pp. 89–101

Bibliography

1973, 'Legatus in medieval Roman law', Traditio, XXIX (1973), pp. 357–78

Perrini, D.A., 1929, Bibliographia Augustiniana, i, Florence, 1929

Perroy, E., 1951, The Hundred Years War, tr. W.B. Wells, London, 1951

1979, 'L'Ars Nova: le point de vue de l'historien' in E. Perroy, Études d'histoire médiévale, Paris, 1979, pp. 21–9

Peters, E., 1970, The Shadow King, London, 1970

Piaia, G., 1980, 'Interpretazione allegorica ed uso ideologico della prima profesia di Daniele agli inizi del trecento', in Zimmerman, 1980, pp. 351–68

Piur, P., 1925, Petrarcas 'Buch ohne Namen' und die päpstliche Kurie, Halle, 1925

1931, Cola di Rienzo, Vienna, 1931

Plumpe, J.C., 1943a, 'Mater Ecclesia': an Inquiry into the Concept of the Church as Mother in Early Christianity, Washington, 1943

1943b, 'Vivum Saxum. Vivi Lapides. The concept of "living stone" in classical and Christian antiquity', Traditio, I (1943), pp. 1–14

Poole, R.L., 1934, 'The names and numbers of medieval popes', in Studies in Chronology and History, ed. A.L. Poole, Oxford, 1934, pp. 156–71

Poquet de Haut-Jussé, B.-A., 1928, Les Papes et les ducs de Bretagne: essai sur les rapports du Saint-Siège avec un état = BEFAR, CXXXIII, Paris, 1928

Post, Gaines, 1964, Studies in Medieval Legal Thought: Public Law and the State, 1100–1322, Princeton, 1964

Posthumus Meyjes, G.H.M., 1978, Jean Gerson et l'assemblée de Vincennes (1329), Leiden, 1978

Powicke, F.M. and Emden, A.B., eds., 1936, The Universities of Europe in the Middle Ages by the late Hastings Rashdall, 3 vols., Oxford, 1936

Pratt, K.J., 1965, 'Rome as eternal', JHI, XXVI (1965), pp. 25–44

Quillet, J., 1977, La Philosophie politique du 'Songe du Vergier' (1378): sources doctrinales, Paris, 1977

1980, 'La Problématique de l'empire et son enjeu doctrinal dans le Mandement Fidem Catholicam (1338)', in Zimmermann, 1980, pp. 427–38

Reaney, G., 1960, 'Ars Nova in France', in The New Oxford History of Music, ii (Oxford, 1960), pp. 1–30

Reese, G., 1941, Music in the Middle Ages, London, 1941

Renouard, Y., 1935, 'Les Minutes d'Innocent VI aux Archives du Vatican', Archivi, II (1935), pp. 14–26

1941, Les Relations des papes d'Avignon et des compagnies commerciales et bancaires de 1316 à 1378 = BEFAR, CLI, Paris, 1941

1970, The Avignon Papacy, tr. D. Bethell, London, 1970

Rieger, F.I., 1885, Die Altarsetzung der deutschen Könige nach der Wahl, Berlin, 1885

Riesenberg, P.N., 1956, Inalienability of Sovereignty in Medieval Political Thought, New York, 1956

Rivière, J., 1922, 'Le Pape est-il un Dieu pour Innocent III?', Revue des sciences religieuses, II (1922), pp. 447–51

1924, 'Sur l'expression Papa-Deus au moyen âge', Miscellanea F. Ehrle, ii=Studi e Testi, XXXVIII, Vatican City, 1924, pp. 278–89

1925, 'In partem sollicitudinis: evolution d'une formule pontificale', Revue des sciences religieuses, V (1925), pp. 210–31

Bibliography

1926, *Le Problème de l'église et de l'état au temps de Philippe le Bel*, Louvain and Paris, 1926

Rodocanachi, E., 1888, *Cola di Rienzo, Histoire de Rome de 1342 à 1354*, Paris, 1888

Roques, M., 1960, 'Le Peintre de la chambre de Clément VI au palais d'Avignon', *Bulletin monumental*, CXVIII (1960), pp. 273–96

Rowley, H.H., 1935, *Darius the Mede and the Four World Empires in the 'Book of Daniel': A Historical Survey of Contemporary Theories*, Cardiff, 1935

Royer, J.-P., 1969, *L'Église et le royaume de France au xive siècle d'après le 'Songe du Vergier' et la jurisprudence du Parlement*, Paris, 1969

Ruello, F., 1965, 'La Notion *Thomiste* de *ratio in divinis* dans la *Disputatio* de François de Meyronnes et de Pierre Roger, 1320–21', *RTAM*, XXXII (1965), pp. 54–75

Russell, F.H., 1975, *The Just War in the Middle Ages*, Cambridge, 1975

Rutledge, D., 1964, *Cosmic Theology. The Ecclesiastical Hierarchy of Pseudo-Denys: An Introduction*, London, 1964

St Clair Baddeley, W., 1897, *Robert the Wise and his Heirs*, London, 1897

Salomon, R.G., 1953, 'A newly discovered manuscript of Opicinus de Canistris', *JWCI*, XVI (1953), pp. 45–57

Sayers, J., 1971, *Papal Judges Delegate in the Province of Canterbury 1198–1254. A Study in Ecclesiastical Jurisdiction and Administration*, Oxford, 1971

Schenk, M., 1965, *Die Unfehlbarkeit des Papstes in der Heiligsprechung*, Freiburg, 1965

Schimmelpfennig, B., 1973, *Die Zeremonienbücher der römischen Kirche in Mittelalter*, Tübingen, 1973

1980, 'Die Funktion des Papstpalastes und der kurialen Gesellschaft im päpstlichen Zeremoniell vor und während des grossen Schismas', *Genèse et débuts*, pp. 317–28

Schmidinger, H., 1978, 'Die Antwort Clemens' VI. an die Gesandtschaft der Stadt Rom vom Jahre 1343', *Miscellanea in onore di monsignor Martini Giusti* = *Collectanea Archivi Vaticano*, VI (Vatican City, 1978), pp. 323–65

1979, 'Die Gesandtschaft der Stadt Rom nach Avignon vom Jahre 1342/3', *Römische Historische Mitteilungen*, XXI (1979), pp. 15–33

Schmitz, P., 1929, 'Les Sermons et discours de Clément VI, O.S.B.', *RB*, XLI (1929), pp. 13–24

1932, 'Un Sermon inconnu de Pierre Roger', *RB*, LXIV (1932), pp. 71–4

Schmugge, L., 1966, *Johannes von Jandun (1285/89–1328). Untersuchungen zur Biographie und Sozialtheorie eines lateinischen Averroisten*, Stuttgart, 1966

Schmutz, R.A., 1972, 'Medieval papal representatives: legates, nuncios, and judges-delegate', *Studia Gratiana*, XV (1972), pp. 443–63

Schneider, R., 1973, 'Karls IV. Auffassung vom Herrscheramt' in *Beiträge zur Geschichte des mittelalterlichen deutschen Königtums=Historische Zeitschrift*, Beiheft II, Neue Folge (1973), pp. 1–24

Schneyer, J.B., 1972, *Repertorium der lateinischen Sermones des Mittelalters*, iv, Münster, Westfalen, 1972

Scholz, R., 1911–14, *Unbekannte kirchenpolitische Streitschriften aus der Zeit Ludwigs des Bayern (1327–1354)*, 2 vols., Rome, 1911–14

Bibliography

Schubert, E., 1985, 'Kurfürsten und Wählkönigtum. Die Wählen von 1308, 1314 und 1346 und der Kurverein von Rhens', in Heyen, 1985, pp. 103–17

Schulz, F., 1951, *Classical Roman Law*, Oxford, 1951

Schütz, A., 1973, *Die Prokuratorien und Instruktionen Ludwigs des Bayern für die Kurie (1331–1345). Ein Beitrag zu seinen Absolutionsprozess*, Munich, 1973

Schwiebert, E.G., 1950, *Luther and his Times*, Saint Louis, 1950

Schwöbel, H.O., 1968, *Der diplomatische Kampf zwischen Ludwig dem Bayern und der römischen Kurie im Rahmen des kanonischen Absolutionsprozesses 1330–1346*, Weimar, 1968

Seibt, F., 1978, *Karl IV. Ein Kaiser in Europa, 1346–78*, Munich, 1978

Seibt, F., ed., 1978, *Karl IV. und sein Kreis = Lebensbilder zur Geschichte der böhmischen Länder*, iii, Munich and Vienna, 1978

Sharon, H., 1958, 'Illuminated manuscripts at the court of King Wenceslas IV of Bohemia', *Scriptorium*, IX (1958), pp. 115–24

Sikes, J.G., 1949, 'John de Pouilli and Peter de la Palu', *EHR*, XLIX (1949), pp. 219–40

Simone, F., 1969, *The French Renaissance. Medieval Tradition and Italian Influence in Shaping the Renaissance in France*, tr. H.G. Hall, London, 1969

Skinner, Q., 1978, *The Foundations of Modern Political Thought*, 2 vols., Cambridge, 1978

Smalley, B., 1954, 'Thomas Waleys, O.P.', *AFP*, XXIV (1954), pp. 50–107
1960, *English Friars and Antiquity in the Early Fourteenth Century*, Oxford, 1960
1961, 'John de Hesdin, O. Hosp. S. Ioh.', *RTAM*, XXVIII (1961), pp. 285–330
1963, 'Jean de Hesdin: a source of the *Somnium Viridarii*', *RTAM*, XXX (1963), pp. 154–9
1975, 'Ecclesiastical attitudes to novelty, *c.*1100–*c.*1250', *SCH*, XII (1975), pp. 113–31

Southern, R.W., 1970, 'Aspects of the European tradition of historical writing: 1. The classical tradition from Einhard to Geoffrey of Monmouth', *TRHS*, series 5, XX (1970), pp. 173–96
1973, 'Aspects of the European tradition of historical writing: 3. History as prophecy', *TRHS*, series 5, XXII (1973), pp. 163–80

Špeváček, J., 1971, 'Die letzte Phase des Kampfes Markgraf Karls (IV) um die römische Krone', *Historisches Jahrbuch*, XCI (1971), pp. 94–108

Stengel, E.E., 1930, *Avignon und Rhens*, Weimar, 1930
1960, 'Baldwin von Luxemburg. Ein grenzdeutschen Staatsman des 14 Jahrhunderts', *Abhandlungen und Untersuchungen zur mittelalterlichen Geschichte*, Cologne, 1960, pp. 180–215

Stickler, A.M., 1977, *Il Giubileo di Bonifacio VIII. Aspetti giuridici-pastorali=Quaderni della Fondazione Camillo Caetani*, ii, Rome, 1977

Storoni Mazzolani, L., 1970, *The Idea of the City in Roman Thought – from Walled City to Spiritual Commonwealth*, tr. S. O'Donnell, London, 1970

Struve, J., 1978, *Die Entwicklung der organologischen Staatsauffassung im Mittelalter*, Stuttgart, 1978

Bibliography

Sussidi per la Consultazione dell'Archivio Vaticano a cura della Direzione e degli Archivisti, i = *Studi e Testi*, xlv, Vatican City, 1926

Swain, J.W., 1940, 'The theory of the four monarchies: opposition history under the Roman Empire', *Classical Philology*, XXXV (1940), pp. 1–21

Synan, E.A., 1965, *The Popes and the Jews in the Middle Ages*, New York and London, 1965

Taylor, L.R., 1931, *The Divinity of the Roman Emperor*, Middletown, Connecticut, 1931

Tessier, G., 1957, 'Les Chanceliers de Philippe VI', *Comptes rendus des séances de l'Académie des Inscriptions et Belles Lettres* (1957), pp. 356–73

Thiriet, F., 1959, *La Romanie vénitienne au moyen âge: le développement et l'exploitation du domaine colonial vénitien (XIIe–XVe siècles)* = *BEFAR*, CXCIII, Paris, 1959

Thomas, A., 1921, 'Bernard Gui, frère, prêcheur', *HLF*, XXXV (1921), pp. 139–232

Thorndike, L., 1934, *A History of Magic and Experimental Sciences*, iii, Columbia, 1934

Thrupp, S., ed., 1965, *Change in Medieval Society*, New York, 1965

Thurston, H., 1900, *The Holy Year of Jubilee: An Account of the History and Ceremonial of the Roman Jubilee*, London, 1900

Tierney, B., 1951, 'A conciliar theory of the thirteenth century', *CHR*, XXXVI (1951), pp. 415–40

1955, *Foundations of the Conciliar Theory*, Cambridge, 1955

1962, '*Tria quippe distinguit iudicia* . . . A note on Innocent III's *Per Venerabilem*', *Speculum*, XXXVII (1962), pp. 48–59

1971, 'Origins of papal infallibility', *Journal of Ecumenical Studies*, VIII (1971), pp. 841–64

1972, *Origins of Papal Infallibility, 1150–1350: A Study on the Concepts of Infallibility, Sovereignty and Tradition in the Middle Ages*, Leiden, 1972

1982a, *Religion, Law and the Growth of Constitutional Thought, 1150–1650*, Cambridge, 1982

1982b, 'Sovereignty and infallibility: a response to James Heft', *Journal of Ecumenical Studies*, XIX (1982), pp. 787–93

Tomasello, A., 1983, *Music and Ritual at Papal Avignon* = *Studies in Musicology*, LXXV, Yale, 1983

Trapp, D., 1957, 'Peter Ceffons of Clairvaux', *RTAM*, XXIV (1957), pp. 101–54

Turley, T., 1975, 'Infallibilists in the curia of Pope John XXII', *Journal of Medieval History*, I (1975), pp. 71–101

1982, 'John Baconthorpe on papal infallibility', *Journal of Ecumenical Studies*, XIX (1982), pp. 744–58

Tyermann, C.J., 1985, 'Philip VI and the recovery of the Holy Land', *EHR*, C (1985), pp. 25–32

Ubald d'Alençon, P., 1911, 'Panégyrique inédit de Saint François d'Assise', *Études Franciscaines*, XXVI (1911), pp. 337–58

Bibliography

Ullman, B.L., 1941, 'Some aspects of the origin of Italian Humanism', *Philological Quarterly*, XX (1941), pp. 212–23

1973, *Studies in the Italian Renaissance*, second edn, Rome, 1973

Ullmann, W., 1949, *Medieval Papalism. The Political Theories of the Medieval Canonists*, London, 1949

1965, *A History of Political Thought: The Middle Ages*, Harmondsworth, 1965

1966a, *Papst und König*, Salzburg and Munich, 1966

1966b, *Principles of Government and Politics in the Middle Ages*, second edn, London, 1966

1967, *The Individual and Society in the Middle Ages*, London, 1967

1969, *The Carolingian Renaissance and the Idea of Kingship*, London, 1969

1970, *The Growth of Papal Government in the Middle Ages*, third edn, London, 1970

1972a, *The Origins of the Great Schism: A Study in Fourteenth-Century Ecclesiastical History*, second edn, Hamden, Connecticut, 1972

1972b, *A Short History of the Papacy in the Middle Ages*, London, 1972

1975a, *Law and Politics in the Middle Ages*, London, 1975

1975b, *The Church and the Law in the Earlier Middle Ages* = *Collected Essays*, i, London, 1975

1976, *The Papacy and Political Ideas in the Middle Ages* = *Collected Essays*, ii, London, 1976

1977, *Medieval Foundations of Renaissance Humanism*, London, 1977

1978, *Scholarship and Politics in the Middle Ages* = *Collected Essays*, iii, London, 1978

Van der Straeten, J., 1964, 'S. Robert de la Chaise-Dieu – sa canonisation – sa date de fête', *Analecta Bollandiana*, LXXXII (1964), pp. 35–56

Van Werveke, N., 1901, 'Itinéraire de Jean l'Aveugle, roi de Bôheme et comte de Luxembourg', *Publications de la section de l'Institut grand-ducal de Luxembourg*, LII (1901), pp. 25–52

Vauchez, A., 1981, *La Sainteté en Occident aux derniers siècles du moyen âge* = *BEFAR*, CCXLI, Rome, 1981

Vernay, E., 1912, 'L'Excommunication et l'interdit en droit canonique de Gratien à la fin du xiiiᵉ siècle', Introduction to Berengar Frédol, *Liber de Excommunication*, Paris, 1912

Villey, M., 1955, 'L'Idée de la croisade chez les juristes du moyen âge', *Relazioni del X congresso internazionale di scienze storiche*, iii, Florence, 1955, pp. 565–94

Vincke, J., 1942, 'Primeras tentativas misionales en Canarias (siglo XIV)', *Analecta Sacra Tarraconensia*, XV (1942), pp. 291–301

Vlasto, A.P., 1970, *The Entry of the Slavs into Christendom: an Introduction to the Medieval History of the Slavs*, Cambridge, 1970

Vodola, E., 1986, *Excommunication in the Middle Ages*, Berkeley, Los Angeles, and London, 1986

Wahl, J.A., 1970, 'Immortality and inalienability: Baldus de Ubaldis', *Medieval Studies*, XXXII (1970), pp. 308–28

Bibliography

Walsh, G.G., 1924, *The Emperor Charles IV: A Study in Holy Roman Imperialism*, Oxford, 1924

Walsh, K., 1980, 'Böhmens Vater – des Reiches Erzstiefvater? Gedanken zu einem neuen Bild Kaiser Karls IV.', *Innsbrucker Historische Studien*, III (1980), pp. 189–200

1981a, *A Fourteenth Century Scholar and Primate: Richard FitzRalph in Oxford, Avignon and Armagh*, Oxford, 1981

1981b, 'Klemens VI. und Stift Stams. Predigttätigkeit in Avignon und Frühhumanismus in Tirol am Beispiel von MS 234 der Universitätsbibliothek Innsbruck', *Studien und Mitteilungen zur Geschichte des Benediktiner-Ordens und seiner Zweige*, XCII (1981), pp. 205–19

Walther, H.G., 1976, *Imperiales Königtum, Konziliarismus und Volkssouveranität*, Munich, 1976

Waquet, H., 1912, 'Note sur les médecins de Clément VI', *Mélanges*, XXXII (1912), pp. 45–8

Wasner, F., 1935, 'De consecratione, inthronizatione, coronatione Summi Pontificis', *Apollinaris*, VIII (1935), pp. 86–125, 249–81, 428–39

Wasner, F., 1958, 'Fifteenth-century texts on the ceremonial of the papal *legatus a latere*', *Traditio*, XIV (1958), pp. 295–358

Watt, J.A., 1965, 'The use of the term *plenitudo potestatis* by Hostiensis', in Kuttner and Ryan, 1965, pp. 161–87

1970, *The Church and the Two Nations in Medieval Ireland*, Cambridge, 1970

1971, 'The constitutional law of the College of Cardinals: Hostiensis to Johannes Andreae', *Medieval Studies*, XXIII (1971), pp. 127–51

1980, 'Hostiensis on *Per Venerabilem*: the role of the College of Cardinals', in *Authority and Power. Studies on Medieval Law and Government presented to Walter Ullmann on his seventieth birthday*, eds. B. Tierney and P. Linehan, Cambridge, 1980, pp. 99–113

Weckmann, L., 1949, *Las bulas alejandrinas de 1493 y la teoría política del papado medieval*, Mexico, 1949

Weider, J., 1978, 'Cola di Rienzo', in Seibt, ed., 1978, pp. 111–44

Weinstein, D., 1972, 'In whose image and likeness? Interpretations of Renaissance humanism', *JHI*, XXXIII (1972), pp. 165–76

Weinstock, S., 1971, *Divus Julius*, Oxford, 1971

Werunsky, E., 1880–92, *Geschichte Kaiser Karls IV. und seiner Zeit*, 2 vols., Innsbruck, 1880–92, repr. New York, 1961

Wetterlöf, V.G., 1975, *Les Ymagiers à la cour des papes d'Avignon et à la cour des rois de France, 1327–1365*, Lund, 1975

Wilkins, E.H., 1955, *Studies in the Life and Works of Petrarch*, Cambridge, Mass., 1955

Wilks, M.J., 1960, 'The idea of the Church as *unus homo perfectus* and its bearing on the medieval theory of sovereignty', *Miscellanea Historiae Ecclesiasticae*, Stockholm, 1960, pp. 32–49

1963a, *The Problem of Sovereignty in the Later Middle Ages*, Cambridge, 1963

1963b, 'The *Apostolicus* and the Bishop of Rome, II', *JTS*, n.s. XIV (1963), pp. 311–54

Bibliography

1966, 'St Augustine and the General Will', *Studia Patristica*, IX = *TU*, XCIV (1966), pp. 487–522

1972, 'Corporation and representation in the *Defensor Pacis*', *Studia Gratiana*, xv = *Post Scripta: Essays on Medieval Law and the Emergence of the European State in Honor of Gaines Post*, Bologna, 1972, pp. 251–92

Willemsen, C.A., 1927, *Kardinal Napoleon Orsini (1236–1342)*, Berlin, 1927

Wolff, R.L., 1948, '*Romania*: the Latin empire of Constantinople', *Speculum*, XXIII (1948), pp. 1–34

Wood, D., 1975, '*Maximus sermocinator verbi Dei*: the sermon literature of Pope Clement VI', *SCH*, XI (1975), pp. 163–72

1983, '*Omnino partialitate cessante*: Clement VI and the Hundred Years War', *SCH*, XX (1983), pp. 179–89

1984, 'Infidels and Jews: Clement VI's attitude to persecution and toleration', *SCH*, XXI (1984), pp. 115–24

1985, '. . . *novo sensu sacram adulterare Scripturam*: Clement VI and the political use of the Bible' in *The Bible in the Medieval World: Essays in Memory of Beryl Smalley*, eds. K. Walsh and D. Wood, *SCH*, subsidia 4 (1985), pp. 237–49

Wrigley, J.E., 1964, 'A papal secret known to Petrarch', *Speculum*, XXXIX (1964), pp. 613–34

1965a, *Studies in the Life of Pierre Roger (Pope Clement VI) and of Related Writings of Petrarch*, unpublished doctoral dissertation, Pennsylvania, 1965

1965b, 'A rehabilitation of Clement VI: *sine nomine 13* and the kingdom of Naples', *AHP*, III (1965), pp. 127–38

1970, 'Clement VI before his pontificate: the early life of Pierre Roger, 1290/91–1342', *CHR*, LVI (1970), pp. 433–73

1982, 'The conclave and the electors of 1342', *AHP*, XX (1982), pp. 51–81

Young, E.J., 1949, *The Prophecy of Daniel: A Commentary*, Michigan, 1949

Zacour, N.P., 1960, *Talleyrand: the Cardinal of Périgord (1301–64)*, Philadelphia, 1960

1975, 'Papal regulation of cardinals' households in the fourteenth century', *Speculum*, L (1975), pp. 343–55

Zimmermann, A., ed., 1980, *Soziale Ordnungen im Selbstverständnis des Mittelalters=Miscellanea Mediaevalia*, XII, 2 vols., Berlin and New York, 1980

Zunzunegui, J., 1940–1, 'Los orígines de las misiones en las islas Canarias', *Revista española de teologia*, I, Madrid, 1940–1, pp. 361–408

INDEX

Figures in italics denote illustrations.

Index

Avignon (*cont.*)
(papal bed chamber, Angels'
Tower) 56–9, *58*, (plan of) *52*,
(Porte des Champeaux) 54, *54*, 55,
71; *see also* Clement VI, pope

Babylon: symbolising Avignon, 47, 68,
81, symbolising hell, 128
Baldmar, canon of Frankfurt, 165
Baldus de Ubaldis, 24, 30, 36n90,
85n57, 153n47
Baldwin of Luxemburg, archbishop of
Trier, 149–51, 154–5, 163
Baluzius, S., *Vitae Paparum
Avenionensium* of, 17
Barlaam of Calabria, bishop of Gerace,
68
Bartholomew of Urbino, 207
Bartolomeo Platina, 1
Bartolus of Sassoferrato, 94n89
Bédarrides, 197n105, 209
Benedict XI, pope, 43, 113
Benedict XII, pope, 11, 13, 33, 40n107,
44, 45, 50, 58–9, 76, 77, 107, 115,
119, 123n9, 132, 139, 143, 155n59,
160, 183, 184
Beneš of Weitmil, 150n29, 151n32,
163n96
Bernard d'Albi, cardinal, 213
Bernard of Clairvaux, St, 16, 21, 24–5,
68, 81n31, 167
Bernard Gui, 207
Bernard de Turre, cardinal, 107n51,
111n69
Bertrand de Déaulx, cardinal, 83n40,
107n51, 109, 109nn60,62, 213, 214
Bertrand de Poujet, cardinal, 108
bishops: inferior to cardinals, 118;
limited to own sees, 81; married to
sees, 155–6; provided by pope, 101
Black Death, 49, 51, 66–7, 74, 191n70,
197; *see also* Clement VI, pope
Boethius, 68
Bohemia, 71, 144, 170, 171
Bologna, 38
Bonagratia of Bergamo, 154n51
Boniface VIII, pope, 23, 26n31, 33, 67,
93, 112n78, 121, 123n9, 125, 132,
159, 192
Bonn, 163–5
Bosporus, 177, 185
Braga, archbishop of, 173
Breslau, episcopal see of, 171
Bridget of Sweden, St, 98

Brittany, 102, 131
bulls, constitutions, and decretals,
papal:
Antiquorum habet fida relatio (Boniface
VIII), 33n75
Coelestis altitudo (Nicholas IV), 113
Constitutio pro Judaeis (Innocent III),
196, 198–9
Cum natura humana (Clement VI-
spurious), 32
Detestandae feritatis abusum (Boniface
VIII), 67n95
Docta sanctorum (John XXII), 69
Fundamenta (Nicholas III), 90
Laudabiliter (Adrian IV), 134
Licet in constitutione (Clement VI),
33n73, 97
Ne Romani (Clement V), 103, 114
Pastoralis cura (Clement V), 38, 146–8
Per Venerabilem (Innocent III), 90,
146, 147
Quia quorundam mentes (John XXII),
9, 37
Solicitudo Pastoralis (Innocent VI),
104nn33,34
Ubi periculum (Gregory X), 103, 104
Unam Sanctam (Boniface VIII), 3,
23n16
Unigenitus Dei filius (Clement VI),
32–3
Vas electionis (John XXII), 8
Burnham, P. E., 1
Byzantines, *see* Greeks

Cahors, 86
Cajetan, Thomas de Vio, cardinal, 33
Calais, siege of (1346–7), 126, 127, 138;
truce of (1347), 138
Canary Islands, *see* Fortune Islands
cardinals, 12, 15, 49, **96–121**, 133, 135–
6, 136, 137, 139, 186, 203–4; and
Benedict XII, 110; ceremonial
order for creation of, 107; College
of, 3, 44, 49, 98–9, 137, 154, 203,
(appointment to) 105–9, 115–16,
(elects pope) 101, 154, (French
character of) 98–9, (instituted by
pope) 117, (instrument of God in
election) 101, (no plenitude of
power *sede vacante*) 103, (*sede
vacante* powers) 99; consulted by
pope, 113–14; duties of, 96–7;
electoral pact of, 104–5, 110–11,
113–14; jurisdictional office of,

246

Index

Clement VI (*cont.*)

majesté) 27; on heretics (outside the Church) 182–3, (subvert Church) 183, (as wild beasts) 183; Holy Land as inheritance of Christ, 191–2, 199; Hundred Years War (attempted mediation) 131–8, (imposes truces) 128, 131, 138, (justice of) 128–30, 140 (partiality for France) 6, 122–3, 131, 134–9, 170 (as peacemaker) 30, 123, 127, 128, 170, (precedence over Holy War) 139–40; infidels (destruction of lordship over Christians) 193, (destruction of lordship over infidels) 194, (dominion of impossible) 194, (forcible conversion of) 195, (lack virtue) 194, (pope should use force against) 196; Jerusalem (as heaven) 20, 128, (New Jerusalem symbolised by Rome) 88–90, (see of transferred to Rome) 88–90, (unnecessary for pope to visit) 89; Jews (forcible baptism of forbidden) 198, (toleration of) 196–201; king of the Romans (approbation by pope) 157, 158, ('canonical' election of) 155–6, (chosen by pope) 161, (confirmation as enthronement) 166, (deposition by pope) 174, (duties of) 160, (election by princes gives no rights) 155–7, (election decrees influenced by pope) 155–7, (election managed by pope) 149–53, (enthroned by pope) 166, (equality with French king) 170–1, (equality with national sovereign rulers) 170–1, (office instituted by pope) 162, (power originates from papal) 145, 157, (promises taken to pope) 153, 167–8, 170, (receives approbation before German coronation) 163–5, (right to administer empire from approbation) 158–9, (rules for pope) 166–7, (special son of pope) 158, 167, (spiritual marriage to pope) 157, (suitability for office examined) 153, 158; patronage, 47, 68, 70–3, (of Matteo Giovannetti) 58–61, 71–3, (of Petrarch) 68–9, (of Philippe de Vitry) 69–70; personal

interests, 64–8, 198; Pope (bishop of Rome) 78–9; (can legislate against determination of predecessors) 37–8, (cannot be judged) 26, (canonises saints) 34, (change of name) 29, (compels subjects to live according to right reason) 195, (claims to be divine) 27, 39–41, (continuity of office) 22, (defines doctrine) 27, (as doctor) 183–4, (duty to promote peace) 127–8, (duty to travel) 81, (exercises clemency) 25–6, (governor of Church) 39, (head of hierarchy) 21, (identified with Holy Ghost) 39, (infallible in matters of faith) 35–40, (living law) 26, (man and office) 27–8, 63, 202, (marriage to church of Rome) 77–81, (marriage to universal Church) 28–9, 35, 77–82, (plenitude of power) 22–6, 34, 173, 194, (possesses all islands) 192, (power of keys) 27, 31–2, 34, 35, 92, (provides to all offices and benefices) 102n25, (represents mystical body of Christ) 24–5, (responsibility for salvation) 22, 128, 181–4, (*sanctus*) 31, (sins as man) 202, (successor of Peter) 22–3, 36, 46, 80, (universality of authority) 46, 192, (universality of care) 122, (universal ordinary) 26, (vicar of Christ) 22–5, 36, 46, 105, 152; portraits of, 61–2, 209–10; postill on *Quia quorundam mentes*, 9, 37–8; on priesthood and laity, 9–10, 21–2; *propria regna* (extension of through crusades) 189, (rulers created and empowered by pope) 172–3, 189, (rulers deposed by pope) 175, (rulers 'feudal' vassals of pope) 172–5, (rulers special sons of pope) 172, (rulers similar to king of the Romans) 173–4, (suitability of rulers examined by pope) 175; registers of, 12–14, 30–1, 186; reputation of, 4–7, (as Renaissance pope) 1–4, 63–71, 202, 204; Rome (bishop of) 78–80, (Lateran basilica as New Temple of Jerusalem) 94–5, 199, (marriage to localised church of) 77–8, (as New Jerusalem) 88–90, 92, 199, (people

248

Index

of epitomise all Christians) 91, (people of as special sons of pope and church) 78; on schism, 182–4; use of demi-bull and title *electus*, 30; works dedicated to or commissioned by, 16, 65–6, 68, 198, 207–8

Cochetus de Cochetis, 82, 84

Cola di Rienzo, 6, 12, 74–5, 78–9, 80, **82–4**, **94–5**, 206: *Libellus* of, 82, 84, 90n73, 109, 142

Cologne, 163

Colonna, family of, 74

Conrad of Halberstadt, 17

Conrad of Megenberg, 33n78, 75, 101, 141, 145n8, 154: on cardinals' *sede vacante* powers, 102; coronation of *rex Romanorum* after confirmation, 164–5; defends Clement VI, 123; on imperial election and confirmation, 157–8, 159–60; papal authority not from cardinals, 101; pope translates kingdoms, 174n147; pope's change of name, 19–20; *regnum Romanorum* and *imperium* same extent, 175; Roman see cannot be changed, 85; superiority of pope to cardinals, 114; where pope is there is Rome, 46

Constance, council of (1415–17), 16

Constantine I, emperor, 85, 90, 93, 94, 124, 192

Constantinople, 85, 177, 178, 185: Latin Empire of, 178

Crécy, battle of (1346), 126, 140

Crete, 178

Crimea, 194

crusade, 12, 126, 139–40, 185; as holy war, 139, 180–1, 190–6; of John XXII, 189; of Louis de la Cerda, 133, 180; of Humbert of Vienne, 186–9; Fourth Crusade, 178; *see also* Clement VI, pope

Cyprian, St, 20n3

Cyprus, 184

Dauphine, wife of St Elzéar of Sabran, 141

Delphine, sister of Clement VI, 99

Déprez, E., 14

Djani-beg, khan of the Crimea, 194

Djerba, island of, 192

Donation of Constantine, 90, 192

Donato Martini, 48

Durazzo, 178

Edward I, king of England, 132, 138

Edward III, king of England, 10, 102, 106, 122, 123, 127–8, **129–40**, 170, 185; *see also* Hundred Years War

Egypt, 177, 178

Elie de Talleyrand de Périgord, cardinal, 107n51, 108, 109, 119, 213

Eltville, 168–9

Elzéar of Sabran, St, 141

Emperor, Roman, 90, 124, 205: appointed, empowered, and controlled by pope, 144; as *dominus mundi*, 147; empowered by Roman people, 142; identity with king of the Romans, 153, 175; marriage to pope, 157; power from election, 154; power no longer universal, 146–8; secular counterpart of pope, 144; *see also* Clement VI, pope: king of the Romans

Empire, Roman, 44, 76, 90, 124, 126, 144, 205; rebirth of, 78; translation of, 86, 89, 142; universal extent of, 144–5

England, 30, 45, 71, 97; *see also* Edward III, king; Hundred Years War

Ernest Pardubitz, archbishop of Prague, 82, 84

Etienne Aubert, cardinal, *see* Innocent VI, pope

Eudes, duke of Burgundy, 126

Europe, continent of, 86

Fécamp, Normandy, Pierre Roger as abbot of, 10, 122

Fidem Catholicam (1338), 153

Firman de Beauval, 66, 207

Flagellants, 67, 197–8, 199

Florence, church of Sta Croce, 62, 209

Fortune Islands, 133–4, 180, 191–2

Fournier, P., 1

Fourth Lateran Council (1215), 196

France, 4, 6, 30, 44, 45, 73, 88, 97, **122–41**, 146, 170–1, 200, 204, 213, 214; *see also* Clement VI, pope; Hundred Years War; Philip VI, king

Francesco of Florence, 60

Francis Petrarch, *see* Petrarch, Francis

Franciscan Order, 9

Index

Index

Index

Index